Library of
Davidson College

YEATS AND A.E.

YEATS AND A.E.

'The antagonism that unites dear friends'

Peter Kuch

COLIN SMYTHE
Gerrards Cross, Bucks

BARNES AND NOBLE BOOKS
Totawa, New Jersey

1986

Copyright © 1986 by Peter Kuch
All rights reserved
First published in 1986 by Colin Smythe Limited
Gerrards Cross, Buckinghamshire

British Library Cataloguing in Publication Data
Kuch, Peter
    Yeats and A.E. : "the antagonism that unites
dear friends".
    1. A.E.—Friends and associates   2. Yeats, W.B.
—Friends and associates
  I. Title
  828'.809   PR5271.R5Z/

ISBN 0-86140-116-6

Library of Congress Cataloging in Publication Data
Kuch, Peter.
    Yeats and A.E.
    Based on author's thesis.
    Bibliography: p.
    Includes index.
    1. Yeats, W. B. (William Butler), 1865–1939—Friends
and associates. 2. Russell, George William, 1867–1935—
Friends and associates. 3. Authors, Irish—20th
century—Biography. 4. English literature—Irish
authors—History and criticism. I. Title.
PR5906.K8 1986   821'.8[B]   85-23028
ISBN 0-389-20603-2

Produced in Great Britain
Printed and bound by Billing & Sons Ltd,
Worcester

For Faye

CONTENTS

PREFACE   xi

ACKNOWLEDGEMENTS   xiii

LIST OF ILLUSTRATIONS   ix

CHAPTER I: ALLIES IN REVOLT   1

    Esoteric Buddhism and The Occult World   8
    Dubliners   13
    The Dublin Hermetic Society   14
    Mohini Chatterjee and the Literature of India 17

CHAPTER II: BREAKING THE SPELL   21

    The Divergence of the Twain   21
    Admiration and Disputation   27
    The Pyrognostics of a Poet   30
    From Dublin to London   37
    'But Friendship Never Ends'   40
    The Search for Unity   42
    The Mask and the Self   47

CHAPTER III: SELF AND SOUL   48

    Spooks and Spirituality   51
    The Household   58
    An Irish Visionary   62
    A Form for Forms   73
    Mage Versus Mystic   79
    Self and Soul   84

CHAPTER IV: POETS AND DREAMERS   92

    Homeward: Songs by the Way   92

Contents   viii

    The *Independent* Review   104
    Evangelism in Eire   106
    'The Castle of Heroes'   117
    Mysticism or Mystification?   125

CHAPTER V: CELTIC AND IRISH   128

    Celtic Propaganda   132
    'Irish' Advice   137
    Poetry and Belief   140
    Moods   146
    Belief and Reincarnation   149
    Farmed out for Poetry   152
    The *Express* Controversy   163

CHAPTER VI: PLAYS AND CONTROVERSIES: ACT I   172

    The Irish Literary Theatre   178
    Enter the Fays   194
    Much Ado About *Where There Is Nothing*   204

CHAPTER VII: PLAYS AND CONTROVERSIES: ACT II   210

CHAPTER VIII: 'BUT FRIENDSHIP NEVER ENDS'   234

NOTES   239

INDEX   285

ILLUSTRATIONS

between pages 146 and 147

W. B. Yeats, by A.E., c. 1884.
W. B. Yeats, by A.E., 1903.
W. B. Yeats, by John Butler Yeats.
Murals at The Household, by W. B. Yeats and G. W. Russell.
G. W. Russell, by John Butler Yeats, 1898.
W. B. Yeats, by John Butler Yeats, 1898.
The front covers of W. B. Yeats's *The Secret Rose* (1897) and *Poems* (1899), designed by Althea Gyles.
The title page of A.E.'s *The Earth Breath*.
A dress rehearsal for A.E.'s *Deirdre*.
A spirit rider, by A.E.
The Serpents of Wisdom, by A.E.
Immortals on their thrones, by A.E.
The philosopher seated on a skull, by A.E.
Murals painted by A.E. at Plunkett House.
Yeats, Russell and J. M. Synge fishing on Coole Lake.
The Library at Coole Park.
G. W. Russell, Lady Gregory and W. B. Yeats in the Library, by Jack B. Yeats.
Yeats and A.E. sketching, by A.E.
Photographs of Yeats and Russell from *The Bookman*.
Portraits of Sir Horace Plunkett, Susan Mitchell, Lady Gregory, and George Moore, by John Butler Yeats.
Poulnabrone Dolmen, Co. Clare.
'The Castle of Heroes', Lough Key, Co. Roscommon.

PREFACE

During his life-time Yeats formed only a few friendships in which he received as much as he gave. His work with Lady Gregory in the Abbey Theatre is his most celebrated association, though over a decade before it began he had established an equally important friendship with George Russell. 'A.E. was my oldest friend', he informed Dorothy Wellesley on Russell's death in 1935. 'We began our work together.'

This book charts the history and evaluates the significance of the first twenty-three years of that work, from the early months of 1884 when Yeats and Russell first met in the Art Schools in Kildare Street, Dublin to their divisive quarrels in 1907 about the policies of the Abbey Theatre. It seeks to gauge the pressures that each man exerted on the other and to understand the way these pressures at once shaped their respective imaginative developments and affected the course of the literary movement. It is a blend of literary history, biography and literary criticism.

I am indebted to many people but especially to Richard Ellmann, who launched my enquiry and criticized drafts of early chapters; to John Kelly, whose encyclopedic knowledge of the period has preserved me from a number of inaccuracies and whose enthusiasm has been a source of encouragement; to Anne Yeats and Senator Michael Yeats for permission to examine their father's library; to Alan Denson for lending me a microfilm of his collection of Russell's letters; and to Colin Smythe for sending me photocopies of manuscripts, several of Russell's personal books, and proof-sheets of books by or about Russell. I am also deeply grateful to Declan Kiberd for his generous support and to Derry Jeffares for guiding me from initial idea to final draft.

My colleagues at the University of Newcastle have been very helpful and encouraging. I am particularly indebted to Hugh Craig, Wayne McKenna, and John Burrows for their excellent advice about style, and to Christopher Pollnitz for an informative discussion on prosody. The Principal of Avondale College, James Cox, and the Head of Department, Donald Hansen, have also been supportive. I am further indebted to Suheil Bushrui, Sir Idris Foster, Monk

Preface xii

Gibbon, Belinda Humfrey, Brendan Kennelly, Anne Knowland, D. E. S. Maxwell, D. A. Rees, Henry Summerfield, Colin Williamson, and John Woodfield for important suggestions. Dennis Porter of the Bodleian Library, and the staffs of the Plunkett Foundation [Oxford] and the National Library of Ireland have been most helpful. I would especially like to thank Kay Winter for typing the final draft, Lorna Ackroyd for entering the corrections, Vicki Salerni for advice about the word processor, Lyndall Hopton for checking the proofs, and my wife Faye, for her valuable assistance.

I am grateful to the Principal, Fellows and Staff of Jesus College, Oxford for their hospitality; to the Board of the Australian Conference Association Limited for the scholarship which enabled me to prepare the thesis on which this book is based; and to the Avondale College Foundation for their generous encouragement and financial support — for a travel grant so I could spend a summer in England and Ireland, and a grant so I could prepare this book for publication.

Peter Kuch
Mirrabooka 1984

Note to the reader. In order to preserve some of the atmosphere of the period I have, in the early chapters, quoted the first published version of Yeats's and Russell's poetry.

ACKNOWLEDGEMENTS

The author and publishers wish to thank Anne Yeats and Michael B. Yeats for permission to publish reproductions of work by John Butler Yeats, and Jack Butler Yeats. They also wish to thank the National Gallery of Ireland, and the Hugh Lane Municipal Gallery of Modern Art for permission to reproduce works of art in their possession, and the Oriel Gallery for permission to reproduce illustrations from their catalogue *Exhibition of Paintings by George Russell, AE, November 26th — December 22nd 1975*.

Extracts from the published work of W. B. Yeats are published by kind permission of Macmillan, London Ltd.

Unpublished letters of W. B. Yeats are published by kind permission of, and are copyright © 1986 by, Anne Yeats and Michael B. Yeats.

Unpublished letters of Lady Gregory are published by kind permission of, and a copyright © 1986 by, Anne de Winton and Catherine Kennedy.

Extracts from the diaries of Joseph Holloway are published by kind permission of the National Library of Ireland.

Unpublished letters of G. W. Russell are published by permission of, and are copyright © 1986 by, the Estate of Diarmuid Russell. Many appear in *Letters from AE* (1961) edited by Alan Denson, and in 'Letters from George William Russell (AE), Selected, Transcribed and Edited by Alan Denson' now housed in the National Library of Ireland. AE's paintings are reproduced by kind permission of Mrs. Diarmuid Russell.

CHAPTER I

ALLIES IN REVOLT

1884 — 1887

'With every new genius a new world is discovered' — A E

When William Butler Yeats first enrolled in the painting class at the Art Schools in Kildare Street, Dublin, in May 1884, his attention was captured by the manner and work of one of the students.[1] This student appeared to be something of an oddity. He was tall and thin. He wore wire-rimmed pince-nez, and had an unruly shock of hair that gave him a dishevelled appearance. He was conventionally but carelessly dressed in a well-worn Donegal tweed suit — so carelessly in fact that one of his closest friends used to quip that his clothes always looked as if they had been put on with the aid of a shovel.[2] His manner seemed kind, gentle, and dreamy. He was quiet, with the quietness of self-absorption. Though he could become animated in discussion, he rarely spoke; not in deference to the many 'Silence is Requested' notices posted around the classroom,[3] but because he had a very bad stammer. Yet even when he spoke, his thoughts were so profuse and clotted that what he said was largely unintelligible. Some of the members of the class thought that he was inspired, others that he was pixilated.[4] Yeats learned that the student's name was George William Russell. He also discovered that Russell had been coming to the art classes irregularly since he had moved to Dublin from the small Northern town of Lurgan about six years before, and that he had gained a reputation for remarkable promise.[5]

What interested him most were Russell's paintings. While the other members of the class, with their vocations as art teachers firmly in mind, dutifully laboured to capture an acceptable likeness to the assigned model, Russell would paint effortlessly, without preliminary sketch or working diagram, representations of the images that apparently rose spontaneously before his imagination. Sometimes there were scenes depicting the spiritual history of other worlds and other incarnations, but mostly his canvasses were peopled with radiant spirit-beings caught in a moment of light-hearted blitheness in some dappled natural setting such as a lake, a seashore, or a forest. At times these paintings displayed a talent for composition which amazed both students and masters. 'I can remember', Yeats recalled over thirty years later in his *Autobiographies*, the 'half-whisper of a student, now a successful sculptor, who said, pointing to the modelling of a shoulder, "That is too easy, a great deal too easy!" For with brush and pencil he was too coherent.'[6] To some, this fluency was further proof that Russell had access to a form of supernatural power.[7]

At first, Yeats shared their awe for this odd Northerner. 'I used to listen to him at that time', he later wrote,

mostly walking through the streets at night, for the sake of some stray sentence, beautiful and profound, amid many words that seemed without meaning; and there were others, too, who walked and listened, for he had become, I think, to all his fellow-students, sacred, as the fool is sacred in the East. . . . We derided each other, told absurd tales to one another's discredit, but we never derided him, or told tales to his discredit. He stood outside the sense of comedy his friend John Eglinton has called 'the social cement' of our civilization; and we would 'gush' when we spoke of him, as men do when they praise something incomprehensible. But when he painted there was no difficulty in comprehending. How could that ease and rapidity of composition, so far beyond anything that we could attain to, belong to a man whose words seemed often without meaning?[8]

Yeats, who was still deciding whether to be a poet or painter, immediately divined a kinship of purpose in these fluent, vision-inspired paintings. He was himself in revolt against Victorian actuality, against the prevailing taste in art for a stolid realism which preferred Carolus Duran and Bastien-Lepage to Blake and Rossetti, and he was struggling to free himself from the influence of his artist father, who, in pursuit of the characteristic and the natural, endlessly reworked whatever he painted.[9] But though he had dismissed all Realism as a 'misunderstanding created by Victorian science', a discipline he professed 'to hate with a monkish hate', he had not yet formulated his own aesthetic beyond a marked preference for the Romantic.[10] Before enrolling in the Art Schools he had tried to paint in the style that his father had first adopted but then abandoned, that of the pre-Raphaelites, where art seemed 'allied to poetry', but he discovered that unaided he was 'too timid' to espouse openly what his father had rejected.[11] He soon realized that he could not expect any guidance from his instructors at the Art Schools, where the only standard was 'a very smooth surface and a very neat outline.'[12] Neither could he turn, like some of his fellow students who affected to follow the latest trends, to the French Impressionists. In his mind they were associated with his father's Rembrandt-like

Allies in Revolt

realism in that both were preoccupied with the physical. Thus, the paintings which Russell produced with the ease and assurance of a visionary inspiration reminiscent of Blake and Shelley offered Yeats both a positive repudiation of what he had himself rejected and an affirmation of what he was striving to achieve.[13] In league with a fellow artist who also seemed to be protesting the untimely death of Romanticism, Yeats believed he could begin his quarrel with his elders and with the present. Russell responded eagerly to the suggestion that they join forces against the prevailing attitudes in art, literature, and religion. So began a fifty-year association that was to be a shaping force in the lives of both men and in the development of the Irish Renaissance. To seal their alliance, the new friends bought themselves brightly coloured neckties which they decided to wear with a flamboyance modelled on a print of Byron.[14]

A broad outline of their revolutionary programme can be derived from the poems that Yeats composed in the two-and-a-half years that he and Russell were at the Art Schools and the Royal Hibernian Academy together. The poems contain only a general plan of campaign, indicating areas where major battles should be fought or skirmishes might be expected. Neither man had formulated his ideas to the point where he could draw up a manifesto, though vagueness may well have been deliberately assumed as the most effective posture. Both were shrewd enough to sense that the *status quo* can be more readily subverted by a gesture of discontent than a detailed plan of attack. All of the poems, as with Russell's visionary paintings, call into question the reality of the phenomenal world, the solid 'matter' that sat so squarely in the Victorian mind. In a poem published in the middle of his art studies, and eventually entitled 'The Song of the Happy Shepherd', Yeats announced that

> The very world itself may be
> Only a sudden flaming word,
> 'Mid clanging space a moment heard
> In the universe's reverie.[15]

If this is so, the poem declares, then subjectivism, and not the current philosophies of empiricism, historicism, positivism, and utilitarianism, is the way to truth.

> there is no truth,
> Saving in thine own heart.[16]

The visionary apprehensions of the artist and the imaginative utterances of the poet, Yeats affirms, are more valid than the decrees of the legislator or the calculations of the scientist. But, as he points out in another poem published towards the end of his art studies, and eventually entitled 'The Sad Shepherd', subjective enquiry must be informed by the imagination if it is to escape the bewildering involutions of solipsism. The chief sources of nourishment for the imagination are dreams, or the visionary faculty; ancient literature and tradition; and folklore. The regions where it should take up residence are the pastoral hinterlands of Mythology such as Arcadia and Ildathach, the Many-Coloured Land of Gaelic myth. These are the literary equivalents of those light-drenched landscapes that so often provide settings for the visionary figures in Russell's paintings. Against the Victorian obsession with utility, an obsession that frequently resulted in the proliferation of ugliness, artist and audience are drawn to gaze on 'The phantom, Beauty, in a mist of tears'.[17] In the art of both men there is a deliberate turning away from the contemporary world of achievement, industry, enthusiasm, and optimism. In 'The Song of the Happy Shepherd', Yeats, with all the solemnity youth can muster, admonishes his readers: 'Then no wise worship dusty deeds'.[18] Instead, they are invited to contemplate the autumnal stillness of a remote past, or share the spring energies of the land of the Sidhe. A recurrent motif is the flight of the weary from doubt, anxiety, and bewilderment.

> Come away, O, human child!
> To the woods and waters wild,
> With a fairy, hand in hand,
> For the world's more full of weeping
>   than you can understand.

Set over against this melancholy is the blitheness of the otherworld, a blitheness reminiscent of many of Russell's paintings of the children of the Sidhe.

> Where the wave of moonlight glosses
> The dim gray sands with light,
> Far off by furthest Rosses
> We foot it all the night,
> Weaving olden dances,
> Mingling hands, and mingling glances,
> Till the moon has taken flight;
> To and fro we leap,
> And chase the frothy bubbles.[19]

Russell came so completely under the spell of his new friend's poetry that even forty years after they had met he could write:

> To re-read *Early Poems and Stories* is to recall my first love in literature. The beauty which overcomes us while sensitiveness is yet virgin and has lost nothing of its poignancy by use, lasts through life for most of us, no matter how many after-loves we may have. Who under the spell can be critical of the enchanter? I was not then, and hardly now can I do anything but surrender myself anew to the music. I find a boy living in me still, affected almost to tears, longing to be remote and winged, flying over the waters listening only to the song of the heart:
>
> 'I would we were changed to white birds on the wandering foam, I and you.'
>
> Or I murmur the benediction sung over Diarmuid and Grania:
>
>> 'Give to these children, new from the world,
>> Silence and love,
>> And the long dew-dropping hours of the night
>> And the stars above.'
>
> And as of old the poetry creates such a loveliness in the heart that I feel I am breathing in a divinely-created nature, air, earth, the stars, ourselves, all fondled by the Magician of the Beautiful, all rapt, all sharing in the benediction. In our first imaginative love there is complete union with the poetry, and I cannot disentangle myself from this early affection or say how much I brought to it, or how much it brought to me.

It always seemed to him that there was an unbroken affinity between his own paintings and his new friend's early poems, and that the fluency of one was often mirrored in the strenuously achieved ease of the other.

> Some of them, like the 'Faery Song', seem breathed on the air by an art as effortless as the art by which flowers unfold, and to be without labour; though I fear the truth-telling artist would confess the anguish of concentration which went to create what seems spontaneous, natural and delicate as the falling of dew.[20]

Part of Russell's inability to 'disentangle' himself from the early poems no doubt came from the fact that in the early days he was often an excited witness of this 'anguish of concentration'. Dublin gossip has it that Russell's father first met Yeats in the early hours of the morning when he went downstairs to accost what he thought was a lout trying to break the upstairs windows of their house. It was merely the poet tossing pebbles against the glass in an effort to rouse his new friend so they could share the final version of a poem they had been discussing on their return from the Art Schools.[21]

Russell's attachment to the early poems was so intense that he came to regard them as an integral part of his own experience. Gifted with a prodigious memory, he could recite everything his friend wrote. In the early nineteen-hundreds he angered Yeats on two occasions by reprinting without permission and lavishly illustrating two poems from their Art School days—'She Who Dwelt Among The Sycamores' (1887) and 'The Solitary Fairy' (1887).[22] The first contains an excellent one-line description of the atmosphere of many of Russell's early paintings:

> Noon wrapped the woods in veils of violet weather.[23]

The second calls the fairies the 'shining ones', an expression that does not occur anywhere else in Yeats's work, but is very common in Russell's accounts of the spirit-beings he saw in his visions.[24] The fact that he had left his mark on both poems and been intimate with their composition seems to have blinded Russell, who was normally an excellent critic, to their mawkishness and immaturity. The refrain of 'The Solitary Fairy', for example, would readily grace any *Stuffed Owl* of pastoral verse.

> Come away while the moon's in the woodland,
> We'll dance and then feast in a dairy.
> Though youngest of all in our good band,
> She is wasting away, little fairy.[25]

Russell could not be critical of the early verse because it was inextricably bound up with his memories of the best period of their literary association. All his life he called Yeats, 'Willy Yeets', and all his life he carried the image of the tall, sallow-faced boy with the lock of black hair falling over his forehead who used to chant his poems to him, the boy who used to wear a beard 'and never again looked so noble as he did with that beard'.[26]

At first, his admiration for his friend's poetry was met with an equal, or perhaps even greater, fascination with his own visionary powers. Yeats's attention was immediately engaged when Russell told him that if he sat silently for a time on 'the Two Rock Mountains, or any spot where man was absent, the scene would change; unknown, beautiful people would move among the rocks and trees'.[27]

Russell's first visionary experience seems to have occurred only months before he and Yeats became friends.[28] While holidaying with some relatives in Armagh, he suddenly began to experience hypnogogic visions—'waking dreams' as he called them—of astonishing power and vividness which seemed to thrust themselves into his conscious mind.[29] They came, he later explained, 'like strangers who suddenly enter a house, who brush aside the doorkeeper, and who will not be denied'.[30] Images of cosmic happenings and what he believed was the history of other worlds passed in rapid succession before his eyes. 'I remember how pure, holy and beautiful these imaginations seemed', he wrote in his spiritual autobiography, *The Candle of Vision*, 'how they came like crystal water sweeping aside the muddy current of my life'.[31] Though he felt cleansed, he was deeply disturbed by these sudden incursions of the spirit. They appeared 'self-begotten', but were they, he wondered, the wisdom of some previous self which sought to incarnate in him? Or were they merely of his own imagining?[32] He discovered that if he told himself he had imagined the vision it would disappear, but if he abandoned himself to it he found that his whole person became charged with expectation, and began to tremble as if on the verge of some awesome revelation. 'The visible world became like a tapestry blown and stirred by winds behind it. If it would but raise for an instant I knew I would be in Paradise.'[33] In spite of their power and promise, the visions never lingered. 'An age of the spirit would fall upon me', Russell recalled, 'and then I would come out of reverie and be the careless boy once more'.[34]

Yeats whose mind was more analytical, and who was more aware of the range of possible explanations for such experiences, was eager to establish the source of these visions. Were they supernatural revelations, as his friend claimed? Or were they, as he first suspected, merely 'a subjective intensification' of images drawn from everyday experience?[35] Were they essentially a way of coping with a chaotic psyche? Or did they provide access to higher planes of reality? Yeats has described his initial responses to the visions in his *Autobiographies*, and in a review of Russell's *Song and Its Fountains*, an autobiographical work exploring the relationship between some of the visions and the poems they inspired. As these two descriptions were written some thirty-five and fifty years after the two men had met, certain allowances should be made. Yeats was probably not as probing or as sceptical as he represented himself, though it was characteristic of him to attempt to test any supernatural event he witnessed. For example, on a visit to the West of Ireland shortly before he met Russell, when he saw what appeared to be a blazing torch climbing Knocknarea, it was typical that he should take out his pocket-watch and time the light's ascent, and that he should note in his diary that the light was approximately seven miles away.[36] The detailed records of the many occult investigations he conducted throughout his life, from his first séance in the mid 'eighties to the years he spent interrogating his wife's 'communicators' for the 1925 edition of *A Vision*, reveal the extent and rigour of his methods.[37] Thus, it is likely that he did display some of the attitudes he said he first adopted towards Russell's visions. He claimed that while the other students in the class accepted 'without hesitation' that the pastel sketches Russell showed them were accurate representations of the beings he saw in vision he reserved his judgment, because he suspected the influence of Gustave Moreau whose work he knew Russell admired.[38] And he also claimed that when he saw him transform a 'study of the nude' which had been assigned as a subject for the life-class into a 'Saint John in the Desert' he allowed for a 'reminiscence of da Vinci'.[39] Yet contemporary accounts of the work done in the Art Schools suggest that the students were not assigned studies of the nude. They were sometimes required to produce a sketch of a statue or a painting, an exercise known as 'drawing from the life', but they were not permitted to hire people to pose for them until 1890, by which time Yeats and Russell had left.[40] Furthermore, the two accounts which Yeats gives of his eventual acceptance of Russell's visions are at variance with one another. In the *Autobiographies* he says that he became convinced that Russell's visions originated in the supernatural and not in his own psyche when several predictions he had made came true.[41] But in his review of *Song and Its Fountains* he says that what convinced him was his ability to confirm for himself 'from the obscure symbolism of alchemy an explanation of the Scourging of Christ implicit in some visionary scene'.[42] It is most unlikely that he would have been conversant with the 'obscure symbolism of alchemy' in 1884. Doubtless, he has embroidered his recollection of the painting with this piece of arcanum to give his verification of Russell's visions greater authority. Yeats did not begin a systematic study of the occult until April 1885, when he read a book entitled *Esoteric Buddhism* (1883), which had been written by A. P. Sinnett, a prominent Theosophist. He immediately showed the book to Russell; and with their joint study of Theosophy their association entered a new phase.

Esoteric Buddhism and The Occult World

Theosophy, in the general sense, is a term used to denote those forms of philosophic and religious thought which claim a special insight into the Divine nature and its creative processes. These special

Allies in Revolt

insights may be the result of supernatural revelations, or they may flow from private speculation. Theosophy is distinguished from most philosophical systems, in which God is generally the *terminus ad quem*, in that it begins with an explication of the Divine essence, and endeavours to deduce the phenomenal universe from the play of forces within the Divine nature itself.[43] In terms of Western thought, its roots are in neo-Platonism and the Kabbalah, while the main trunk is comprised of the speculative mysticism of writers such as Plotinus, Paracelsus, Boehme, Eckhart, Nicholas of Cusa, the Cambridge Platonists, and Swedenborg.

As a modern cult, Theosophy was first taught in America in 1875 by Madame Blavatsky, a remarkable Russian émigré who seems to have possessed most of the ambitions but none of the mummified pedantry of George Eliot's Reverend Casaubon. In addition to scores of articles, she produced two major works, *Isis Unveiled* (1877) and *The Secret Doctrine* (1888), in which she attempted to synthesize the main religious, philosophical, and scientific traditions of the East and West and of the Ancient and Modern worlds. This synthesis was then boldly offered as a means of solving the major problems thrown up by the Nineteenth century debates on Science, Religion, and Philosophy. Science and Religion were reconciled by declaring that evolution took place in both the physical and the spiritual worlds, and that Darwin and Huxley were in harmony with the Ancients and with the Buddhist scriptures. Contemporary discoveries in thermodynamics, electromagnetism, and physics were related to the occult and to research being conducted in Spiritualism. The faith-corroding problems raised for traditional Christianity throughout the century by Higher Criticism—especially works like Feuerbach's *Das Wesen des Christentums* (1841) and Renan's *La vie de Jésus* (1863) —were solved by advancing a theory of exoteric and esoteric interpretation, and by expounding the Bible in terms of the Kabbalah and the Vedas. The widespread belief that a knowledge of Eastern literature was necessary for true self-understanding, a belief evident in the popularity of translators such as Edward Fitzgerald and Edwin Arnold, in the monumental labours of Max Müller, and in the pervasive influence of Schlegel, Hegel, Schopenhauer, and Schelling, all of whom drew heavily on the *Upanishads*, was adopted as one of the fundamental tenets of Theosophy. In short, it offered itself, as the sub-title of *Isis Unveiled* declared, as 'A Master-Key to the Mysteries of Ancient and Modern Science and Theology'.

Madame Blavatsky claimed that she had been granted her spiritual authority by a Brotherhood of Masters which had existed for thousands of years in Tibet. She professed to be their chosen medium, called to reveal important truths for what was soon to be a crucial period in the world's spiritual history. To signify her election, the Masters were alleged to have given her the power to materialize objects, purify water, and cause the astral bells to ring.[44] These powers were not 'supernatural', she said, but were the result of special revelations concerning the cosmic rhythms of natural laws.[45] She declared the Masters had shown her that the Divine life of the Great Being had been obscured by the dense forms of matter, and that it could only be revealed again through a process of physical and spiritual evolution, by which man could become perfect. For most, perfection could only be attained after numerous incarnations; but those who studied Theosophy were able to accelerate the process, because they were taught how to liberate themselves from natural law.[46]

Most of Madame Blavatsky's claims were briefly set out and allegedly substantiated in two books, *The Occult World* (1881) and *Esoteric Buddhism* (1884). Both were written by A. P. Sinnett, an English journalist she had met in India. In *The Occult World* Sinnett told of the various experiments he had devised to test Madame Blavatsky's powers, of his conviction that she was the chosen prophetess, and of his conversion to Theosophy. *Esoteric Buddhism* was principally an exegesis of the doctrines outlined in *The Occult World*. Its importance, as Madame Blavatsky pointed out, was that 'it was one of the first European attempts to sketch the approximate outline of archaic cosmogony.'[47] According to Sinnett, matter and spirit share a common origin. Both were spawned from primordial chaos, and both are involved in a process of constant evolution, the ratio of spirit to matter gradually increasing as the soul proceeds up the evolutionary chain. In all, the soul passes through some eight hundred incarnations, in multiples of seven incarnations per round, each round being distinguished by a discreet change in the ratio of spirit to matter. At the beginning of each round, one of the Planetary Spirits or Avatars, a being from a higher round, incarnates to teach 'to some receptive minds the outlines of the Esoteric wisdom'.[48]

Yeats first read *Esoteric Buddhism* after his aunt Isabella Pollexfen had sent him a copy.[49] He showed the book to Russell, and to a mutual friend, Charles Johnston. Already familiar with *The Occult World* which he had found 'admirable' and 'wholly credible', Johnston read *Esoteric Buddhism* and was promptly converted to Theosophy.[50] Russell was also impressed by the book, but he was more guarded in his response. When he recommended it to his friend Carrie Rea, he cautioned her that it was not all 'authentic'.[51] Nevertheless, as his unpublished correspondence with her shows,

Esoteric Buddhism contained a number of teachings which he found considerably more agreeable than the doctrines of the church he attended regularly every Sunday with his parents, the Church of Ireland. The idea that it was an avatar who had incarnated in him when he began to see visions appeared to fit his experience more closely than the suggestion that he had been visited by the Holy Spirit. The principles of Karma and Reincarnation, when compared with the doctrines of Sin and Judgment, seemed more logical and more equitable. He wrote to his friend.

You must come to the conclusion that you have existed before, that your character is the result of your thoughts and ideas in the last incarnation. When you once accept this idea, though it destroys the nice comfortable feeling of going to heaven once you die, it explains all that seems unjust in the condition of children born in the slums of great cities like London or Paris, with the worst qualities of man instinctive in them and no chance of being trained to better things. The charitable minded Christian of today sends all these poor folk to hell forever. I have no patience with them.[52]

His own visions affirmed the existence of an omnipresent and immediate spirit-world as taught by the Theosophists rather than the remote hereafter promised by Christianity. And Sinnett's explanation of evolution was more attractive to him than the Genesis account of creation. 'It is far more beautiful', he assured his friend, 'to think that the world evolved itself than to think that it was violently constructed by a deity very much in a hurry.'[53] But even though he found *Esoteric Buddhism* more congenial than The Bible and The Book of Common Prayer, Russell did not officially join the Theosophical Society for another five years; though when he did, he enjoyed stigmatizing Christianity as a diminished religion which 'possessed no cosmogony, no psychology, only a most perfect ethic'.[54]

Yeats claimed in the *Autobiographies* that he too greeted Sinnett's *Esoteric Buddhism* with caution, adopting a position somewhere between it and what he then saw as the epitome of agnosticism, Renan's *La vie de Jésus*. He surmised he was 'held there perhaps by [his] father's scepticism'.[55] Compared with Russell, who moved easily though slowly from an evangelical confidence in pious emotionalism to mystical intensity, Yeats had the complex task of discovering a form of belief that could withstand his father's philosophy of Utilitarianism. While his father appeared to him unassailably secure, 'full always of Mill and humanitarianism'[56], he felt compelled to consider the problem of religious belief 'perpetually with great anxiety' for he did not think that he could 'live without religion.'⁵⁷ Because a schoolboy enthusiasm for evolution had destroyed his faith in traditional Christianity, Yeats had first turned to literature, confident that even if he could not readily find the spiritual assurance he sought he could make himself 'a new religion', 'almost an infallible Church' from the imaginative creations of successive generations of poets and painters. Since imaginary characters, he argued, 'are created out of the deepest instinct of man, to be his measure and his norm, whatever I can imagine those mouths speaking may be the nearest I can go to truth'. Undeterred by the fact that this approach was indefensibly subjective, Yeats concluded that the unanimous pronouncement of literature was that life was 'steeped in the supernatural'.⁵⁸ This appeared to be confirmed by his own experience, and by Russell's visions.

So while Russell turned to Sinnett's books for moral exhortation and greater spiritual understanding, Yeats read them to study the supernatural. Theosophy, as far as he was concerned, was one way of investigating an issue that was central to human experience. It provided him with a form of religion and a synthesis of ancient tradition, a means of formulating an antithesis to scepticism. Above all, he hoped his study would acquaint him with images and symbols that would impart resonance to the poetic expression of his own ideas, just as many years later his wife's 'communicators' were to announce that they had come to give him 'metaphors for poetry'.⁵⁹

In his account of their response to Sinnett's books Russell does not represent Yeats as cautious. In fact, he alleged that his friend was enthusiastically attracted to *The Occult World*. Yeats, he recalled,

had a marvellous collection of tales about Madame Blavatsky, whose Masters, he said, lived in the Himalayas amid the snows meditating through long centuries, and their beards grew and grew, and lay upon the mountain sides, and the birds built their nests in their beards.

Russell remembered his friend openly recounting these and other stories with delight, 'as if to say, what more enchanting universe could one desire to live in than a universe where such things were possible?' To him it seemed that Yeats thought 'earth was all fairy, and he tried to use a phrase of his own, "to light every cigarette at the stars" '.⁶⁰

Yeats's desire to combat scepticism and materialism with the world of fairy and miracle found expression in poems like 'Anashuya and Vijaya', which contains a description of Madame Blavatsky's Masters in a setting modelled on Kalidasa's *Sakuntala*.⁶¹ Anashuya makes Vijaya

> Swear by the parents of the gods
> . . . who dwell on sacred Himalay —
> On the far Golden Peak — enormous shapes, . . .
> Their hair along the mountains rolled and filled
> From year to year by the unnumbered nests
> Of aweless birds . . .[62]

Yeats later defined the function fulfilled for him by his early poetry in one place as 'the revolt of the soul against the intellect'[63], in another as 'the cry of the heart against necessity'[64], and in another as 'the call of the heart, the heart seeking its own dream'.[65] Eschewing credulity as much as scepticism, he looked to his study of Theosophy with Russell to enlarge his world for the purposes of poetry.

Dubliners

A month after Yeats and Russell began their study of Theosophy, the Yeats family moved from 'Island View', Howth, on the outskirts of Dublin, to 10 Ashfield Terrace, a red brick villa in Rathmines that was within easy walking distance of Russell's home at 67 Grosvenor Square. For the two years they lived there Russell was a frequent visitor, despite parental opposition to the friendship from both families.[66] Russell's parents disapproved of Yeats because they thought he was robbing their son of his religious faith.[67] J. B. Yeats was critical of Russell's influence. 'You can only pretend' an interest in religion, he would taunt his son; 'Your interest is in mundane things, and Heaven to you is this world made better, whether beyond the stars or not.'[68] He considered that mysticism was merely a refuge for relaxed intellects, and grudgingly allowed Russell holiness, but little else.[69] 'A saint, but raised in Portadown', he would say, consistently confusing Russell's real birth place, Lurgan, with a town notorious in those days for its religious intolerance. 'He has no love, no admiration for the individual man. He is too religious to care for really mortal things, or rather, for he does care, to admire and love them.'[70]

Not all the family made such disparaging remarks. Yeats's sisters, who dubbed their unwelcome visitor 'The Strayed Angel', looked forward to his visits.[71] Lily Yeats remembered Russell running down the street to their house, 'full of vitality and enthusiasm', his 'great overcoat flying open'.[72] He mostly came in the evening, and when the maid and the rest of the family had gone to bed, the two friends would retire to the kitchen, put their inkpots and lamp on a bench top and settle to a night of writing or discussion. Sometimes they would cook a late meal and chant their verses to one another. Sometimes they composed plays in friendly rivalry. Russell wrote confidently to Carrie Rea in 1886:' [Yeats's] great drama *The Equator of Olives* is finished. The episode of the Sculptor's Garden is in it. It will appear shortly after his first volume is published.'[73] In another letter, he analysed some lines from this episode to show her how a mood can be created by careful attention to rhythm and syntax. Such skills, he assured her, would only come from an arduous apprenticeship.

> You should get practice by writing continuously for two hours every day, or at least an hour, whether you feel inclined or not, even if you feel disgusted with what you do and burn everything you write for months. Nothing else I know will give you freedom and absence from conventionality. Yeats does so, and some other literary acquaintances of mine. They do not mind tearing up.[74]

Apart from their literary endeavours, the most common topic of conversation at 10 Ashfield Terrace was the supernatural. They often spent all night speculating about subjects as strange as 'what cosmic sounds make mushrooms grow'[75], experimenting with thought transference and astral travel, or discussing books as various as Tyndall's *Fragments of Science*, Whitman's *Specimen Days*, and Higgins' *Anacalypsis*.[76] After they had been working together for about two months, Yeats suggested to Russell, and to several mutual friends, that they form a Hermetic Society so they could pursue their investigation of psychic phenomena in a more systematic and public manner.

The Dublin Hermetic Society

The inaugural meeting of The Dublin Hermetic Society was held on 16 June 1885.[77] The title was derived from a branch of the London chapter of The Theosophical Society which had been granted special permission by Madame Blavatsky to conduct independent psychical research[78], and was thus a declaration of the Dublin members' aim to study more than Theosophy. Yeats was elected President. The foundation members included Charles Johnston, by now a committed Theosophist, Claude Falls Wright, who was to spend the rest of his life working for Theosophy, and Charles Weekes, a close friend of Russell's who wrote much verse. Russell refused to join, though he may have attended some of the meetings.

Yeats later told Ernest Boyd, when Boyd was collecting information for his book, *Ireland's Literary Renaissance*: 'George Russell was not a member. He was then very young.'[79] Russell was not quite two years younger than Yeats, who turned twenty shortly before The Dublin Hermetic Society was launched, so perhaps age was not the principal reason for his refusal to join, though, as an eighteen year old still living at home, he may not have felt sufficiently confident to break publicly with his parents' religion. When Carrie Rea, in whom he confided openly and fully, queried his desire to keep their correspondence secret, he replied: 'The only reason I have for not wishing you to show my letters to anyone is that I would not like auntie to be holding prayer meetings over me if ever I went to the North again, as she certainly would if she heard any of my opinions.'[80] It is more likely that Russell did not join because he did not approve of the constraints that organizations placed on spiritual enquiry. The longest period of time he was a member of an official religious organization throughout his entire life was nine years. Like a Protestant he consistently put independence before institutionalism, and like a Protestant he preferred moral admonition to the study of tradition. He told the members of Yeats's Society that it would be better for them to train their minds in the techniques of transcendental meditation than to waste their time debating 'the absolute and the alcahest'.[81] And he countered Sinnett's *The Occult World* with Mabel Collins's *Light on the Path*, a book that teaches 'an austere doctrine of complete self-conquest, including the annihilation of all ambition and sensual or personal desires'.[82] He declared to a friend: 'I can have no friends outside those who are not in earnest about life, *in terrible earnest*.'[83]

Yeats was upset by Russell's attack. Spiritual enquiry for him was not the study of what men should believe or how they should act. In some notes on George Eliot, whom he was reading at the time, he observed testily: 'There is too much talk of the moral law. Surely the tongue of the poet is for other teaching. Is there not a pulpited million of disconsolate voices shouting the moral law for so much a day?'[84] Like Blake, he believed that 'good' and 'bad' as commonly used were merely 'nets of convention.' He declared in one of his poems:

> Out-worn heart, in a time out-worn,
> Come clear of the nets of wrong and right.[85]

While Russell's preoccupation with morals was not his style, Yeats was equally unwilling to go to the other extreme and side with his father, who thought that the 'true poet was neither moral nor religious.'[86] Instead, he chose a position between the two, though his stance was not a compromise. Against his father he argued the common concern of poetry and religion for 'old faiths, myths, dreams'[87]; while against Russell he proposed a distinction between religion and morality. In fact, Yeats believed that religion and morality were antagonistic. In 1887 he wrote to a friend: 'The moral impulse and the religious destroy each other in most cases.'[88] In revolt against what he saw as the sterility and earnestness of his outworn age, Yeats looked forward to a time when an alliance between religion and the arts would renew the imagination and release poetry from its obsession with morality and issues of belief.

Despite Russell's condemnation of their aims, Yeats continued to chair regular meetings of The Dublin Hermetic Society. He managed to keep the programme of study free of ethical speculation, but he was not able to direct it to the extent that he would have liked. In his inaugural address he had asserted that 'whatever the great poets had affirmed in their finest moments' was the nearest man 'could come to an authoritative religion, and that their mythology, their spirits of water and wind, were but literal truth'.[89] Having just read Shelley's *Prometheus Unbound* with this idea in mind, he proposed that the Society should systematically study the works of all the major writers. The other members agreed for a time, but they did not really share his exaltation of the literary way to truth.[90] Instead, they turned to Theosophy. Two weeks after Johnston had joined the Hermetic Society, he travelled to London to meet Sinnett and Madame Blavatsky, and on his return suggested that the Dublin group should reorganize as a Theosophical Society.[91] Yeats resisted the recommendation, and preserved the title and independence of the Society for a further nine months. By April 1886 all the members except Yeats had been converted to Theosophy, so that Johnston had no difficulty in obtaining a charter for a Dublin Lodge, signed by Sinnett himself. The Hermetic Society accordingly dissolved and reconstituted itself as The Dublin Theosophical Society. Yeats and Russell were invited to join, but they declined.[92]

Both were uneasy about organizations which threatened their independence.[93] Russell was probably afraid that he might be forced to compromise the truths revealed to him in vision; Yeats was jealous of his freedom to conduct his own psychical research. Russell's reticence was the more ambiguous. On 31 October 1887 he confided to Carrie Rea: 'I call myself a Theosophist because I believe in internal

Allies in Revolt

illumination — its principles — and because I have found that my own intuitions about things agree in the main with theirs.'[94] But he refused to identify himself publicly with the movement. At the conclusion of an article he co-authored with Charles Johnston entitled 'The Speech of the Gods', and published in *The Theosophist* in December 1887, he took care to make it clear that he was not a member of the Society.[95] And in a letter he wrote to Madame Blavatsky, dated 6 November 1888, he asserted: 'I am not a proclaimed Theosophist. I do not belong to the Society.'[96] Though Yeats and Russell sought different ends in their spiritual quest, the bond between them was for a time strengthened by their joint refusal to acquiesce in a formal commitment to Theosophy.

Mohini Chatterjee and the Literature of India

Their resolution to remain aloof from The Theosophical Society was partially weakened by the visit of a Theosophist who came from London to help to consolidate the Dublin branch. This was Madame Blavatsky's Indian chela, Mohini Chatterjee. He was asked by the new branch to explain *Esoteric Buddhism*, but he went beyond it to discuss his own study of the Indian philosophy of Sankara, a system of metaphysics which grew out of a radical critique of the *Upanishads* offered in the late seventh century by Śankara Āchārya. Unlike many Eastern philosophies, Sankara views the soul as an individual entity, and not an emanation from the world-soul. It also enforces the distinction between what is said to be illusory and what is said to be real more rigidly than other systems. The theory that the material world has no real existence, but is a mere illusion [mâya] of the individual soul wrapped in ignorance, and that it therefore has only a practical or conventional [vyâvahârika] reality and not a true [pâramârthika] reality, is thoroughly developed. Thus the whole emphasis of Sankara is on inner realization, and not on any outer action or desire that might ultimately lead to action. The only 'real' life is that of the imagination, of dreaming and contemplation. Only the self is worth pondering, for all that matters is said to be centred in it.[97]

Yeats was dazzled by Mohini Chatterjee, and was fascinated by his teachings. For a short time he adopted Sankara as a philosophy that confirmed his own speculations, helped give his 'vague thoughts shape'[98], and 'seemed at once logical and boundless'.[99] Mohini's exposition inspired him to write several poems,[100] and one of his talks, 'The Common Sense of Theosophy', which was softly persuasive, did much to allay his fears, as well as Russell's, about joining The Theosophical Society.[101] Yeats joined a little over a year after his visit; Russell two or three years after.

While Russell was also impressed by Mohini, and considered him to be 'a very wonderful fellow', he did not come under his spell to the same extent.[102] The most important result of their brief acquaintance was the encouragement he received to pursue his study of Indian philosophy and literature, which he had first discovered the previous year. He may have turned to the Indian Scriptures after reading Thoreau's enthusiastic endorsement of *The Bhagavad Gita* in *Walden*[103] — a work that almost had the status of a sacred book for both Russell and Yeats — or he may have become interested as a result of Edwin Arnold's *The Light of Asia, The Indian Song of Songs,* and *Indian Idylls,* all of which he pressed Carrie Rea to read.[104] In the months following Mohini's visit, Russell seems to have slowly worked his way through *The Bhagavad Gita, The Sutras* of Patanjali, *The Great Jewel of the Wisdom of Sankara,* and as he told Sean O'Faolain, 'every scrap [he] could get in almost every school of Indian thought, Buddhist, Brahmin, Yoga, Vedanta, and Vaishnava.'[105] He came to call Indian thought his 'aid to understanding'[106], and he studied it as assiduously for spiritual guidance and moral admonition as his parents studied the Bible. It gave direction to all his reading, was a foundation for his thoughts and literary judgments, and provided inspiration for poetry. When he learned that his first volume of poems was being translated into Bengali, he told his American publisher: 'I will come into my proper audience at last.'[107] In 1905 he assured the young writer Clifford Bax:

> I agree with you about English poetry [that] for all its splendour it moves in a world of illusion because of its lack of fundamental ideas. I except Shelley, Wordsworth, and Blake. Myself, I prefer the Sufi poetry to anything because of its intoxication with divine things; because romance and beauty and love which in our literature moves on a path of their own are in Eastern mystical poetry rapt up into eternal things. I read hardly anything else when I was young but Eastern literature, and I have never since been able really to enjoy the literature of Europe. I thought when I was young I would be able to bring into our literature in Ireland that interior life.[108]

In later life, however, Russell often asserted that he 'had never tried to put Eastern mysticism into poetry' because he had 'a natural mysticism' of his own.[109] This contention is partly supported by *Song and Its Fountains* where he shows how a number of his poems

Allies in Revolt

came directly from his own visionary experiences. But there are several, particularly in the first two volumes, that are clearly indebted to his close study of the *Upanishads*. They seem to have inspired him in different ways. Sometimes the governing metaphor for a poem is drawn from one of the texts. In the *Khandogya-Upanishad*, fifth prapâthaka, tenth khanda, verses three to six, the devout are imaged as smoke that rises from a village and mingles with the air, where it is inexorably caught up in the water cycle, a metaphor for the process of reincarnation.[110] Russell's poem, 'Dusk', is constructed around the same image.[111]

> Dusk wraps the village in its dim caress;
> Each chimney's vapour, like a thin grey rod,
> Mounting aloft through miles of quietness,
>   Pillars the skies of God.
>
> Far up they break or seem to break their line,
> Mingling their nebulous crests that bow and nod
> Under the light of those fierce stars that shine
>   Out of the calm of God.
>
> Only in clouds and dreams I felt those souls
> In the abyss, each fire hid in its clod;
> From which in clouds and dreams the spirit rolls
>   Into the vast of God.[112]

The *Khandogya-Upanishad* seems to have given Russell the idea of using smoke mingling with clouds as a symbol for the absorption of the individual into the Infinite. Similarly, the *Brihadâranyaka-Upanishad*, fourth adhyâya, fourth brâhmana, verse thirteen, contains an image that provides the governing metaphor for 'The Vesture of the Soul'.[113] In other cases, Russell is indebted to an *Upanishad* for part, rather than all, of a poem. The contrast between the spiritual vision of the poet and the myopic, earth-bound sight of his contemporaries in 'On a Hill-top' echoes the contrast drawn in the *Brihadâranyaka-Upanishad*, fourth adhyâya, third brâhmana, verses six to thirty-two.[114] The image of the 'Unknown Archer' in 'Sung on a By-Way' may have been taken from the *Mundaka-Upanishad*, second mundaka, second khanda, verses two to six[115], while the image of the symbol as a chariot in 'Symbolism' is probably taken from the *Katha-Upanishad*, first adhyâya, third vallî verses three to nine.[116] It is also necessary to consult the *Upanishads* to understand Russell's use of terms such as 'soma'[117], 'om'[118], and 'maya'[119] and to appreciate the message of poems like 'Magic'[120] and 'The Secret'.[121] Yeats claimed that the 'only influence' he could detect in Russell's first volume of poems was his 'well-loved *Upanishads*'[122], though the image of the symbol as a chariot might equally have been borrowed from Plato's *Phaedrus*[123], while 'Destiny' is heavily derivative of Wordsworth's 'Lucy' poems.[124] But Yeats is undoubtedly correct when, in his Introduction to the *Oxford Book of Modern Verse*, he grouped Russell with the 'nineties poets who turned to religion and liturgy for their symbologies. He held the opinion that Russell 'found in Vedantic philosophy the emotional satisfaction found by Lionel Johnson, John Gray, [and] Francis Thompson in Catholicism', and that 'he went to the *Upanishads*, both for imagery and belief'.[125]

By comparison, his own poetry shows little sign of Indian influence. A few early poems reveal his passing enthusiasm for Sankara, and one, 'Anashuya and Vijaya', his brief interest in the drama of Kalidasa, a Romantic whose style is famed throughout India for its clarity and elegance.[126] But he confessed he found it difficult to share his friend's 'ceaseless' and 'vague' enthusiasm for the *Upanishads*.[127] The clumsy, archaic language of the translations repelled him, and the doctrine that words were chiefly important as aids to meditation offended his keen sense of the intrinsic worth of language.[128] While Russell declared in a letter to Carrie Rea, that 'what can be put into words is useless — what is a thing that has boundaries to one who longs to escape from them?'[129], Yeats unequivocally asserted in a poem: 'For words alone are certain good'.[130] During his early study of the Indian Scriptures with Russell, Yeats looked principally for traditions, for glimpses of 'some fibrous darkness' concealed in the 'dim folds' of that great tapestry of religious thought which he believed formed the backdrop to the Irish mind.[131] He turned to the East because he was convinced that the pre-Christian Irish and the Indians had once shared a mythology.[132] In 1889 he wrote in an article: 'Tradition is always the same. The earliest poet of India and the Irish peasant in his hovel nod to each other across the ages, and are in perfect agreement.'[133] He repeated the assertion in 1893 in the first volume of his edition of Blake[134]; in 1902 in 'The Celtic Element in Literature'[135]; and in 1939 in *A General Introduction for My Work*.[136]

And so, while Yeats and Russell were united in a warm friendship by their revolt against the Victorian despotism of fact, by their search for an alternative to their parents' attitudes to religion, and by their refusal to acquiesce immediately in a formal commitment to Theosophy, they viewed their association as strengthening rather than moulding their own imaginative developments.

CHAPTER II

BREAKING THE SPELL

1887 — 1890

'The more powerful and original a writer, the more dangerous he is to lesser talents who are trying to find themselves.'

-- W. H. Auden

The literary association that was formed in the early years of their friendship was very strong, but it was not binding on all their interests. Russell in particular seems to have felt the need to devise unilaterally several articles of exclusion to guarantee his own sovereignty.[1] And though these articles were invoked very early, they were not formally declared until the end of his life. In a long letter he wrote shortly before he died, he confided to Yeats that for him their entire literary association had been governed by his dread that 'a nature more formidable and powerful' than his own would draw him away from his 'own will and centre.'[2] At the beginning, this dread prevented him from sharing an enthusiasm that was seminal to his friend's imaginative development—the establishing of a true literary expression of Irish nationality. While Yeats busied himself formulating a view of Irish literature, redefining the national tradition, and forging an image of himself as an Irish poet in a rush of poems, plays, articles, and debates, Russell, in an effort to realize his own spiritual identity, withdrew into the stillness of his soul to contemplate the nature of the spirit-being he believed had incarnated in him.

The Divergence of the Twain

The first influential nationalist Yeats came to know was Charles Hubert Oldham, a young Trinity College graduate with a passion for literary and political discussion.[3] In February 1885 Oldham founded the *Dublin University Review,* a liberal arts magazine that was avowedly apolitical and that aimed to promote new Irish writing without seeming merely to endorse parochialism.[4] The *Review* was out of the first magazines to publish Yeats's poems and plays.

In November of the same year, Oldham also founded the Contemporary Club.⁵ This was a loose association of intellectuals who met once a week in his rooms for vigorous, and sometimes heated discussions about the main 'social, political, and literary questions of the day'.⁶ The Contemporary Club brought Yeats into frequent contact with many of Ireland's leading nationalists, a contact Russell denied himself.⁷ Less assured of his literary powers, hesitant and shy, hampered by a bad stammer, and less interested in 'the politics of time than the politics of eternity', he neither attended the Club nor published in the *Review*.⁸ To some extent he was also debarred from identifying with the nationalists by his conventional, lower middle class, Northern Irish upbringing. By contrast, Yeats received active support for his membership of the Club from his father, who was on first name terms with most of the members from his own days at Trinity and at the Bar. They regularly attended meetings together, for J. B. Yeats was a talkative, gregarious man and was delighted to have the chance to enjoy himself and advance his son's literary ambitions.⁹

One valuable friendship Yeats formed through the Contemporary Club was with Douglas Hyde, a committed student of Gaelic who had begun to master its folklore, mythology, and literature. Hyde's diaries provide a detailed record of the social life of literary nationalism in Dublin in the mid to late 'eighties, listing the names of those who attended the various 'at homes' and literary clubs, and sometimes giving a short summary of the evening's discussion. From them it is possible to capture some of the feeling of purpose and enthusiasm that must have animated the young nationalists. There is only one entry for Russell, who is simply listed as 'a friend of Yeats's . . . an art student'.¹⁰ But there are numerous entries reporting conversations with Yeats. For example, the entry for 18 December 1885 reads:

Went with Joynt to Young Ireland. Very good paper from Oldham. Gregg, A. Webb and Joynt spoke. I went back to Oldham's rooms where I drank a glass of punch and spent three hours talking to Yeats.¹¹

Other entries, made in the course of 1886, tell of long walks together to Katharine Tynan's home, 'Whitehall'; visits to literary clubs; and details of discussions, some lasting well into the morning, about oral poetry, Gaelic culture, and historical drama.¹² The main benefit of this friendship, though it was never as close as the one with Russell, was that Hyde was able to guide Yeats expertly to areas

Breaking the Spell

of Gaelic literature otherwise closed to him, such as the hidden Ireland of eighteenth century Munster, on which Yeats wrote with apparent authority as early as 1887.[13]

The nationalist whom Yeats himself claimed made the greatest impact on him was John O'Leary.[14] They met at the Contemporary Club toward the end of 1885, O'Leary having recently returned from Paris where he had been exiled by the British Government for his part in the '48 rebellion.[15] His commanding appearance, exploits as a Fenian, and association with the writers of Young Ireland made him a compelling figure.[16] It was probably Yeats who introduced Russell to him, for Yeats became a frequent and Russell an occasional visitor to his house.[17] O'Leary invited them both to join the York Street Branch of the Young Ireland Society, of which he was President. Russell declined, but Yeats, who had been to one or two meetings with Oldham and Hyde before O'Leary's return, accepted, and began to attend regularly.[18] With the encouragement of his new mentor, he rapidly gained a reputation as a passionate and at times stubborn debater on Irish affairs.[19] He also began to read extensively in Anglo-Irish literature, for, as he later claimed with some indulgence, O'Leary had a 'fine collection of Irish books—the best I know'[20], and an 'unequalled familiarity with the Irish literature of the past.'[21] O'Leary further performed the service, valuable to any young writer, of securing introductions to the editors of *The Gael*, a penny weekly that had a wide circulation in Ireland, and to two American magazines,[22] *The Boston Pilot* and the *Providence Sunday Journal*.

His membership of a Young Ireland Society and the encouragement he received had important consequences for his view of poetry. They persuaded him to attempt a national poetry drawn from 'the common thought of the people', with the result that he began to search for subjects among Irish folklore and legend.[23] In July 1887 he wrote a long rambling article on the 'Popular Ballad Poetry of Ireland' in which he argued that all poetry should be passionate, syncretic, and direct[24]; and in the following year, in order 'to carry on the ballad literature of Ireland according to the tradition of 1848', he helped O'Leary edit *Poems and Ballads of Young Ireland*.[25] But his endorsement of Young Ireland was not uncritical. In his article he noted that the immediacy of their response often led to triteness: 'The grass is merely green to them and the sea merely blue, and their very spontaneity has made them unequal.'[26] Furthermore, his own contributions to *Poems and Ballads of Young Ireland* reveal more of a debt to the Gaelic forms Douglas Hyde had shown him than to the overtly propagandist verse of Davis.

As Yeats gradually refined his view of national literature he became increasingly dissatisfied with Young Ireland, and though he always retained his admiration for their attempts to 'speak out of a people to a people'[27], he came, by the early 'nineties, to reject much of their verse as political bombast. He was particularly concerned that the efforts made by Sir Charles Gavan Duffy and others to reimpose the canon of Young Ireland through the New Irish Library, a series of shilling reprints, would prove detrimental to any true literary revival, reducing it to 'argument and oratory.'[28] To counter this, he advanced the idea that national literature should be written from, and not at, the people. The true poet should neither versify a political point of view, nor allow the political implications of an event to dictate his response. He should, as he himself showed, by his initial insistence on the 'Celtic' note, by early poems such as 'The Dedication to a book of Stories selected from the Irish Novelists', and 'To Ireland in the Coming Times', and in maturity, by 'Easter 1916', and 'Meditations in Time of Civil War', write poems in which the life of the nation had been creatively assimilated into the personal life of the poet.[29]

In order to explain his stance and encourage poets to write his type of Irish poetry, Yeats began during the late 'eighties to 'put forward a nationality that [was] above party'.[30] In a series of reviews and articles which displayed a criticism he later characterized as 'remorseless and enthusiastic'[31], he attempted to re-educate public taste by acquainting his fellow countrymen with an 'imaginative tradition in Irish literature'[32], a 'national literature that made Ireland beautiful in the memory'.[33] He began with a reappraisal of Ferguson's poetry, suggesting that perhaps 'reading and reasonable Irishmen' should put Ferguson at the head of their poets.[34] He dismissed the popular poets of the day, Moore, Lever, and Lover, for not being 'poets of the people'[35], and he criticized Allingham for not taking the people 'seriously.'[36] Mangan's best poems, he argued, were not those in *The Nation*, but some 'half-dozen lyrics of indescribable, vehement beauty' scattered through various anthologies.[37] In conclusion, he suggested that the poems of R. D. Joyce, who 'went for his subjects to that simple and legendary past' associated with his native county of Limerick, merited wider recognition.[38]

These reviews and articles, which were published in 1886 and 1887, are not 'criticism' as Yeats claimed at the time, but propaganda. Like all propaganda, they were periodically revised to meet emerging needs. The 'great tradition' of Irish writers advanced in 1887 was significantly redrawn in 1892, and then again in 1895.[39] What is important, however, is the purpose. Each series of articles shows Yeats establishing precursors, creating an Anglo-Irish tradition to give weight to his own theory of nationality. 'A poet', he later wrote, 'is justified not by the expression of himself, but by the public he finds or creates.'[40] In the late 'eighties and early 'nineties Yeats sought to justify himself, both as a poet and a nationalist, by reappraising existing movements and so creating his own. This involved him writing poems and plays, giving talks, publishing reviews and articles, and helping to found literary societies — The National Literary Society [Dublin] in 1891 and the Irish Literary Society [London] in 1892.[41] All his attempts to involve Russell in these projects were in vain.

Russell only partly shared his friend's ambition to be an Irish writer. He was more interested in achieving ultimate reconciliations than in defining local differences. When he began to write he did not feel compelled to formulate a theory of nationality to prove the existence of a poetic tradition. He believed his poems belonged less to time than to eternity, and less to Ireland than to Ildathach. While he was establishing himself as a writer, he felt severely threatened by the vigour and insistence of his friend's theories about literary nationalism. Even after he had secured the independence of his poetic voice with the success of his first volume of poems, he adopted the same stance towards literary nationalism as he eventually took towards the hierarchy of the Theosophical Society — a characteristically Protestant assurance in his own inner light coupled with a serene disrespect for authority and bureaucracy. As he said in the Preface to *Imaginations and Reveries*:

Birth in Ireland gave me a bias towards Irish Nationalism, while the spirit which inhabits my body told me that the politics of eternity ought to be my only concern, and that all other races equally with my own were children of the Great King. To aid in movements one must be orthodox. My desire to help prompted agreement, while my intellect was always heretical.[42]

This compulsion not to be hedged about by the national and the temporal led him to praise writing that transcended Irishness. For example, he wrote to Stephen Gwynn on the publication of his *A Lay of Ossian and Patrick*:

I like especially 'The Ash Walk' in your book because it makes me forget Ireland. I love Ireland because I find it possible here to think of other things than its history, and I like your poem because it reminds me that there is a beautiful world where I could be happy whether there was an Ireland or not. You see I am only half an Irishman, and I suspect in myself a capacity to be well pleased in any wild nature, even if it were in the Southern Hemisphere, and love the poetry most which suggests the thoughts I might have living anywhere. Don't suppose that I do not love Ireland. I am only afraid of liking it too much and of making its history and traditions too much a part of my soul to have anything to carry back to the stars where I must go.[43]

In contrast to Yeats, who constructed and reconstructed a number of ideal nationalities to harmonize with his poetry and his self-image, Russell doggedly followed what he believed were the promptings of the spirit. 'I have written out of every mood, and could not retain any mood for long', he explained.

If I advocated a national ideal I felt immediately I could make an equal plea for more cosmopolitan and universal ideas. I have obeyed my intuitions wherever they drew me, for I felt that the Light within us knows better than any other the need and the way.[44]

Yet, even when he advocated the national, it was generally in terms of the ideal. In an article on his fellow art student, John Hughes, published in the *New Ireland Review* in 1898, he wrote:

The sculptor of the Orpheus and Eurydice may smile a little if he hears that I claim him as representing, more than any of his contemporaries in art, the movement known as the Celtic renaissance; and that I place him in that position, not on account of any interpretation of Celtic tradition, history, or character, but because of his most tender and beautiful treatment of the world-famous myth of ancient Greece. But the Celtic renaissance of Ireland, as I conceive it, has not come about through the appearance of a number of excellent works dealing with Irish subjects mainly, but through the almost simultaneous awakening of a number of Irishmen to a higher ideal of beauty and perfection in their art than hitherto; . . .[45]

In his spiritual autobiography, *Song and Its Fountains*, he entered the plea that he was fated to be a mystic:

However I might wander in imagination, misled by desires, fantasy or ambition, an uneasy undercurrent set in, and I was guided back to the path from which I had so often strayed. I came at last almost to believe that, like Ulysses in the Platonic myth, I had chosen before birth a life in which I was primarily to be mystic, and I could not conflict with that primal will without finding many of the inhabitants of the soul deserting me.[46]

Throughout their entire association Russell not only saw Yeats's campaign for literary nationality as a threat to his 'own will and centre', but he also came to believe that his search for spiritual wisdom prevented him from achieving the understanding of Ireland which Yeats possessed and which he argued was necessary for the Irish writer. Russell wrote to him on the occasion of his seventieth birthday:

> I think you will be the pivot round which Ireland will turn from its surfaces to more central depths. There are deeps in the Irish character to be sounded. I could not sound them. I could only find intermittently access to some spiritual nature which is not more Irish than Hindu, but to find access to that however intermittently was the only thing I really cared about in life and it is the reason why so often I could not or would not be with you in your work or policies for I dreaded that a nature more formidable and powerful than my own would lead me away from my own will and centre.[47]

His refusal to work with Yeats in generating a new Irish literature, a refusal which he consistently attempted to excuse by claiming that he 'could not' be an Irish writer, explains why Yeats never celebrated Russell as one of the seminal figures of the Renaissance. As a friend, Russell was for several years as close to Yeats as Lady Gregory, and much closer than Synge, but he is not even mentioned in any of the great retrospective meditations: 'All Souls' Night'; 'Coole Park, 1929'; 'Coole Park and Ballylee, 1931'; and 'The Municipal Gallery Revisited'; nor in the speech Yeats delivered when he received the Nobel Prize in 1923, 'The Irish Dramatic Movement'. By removing himself from an influence which he felt would be injurious to him as a writer, Russell also removed himself from the mainstream of the Irish Literary Renaissance.[48]

Admiration and Disputation

Russell's decision not to join Yeats in his campaign to advance a literary expression of nationality, and his fear that nationalism would prove a malign influence on his writing did not prevent him from enjoying a close friendship with Yeats. In fact, the three years, from May 1884 when they first met to May 1887 when Yeats moved to London, were probably the best years of their long association. Russell is said to have once remarked that the happiest days of his life were the times that he and Yeats had 'sat up to all hours talking about everything in heaven and earth'.[49] Their proximity to one another in Dublin enabled an immediate and enthusiastic exchange of ideas. On one occasion Yeats was so anxious to learn his friend's reaction to a new poem that he rushed around to his home at 'three or four in the morning'. In his efforts to rouse Russell he also woke the rest of the family, who were annoyed by the intrusion.[50]

This enthusiastic admiration for one another's abilities attracted the notice, and on one occasion the ridicule, of their contemporaries. They were both singled out for attack by Hannah Lynch, a minor novelist who met them at an informal party given by Katharine Tynan. She had invited Russell, Douglas Hyde, James Sheehan, the Lynch sisters, and Yeats, who had recently come over from London for a few weeks, to visit 'Whitehall' one Sunday early in December 1887.[51] In the course of the afternoon Hannah Lynch, as Russell later told Charles Johnston, proceeded 'to pump' Yeats and himself for their 'religious, political and artistic opinions'. Several days later Yeats returned to London to spend Christmas with his family, and so missed the long, thinly-disguised account of their Sunday afternoon entitled 'A Dublin Literary Coterie' that was printed in the Dublin *Evening Telegraph* for 14 January 1888. Johnston read the article to Russell, who confided to Carrie Rea: 'I believe I made an hysterical attempt to laugh which did not impose on him, but about ten minutes after, when I thought of what poor Willie Yeats would think, I began to scream with laughter and enjoyed it immensely.'[52]

After half a column of snide remarks about their 'Aestheticism', which Hannah Lynch says any 'hardy patriot' would recognize as effete and English, and a jibe at their deliberately out-moded style of dress (their Byronic neck ties?), she describes Yeats introducing Russell:

Do you know that . . . is an artist of splendid genius and promise? . . . He excels Blake in weird and mystical fancies, and neither Puck nor Ariel is a more delicately inhuman and sprightly creation than one of his fairies. Look at this lovely little sketch of his. Is not it quite precious and spiritual? You mark the allegory. It was a dream, and you see that it is more exquisite far and more unseizable than anything Blake did.

Most of the article is devoted to Russell's stammering admiration for Yeats reading his own poetry.

'His r-reading is-is quite re-remarkable. He is v-very proud o-of it . . .'
'But he doesn't read at all correctly. It is impossible to understand him.'
'Oh, b-but no one w-wants t-to understand him. . . . I-It isn't t-the sense, you know, b-but the a-atmosphere. I-It's like l-listening to m-music you don't un-understand. H-He envelops h-his l-listeners in a de-delicious atmosphere. Y-You f-feel it all t-there, b-but you don't understand, a-and the a-agitated n-nerves are calmed, the un-unrest of the s-soul is soothed, a-and th-the tremulous un-unutterable yearnings of-of the h-heart are s-stilled.'

Russell is reported to claim that 'Ireland has produced no such poet hitherto'; that some of Yeats's 'unpublished songs are equal to Shakespeare, that in music he ranks with Shelley, in colouring with Keats; and that Coleridge himself was not more saturated with deep and transcendental philosophy'.

Though their mutual admiration has been made ludicrous, the two men did discuss one another's work in this manner. Yeats described Russell to Lady Gregory in the late 'nineties as having been 'the most promising student in the Dublin Art schools'[53]; while in *The Sketch* for August 1898 he called Russell's painting 'very fantastic' — an accomplished attempt 'to make of unmoving and silent paint a mirror for the wandering, exultant processions that haunt those margins of spiritual ecstasy, where colours are sounds, and sounds are shapes, and shapes are fragrances'.[54]

Russell, for his part, wrote admiringly in *The Irish Statesman* in 1925: 'The poetry of Yeats is the greatest spiritual gift any Irishman has made to his tribe. He is the finest artist in Irish literature.' To which he added, in words that are strikingly similar to those ridiculed by the authoress of 'A Dublin Literary Coterie': 'Who under a spell can be critical of the enchanter? I was not then, and hardly now can I do anything but surrender myself anew to the music.' In the 1925 article he even makes some of the same comparisons that he was reported making in 1887:

No poet since Keats and Shelley has so completely realized for us the stranger regions of imagination, has convinced us more of the authenticity of his vision, that the words depict things which were present to the interior sense.[55]

But this open, and at times extravagant admiration for one another's work did not mean that their literary association was based on cosy reassurance. Russell, as has already been shown, was sufficiently self-possessed and sufficiently distant not to ally himself with his friend's campaign to promote a literary expression of Irish nationality. They often held opposing views. In one of those trenchant phrases so characteristic of his poems, Yeats perceptively described the force that drew and bound them together as that 'antagonism that unites dear friends'.[56] His quarrels with Russell, though not as noisy as his much publicized disputes with his father,[57] were probably as frequent, for the differences between the two young men were in some ways far greater than those between son and father. Yeats came to share many of his father's views on topics such as 'belief, doubt, style, personality, emotion, intellect'[58], while he quarrelled doggedly and eventually divisively with Russell about mysticism, poetry, drama, autobiography, politics, artistic patronage, and literary nationalism.

In fact, though it may seem paradoxical, the antagonism that united them as dear friends would appear to have been a necessary stimulus for Russell's creativity. It prevented him from evaporating away in mysticism, it drove him to develop and defend his ideas, and it fired him with the desire to produce his own work. As Yeats himself observed: 'All creation is from conflict, whether with our own mind or with that of others.'[59] And even if this assertion does not hold true as a generalization, it was certainly true for Russell. Twenty years after he had met Yeats, he admitted to a friend: 'I will be very glad to see W.B.Y.' when he returns to Ireland. 'I am always fighting with him, but if I hadn't him to fight with it would make a great gap in my life.'[60] As late as 1929 he wrote to Yeats: 'I am very glad to know that you will soon be back again in Ireland. There is a distinct lowering of intellectual vitality whenever you are away.'[61] Antagonism and exclusion were as necessary for their literary association as admiration and enthusiasm.

The Pyrognostics of a Poet

Yeats's sudden move to London in the summer of 1887 deprived Russell of his most vital source of intellectual and artistic stimulus. Within months he began to renounce most of the interests which he had so enthusiastically shared with Yeats during the first three years of their friendship. Yeats believed that 'if you are separated from your opposite, you consume yourself away',[62] and this is exactly what happened to Russell. Between the summer of 1887 and the beginning of 1890 he burned all his manuscripts, gave up reading for nine months, stopped writing plays, poems and fairy tales, abandoned painting, left the Dublin Art Schools, and even made plans to quit Ireland of America. By 1890, as Yeats wrote, 'he was the religious teacher, and that alone'.[63]

This dramatic surge of renunciation was brought on by a profound spiritual and artistic crisis that seems to have begun in the summer of 1887. Evelyn Underhill, in her classic account of the mystic life, has shown that 'awakening' is generally followed by a period of great upheaval and dislocation. After some time the feelings of exaltation and power that have flowed from the onset of ecstasy begin to break

Breaking the Spell

up and become turbulent, so that the mystic finds himself swinging uncertainly between bouts of depression and bursts of radiance. The characteristic response is to try to strip the self down to the essentials, to practise what is called 'mortification', in order to restore equilibrium and harmony. As Evelyn Underhill explains:

> Mortification takes its name from the reiterated statement of all [mystic] writers that the senses, or 'body of desire', with the cravings which are excited by different aspects of the phenomenal world, must be mortified or killed; which is, of course, a description of psychological necessities from their point of view. All those self-regarding instincts — so ingrained that they have become automatic — which impel the self to choose the more comfortable part, are seen by the awakened intuition of the embryonic mystic as gross infringements of the law of love.[64]

This painful and sometimes violent paring down of the self is an attempt to reduce the disparity between the mystic's own 'clouded contours and the pure sharp radiance of the Real'.[65]

In Russell's case, the compulsion to 'mortify' the self seems to have coincided with and been intensified by Yeats's unexpected departure, an event which, he confided to Carrie Rea in a long anguished letter, had thrown him into 'a state of desolate and spiritual blackness. . . the only way out of which is to reflect that both good and evil in life are the fulfilment of one's own wishes and thoughts, and that if I hold to the true I shall again meet the true and the real in humanity.'

The same letter also reveals that part of his despair was caused by his frustration at not being able to express his visionary insights. He confided to Carrie Rea that he sincerely wanted to emulate the 'vitality' and 'wisdom' of the poetry of 'Arnold, Goethe, Wordsworth, Emerson, and Thoreau'. By 'vitality', 'I do not mean mere wisdom', he explained,

> but an inward consciousness of [the poet's] true relations to the universe and to man, to the 'eternal' which he feels within him and its manifestations without. By his wisdom I do not mean his philosophy, metaphysics, or learning, but those few precious sayings, a page or two would contain them, no man ever leaves more, which are the result of the conflict of the eternal and the transitory within him, and when the former has conquered.

He was convinced, he told her, that the best way to prepare himself to write the poetry of vitality and wisdom was to study the sacred writings of the East.

The *Bhagavad Gita* and *Upanishads* contain such God-like fullness of wisdom of all things that I can feel the authors must have looked with calm remembrance back through a thousand passionate lives full of feverish strife for and with shadows, ere they would have written with such certainty of things which the soul feels to be sure.

The poems that came to him from the visions that broke into his own clouded life seemed equally profound, but when he wrote them out they appeared chaotic, trite, and commonplace. I write 'much feverish verse', he admitted,

which practice shall have to be given up until I have something worth saying, my 'one or two precious pages.' This verse writing is the sort of thing which does no good as it is only a reiteration of that which does not want reiteration, action being necessary.[66]

Even the good verse that he wrote seemed to him to be derivative of Yeats. He later told Cecil French in a candid letter that is central to understanding his attitude to the literary association:

When I was young and much in company with Yeats and when I found I was writing lines that seemed to be more the offspring of his mind than my own I deliberately broke the spell, read little for a while of Yeats, and much of the Sacred books and came to be myself, perhaps a less exquisite artist than I might have been had I allowed this tutoring to continue but at least I came to act from my own will and centre and found my own way of saying what I felt and thought.[67]

The talisman for protecting himself against Yeats's spell was the slow discovery and establishment of his own 'will and centre'. As he said in his review of *Early Poems and Stories*, he only became 'less yielding' after he 'had gone on a way of [his] own and had become self-conscious'.[68]

The dread that he would yield to the potentially distorting influence of his friend's work remained with him all his life. He wrote to Yeats in 1902, for example, to explain why he had not read his play *Where There is Nothing*:

I limit my own mind and keep within my own circle as much as possible and hate going out of it. The mind of another is full of dangers. The mould of the imagination which we stamp on what we write is a very delicate thing and to reshape it, even to enlarge its scope, is liable to blur the distinctness and beauty of impression.[69]

The same fear lay behind his admission to Yeats in 1935 that their literary associations had been governed by his dread that 'a nature more formidable and powerful than my own would lead me away from my own will and centre'.[70] Throughout his life, Russell reserved some of his most biting criticism for those who had succumbed to the spell, who merely 'reiterated' his friend's images and ideas.[71]

The strain of distancing himself from Yeats can be detected in the apology he wrote to Katharine Tynan for missing the farewell party she had organized for Yeats on his return to London to spend Christmas with his parents. There is, for this early in their association, an uncharacteristic tinge of sarcasm in his parodies.

67 Grosvenor Square
[Late December 1887]

My Dear Miss Tynan,

I am sorry that I was unable to come to Mr O'Leary's last evening. But it will not make much difference about my not seeing Willie Yeats as I intend opening communication with him through the medium of the astral light — that is — try thought transference between Grosvenor Square and Eardley Terrace. No doubt he will have imagination enough to think he is receiving messages from me and whenever I write to him about these airy conversations I will use expressions which will suit his conversation at any time. 'Your poem is splendid' 'Your paradoxes are getting more startling every day' and 'You should not say such hard things of your friends.' These remarks will convince him more than ever of my occult powers and he will tell everyone that I can hear his smallest whisper over a thousand miles away and exalt me generally above M. Blavatsky . . .[72]

Shortly after Yeats left for London, Russell burnt all his manuscripts.[73] This symbolic act of self immolation was meant to rid him of Yeats's poetic spell and be the funeral pyre for his own literary ambitions. He also told Carrie Rea that the discovery that his 'knowledge of occultism' was incomplete had given him an additional reason for burning his manuscripts. 'I found I was merely a child', he confessed dejectedly, 'when I thought I was an advanced student.' He explained that he had been reading Blake and Boehme and had come to realize that they had anticipated all his ideas. 'This was enough', he wrote. 'I found it was possible that I might after years of thought arrive at their knowledge, but mere knowledge of possibilities was not what I wanted.' He was convinced that he should try to purify his soul. Perhaps when his soul was strong enough it would 'melt' the 'body' and poetry would 'come through.' 'I need not tell you', he continued his letter, that I believe . . . our situation in the world is the result of our actions in a past existence, that every intellect commences the struggle where it left off before, that if I fill myself with poetry at present, in my next life I shall be a poet.[74]

When Carrie Rea, with a good deal of shrewdness, jokingly accused him of hankering after literary fame, he retorted: 'I never said that I would be a poet in my next life. I have no desire to be famous, fame is such a very foolish thing. I would like, if I could, to raise some of the people I know to a higher level of existence.'[75] A few months later he reiterated:

I do not think I will ever try to get either literary or artistic fame. Art and literature do not interest me now. Only one thing interests me and that is life or truth. I want to become rather than know.[76]

Either later that year, 1888, or early the next, he stopped attending art classes at the Royal Hibernian Academy.[77] It had been his earliest ambition to be a painter. Despite the promising work he had already produced, the prizes he had won, and despite his fellow students' belief that there was a great artist in him, he put down his brushes and paints and did not take them up again for nearly twenty years.[78] He told Yeats

that the will is the only thing given us in this life as absolutely our own, and that we should allow no weakening of it, and that Art, which he cared for so much, would, he believed, weaken his will.[79]

Yeats said he greeted the decision with irony and indignation.[80]

Russell also renounced literature. He did not publish anything creative or critical between December 1887, when his article on 'The Speech of the Gods' was printed in the Madras *Theosophist*, and October 1892, when he became editor of *The Irish Theosophist*, a small monthly that had a very limited circulation in Dublin. He later told Yeats that he gave up writing poetry and prose because he felt that creative writing also encouraged self-indulgence.[81] Instead of writing and painting he spent long periods of time poring over *The Bhagavad Gita* and the *Upanishads*, and when his mind became so tired that he felt completely drained of concentration, he would go for long walks in the hills around Dublin, where, as he later told a friend, he would lie 'for hours letting what would come out of myself'.[82]

During these five years of artistic silence, he found refuge from despair in his visions. He wrote to Carrie Rea early in 1888:

Breaking the Spell

I am afraid that I will never be of any use in this Western World. I will try some time to go out to India to become a pupil of the adepts. My dreaming propensities would not be so much out of place there, but to dream is delightful, it is the only thing that makes me happy, for even a short time. I seem to rise higher within myself and come to a white circle of consciousness where I feel blind with joy as if I am united with an existence greater than my own, and one finds out such beautiful ideas.[83]

This does not mean that he simply exchanged the emotional self-indulgence that he associated with poetry and painting for a different type of emotional self-indulgence, 'blind' feelings of joy. His visions were chiefly important to him as a source of 'beautiful ideas'. As he pointed out in *Song and Its Fountains*, he believed visions were one of the means the incarnating spirit chose 'to tune the body' to receive esoteric wisdom.[84] Even so, he persistently held to the hope that once he had attained a measure of spiritual maturity his visionary revelations would be sufficiently profound for him to write wise, vital poetry. In 1888 he informed Carrie Rea that he would begin to write again as soon as he was convinced that his knowledge was 'universal'.[85]

In the same year that Russell began preparing himself to receive 'universal' truths, Yeats wrote an article on the poet Allingham in which he argued that the particular and the national were the only means a poet had of understanding and expressing the universal.

To the greater poets everything they see has its relation to the national life, and through that to the universal and divine life: nothing is an isolated artistic moment . . . the grass blade carries the universe upon its point. But to this universalism, this seeing of unity everywhere, you can only attain through what is near you, your nation, or . . . your village and the cobwebs on your walls.[86]

Yeats's own early poems are full of details which show how closely he observed village life and the Irish countryside.[87] He knew that the grass grew longest on the weirs; that the light of the West made the water seem 'mouse-grey' and the sand 'dove-grey'; that a heavy creel of fish made the wheels of the cart creak; and that the fishermen laid their nets on the pebbly beaches when they wished to mend or dry them. The poems are full of the wild creatures that populate the West: cranes, swans, curlews, herons, osprey, and ousels; cormorants shivering on the rocks, mice in the barley sheaves, drowsy water-rats, slumbering trout, wise owls in their downy caps, swallows flashing their white breasts, dreaming water fowls; and foxes, weasels, squirrels, badgers, spiders, glow-worms, rabbits, otters, lizards, hares, bats, and frogs. There are marigolds and foxgloves and gillyflowers, dew-tongued daisies, lemon daffodils, wet wild-strawberry leaves, hawthorn, sorrel, spear-grass, hazel, sloe berries, and even puff-balls. This abundance is not for ornament, but to fix the poems to a known locality.[88] Their enumeration belongs to that love of place that Robin Flower has shown is an essential quality of the Gaelic literary tradition.[89] Much of the force of a poem like 'The Stolen Child' is derived from the savouring of the local features that provide a landscape for the poem.

> Where the wandering water gushes
> From the hills above Glen-Car,
> In pools among the rushes
> That scarce could bathe a star.[90]

Within little more than a decade, Russell regretted that he had not followed Yeats's example and sought to express the universal through the medium of the local and the particular, to write poems about local flowers and wildlife, the 'village' and the 'cobwebs' on the walls. In 1901, when he himself had only published his first two volumes of poems, he wrote to William Byrne on the release of his *A Light on the Broom*:

I have read with much pleasure your book of poems which has a quite distinct note of its own . . . I find all through your poems an atmosphere which recalls Catholic Ireland at its kindliest; an atmosphere I always think of with pleasure, remembering many cottages where I have sat on the hearth, the kindly people, the bogs I have walked over, and the colour of Irish twilights, and the dream of another world which is never far from any of us, Catholic or not. I find many beautiful lines which picture perfectly this average Irish life, and I sincerely envy you your poetic 'properties': bogland, turf fire, sweet milk, crickets, corncrakes, furze land, and cabin smoke, which no one could introduce so fitly as you do unless they were not only familiar but were also part of the dream of life. *I am too old now to get at these everyday things which must always be the subject of the best art. I started from the stars and never succeeded in getting my feet firmly on the earth, but if you start from the earth you can go as far as you like.*[91]

Many years later, he confided to Monk Gibbon that he had wasted much of his youth gathering 'rootless flowers'[92] — a metaphor for his intensive study of Eastern mysticism. And when the young poet sent him verses which he thought were derivative, Russell replied:

I cannot find the likeness you surmise to other poets. I fancy it is imaginary. Besides as Goethe says it is open to any poet to take from another so long

Breaking the Spell

as he can use the idea and make it his own . . . I think it might be well if you watched Nature closely to get precise images of things . . . Yeats's verse owes much to his observation of Nature. 'The Wild Swans at Coole' is an instance. I am not suggesting pictorial poetry but it is well to have clear images showing precision of observation and not to generalize too much when referring to Nature.[93]

Monk Gibbon followed his advice, and when *The Seals* was published, Russell singled out for praise his 'intentness of eye and mind.' 'How good it is', he wrote, 'to come upon this consuming interest in what the eye casually rests on.'[94]

Had Russell himself been more assured when he began to write, and had he been less ready to see his friend as a threat, he might have written vital poetry that drew from all parts of his richly-varied experience. But he chose instead to limit his own mind and keep within his own circle as much as possible, to succumb to that self-induced dread that his friend's more formidable and powerful nature would entice him away from his own will and centre. To be the admirer and friend of Yeats at once stimulated and stifled him. It inspired him to write poetry, but it made him excessively, and perhaps unnecessarily, anxious about going beyond what he arbitrarily designated was his own. The mistake of his life as a poet was that he drew this self-limiting circle before he had published anything.

From Dublin to London

While Russell concentrated solely on spiritual improvement, Yeats devoted his energy to writing. His vigour and industry provide a sharp contrast with Russell's withdrawal. As he later disclosed, all his twenties were 'crammed with toil'.[95] Between 1887 and 1892 he contributed over one hundred items, comprising poems, reviews, articles, and letters to Irish, English, and American newspapers and periodicals. He edited two volumes of fairy tales, two volumes of stories and a selection entitled *Stories from Carleton*. He began a 200 page history of Irish literature that was to be 'systematically political or national . . . throughout',[96] and he published his only novel, *John Sherman*, in which he juxtaposed and contrasted his own emotional responses to London and the West of Ireland; a short story, modelled on William Morris's *Gettir the Strong*;[97] and his first full-length play. He contributed poetry to *Irish Minstrelsy, Poems and Ballads of Young Ireland,* and *The Book of the Rhymers'*

Club, as well as publishing two volumes of his own poems, *The Wanderings of Oisin and Other Poems*, and *The Countess Cathleen and Various Legends and Lyrics*. And, in collaboration with Edwin J. Ellis, he began work on a three volume edition of Blake's works, supplemented by a biographical *Memoir* and extensive critical notes.[98]

He was able to produce this impressive quantity of work because he devoted all his time to writing. Shortly after he left Dublin he decided not to seek regular employment but to see if he could support himself from editorial work and criticism. He believed that this would prove best for poetry, and though his decision plunged him into poverty, he held to his independence. The bottom line of many a literary project in the late 'eighties and early 'nineties involved the repayment of borrowed pounds, or the raising of money to buy food and meet other household bills. His father, whose own ability to earn money from painting was at its lowest ebb, at least gave his son an abundant supply of moral encouragement. The odd times Yeats dreamed of a weekly pay packet he was warned it would cost him his 'mental liberty'.[99] When he refused York Powell's offer of a recommendation for a sub-editorship on the *Manchester Courier*, his father reassured him: 'You have taken a great weight off my mind.'[100]

Russell's situation was the reverse. His father, a book-keeper for a firm of chartered accountants, obtained a clerkship for his son, who dutifully spent the final month of his last school vacation improving his 'totting up'.[101] For the rest of his life Russell moved cautiously, especially after he had acquired a wife, two children and a mortgage, from one form of regular employment to another, though he frequently complained to Yeats: 'I [have] such a tired and busy life that I never get a chance of dreaming a little and making myself at home in my themes.'[102]

The move to London also meant that Yeats came increasingly to leave behind the way of life that he and Russell had shared as art students together at the Royal Hibernian Academy. So significant was the change that when he wrote his *Autobiographies* he devoted an entire section to his first four years in London. The rich variety of treatment and style of the large volume of work he produced at this time reflects the new literary society to which he was disposed and obliged to respond. Living in Bedford Park, an artistic enclave for respectable bohemia, brought him into contact with York Powell, the Regius Professor of History at Oxford, the publisher Elkin Mathews, the artists Paget and Nash, and Dr John Todhunter, whose productions of his own plays whetted his appetite for the theatre.[103] He spent his first London Christmas, 1888, with Oscar Wilde, who graciously invited him to dine with the family and then read to him from the proofs of *The Decay of Lying*.[104] Barely a mile from Bedford Park was William Morris's Kelmscott House, where he was a frequent and welcome visitor, and where he met George Bernard Shaw, Walter Crane, Emery Walker, Henry Hyndman the socialist, and Prince Kropotkin the anarchist.[105] A quarter of an hour's walk from Bedford Park, out on the high road to Richmond, lived W. E. Henley, who introduced him to several literary figures, including Arthur Symons and Edward Garnett, and published his poems, reviews and articles in the *National Observer*. 'He made us feel always our importance', Yeats later wrote of him.[106] It was Henley who enhanced the reputation Yeats had achieved for himself with *The Wanderings of Oisin* by publishing and praising the two poems that secured his literary standing in London: 'The Lake Isle of Innisfree', and 'The Man Who Dreamed of Faeryland'.[107]

Living in London also gave him the opportunity to visit Madame Blavatsky, who established her headquarters there in 1889. It was at her rooms that he met Annie Besant and the Countess Wachtmeister.[108] From working in the British Museum he met MacGregor Mathers;[109] and through the Hermetic Order of the Golden Dawn came in time to know and to contend with occultists such as A.E. Waite and Aleister Crowley.[110] Early in 1891 he helped found the Rhymers' Club, which brought together in his phrase, 'well nigh all the poets of the new generation': Ernest Dowson, John Davidson, Lionel Johnson, Arthur Symons, Ernest Rhys, Edwin Ellis, Victor Plarr, Richard Le Gallienne and Aubrey Beardsley.[111] His association with the Rhymers' further increased his literary and social standing. In 1892 the editor of the *Bookman* sought out Yeats as one of four distinguished poets to express an opinion on the election and office of the Laureate following the death of Tennyson.[112]

And the women he met in London made his Dublin friendship with Katharine Tynan seem conventional, domestic and amiable. Some twenty minutes walk from Bedford Park lived the young actress and divorcee, Florence Farr. Especially in his first year in London he called on her frequently, ostensibly to talk about the plays that he would some day write for her.[113] But her 'tranquil beauty' was soon eclipsed by Maud Gonne, who called on him at Bedford Park in 1889, a woman of 'so great beauty' that she seemed to belong 'to famous pictures, to poetry, to some legendary past'. 'She brought into my life', he later wrote, 'the middle of the tint, a sound as of a Burmese gong, an overpowering tumult that had yet many pleasant secondary notes.'[114] When his love for her seemed unattainable and desperate, he formed a brief, consoling liaison with Olivia Shakespear, a beautiful young married novelist.[115]

Many of the letters he wrote to friends in Dublin reveal his hatred of London: his initial dislike of soirées and coteries, his revulsion for city crowds, his money worries, his ill health from overwork, his gnawing sexual frustration, and his difficulties with editors and publishers; but they also show his burgeoning self-confidence and his growing skill in self-advertisement.[116] From his London friends he learned something of French writers, and when he visited Paris in the early 'nineties he was stimulated by its literature and theatre. For most of his life he moved impecuniously between England, Ireland, and the Continent. Altogether, he spent thirty-four of his seventy-three years outside Ireland, and in the process created, as Sean O'Faolain has rightly said, 'a new type of Irishman — the Irish-European.'[117]

Russell, on the other hand, despite the breadth of his reading and interests, remained stolidly provincial. He rarely left Ireland, and when he did was conspicuously uncomfortable. He made several trips to England, late in life lectured in America, but his only trip to the Continent, a visit to Paris in the 'twenties, was a disaster.[118]

Frank O'Connor, who knew both men well, has memorably evoked that initial divergence that must have taken place as a result of the move to London.

> Yeats was the small-town boy who had travelled; AE the one who had remained at home. I could almost imagine the moment of the first rift, when Yeats, back from London, spoke of some writer who kept a mistress. And AE, dumbfounded, would repeat, 'a mistress, Willy?' And after that Yeats would think his old friend narrow-minded, and AE would say that Yeats had disimproved since his early days. It is a little tragedy that takes place in every provincial town every day of the week.[119]

'But Friendship Never Ends'

Russell's struggle to free himself from his friend's poetic influence, and the physical and cultural distances separating them, must have imposed a heavy strain on their literary association. It would have been easy for them to drift apart, but Yeats made a concerted effort to keep in touch. Shortly after he had arrived in London he was asked by Ernest Rhys, the editor of the Camelot Classics, to compile a selection of Irish fairy and folk tales for the series. As not all the material he wanted was available in the British Museum, he wrote

Breaking the Spell

to Russell in Dublin and asked him to transcribe various folk-tales from back numbers of Irish journals.[120] Russell copied them out for him, and though Yeats also received help from Katharine Tynan and Douglas Hyde, he dedicated his book, *Fairy and Folk Tales of the Irish Peasantry* 'to my mystical friend, G.R'.[121] By wording his dedication in this way, he wished both to signify his appreciation for Russell's friendship and assistance, even though it had been rather menial, and acknowledge him as a fellow-believer in the world of faery.

From the few letters which have survived from the late 'eighties and early 'nineties it would seem that Yeats initiated most of the correspondence. And though his letters lack the familiarity of those to John O'Leary or the ease between fellow writers that mark those to Katharine Tynan, they nevertheless reveal that Yeats was anxious to preserve his friendship with Russell. They generally show him brushing over his own accomplishments, asking questions, soliciting news, and eagerly requesting a reply. For example, he wrote to Russell on 8 February 1889, following the publication of *The Wanderings of Oisin and Other Poems*:

> Write and tell me what you like best and what worst, and what other students who got copies think. The people of my own age are in the long run the most important. They are the future. I am starting a new drama founded on an Irish folk-tale. The best plot I [have] ever worked on. So much about myself. What are you doing? You have not written lately. Where is Hughes? Is he your companion in that projected American trip? Is it still projected? I have heard many regret your coming departure and one names Hughes as your probable fellow traveller. Are any dates or other matters decided on?[122]

Russell's reply has been lost; but early in the 1900s he wrote in an article entitled 'A Poet of Shadows' of his response to *The Wanderings of Oisin*:

> I am too often tempted to wander with Usheen in Tirnanoge and to forget my own heart and its more rarely accorded vision of truth. I know I like my own heart best, but I never look into the world of my friend without feeling that my region lies in the temperate zone and is near the Arctic Circle; the flowers grow more rarely and are paler, and the struggle for existence is keener.[123]

While apparently envious of Yeats's seeming facility, Russell did not believe that he should venture beyond his own spiritual experiences for inspiration.

The Search for Unity

While he 'could not endure' the idea of 'an international art, picking stories and symbols where it pleased',[124] and while he increasingly came to see himself as an Irish writer, Yeats's exposure to some of the principal figures and movements of the day meant that his point of view was never simple. Russell's first volume of poetry has a single preoccupation and a homogeneous style. Yeats entitled the selection of his earliest poetry 'Crossways', because he said he had 'tried many pathways'.[125] In his *Autobiographies* he described himself in the late 'eighties as being 'in all things Pre-Raphaelite'[126], yet in the Introduction to *Early Poems and Stories* he retrospectively identified himself with the Young Ireland poets,[127] though, as he himself acknowledged elsewhere, many of the 'Irish' poems have an occult dimension which sets them apart from Young Ireland. In 'To Ireland in the Coming Times' he cautioned his readers that while he wished to

> be counted one
> With Davis, Mangan, Ferguson . . .
> [his] rhymes more than their rhyming tell
> Of the dim wisdoms old and deep,
> That God gives unto man in sleep.[128]

Because many of the poems evoke a dim, dream-like atmosphere, some critics have mistakenly identified Yeats with fin-de-siècle aestheticism.[129] Several of the early poems are ostentatiously languid and world-weary, as MacNeice[130] and Clarke[131] have shown, but Yeats was not an escapist who rejected the world of experience, a poet who believe that art should be purged of everyday life. In fact, it was during the late 'eighties that he conceived the idea that the poet should seek and achieve 'unity of being', by which he meant that he should cultivate the ability to write from an 'inherited subject-matter known to the whole people.'[132] George Moore commented when he first met Yeats in the late 'eighties that his early poems only sparely represented the profusion of his interests.[133] It was as though he had achieved, without particularly desiring it or striving for it, that state described by Pater in the last chapter of *The Renaissance*, where Art is proclaimed as the end of life because it gives 'a quickened, multiplied consciousness'.[134]

Yeats later confessed that he was extremely worried by the variety and seeming incompatibility of his concerns. 'I had three interests; [an] interest in a form of literature, a form of philosophy, and a belief in nationality', he wrote:

None of these seemed to have anything to do with the other, . . . [then] when I was twenty-three or twenty-four this sentence seemed to form in my head, without my willing it, much as sentences form when we are half-asleep; 'Hammer your thoughts into unity.' For days I could think of nothing else, and for years I tested all I did by that sentence.[135]

Both the enumeration of his interests and his self-analysis are more tidy and purposeful than they would have been in 1888 or 1889, when he was twenty-three or twenty-four. At that time his aesthetic theory was as inchoate as his poetry. But the purpose of the statement is not to report accurately a factual event, but to sketch in the magnitude of a need, and to provide the reader, and incidentally Yeats himself, with a point of entry into a difficult period of his life. The means he chose to achieve this unity contrast sharply with those chosen by Russell, for while Russell strove to gain coherence by renouncing most of his interests — 'to summon', as Yeats shrewdly remarked, 'a creator by revealing chaos'[136] — Yeats himself preferred to experiment with a variety of stances that allowed his interests free and rewarding play.

One of his earliest was his theory of the bifurcated self — a theory that essentially the consciousness is divided, and that a type of unity could be achieved by pitting one self against the other or by employing one self to interrogate the other. According to Russell, Yeats already possessed some notion of this when they were art students together in Dublin. 'I remember', he recalled in *Song and Its Fountains*,

showing the poet some drawings I had made and wondering why he was interested most of all in a drawing of a man on a hill-top, a man amazed at his own shadow cast gigantically on a mountain mist, for this drawing had not seemed to me the best. But I soon found his imagination was dominated by his own myth of a duality in self . . .[137]

In terms of his move to London, Yeats successfully exploited the artistic and psychological possibilities of this theory of the self in the short novel published in 1891 entitled *John Sherman*. Through the antithesis between the two main characters, Sherman and Howard, which is extensively worked out, he was able to express the emotional turmoil he had experienced in moving to London while he simultaneously explored two self-images — that of a rural dreamer who is nourished by the calm of Sligo, and that of a self-possessed cosmopolitan who enjoys living in London.[138]

Another method of achieving unity which preoccupied Yeats throughout the 'nineties was style. He said himself that he began his search for a style with a 'deliberateness' which even in his later years surprised him.[139] In the main, he seems to have taken his bearings from the younger Hallam's essay on the lyrical poems of Tennyson[140] and from Walter Pater's seminal and much-discussed essay, 'Style', first published in the *Manchester Guardian* in 1888.[141] Both, allowing for their distinctive emphases, belong to the Romantic view of style derived from Longinus' treaties *On the Sublime* and expounded in Coleridge's *Biographia Literaria*, rather than the neo-classical view of style, championed by Renaissance theorists such as Puttenham, Sir William Alexander, and Chapelain. The Romantic view proposes that style is organic rather than ornamental, that it grows out of the symbiotic relationship between perception and expression rather than the separate and perhaps belated addition of ornament. Essential to any discovery of a style, the Romantics assert, is the realization of a self.[142] In his essay, the younger Hallam argued that Keats and Shelley, poets Yeats often set before himself, should be thought of as 'poets of sensation rather than reflection', for while

other poets seek for images to illustrate their conceptions; these men had no need to seek; they lived in a world of images; for the most important and extensive portion of their life consisted in those emotions, which are immediately conversant with sensation.[143]

In his essay, Pater went further to argue that in an important sense style is comprised of the arduous, painstaking quest for the Flaubertian *mot juste*, for 'the unique word, phrase, sentence, paragraph . . . absolutely proper to the single mental presentation or vision within'.[144] Quoting Buffon, he reasserted: ' "The style is the man", complex or simple, in his individuality, his plenary sense of what he really has to say, his sense of the world.'[145] From both essays, Yeats realized that his search for style involved a parallel search for a self.

Russell, who was an ardent exponent of being true to the depths of one's being, and who thought that 'life creates the form', believed that his friend's obsession with style was a mistake. He later confided to George Moore that Yeats seemed to think that 'if you have a style . . . you will have something to say'.[146] As far as he was concerned, style either came naturally, as the form in which the 'oracles out of the psyche' were delivered, or it did not come at all.[147]

His misunderstanding of Yeats's conception of style can be seen from the way he unwittingly but consistently employed the stock metaphors of the neo-classical view whenever he criticized his friend's work. For example, his complaint that finding a new style on an old poem was 'as disconcerting as for a lover to find his mistress had powdered the hair or tinted the face he had come to love for its natural beauty'[148] echoes Puttenham's metaphor that style is 'the crimson taint . . . laid upon a lady's lips'.[149] Similarly, his mistaken belief that Yeats thought style was the fine clothes that made the fine manner, a belief given expression in a reported conversation in George Moore's *Vale*, also echoes Sir William Alexander's contention that 'language is but the apparel of Poesy, which may give beauty but not strength'.[150]

AE thought that Yeats had discovered a style, and a very fine style indeed, and compared it to a suit of livery which a man buys before he engages a servant; the livery is made of the finest cloth, the gold lace is the very finest, the cockade can be seen from one side of the street to the other, but when the footman comes he is always too tall or too thin or too fat, so the livery is never worn.[151]

The metaphor, and hence the criticism, are as misplaced as they are mischievous.

Finally, Russell was just as intolerant of and uninformed about the third method of unification which Yeats pursued throughout the 'nineties: his conviction that he could bring together some of his interests and increase his range of expression by adopting various poses. 'I was about to learn', he wrote in the *Autobiographies*,

that if a man is to write lyric poetry he must be shaped by nature and art to some one out of half a dozen traditional poses, and be lover or saint, sage or sensualist, or mere mocker of all life.[152]

He began by transforming his appearance. To the consternation of Russell, who protested perversely that he did not look as noble, and Madame Blavatsky, who promised him a bad illness through the loss of the mesmeric forces, he shaved off his beard, and then his moustache.[153] He also exchanged the brightly-coloured neckties that were a sign of his pact with Russell for loosely knotted silk ties in grey, dark blue, or black. And while his friend continued to amble around Dublin in his well-worn Donegal tweed suit, its charred pockets showing how often he had absent-mindedly put his lighted pipe in them, Yeats took to wearing velveteen and dressing inexpensively but elegantly in grey or black.[154] The pictures of him from this time show him to be deliberately the poet, even to the point of appearing theatrical. When Katharine Tynan came to see him late in 1893, she could not help but remark the new tendency towards 'literary dandyism'.

> In the old Dublin days he was as untidy as a genius newly come from the backwoods. He was an art student then, and generally bore the stains of the studio . . . He used to affect scarlet ties, which lit up his olive face. They were tied most carelessly. Ordinary young men who had been at school with him, and resented his being a genius, used to say that the carelessness was the result of long effort; but one never believed them. Now he wears the regulation, London costume, plus a soft hat, and his ties are dark silk, knotted in a soft bow.[155]

In transforming his appearance, and hence himself, Yeats was influenced to a degree by Lionel Johnson,[156] but mostly by Oscar Wilde.[157] He spent the Christmas of 1888 with Wilde, and about then, or a little later, began to irritate Russell by 'vigorously defending Wilde against the charge of being a poseur. He said it was merely living artistically, and it was the duty of everybody to have a conception of themselves, and he intended to conceive of himself.' To Russell's mind however, the poseur committed the same error as the stylist in thinking that form created life. 'The error in [Yeats's] psychology', he told George Moore, is that he thinks that if 'you make a picturesque or majestic personality of yourself in appearance, you will become as wonderful inside as outside.'[158] But this account seems to fit only the early, simple form of the idea. When he was rallied by Russell for appearing in a top hat at the Horse Show, Yeats wrote of his response: 'I read in that book which I still think the wisest of all books, *Wilhelm Meister* by Goethe, "The Poor are; the rich are enabled so to seem". I was then shy and awkward, and I set myself to acquire this technique of seeming.'[159]

Though Russell's criticism exposes the Wildean pose for its sterility, it misrepresents the developed form of Yeats's idea. For Yeats the pose, which in time became transmuted into the Mask, represented an allegorical victory of imagination over circumstance which went far beyond mere attudinizing.[160] Whereas Wilde thought of the pose as a perpetually performed play,[161] a 'kind of gambling with one's public aspect',[162] Yeats advanced the idea that the self takes its cue from an historical and daemonic counterpart, the 'Mask'. The Wildean pose is fabricated; the Yeatsian Mask is discovered.[163] The pose saps the creative vitality of its actor; the discovery of the Mask is an 'occasion for a sudden unleashing of energy',[164] 'a crisis that joins that buried self for certain moments to [the] trivial daily mind.'[165] The poseur is confined by his pose, but the writer who discovers his Mask is free to contemplate 'the image of what [he wishes] to become.'[166] The pose is a dramatization of the 'opposite of all that [has been] known in childhood and early youth'.[167] The Mask is a preternatural self whose 'lineaments permit the expression of all the man most lacks, and . . . may be dreads . . .'[168]

The Mask and the Self

In Yeats's final aesthetic there are two Masks: 'There is a form of Mask . . . that comes from life and is fated, [and] there is a form that is chosen.'[169] The idea that there is a Mask that is fated had its roots in Yeats's study of folklore and the occult, and is similar to Russell's idea that one may be dominated by a supernatural being, or 'daimon', which incarnates as the result of a specific spiritual experience.[170] Russell wrote in 'Germinal':

> In ancient shadows and twilights
>   Where childhood had strayed,
> The world's great sorrows were born
>   And its heroes were made.
> In the lost boyhood of Judas
>   Christ was betrayed.
>
> Let thy young wanderer dream on:
>   Call him not home.
> A door opens, a breath, a voice
>   From the ancient room,
> Speaks to him now. Be it dark or bright
>   He is knit with his doom.[171]

Yeats did not believe that a person need passively accept being 'knit with his doom'. 'I think of life', he asserted, 'as a struggle with the Daimon',[172] as a conflict between the self and apparently imposed images of the self. A person could oppose the tyranny of his fated self or Mask by consciously assuming a Mask or Masks that were the opposite of all that he was. 'A writer', he declared in his *Autobiographies*, 'must die every day he lives, be reborn, as it is said in the Burial Service, an incorruptible self, that self opposite of all that he has named "himself" '.[173]

The complexity of Yeats's conception of himself, his many changes of Mask, his deliberate poise, his cultivation of a dignified and distant personality, and the apparent ease with which he ranged over a wide field of interests in search of material for poetry, when combined with Russell's perennial fear of succumbing to his influence, meant that their literary association fluctuated and was never simple.

CHAPTER III

SELF AND SOUL

1890 — 1894

'Le mysticisme de Yeats est plutôt poétique, instinctif; celui de A.E. est conscient, réfléchi.'
— Simone Téry

In the early part of the 1890s Yeats and Russell slowly began to realize that their attitudes to spiritual enquiry were fundamentally opposed. The process was gradual because both men took several years to establish their own orientations and because both were more aware of what united them than they were of what threatened to, and eventually did, divide them. But their differences were fundamental. Russell was essentially a mystic. He believed that by practising austerities and developing his powers of concentration he could subjugate his present self and so hasten his reunion with the Infinite. Yeats was essentially a symbolist poet in search of powerful, sudden, momentary disclosures of the supernatural — what Goethe has called 'eminent instances'. He sought for them through a careful investigation of psychic phenomena, a close study of the arcane, and the life-long practice of Ceremonial Magic. He wanted to obtain insights into the natural and the supernatural world, and he wanted to intensify his own personality. In terms of the language often used to describe the traditions that each man immersed himself in, Russell chose the 'path of being', while Yeats chose the 'path of knowing'.[1]

The conflict that has always existed between mysticism and magic was without doubt one of the most important forces generating the antagonism that eventually divided Yeats and Russell. An excellent description of the principal characteristics of each tradition and of the distinctive habits of mind that each tends to encourage has been given by Evelyn Underhill. According to her the mystic temperament is characterized by a disciplined will, subservient emotions, strongly developed intuitive powers, an avidity for moral perfection, and a deep yearning for a transcendent love relationship with the Infinite. 'In mysticism', she explains,

Self and Soul

the will is united with the emotions in an impassioned desire to transcend the sense-world, in order that the self may be joined by love to the one eternal and ultimate Object of Love; whose existence is intuitively perceived by that which we used to call the 'soul', but now find it easier to refer to as the 'cosmic' or 'transcendental' sense. This is . . . the religious temperament acting upon the plane of reality.[2]

For the mystic, the self is a soul, whose value is realized only in service for others and in union with the Infinite.

Magic, on the other hand, is utterly egocentric. 'The Great Work', Eliphas Levi, an eminent authority on the occult, has written, 'is, before all things, the creation of man by himself, that is to say, the full and entire conquest of his faculties and his future.'[3] Magic claims to be a practical, intellectual, and very ancient science whose secret formulae and doctrines enable an initiate to dominate and control all natural and supernatural powers. This dominance is achieved by intensifying and extending the powers of the will, and by manipulating the two fundamental laws that are said to govern the whole universe — the law of cause and effect, and the law of analogy. The first is a crude application of a Newtonian-like causality, while the law of analogy is said to have been taken from the Smaragdine Tablet buried with the body of Hermes Trismegistus: 'what is below is like that which is above, and what is above is similar to that which is below to accomplish the wonders of one thing.'[4] Mastery of hidden rituals and secret incantations give the initiate power to control these laws to his own purposes. 'In magic', as Evelyn Underhill has pointed out, 'the will unites with the intellect in an impassioned desire for supersensible knowledge. This is the intellectual, aggressive, and scientific temperament trying to extend its field of consciousness, until it includes the supersensual world.'[5] Certain habits of mind are considered essential for the successful study of magic. 'To attain the SANCTUM REGNUM, in other words, the knowledge and power of the Magi', declares Eliphas Levi, 'there are four indispensible conditions — an intelligence illuminated by study, an intrepidity which nothing can check, a will which cannot be broken, and a prudence which nothing can corrupt and nothing intoxicate. TO KNOW, TO DARE, TO WILL, TO KEEP SILENCE.'[6] In magic, the soul is entirely subsumed to the purposes of self, as the mage attempts to realize to the full the divine potential of his humanity.

Mysticism is concerned with attempting to transcend the phenomenal world; magic with attempting to enlarge its boundaries. The mystic abjures self; the mage intensifies self. The mystic humbly and passively accepts any supernatural revelations, such as visions, clairaudience, or automatic writing as a spiritual gift, a sign of Divine grace. The mage appropriates all supernatural revelations to himself as objective proof of the success of his incantations, and through the extension of his powers he attempts to force the spirits to yield up their secrets. The mystic does not trust his own faculties — his intellect, reason, and senses — for he sees them as nothing more than the obedient slaves of the phenomenal world he believes he has indisputably transcended. 'Initiation' into magic, Eliphas Levi asserts, 'is a preservative against the false lights of mysticism; it equips human reason with its relative value and proportional infallibility, connecting it with supreme reason by the chain of analogies.'[7] Mysticism is active and practical. The great mystics, like St Francis, St Teresa, and St Catherine, busied themselves with the day-to-day needs of their fellow-men. Magic is combative and secretive. Of the 'Knowledge of Quaternity', Eliphas Levi says: 'To know it and have the courage to use it is human omnipotence; to reveal it to a profane person is to lose it; to reveal it even to a disciple is to abdicate in favour of that disciple, who, henceforward, possesses the right of life and death over his master — I am speaking of the magical standpoint — and will certainly slay him for fear of dying himself.'[8] Finally, language always seems inadequate for the mystic, whose special *differentia* is the power of apprehending simultaneity. As the great neo-Platonic mystic Plotinus observed: 'This is why the vision baffles telling; we cannot detach the Supreme to state it; if we have seen something thus detached we have failed of the Supreme which is to be known only as one with ourselves.'[9] The *Memorial* of Pascal is an excellent example of the way a great religious philosopher, whose writing is distinguished by its lucidity, can be put utterly to rout by a mystical experience.[10] As Dante was made aware at the height of his greatest vision:

> Non che da se sien queste cose acerbe:
> Ma e difetto dalla parte tua,
> Che non hai viste ancor tanto superbe.

> Not that these things are themselves imperfect:
> But on thy side is the defect,
> In that thy vision cannot rise so high.[11]

Magic, on the other hand, exploits the denotative and imperative power of language. It is a 'magical axiom', states Eliphas Levi, that 'within the circle of its action, every word creates that which it affirms'.[12] These traditional areas of conflict between mysticism and magic provide, as will be shown in this and subsequent chapters, important points of reference for understanding and charting Yeats's and Russell's literary association.

Spooks and Spirituality

Many of those who have written about the literary association have unquestioningly accepted Russell's claim that he did not share Yeats's initial enthusiasm for investigating the occult. They have believed this to be true on the evidence of several humorous stories that were circulated in Dublin around 1910 about experiments the friends had conducted in their youth, experiments in which Russell always seems to have played the role of an amused observer. His lack of participation, it has been argued, provides clear proof of his lack of interest.[13] But those who have accepted this view have overlooked a number of facts. Most of the stories seem to have originated with Russell himself. There is a gap of almost twenty-five years between the stories and what they describe, a gap that defies accurate recall. Russell is probably the only writer from the period who felt it necessary to report what had taken place, and report it humorously. As the sole chronicler, he would have been open to the temptation to choose the role and the point of view that were most flattering to his image of himself as a mystic. Finally, the fact that he possessed a collection of stories indicates that he must have been sufficiently interested in his friend's investigations to be present for several of them. The humorous stories Russell entertained Dublin with in the 1900s cannot be taken as proof of his lack of enthusiasm for Yeats's enquiry; what they probably show is the role that he wished he had played.

The original version of one story can be found in Russell's autobiographical fragment, 'Some Characters of the Irish Literary Movement'. The section on Yeats contains a description of a farcical attempt to raise the spirits, an attempt that was apparently prompted by Professor Dowden's account of Shelley's expulsion from Eton for allegedly evoking the Devil.[14] Dowden, who was a close friend of the Yeats family, had begun his comprehensive biography in 1883 and had completed it by 1886, so the séance that is described probably took place some time in the mid 'eighties. Russell claimed he could remember Yeats instructing himself and some others about the right ritual for . . . evocations. All must be done according to ancient formula. The Gods must be evoked with dignity and dismissed with thanks and a high courtesy, or in their anger they might make the rash magician insane. Then he took the most likely of our group, told her to mutter certain words of power making them mentally vibrate within her, and himself walked round the room with a sword pointed solemnly to the four quarters one after another, muttering words of power. Just as the divinity was evoked a rap came at the door. 'Oh', said Yeats cheerfully, 'here is the tea', and went off leaving the dread deity undismissed.[15]

Needless to say, no-one was stricken with insanity for irreverence; and no-one, once the story was out, was inclined to take Yeats's mediumship seriously.

Other stories in Russell's repertoire designed to show his amusement at his friend's ludicrous proceedings include an account of the time Yeats had been hurriedly forced to abandon a magic ceremony because the ritual killing of a black cock and the sprinkling of its blood had made him nauseous.[16] Then there was the occasion when Yeats's rapturous description of a gesticulating spirit he claimed he could see in a crystal ball had been embarrassingly cut short by the information that the real object of his vision was none other than the cleaner who was polishing the front of the pharmacy immediately opposite.[17] Finally, there was the story of Yeats's walking round and round a room, sword in hand, muttering spells to ward off evil spirits, and every time he passed a plate of plums taking one, until Russell protested that not even the spirits could distinguish between the chewing and the chanting.[18]

There are several possible explanations for Russell's desire to ridicule Yeats in this way. He did not begin circulating his stories until at least three or four years after their literary association had broken up. By then, he had become irritated with Yeats's grand manner, represented by the published boast that there was 'not a fool' could call him 'friend'.[19] He may have decided that a collection of humorous anecdotes was the best device for puncturing this pretence. On the other hand, he may not have made a deliberate decision; he may have just been caught in a situation where he couldn't resist being the person with the funniest story. Every major biographical sketch of Russell makes some reference to his impish sense of humour. Aware too that his own mysticism had become a source of merriment in certain parts of Dublin, and that his visions had been held up to ridicule by writers as widely quoted as Joyce, he may have felt that telling stories about someone else's eccentricities was an effective way of diverting laughter away from himself. All

Self and Soul

his stories, it will be noted, poke fun at either Yeat's pontificating or bungling. Finally, his humorous stories may have been a small part of that process of reassessment that followed the break-up of the association in 1907. In his own *Journal* for 5 April 1909, Yeats confessed to belittling Russell to a mutual friend, and added: 'a not very amiable desire'.[20] Doubtless, Russell was engaged in the same exercise. His satires in the *Homestead*, and in Susan Mitchell's two books of humorous verse, *Aids to the Immortality of Certain Persons in Ireland* (1913), and *Secret Springs of Dublin Song* (1918), indicate that after 1910, or thereabouts, he often found his former friend an inviting target for derision.[21]

But, whatever personal purposes these stories may have served him, their general effect has been to reinforce the belief that he was not seriously engaged in his friend's earliest experiments with magic. The model of the association that has been most commonly advanced is one of Russell as an earnest mystic with a devout reverence for the other-world, and Yeats as an essentially serious if somewhat amateur mage.[22] Yet the unpublished correspondence from the period proves this wrong. In particular, the years 1885 to 1887 emerge as a time of indiscriminate and enthusiastic experimentation, when neither Russell nor Yeats were particularly concerned, or for that matter well-informed, about the antipathy that has traditionally existed between mysticism and magic. A long letter Russell wrote to his friend Carrie Rea late in 1885 or early in 1886 indicates that by then he had willingly joined Yeats and their mutual friend, Charles Johnston, in a close study of various occult books, including, it seems, such classics as Eliphas Levi's *The Mysteries of Magic* and Baron von Reichenbach's *Researches on the Dynamics of Magnetism*. Together, the three friends devised a number of experiments to investigate the phenomena of odic force, thought transference, materialization, and astral travel.[23] A measure of Russell's excitement about these projects can be taken from another unpublished letter to Carrie Rea written some time in 1886.

My second experiment is a delightful one and has often been done before by Adepts and black magicians. It is to try and separate my astral body consciously from my physical body. When I can do this I can wander away with the speed of thought from land to land over the world.[24]

In other letters there are reports of astral travel to distant worlds and other incarnations, and accounts of the successful thought transference of symbols, images, and sacred words. Yet interspersed among all this enthusiasm are passages that indicate that Russell felt some unease about what he was doing. In one letter, he tried to reassure his friend, a devout member of the Church of Ireland, that the type of magic he had been investigating could be fitted into the framework of Christianity,[25] while in another he cautioned her not to say anything to her family about his activities for fear they would promptly notify his parents and make him the subject of public prayer at the next mid-week meeting of the local Church.[26]

Exactly what caused him to change from an enthusiasm that was partly checked by uneasiness to an open hostility towards the occult is difficult to say. The turning point may have come in December 1887 when he and Yeats were invited to attend a séance that was being organized by some Dublin Spiritualists. Charles Johnston heard about the invitations and persuaded Russell, though somewhat against his will, to stay at home.[27] He was not able to influence Yeats, who went, and who came so completely under the control of the spirits that he was thrown violently about the room. In a frantic attempt to exorcise them, Yeats tried to recite the Lord's Prayer, but he discovered to his horror that the only thing remotely scriptural he could remember was the opening passage of *Paradise Lost*. Fortunately, it put the spirits to rout, but he came away so shaken that he did not attend another séance for ten years.[28] Russell also took fright. The spirit-possession of his best friend probably confirmed a fear he had expressed to his cousin several months before that their investigations might bring them into contact with a malevolent black magic. Like many mystics, Russell drew a sharp distinction between black magic and white magic. Black magic was evil, he told Carrie Rea, because it affected one's spiritual development in both present and future lives: 'it is purely selfish, and after death pushes back the user of it farther from the goal' of reunion with the Absolute 'than when he started.' By comparison, white magic, he informed her, 'has the same or greater powers, but they are applied for the benefit of mankind, not for the benefit of an individual.'[29] At all times the emphasis must be on spiritual preparation rather than personal aggrandizement.

The change in Russell's attitude to the occult can be traced in his correspondence. While some of the letters after 1887 contain brief references to occult experiments and occult literature, none of them contain any passages comparable with the enthusiastic accounts scattered through the correspondence from 1885 to 1887. His first public condemnation of the occult, however, did not come until November 1888, a few days after he had learned that Yeats had decided to join The Esoteric Section of the Theosophical Society. The Section had been specially formed by Madame Blavatsky to secure

Self and Soul

an inner circle of disciples and to meet the growing demands of some of the London members for instruction in Ceremonial Magic. When the news of the Section's formation reached Russell in Dublin, he wrote two vigorous letters to *Lucifer*, the Society's newspaper, protesting the denigration of Theosophy, though he was not, as he took pains to point out, an official member of the Society.

I recognize the essentiality of establishing the scientific basis of Theosophy . . . but [must we have] toys and picture books. . . . I do not 'hope' to see spooks. . . . My baser part sometimes desires manifestations, but I recognize such desire to be impure. I earnestly trust no Member of the Society will ever indulge in the evocation of phenomena, whether for curiosity, or for the gratification of the intellect.

The major part of the first letter is devoted to the evils of spiritualism, and was doubtless meant as a covert warning to Yeats, for it accurately charts the course his investigations had taken since the two friends had first encountered Theosophy in 1884.

A young man, whose intellect is of the keenest, and with great power of assimilating and applying knowledge . . . feels there may be something beyond the facts of material science, beyond the anthropomorphic religions of the day. Drifting into that mysterious current which is now flowing through the century, he becomes attracted by Theosophy. For a while he studies it with avidity, strives to live 'the life', to permeate himself with its teaching.

His intellect is satisfied for the time.

But, alas! he commits the fatal fault of forgetting that he has a soul. . . . Mystic Union with the Higher Self becomes more and more phantasmal. He recognizes its necessity, but postpones the ordeal.

'First let me prove the lower realms of Nature' he cries, and plunges into the phenomena of spiritualism, table rapping, and the evocation of spooks. He declares that Knowledge is Power . . . .

He is remonstrated with. He replies that it is necessary to test all experience, and construes that axiom into a law that Karma is to be moulded and shaped by the conscious Ego. Carried to a logical conclusion, his rendering of the axiom would lead him into the lowest depths of vice to the hurt of his higher nature. He would seek in this transient incarnation to gratify every lust, passion and ideal of his personality.[30]

Yeats immediately denied Russell's charges, protesting to a mutual friend who had accompanied him to the Dublin séance: as for Madame Blavatsky, 'you need not fear for a spiritualistic influence coming to me from that quarter.'[31] He reassured another mutual friend: 'No fear of Madame Blavatsky drawing me into such matters

— she is very much against them and hates spiritualism vehemently — says mediumship and insanity are the same thing.'[32] It may even have been at his insistence that Russell visited London late in 1888 or in 1889 to meet Madame Blavatsky, and observe the Esoteric Section at first hand.[33]

Madame Blavatsky herself responded to Russell's letters of protest by reassuring him that she was utterly opposed to Spiritualism. In the issue of *Lucifer* in which she published his letter, she asserted: 'It is not in the Theosophical Society that our correspondent can ever hope to evoke spooks or see any *physical* phenomena.'[34] She also pointed out that prospective members of the Esoteric Section were required to take vows of humility, abstinence, asceticism, and philanthropy. Her reply in fact repeats some of the advice that she was giving prospective initiates in an article in *Lucifer*, where she was presenting an exegesis on a selection of the seventy-three rules for effective chelaship. For example, rule 11 states:

Meditation, abstinence in all, the observation of moral duties, gentle thoughts, good deeds and kind words, as good will to all and entire oblivion of Self, are the most efficacious means of obtaining knowledge and preparing for the reception of higher wisdom.[35]

Russell was deeply impressed by this emphasis on practical, spiritual development, which corresponded closely with his own orientation. But he was even more impressed by Madame Blavatsky's presence when he visited her in London some time in 1888 or 1889. Like Yeats, who said he regarded her as some 'sort of old Irish peasant woman with an air of humour and audacious power',[36] he was fascinated by the force of her personality, and amazed at her erudition. Charles Weekes, who was present at one of his visits, remembered him appearing 'awestruck',[37] while Russell himself told a close friend that he had witnessed her 'do some wonderful things'.[38] Several years after his visit, when her reputation was under attack, he wrote to Carrie Rea in defence of his reverence for her:

The enthusiastic love which is felt for her by those who lived with her, some of them personal and old friends of my own, is quite sufficient guarantee of character even if her vast learning [and] her public conduct were not of themselves sufficient to persuade me about her sincerity.[39]

In later years he deeply regretted that he had not met her at a more opportune time. 'I was too immature — too small', he told a friend, 'and she too remote — a Cosmos in an ailing woman's body.'[40] At the time, however, she made such an impact on him that he immediately joined the Theosophical Society, a decision that he had hesitated making for almost half a decade. Even though his unpublished correspondence from the late 'eighties shows that he had gradually been arguing himself towards a close identification with Theosophy, it was most likely the deep impression which Madame Blavatsky made on him that finally persuaded him to request official membership of the Theosophical Society. Unlike Yeats, who had been sceptical of her claims to the point of keeping a record of his doubts in a private diary,[41] and who was soon to dismiss her as 'simply a note of interrogation',[42] Russell remained unfailingly loyal to her, though not to her organization, for the rest of his life.[43] But even though she had quieted his fears about the Theosophical Society's attitude to Ceremonial Magic and Spiritualism, he held back from requesting membership of the Esoteric Section for a further year — until 9 December 1890.[44]

By then, Yeats had been excommunicated from the Section. He had criticized *Lucifer* in an article he had written for *The Weekly Review*, and his research, which included the evocation of the ghosts of flowers, had been judged to be not in harmony with Theosophical 'methods' or 'philosophy'.[45] His excommunication did not disturb him unduly, for by then he had joined another society formed especially to study Ceremonial Magic — The Hermetic Order of the Golden Dawn. He was initiated into the Golden Dawn on 7 March 1890.[46] It suited his needs. He liked the freedom to experiment, and he was attracted by the sonorous Latin titles given to initiates, the complicated rituals, 'full of the symbolism of the Middle Ages and the Renaissance', and the frequent allusions to a mysterious 'sacred book.' 'One passes from degree to degree', he noted, 'and if the wisdom one had once· hoped for is still far off there is no exhortation to alarm one's dignity, no abstraction to deaden the nerves of the soul.'[47] Yeats remained a member of a branch of the Golden Dawn for thirty-three years, contributing significantly to its internal organisation with a number of circularized letters and a pamphlet entitled, *Is the Order of R.R. & A.C. to Remain a Magical Order?*[48] Though he encouraged several of his friends to join, there is no evidence that he ever tried to interest Russell in any of its activities.

1890 thus marks an important point of divergence in Yeats's and Russell's literary association. Oddly enough, neither of them, nor anyone else who has written about them, has drawn attention to the significance of this date. But, by leaving the Theosophists for The Hermetic Order of the Golden Dawn, Yeats clearly signalled his intention of taking the occult way, or the 'path of knowing'; and by openly aligning himself with the Theosophists, Russell affirmed his commitment to the mystic way, or the 'path of being.' Their decisions did not provoke any immediate disagreement, though they did sow the fertile seeds of future antagonism. That there was no sudden crop was probably due to two factors. Firstly, the long periods they spent apart meant that their brief reunions were mainly spent exchanging gossip and ideas, and enthusiastically discussing their latest work. This left little time for disagreement. Secondly, Yeats was very guarded about his commitment to the occult. He feared ridicule, was anxious not to alienate the small popular audience he had begun to create, and was aware of the difficulties he would encounter in Ireland if he antagonized the Catholic Church. Unlike Russell, who quickly and openly declared himself an ardent Theosophist, Yeats took eleven years from the time he was initiated into the Golden Dawn before he publicly declared his belief in magic.[49] In this respect, the literary association could be said to have been nurtured for much of the early 'nineties by unfamiliarity and distance.

The Household

In his biography of the poet, Joseph Hone has claimed that by 'joining the Order of the Golden Dawn Yeats braved the reproaches of George Russell and the Dublin visionaries'.[50] This is unlikely. Russell would not have been *au fait* with what was happening in occult circles in London. Even if he had asked about the Golden Dawn, and there is no evidence that he did, he probably would have received the same vague, reassuring reply that Yeats gave his English friend, W. T. Horton, when he protested about his study of magic.[51] It is more likely that Russell, the next time they met in Dublin, was disappointed to find that Yeats no longer shared his enthusiasm for Theosophy. Since meeting Madame Blavatsky, Russell had become a fanatical convert. As a close friend later recalled, 'A.E. was aflame with Theosophy' during the 'nineties; 'a red hot missionary'.[52] In April 1891 he moved out of his parents' home and took a room at the headquarters of the Dublin Lodge of the Theosophical Society, located at No. 3 Upper Ely Place and known affectionately as 'The Household'. It was to be the centre of his life until his marriage to Violet North, one of the members, in 1898.[53] 'The seven years I lived there', he wrote, 'were the happiest in my life. How fortunate I was to be drawn into companionship

Self and Soul

with six or seven others all as I think wiser and stronger than I then was.'[54]

Yeats was also, despite his later denial, an official member of The Household for a short time.[55] He did not share Russell's idealized view of its mission or its members,[56] though he was grateful to be able to use it as a cheap place to stay on his periodic visits to Dublin. To come from the Rhymers' Club and the other literary societies of London to the Theosophists' meeting house in Dublin must have made him aware of the growing contrast between his own and his friend's way of life. It seemed to him, when he came to review this period for the *Autobiographies*, that Russell had surrounded himself with 'a little group of infirm or unlucky persons, whom he explained to themselves and to others, turning cat to griffin, goose to swan'.[57] He possessed 'the religious genius', he concluded,

and it is the essence of that genius that all souls are equal in its eyes. Queen or apple woman, it is all one, seeing that none can be more than an immortal soul. Whereas I have been concerned with men's capacities, with all [that] divides man from man.[58]

His contention is supported by their different accounts of members of The Household. Russell's memories of the people he alleged were crucial to his imaginative and spiritual development are heavy with sentiment and breathless admiration. He described Edmund King as

> that handsome youth
> From reverie that seemed like indolence
> Waking with haughty transcendental speech
> That whipt the will.[59]

To Yeats, Edmund King was merely 'a medical student who read Plato and took hashish', and lived in a room 'at the top of the house.'[60] While Russell's reminiscences are indiscriminately scattered through his correspondence and his poems, Yeats's are concentrated in a vivid, sardonic account, comprising almost one third of *Ireland After Parnell*.

The house had been taken in the name of the engineer to the Board of Works [F.J. Dick] a black-bearded young man, with a passion for Manichaean philosophy, and all accepted him as host; and sometimes the conversation, especially when I was there, became too ghostly for the nerves of his young and delicate wife, and he would be made angry.... At the top of the house lived ... a young Scotsman [Arthur Dwyer] who owned a vegetarian restaurant, and had just returned from America, where he had gone as the disciple of the Prophet Harris, and where he would soon return in the train of some new prophet. . . . On a lower floor lived a strange red-haired girl [Althea Gyles], all whose thoughts were set upon painting and poetry, conceived as abstract images like Love and Penury in the *Symposium*; and to these images she sacrificed herself with Asiatic fanaticism. . . .[61]

The Household was probably more mundane than Yeats's account suggests.[62] Perhaps he allowed his assessment of its members to be excessively influenced by the theory of personality he had begun to explore in the early drafts of *A Vision* at the time he was writing 'Ireland After Parnell'. His attention to eccentricity and religious enthusiasm reflect his conviction that only a few of his fellow countrymen had achieved that *discordia concors* he believed to be necessary for personal fulfilment. Perhaps he deliberately chose to emphasize the exotic aspects of some of the members to draw a comparison between The Household as a loose collection of religious fanatics held together by an ill-defined interest in Platonism and Theosophy, and the Golden Dawn as a carefully planned, closely-knit Society, committed to the diligent study of an ancient tradition.

Whatever his reservations, Yeats spent several weeks of the autumn of 1891 at The Household, where he quickly became involved in some of its activities. He took an interest in the vegetarian restaurant that was run by the Theosophists and managed by Charles Johnston's sister, and, with Russell, made plans to use it as a meeting place for a social and literary club. The novelist Richard Ashe King was invited to open the club, but it never met.[63] At some of the evening meetings held at The Household, he talked about his work on his three volume edition of Blake, no doubt fascinated and perhaps even slightly amused by Russell's claim to have known Blake personally in a previous incarnation and to be the only one who had 'any idea of the meaning of some of Blake's wilder poems'.[64] From the evidence of the final text, however, it seems that Yeats chose to pass up his friend's generous offer of this 'higher criticism', even when it would have been directly relevant to his commentary. For example, the section on 'Names' in 'The Symbolic System' in Volume II openly acknowledges his indebtedness to the speculations of 'Boehmen [sic], Swedenborg, and the Kabalists' rather than the equally relevant findings published by Russell and Johnston in their article, 'The Speech of the Gods'.[65] But Yeats was deeply impressed by a vision which Russell recounted of one of Maud Gonne's previous lives, and when he returned to London was amazed to discover that Mrs Mathers had seen a similar vision. 'Hers was not absolutely identical in its details but curiously alike in total effect', he later informed his friend.[66] While at The Household he also asked Russell

Self and Soul

to illustrate *Dhoya*[67], and discussed Rousseau's *Confessions*,[68] his own *Fairy and Folk Tales of the Irish Peasantry*, and an article on the Hellfire Club which he had published in the 12 September issue of *United Ireland*.[69] His research into the origins and activities of the Club, a meeting place for the wealthy young rowdies of eighteenth century Dublin, aroused so much interest among The Household that he was able to persuade Russell and some of the other members to join him in exorcising the 'drunken phantoms' that were said to haunt its ruins.[70]

In addition, Yeats prepared an article on Russell which he entitled 'An Irish Visionary' and submitted to the *National Observer*. It was published on 3 October 1891. In terms of the history of the literary association this article is very significant for it is the first published account of either writer about the other, and it is the first time that one of Russell's poems had appeared in print. The article is essentially a personal response to selected aspects of Russell's life and work. He is not, apparently at his own request, mentioned by name, and there is no reference either to his commitment to Theosophy or his membership of The Household. That Yeats chose to depict him as 'An Irish Visionary', and not, say, 'A Dublin Theosophist', shows that he was less interested in describing Russell's current situation than in creating an image of him as representing a particular aspect of Ireland. The word 'Irish' in the title is somewhat misleading, for in several places in his article Yeats rather awkwardly emphasizes the Celtic quality of Russell's visions, temperament and writings. The criteria he employs for this are not his own, but have been borrowed unacknowledged from Ernest Renan's *The Poetry of the Celtic Races* and Matthew Arnold's *On the Study of Celtic Literature*. For the most part the article has been written in the style of a type of folk-tale which Douglas Hyde, whose work Yeats was thoroughly familiar with and greatly admired, called a 'folk-belief'. According to Hyde the folk-belief consists of a narrative of anything from some hundred to a few thousand words that recounts, in a conversational manner, several anecdotes about a person's encounters with the Sidhe.[71] What distinguishes Yeats's folk-beliefs from those written by Hyde and others is the lack of deliberately interpolated Irishisms and the unusual narrative tone. Instead of being unblushingly forthright and jovial like them, the narrator of 'An Irish Visionary' is sometimes aloof and sometimes mildly indulgent, perhaps even a trifle condescending. 'An Irish Visionary' is one of a number of folk-beliefs that Yeats gathered between 1888 and 1893, when he published them collectively as *The Celtic Twilight*.[72] It concentrates on four areas: biographical details, visions, poetry, and Celticism, all of which are introduced in the first paragraph. The rest of the article is organized in the same way, and by skilful juxtaposition Yeats is able to generalize about Russell without sacrificing the force and immediacy of the particular.

An Irish Visionary

A young man came to see me at my lodgings the other night, and began to talk of the making of the earth and the heavens and much else. I questioned him about his life and his doings. He had written many poems and painted many mystical designs since we met last, but latterly had neither written nor painted, for his whole heart was set upon making his mind strong, vigorous and calm, and the emotional life of the artist was bad for him he feared. He recited his poems readily, however. He had them all in his memory. Some indeed had never been written down. They, with their wild music as of winds blowing in the reeds, seemed to me the very inmost voice of Celtic sadness, and of Celtic longing for infinite things the world has never seen. Suddenly it seemed to me that he was peering about him a little eagerly. 'Do you see anything, X-?' I said. 'A shining, winged woman, covered by her long hair, is standing by the doorway', he answered, or some such words. 'Is it the influence of some living person who thinks of us and whose thoughts appear to us in that symbolic form?' I said; for I am well instructed in the ways of the visionaries and in the fashion of their speech. 'No', he replied; 'for if it were the thoughts of a person who is alive I should feel the living influence in my living body, and my heart would beat and my breath would fail. It is a spirit. It is some one who is dead or who has never lived.'

In spite of the anonymity of his subject, Yeats immediately focuses the opening sentences of his first paragraph on a personal issue that had preoccupied Russell for the last four years — would the 'emotional life of the artist' harm his spiritual development? Fears that it might had led him to burn all his manuscripts in 1887 in the belief that 'verse writing is the sort of thing which does no good',[73] and leave the Art Schools in 1889, convinced that Art was weakening his will.[74] In February 1891, seven months before Yeats wrote his article, Russell had sent Carrie Rea 'the last verses I wrote or am likely to write', adding, 'Now and then the old passion overtakes me and I write — anything — for the sake of getting rid of the temptress'.[75] Yeats noticed the effect that these guilt feelings were having on Russell's verse, and when he revised the article for *The Celtic Twilight* (1893)[76] he added the sentence: 'At times the beauty of thought is obscured by careless writing as though he had suddenly doubted if writing was not a foolish labour.'[77] In 'An Irish Visionary' Yeats uses an incident arising from his composition of the article to dramatize Russell's dilemma.

I told him I would write an article upon him . . ., and was told in turn that I might do so if I did not mention his name, for he wished to be always 'unknown, obscure, impersonal.' Next day a bundle of his poems arrived, and with them a note in these words: 'Here are copies of verses you said you liked. I do not think I could ever write or paint any more. I prepare myself for a cycle of other activities [in some other life].[78] I will make rigid my roots and branches. It is not now my turn to burst into leaves and flowers'.

The last two lines of Russell's note seem to have captured Yeats's imagination when he was revising 'An Irish Visionary' for the fifth volume of his *Collected Works*, for they provided him with the central image for the quatrain, 'The Coming of Wisdom with Time'.

> Though leaves are many, the root is one;
> Through all the lying days of my youth
> I swayed my leaves and flowers in the sun;
> Now I may wither into the truth.[79]

The assertion that he makes about the Celtic quality of Russell's poems and paintings in the first paragraph of his article is also something that subsequently caught his attention. 'They, with their wild music as of winds blowing in the reeds, seemed to me the very inmost voice of Celtic sadness, and of Celtic longing for infinite things the world has never seen.' In 1899, when he wanted to suggest the implicit Celticism of a collection of his own poems, he revived this image for the title: *The Wind Among the Reeds*.[80] But after he had mined the sentence for his own poetry, he became increasingly uneasy about the assumptions it contained. In the 1902 edition of *The Celtic Twilight* he informed his readers:

I wrote this sentence long ago. This sadness now seems to me a part of all peoples who preserve the moods of the ancient peoples of the world. I am not so preoccupied with the mystery of the Race as I used to be, but leave this sentence and other sentences like it unchanged. We once believed them, and have, it may be, not grown wiser.[81]

Despite this prevarication, he kept returning to his sentence. In 1914 he deleted the adjective 'wild' from his description of Russell's 'music'; and in 1921 he dropped the comparison between Russell's 'music' and the 'winds blowing in the reeds', probably to dissociate his own early poetry from Russell's and to distance it from his youthful speculations about 'the mystery of the Race'.[82]

The assertions that Yeats makes in the 1891 'An Irish Visionary' about what he considers to be quintessentially Celtic are most likely based on borrowed criteria. The phrase 'inmost voice of Celtic sadness' seems to echo Matthew Arnold's contention that the Celt is distinguished by his 'passionate, penetrating, melancholy';[83] while the idea that the Celt longs 'for infinite things the world has never seen' appears to have been influenced by Renan's *The Poetry of the Celtic Races*. 'The essential element in the Celtic imagination', Renan declared, 'is the pursuit of the unknown; . . . their profoundest instinct . . . is their desire to penetrate the unknown.'[84]

This desire to penetrate the unknown, Yeats says in his article, drew people to Russell.

. . . when I was with him in his own lodging, more than one turned up to talk over their beliefs and disbeliefs, and sun them as it were in the subtle light of his mind. Sometimes visions come to him as he talks with them, and he is rumoured to have told divers people true matters of their past days and distant friends, and left them hushed with dread of their strange teacher, who seems scarce more than [a] boy and is so much more subtle than the oldest among them.

When he re-worked this passage for 'Ireland After Parnell', he added two examples of the objective corroboration of Russell's visions:

Walking with some man in his park — his demesne, as we say in Ireland — he had seen a visionary church at a particular spot, and the man had dug and uncovered its foundations; then some woman had met him with 'O, Mr Russell, I am so unhappy', and he had replied, 'You will be perfectly happy this evening at seven o'clock', and had left her to her blushes. She had an appointment with a young man for seven o'clock. I had heard of this a day or so after the event, and I asked him about it, and was told it had suddenly come into his head to use those words; but why he did not know.[85]

While he was willing to 'give endless time to a case of conscience', his Visionary's chief 'pleasure', Yeats informed his readers, 'was to wander about upon the hills, talking to half-mad and visionary peasants'.[86] He describes one of these encounters in his article.

A winter or two ago he spent much of the night walking up and down upon the mountain talking to an old peasant who, dumb to most men, poured

Self and Soul

out his cares for him. Both were unhappy: X- because he had then first decided that art and poetry were not for him,[87] and the old peasant because his life was ebbing out with no achievement remaining and no hope left him. Both how Celtic! how full of striving after a something never to be completely expressed in word or deed. The peasant was wandering in his mind with prolonged sorrow. Once he burst out with — 'God possesses the heavens' — but he 'covets' the world; and once he lamented that his old neighbours were gone, and that all had forgotten him; they used to draw a chair to the fire for him in every cabin, and now they said: 'Who is that old fellow there?' 'The fret (Irish for doom) is over me', he repeated, and then went on to talk once more of God and Heaven. More than once also he said, waving his arm towards the mountain, 'Only myself knows what happened under the thorn tree fortyyears ago': and as he said it the tears upon his face glistened in the moonlight.

The way Russell and Yeats subsequently responded to this encounter illustrates the difference between their two temperaments. Russell, with the mystic's passivity in the face of experience and his concern for its immediate spiritual significance, allowed the incident to lapse into imprecise memory, merely recalling it as an exercise in casuistry in a fragment of an unpublished autobiography[88] and a paragraph in a novel.[89] Yeats, with the mage's compulsion to impose order on circumstance and submit experience to the shaping power of his own will, formed the encounter into a poem. Entitled 'The Old Pensioner', it was first published in *The Scots Observer* on 15 November 1890.

> I had a chair at every hearth,
> When no-one turned to see
> With 'Look at that old fellow there;
> And who may he be?'
> And therefore do I wander on,
> And the fret is on me.
>
> The roadside trees keep murmuring —
> Ah, wherefore murmur ye
> As in the old days long gone by,
> Green oak and poplar tree!
> The well-known faces are all gone,
> And the fret is on me.[90]

In a note, Yeats admitted that his poem was 'little more than a translation into verse of the very words of an old Wicklow peasant.'[91] His choice of the simple ballad form of alternating tetrameters and trimeters and his use of reported speech emphasize his desire to offer the poem as a piece of accurately recorded folklore. He has achieved only partial success. The last line of each verse, though it closely echoes the old peasant's cry, lacks most of its dramatic intensity. The second verse is perhaps more effective. The pathetic fallacy in the first line, the vagueness and menace evoked by the alliteration of 'murmuring' and 'murmur', and the contorted structure ending with the archaic 'ye', realistically convey a sense of the old man's distraction.

Yeats's drastic rewriting of this simple ballad in 1925 when he revised 'An Irish Visionary' for *Early Poems and Stories* demonstrates his lasting compulsion to appropriate the encounter to his own poetic. While the final version retains the original rhyme scheme, the iambic metre has been considerably strengthened to bring out the old man's contempt for the timid passions of the present. And what was a lament about the past, when he had been welcome at every hearth, has been transformed into a jeremiad against the fact that he can no longer command the love of women. The shift in emphasis probably owes as much to Synge's description of the Old Pensioner in 'The Vagrants of Wicklow', which includes an account of his numerous and turbulent marriages,[92] as it does to the arrogant sexuality of *The Last Poems*. Finally, the greatest weakness of the original ballad, the Old Pensioner's repeated, passive complaint that he is doomed, becomes one of the greatest strengths of the final version, a scornful gesture of defiance that is as universal as it is physical.

> Although I shelter from the rain
> Under a broken tree
> My chair was nearest to the fire
> In every company
> That talked of love or politics,
> Ere time transfigured me.
>
> Though lads are making pikes again
> For some conspiracy,
> And crazy rascals rage their fill
> At human tyranny,
> My contemplations are of Time
> That has transfigured me.

Self and Soul

> There's not a woman turns her face
> Upon a broken tree,
> And yet the beauties that I loved
> Are in my memory;
> I spit into the face of Time
> That has transfigured me.

The appropriation of protagonist and setting are complete. The 1925 'Old Pensioner' no longer resembles the 1891 'old peasant' that Russell had wandered the Wicklow mountains with in 'An Irish Visionary'. He is now one with Crazy Jane, Tom the Lunatic, Ribh, several nameless religious beggars, and the raging, spitting Old Man who introduces Yeats's last play, *The Death of Cuchulain*.[93] The old peasant's cry that Russell had repeated to Yeats before he wrote his article: 'Only myself knows what happened under the thorn tree forty years ago' is transformed into a passionate lament for lost love that not only echoes through 'The Lamentation of the Old Pensioner' but also recurs in 'Summer and Spring' (1926)[94] and again in 'Love's Loneliness' (1930).

> The mountain throws a shadow,
> Thin is the moon's horn;
> What did we remember
> Under the ragged thorn?
> Dread has followed longing,
> And our hearts are torn.[95]

The poet, unlike other men, Yeats implies in his essay entitled 'Magic', does not 'accept the days as they pass, simply and gladly.'[96] He gives shape to the events that have shaped him. To write is to fashion a reality. The distinction, of course, applies as much to Yeats's desire to arrest and mould Russell's experiences into an article entitled 'An Irish Visionary' as it does to his wish to form the encounter between Russell and the old peasant into a poem that he progressively appropriated to himself.

In the 1891 'An Irish Visionary', Yeats uses the meeting between Russell and the old peasant to illustrate his contention that 'the pursuit of the unknown' is characteristically Celtic.

This old man always rises before me when I think of X-. Both seek, one in wandering sentences, the other in symbolic pictures and subtle allegoric poetry, to express a something that lies beyond the range of expression; and both, if X- will forgive me, have within them the vast and vague extravagance that lies at the bottom of the Celtic heart. The peasant visionaries that are, the landlord duellists that were, and the whole hurly-burly of legends — Cuchulin fighting the sea for two days until the waves pass over him and he dies, Caolte storming the palace of the gods, Oisin seeking in vain for three hundred years to appease his insatiable heart with all the pleasures of fairyland, these two mystics walking up and down upon the mountain uttering the central dreams of their souls in no less dream-laden sentences, and this mind that finds them so interesting — all are a portion of that great 'Celtic' phantasmagoria whose meaning no man has discovered, nor any angel revealed.

In fact, the examples Yeats has assembled here are a compendium of his own interests and have little or nothing to do with Russell. The curious pairing of peasant visionaries and landlord duellists arises from his simultaneous interest in Russell and the swashbuckling gentry of the Hellfire Club, on whom he had published an article entitled 'A Reckless Century. Irish Rakes and Duellists'. The cavalier rowdyism of the Hellfire Club, he argued, was essentially a display of 'the Celtic intensity, the Celtic fire [and] the Celtic daring', and the same 'vast energy' that had once filled Ireland with bullies would now give her 'great poets and thinkers.'[97] The extravagance of this claim demonstrates the force of his compulsion to construct a context for his friend's visions and his own poetry. The figures of Cuchulain, Caolte, and Oisin named in the final paragraph of 'An Irish Visionary' are prominent in the poems Yeats himself composed in the late 'eighties and early 'nineties;[98] while the idea expressed by the image of the 'great Celtic phantasmagoria' was one that he retained throughout his work. It reappears, for example, as the 'great tapestry' hanging behind 'all Irish history' that is described in *A General Introduction for my Work* (1937).[99]

The 1891 'An Irish Visionary' also contains Yeats's first use of the word 'phantasmagoria'. This was a word he came increasingly to employ in his own symbology and incorporate in his view of himself as a poet. As late as the 1919 Preface to *The Wild Swans at Coole*, when most readers would rightly feel he had left the Celtic 'nineties far behind, he was still asserting his need for that 'phantasmagoria through which I can alone express my convictions about the world.' Perhaps the strongest proof of its importance is that it is the first term to be explained in *A General Introduction for my Work*.

The word phantasmagoria itself was originally coined in 1802, in much the same way as the modern word television was coined, to describe 'an exhibition of optical illusions' produced chiefly by the then recently improved magic lanterns. It was soon appropriated by writers to designate 'a shifting series or succession of phantasms or imaginary figures, as seen in a dream or fevered condition as called up by the imagination, or as created by literary description.'[100] Yeats may have encountered it in the writings of the Romantics, for it was used by Landor, Hazlitt, Byron, Coleridge, and Poe; or in translations of Baudelaire and Rimbaud; or in essays and books known generally to him such as Matthew Arnold's 'Literature and Dogma' (1876), John Todhunter's *A Study of Shelley* (1880), Standish O'Grady's *History of Ireland: Critical and Philosophical* (1881), Edward Dowden's *Life of Shelley* (1886), or Madame Blavatsky's *The Secret of Doctrine* (1888).[101]

Whatever his source or sources, Yeats made the word distinctly his own by giving it a structural connotation and by relating it firmly to his own views about the nature and function of consciousness. Primarily, a phantasmagoria designated for him a pattern of related images, some traditional and some still being invented, which were part of the collective consciousness, or what he eventually called 'Anima Mundi'. His belief both in the existence of a phantasmagoria and the need for poets to draw from it arose, in the early 'nineties, from his reading of Pater, his association with the Rhymers' Club, his work on his edition of Blake, especially the section entitled 'The Symbolic System', and his membership of the Golden Dawn, where successive grades of adeptship were distinguished by specific complexes of imagery.[102] 'When a man puts only his contemplative nature and his more vague desires into his art', he declared, 'the sensuous images through which it speaks become broken, fleeting, uncertain, or are chosen for their distance from general experience, and all grows unsubstantial and fantastic.'[103] For a poem to be substantial, and its meaning to be fully accessible, the poet's personal experience must be expressed through 'a system of ordered images' drawn from those aspects of human experience that had been preserved in folklore and literature or recorded in Anima Mundi. Since these images were rich in associations they would function as symbols. And if the poet took account of their original context, he could tie the rhythms of his own experience to those of the rest of humanity. This anchoring of the personal to the universal was possible, Yeats pointed out in a section of his Blake commentary that he probably discussed with Russell during the visit of 1891, because all minds were in essence 'portions of the one great mind or imagination.'[104] By employing symbols the poet could tap the universal mind, giving his own poetry a much broader context and a much greater resonance than if he were merely writing out of his own private set of images.

Yeats further argued the need for every poet to write out of a phantasmagoria by contending that it is only by ancient symbols, by symbols that have numberless meanings besides the one or two the writer lays an emphasis upon, or the half-score he knows of, that any highly subjective art can escape from the barrenness and shallowness of a too conscious arrangement, into the abundance and depth of nature.[105]

The selection and deployment of these ancient symbols were important for Yeats believed that it was the symbols themselves which mediated between the individual consciousness, that would otherwise be solipsistic, and the universal mind, that would otherwise be alien.[106] Only through a phantasmagoria could the poet weld what was personal and transitory to what was shared and permanent, could he bring 'the dream and the reality' to face 'each other in visible array'.[107] This conjunction, however, was to be evoked rather than stated, for the poet's art should be devoted to essence, to filling the minds of his readers with 'the essences of things, and not with things'. His chief instrument for achieving this was a rhythm that kept his readers 'in that state of perhaps real trance, in which the mind liberated from the pressure of the will is unfolded in symbols'.[108] The making and understanding of a work of art should be a form of subtle enchantment. Thus, the key elements in Yeats's poetic idiom of the 'nineties were the need to write from a phantasmagoria, and the need to evoke the essence of experience through the use of symbols and the use of 'wavering meditative rhythms'.

The way that Yeats employed these principles, both as a basis for the writing of his own poetry and as standards for literary criticism, can be seen in his comments on the example which he selected from 'the bundle of poems' that Russell had given him for 'An Irish Visionary'.

Among the poems one seemed to me of especial beauty. It is addressed to some girl, and, despite a careless arrangement of the rhymes, has haunted me these three weeks. Surely it is worth preserving in *The National Observer*, safe from the caprices of the gods who rule over a mystic's manuscripts:

> 'I know I could see thro' and thro' you,
>   So unconscious, tender, kind,
> More than ever was known to you
>   Of the pure ways of your mind.
>
> For us who long to rest from strife,
>   Yet labour sternly as a duty,
> A magic charms us in your life,
>   So unknowing of its beauty.

Self and Soul 71

> We are pools whose depths are told,
>   You are like a mystic fountain
> Issuing ever pure and cold
>   From the hollows of the mountain:
>
> We are men by anguish taught
>   To distinguish false from true;
> Higher wisdom we have not,
>   But a joy within guides you.'[109]

One or two others have a like perfection of feeling, but deal with more impalpable matters. There are fine passages in all, but these will often be imbedded in thoughts which have evidently a special value, to 'the writer's' mind, but are to other men merely the counters of an unknown coinage. To them they seem merely so much brass or copper or tarnished silver at the best.[110]

Though it is somewhat perverse to save a poem only to damn it, Yeats's criticisms, particularly of the imagery, are justified. The 'pools' and 'fountains' of the third verse are excellent examples of what he described as 'broken, fleeting, and uncertain' images in the sense that they seem to have been derived wholly from Russell's own 'contemplative nature' and his 'more vague desires'. Their association with the central theme of profundity is contrived, and they do little to reinforce the 'message' of the final verse. Instead of the poem itself giving expression to 'a system of ordered images', a phantasmagoria, the images of 'pools' and 'fountains' have been used to illustrate a personal observation about comparative spirituality. Hence the criticism that many of Russell's thoughts, while they may have a 'special value' for him, are 'to other men merely the counters of an unknown coinage'. In short, the poem exemplifies that 'highly subjective art' that has not been able to 'escape from the barrenness and shallowness of a too conscious arrangement, into the abundance and depth of Nature'; the sense of conscious arrangement, of course, owing as much to the almost unvaried use of exact alternate end rhyme and the dogged paralleling of metrical and rhetorical rhythm as to the arbitrary and personal collection of images placed in the poem. For that matter, Yeats himself soon changed his opinion about the worth of this particular example of Russell's verse. When he revised 'An Irish Visionary' for the 1893 edition of *The Celtic Twilight* he substituted the poem 'Parting', and focused his criticism of Russell's unsystematic imagery into a single pithy sentence. 'The poems', he said, 'are all endeavours to capture some high, impalpable mood in a net of obscure images.'[111]

The 1891 'An Irish Visionary' thus tells the reader more about

Yeats's poetic concerns and more about his attitude to Russell's mysticism than it does about Russell himself. The extent to which Yeats employed his friend to express his own interests can be gauged by his anxiety to prove the existence of a Celtic tradition, which was important only to his view of himself as a poet; by his drawing attention to the mythical heroes who people his own poetry; by his use of the term phantasmagoria; and by the fact that at various times he quarried the article for at least four of his own poems. 'An Irish Visionary' also signals a change in his attitude to his friend's choice of the mystic way. In the late 'eighties Yeats had enthusiastically employed Russell's visions to combat his father's scepticism and to counter his friends' preoccupation with materialism and science. And though he may have had some doubts about the origin and nature of these visions, he had fallen under their spell to the point that he had written several poems and plays celebrating dream states and visionary wisdom. The 1891 article, however, contains a number of indications that his enthusiasm had begun to wane, and that his appraisal of his one-time ally had taken a critical turn. The location of Russell among 'half-mad and visionary peasants' and 'queer and conscience-stricken persons', the choice of a narrative stance that alternates between the aloof and the condescending, and the criticism of the poem reproduced in the article all firmly point to Yeats's growing conviction that Russell's visionary powers were dissipating themselves in fruitless moralism and in the exaltation of life over art. His preference for perfecting his life, making his 'mind strong, vigorous and calm', at the expense of perfecting his poetry is noted with disapproval. In 1891 he wrote that Russell sometimes 'illustrates his verses with Blake-like drawings, in which rather incomplete anatomy does not altogether hide extreme beauty of feeling'. In 1902 he removed the comparison with Blake and changed 'rather incomplete' to 'imperfect', and in 1925 he deleted the word 'extreme' and changed 'hide' to 'smother'. The final version reads: 'He had frequently illustrated his verse with drawings, in which an imperfect anatomy did not altogether smother a beauty of feeling.'[112] The general impression gained from the 1891 article is of unrealized potential, of spiritual and creative powers at loose in a tradition that seems itself to have lost most of its coherence and shaping power. One would never think from reading 'An Irish Visionary' that within three years Russell would produce a volume of poems that Yeats would widely praise as 'about the best piece of poetical work done by any Irishman this good while back'.[113] That Yeats himself was taken by surprise not only indicates the degree to which he had lost contact with Russell's poetry, but also the way in which he had become effectively imprisoned by his own image of him.

A Form for Forms

The attention which Yeats paid to the obscurity of Russell's poetry and painting in 'An Irish Visionary' reflects his anxiety about the same problem in his own work. In a poem written in September 1892, 'To the Rose Upon the Rood of Time', he publicly expressed the hope that his quest for

> the strange things said
> By God to the bright hearts of those long dead

would not blind him to the Natural and human world and cause him 'to chaunt a tongue men do not know.'[114] Yet, in spite of his good intentions, he frequently puzzled his readers. Throughout the early 'nineties his fellow Rhymers often took him to task for obscurity, while many of his friends in Ireland quizzically raised one eyebrow when they read his work.[115] 'I [had begun] to write love poems', he later admitted ruefully, 'which my fellow countrymen, discerning the presence of some abstraction plainly not "the finest peasantry above earth", found very obscure'.[116]

The love poems that he is referring to, which were later collected in 'The Rose', are similar in intention to Russell's 'Parting', the poem he had selected for the 1893 revision of 'An Irish Visionary' for *The Celtic Twilight*.[117] 'Forgiveness', 'Pity', 'To One Consecrated', and 'Echoes' are further examples of Russell's poetry from the early 'nineties in the same mode.[118] They are all love poems apostrophizing the beloved as a spiritual ideal, and they are difficult to understand because in most of them the beloved has almost been idealized out of existence. Naturally, any poetry that consciously devotes itself to expressing the 'essence of things' rather than the 'things' themselves needs to be skilfully written to be understood. In the case of some of Yeats's love poems, part of the obscurity is due to the patterns of related images that he had taken from Irish mythology and the rituals of the Golden Dawn.

A measure of obscurity was perhaps unavoidable with the type of poetry they were attempting to write. 'We preferred the love poetry when one sang at the same moment not [only] the sweetheart but some spiritual principle', Yeats wrote of his own and Russell's taste: 'all must be *vita nuova*'.[119] Like Dante, their passion for the ideal arose partly from sexual frustration — Russell formed an unrequited attachment for a girl at Pim's in 1891, which was the year Maud Gonne rejected Yeats's first proposal of marriage[120] — and like the pre-Raphaelites whose poetry they admired, their idealization of love was partly due to the influence of Plato. 'We were full of Platonism', Yeats wrote in an account of The Household, and wishing to emphasize that their enthusiasm had been ill informed, added 'not of Plato but of current conversation'.[121] But Russell told a friend he had studied Taylor's translation of *The Dialogues* carefully in 1890 or 1891, and emphasized that he had been particularly impressed by Socrates' account of the hierarchy of beauty in *The Banquet*, an account which he accurately summarized:

First he says we are in love with a single person or form; then, as the soul becomes wiser, it realises that the beauty in one form is akin to the beauty in all other forms. We are released from this mean idea of beauty in one person or form only. Our search goes into the depths, and in this second stage of initiation into beauty we pass from the beauty of form into perception of the beauty of ideas, and at last we are led to see beauty in its very essence.[122]

The movement from contemplating a particular woman who is loved to perceiving the spiritual essence she either embodies or reveals is characteristic of Russell's and Yeats's love poems from the early 'nineties. In 'Forgiveness', for example, Russell begins with a particular woman, located in time and space, 'at dusk' in a 'little room', and then proceeds to apotheosize her.

> At dusk the window panes grew grey;
> The wet world vanished in the gloom;
> The dim and silver end of day
> Scarce glimmered through the little room.
>
> And all my sins were told; I said
> Such things to her who knew not sin —
> The sharp ache throbbing in my head,
> The fever running high within.
>
> I touched with pain her purity;
> Sin's darker sense I could not bring:
> My soul was black as night to me;
> To her I was a wounded thing.
>
> I needed love no words could say;
> She drew me softly nigh her chair,
> My head upon her knees to lay,
> With cool hands that caressed my hair.

> She sat with hands as if to bless,
> And looked with grave, ethereal eyes;
> Ensouled by ancient Quietness,
> A gentle priestess of the Wise.[123]

The poem moves from particular to universal and from sexual to spiritual, the woman who comforts the poet becoming a 'gentle priestess' who has been 'ensouled by ancient Quietness'.

Yeats's poem 'The Rose of the World' follows a similar pattern of development, though the transition from particular to universal is much swifter. He starts with a particular woman, 'these red lips', whom he then associates with Helen of Troy and Deirdre of the Sorrows, two mythological women whose great beauty brought suffering to themselves and their worlds. In the second verse the woman is accorded the status of an archetype — untouched by the flow of events on earth or the passing of the stars in the heavens; while in the final verse she becomes beauty herself before God's throne, a conception indebted to the 'Kabbalistic and neo-Platonic theory that the *Shekhinah* or eternal womanhood is coeval with God'.[124] There is a progression from 'these red lips' to the eternal essence of beauty which they manifest.

> Who dreamed that beauty passes like a dream?
> For these red lips with all their mournful pride,
> Mournful that no new wonder may betide —
> Troy passed away in one high funeral gleam,
> And Usna's children died.
>
> We and the labouring world are passing by:
> Amid men's souls that day by day give place,
> More fleeting than the sea's foam-fickle face,
> Under the passing stars, foam of the sky,
> Lives on this lonely face.
>
> Bow down archangels in your dim abode;
> Before ye were, or any hearts to beat,
> Weary and kind one stood before His seat,
> He made the worlds to be a grassy road,
> Before her wandering feet.[125]

Russell's poem is obviously simpler. It recounts a specific experience that has led to a greater understanding of Quietness and Wisdom. The experience itself is first given a sexual and a physical context. The moment of contact between the poet and his beloved, while rendered timeless and ethereal by her caresses, occurs 'at dusk' and in 'the little room'. The predominance of simple tenses, especially the present and preterite, and the use of verbs such as 'vanished' and 'drew', which imply a specific moment, reinforce the particularity of the experience. The word 'ancient', which occurs in the final verse, does not detract from this sense of the particular, because it is not used to denote the passage of time but as an epithet to acknowledge the dignity of the beloved. The imagery, which is subdued, sparse, and for the most part conventional, serves two main functions. It helps the reader to visualize the scene, and it suggests a hierarchy of values. For example the trite images,

> My soul was black as night to me;
> To her I was a wounded thing

prevent the reader from identifying with and concentrating on the poet's past sins. They also indicate that the meaning and the significance of the encounter lie not with him, but with his beloved, 'The gentle priestess of the Wise'. Imagery is principally used to illustrate and order the sequence of events that provide the basic narrative structure of the poem. Russell's poem simply recounts a spiritually significant experience.

Yeats immediately creates a distance between himself and his readers by posing a question in the first line: 'Who dreamed that beauty passes like a dream?' His poem neither recounts an experience nor explains an idea. [The poet] never speaks directly as to someone at the breakfast table', he asserted, 'there is always a phantasmagoria.'[126] The system of ordered images which mediate between the poet, subject, and reader are the images of two beautiful, world-shaping women. The opening verse of the poem dramatizes the past incarnation of divine beauty in Helen of Troy and Deirdre of the Sorrows, and challenges the reader to recognize its reincarnation in Maud Gonne. The association of Helen and Deirdre as paragons of beauty is not an idle fancy on Yeats's part — it was traditional in folk literature. The blind poet Raftery, for example, jointly celebrates their great beauty in the first quatrain of 'Maire Standun'.[127] In fact, the practice of mixing classical and local mythology, as the eminent philologist Georges-Denis Zimmermann has shown, was very common in traditional Irish songs.[128] So the imagery for Yeats's poem has been drawn from a phantasmagoria, since the images themselves and their association with one another are deeply rooted in Irish tradition. They are truly 'ancient symbols.' In the first verse they are used to link the present to the heroic age in Maud Gonne. But the poem pauses only briefly in the present.

Self and Soul

The reader is quickly taken from there, through the heroic past, to the beginning of time, as he moves from Troy, to the world, the stars, and finally to the throne room of Creation. The effect of these transitions is to enrich the present by showing its relation to the past. The emotions aroused by 'these red lips', a masterful use of synecdoche, which eases the transition from the particular to the general, gain significance as they are linked to the emotions which previous manifestations have aroused. The persistent vitality of this divine beauty is emphasized in the second verse, even if somewhat tortuously, by another 'ancient symbol', the neo-Platonic symbol of the sea as representing the impure chaos of human affairs or the turbulent flux of history.[129] The predominant tone of the poem, however, is subdued. Both imagery and diction, especially through words such as 'dream', 'mournful', 'gleam', and 'dim', help to evoke a 'Celtic' atmosphere. Russell later described the poem as a perfect blending of 'Celtic memories and Platonic mysticism',[130] though he would have been more accurate if he had said neo-Platonic symbolism.

In 'Forgiveness' Russell recounts a mystical experience. In 'To the Rose of the World' Yeats as a poet, in the words of *A General Introduction for my Work*, has been 'reborn as an idea, something intended, complete'. Russell's poem, in its approach to its subject, is essentially Platonic. As the poet James Cousins, who knew both Yeats and Russell very well, has rightly pointed out:

To A.E. the Fundamental Beauty, which is the first garment of the Divine Unity, is not — as Yeats figures it — a wanderer, but self-existent now. All things disclose it according to the measure of their possibility. Even the beloved of the human heart may not claim to be beautiful in her own right, but as an intermediary.[131]

Russell expected his own poetry to function in the same way. In 'Forgiveness' the reader is led, as was Plato's neophyte, from an awareness of an individual manifestation of purity to share in a realization of the essence of purity. He once declared to Yeats, in the middle of an argument about the stance a poet should adopt towards his audience, that

To quote Plato in *The Banquet*, the aim of the [poet] is to lead the neophyte from the perception of the beauty of forms or sounds or colours to the beauty of laws and of ideas until at last he attains a vision which is equal to a beauty so vast.[132]

His primary concern in 'Forgiveness', which is reflected in his choice of the lyric mode, is the experience.

Yeats, who at the time he wrote his poem was more concerned with modes of expression than narrating individual experiences has broken the restraints of the lyric by constructing his poem around a phantasmagoria. His two main points of departure are his use of 'ancient symbols' and his view of himself as the register of the experience.[133] If, as Joyce says, lyric poetry is 'the form wherein the artist presents his image in immediate relation to himself'[134] then Yeats in 'To the Rose of the World' has neither presented his image solely or immediately in relation to himself. By drawing from a phantasmagoria he has been able to enmesh his own experience with universal traditions, and he has been able to express indirectly, rather than immediately, his emotional response to the ideas that have become associated in his mind with the experience that inspired the poem. Perhaps the best way to understand how Yeats has been able to write about the 'essence' of his experience, rather than the raw, private experience itself, is to compare the first verse of his poem:

> Who dreamed that beauty passes like a dream?
>   For these red lips with all their mournful pride,
>   Mournful that no new wonder may betide —
> Troy passed away in one high funeral gleam,
>   And Usna's children died.

with a passage from his autobiographical novel, *The Speckled Bird*:

> . . . at night he went over her words and her looks, fixing upon his imagination that face where great beauty was half dependent upon something so impersonal that it almost suggested a pattern, a rhythm, rather than an individual soul.[135]

The prose passage, where Yeats does present his image in immediate relation to himself, recounts the experience; the poem attempts to capture the essence of the experience. 'The Rose of the World' is a Symbolist poem. It is written from an aesthetic which proposes that reality inheres in form and symbol, and that the world is constructed by the imagination, rather than apprehended, as Russell's poem implies, through vision, meditation, or intuition.

This distinction is one of the fundamental differences between mysticism and magic. For the mystic the spiritual world simply exists. It does not necessarily have to be approached through images or symbols. As Russell explains in *The Candle of Vision*, 'Imagination

... is an act of vision, a perception of images already existing breathed on some ethereal medium which in no way differs from the medium which holds for us our memories'.[136] The mage, on the other hand, attempts to master various rituals and symbols in the belief that they will give him the power to shape and control his world. Note, for example, the imperative in the first line of the last verse of Yeats's poem: 'Bow down archangels in your dim abode'. 'The central principle of all the Magic of power', Yeats said, 'is that everything we formulate in the imagination, if we formulate it strongly enough, realises itself in the circumstances of life, acting either through our own souls, or through the spirits of nature.'[137] Elsewhere, he declared:

All art that is not mere story-telling, or mere portraiture, is symbolic, and has the purpose of those symbolic talismans which medieval magicians made with complex colours and forms, and bade their patients ponder over daily, and guard with holy secrecy; for it entangles, in complex colours and forms, a part of the Divine Essence. . . . I cannot now think symbols less than the greatest of all powers whether they are used consciously by the masters of magic, or half consciously by their successors, the poet, the musician and the artist.[138]

Through the manipulation of symbols, the forces of the imagination, and the imperative power of language, Yeats believed the mage and the poet could shape reality.

Mage Versus Mystic

While Yeats was developing his theory of symbolism, he conducted a wide range of experiments in which he tried to determine the types of images, emotions, and ideas evoked by specific symbols. He was motivated by a desire to utilize for poetry the various doctrines of correspondence which he had studied in The Esoteric Section of The Theosophical Society, the writings of Blake, and the manuals of the Golden Dawn. He also hoped that a precise symbolism would make habitable his Celtic Twilight—that borderland between the physical and the metaphysical where 'heaven and earth so mingle that each seems to the other to have taken upon itself some shadow of the other's beauty'.[139] Yeats believed that once he had discovered the principal associations of a number of traditional symbols he would be able to write poems, plays, and stories which evoked a range of precise yet indefinable emotions. But this desire to measure and arrange eventually brought him into conflict with Russell, whose mind was not diagrammatic and whose aims were spiritual rather than poetic.

Perhaps the 'intellectual chief influence' on his life throughout the 'nineties, Yeats later claimed, was a technique of controlled vision stimulated by pictorial symbols taught him by MacGregor Mathers, one of the chief adepts of the Golden Dawn.[140] 'I was made to look at a coloured geometric form', he recounted,

and then, closing my eyes, see it again in the mind's eye. I was then shown how to allow my reveries to drift, following the suggestion of the symbol. I saw a desert, and a gigantic Negro raising up his head and shoulders among great stones.[141]

Yeats was told that he had seen a being from the Order of the Salamanders, whose symbol he had been shown.[142] Excited by this new form of psychic experience, he began his own experiments in the hope that the visions he saw would provide him with subjects, and would make his writing more sensuous and vivid. No longer was access to the other world solely the province of his visionary friend.

Two of the stories Yeats included in the first edition of *The Celtic Twilight*, 'Regina, Regina Pigmeorum, Veni' and 'The Eaters of Precious Stones', were vision-inspired.[143] He told a fellow occultist that many of the stories he collected in *The Secret Rose* were not 'mere phantasies but the signatures . . . of things invisible'.[144] One of them, entitled 'Out of the Rose', probably had its origin in a vision which he saw using Mathers's method as early as 1890. 'It arose in three minds', he recalled, 'without confusion, and without labour . . . and more swiftly than any pen could have written it out.'[145] The narrator of 'Rosa Alchemica' is deeply moved by a 'certainty of vision' in which he glimpses 'that Death which is beauty herself' and that 'Loneliness which all the multitudes desire without ceasing';[146] and the autobiographical hero of *The Speckled Bird*, in which Mathers's technique is described, sees several visions.[147] The idea for 'The Cap and Bells', a poem that by his own admission meant a lot to Yeats, was revealed in a 'beautiful and coherent' vision that gave him a 'sense of illumination and exultation',[148] while another vision seen about 1897, provided him with the motif for *At the Hawk's Well*.[149] Other plays based to some extent on induced visions include *Cathleen ni Houlihan* and *The Shadowy Waters*.[150]

Russell was greatly impressed by some of the results of this new system and decided to test it himself. He painted on a sheet of cardboard a symbolic representation of Mananaan MacLir and the

Self and Soul

Nuts of Knowledge, which he thought would not be recognized, and sent it to Gerald Balfour, the President of the Society for Psychical Research. Balfour gave it to a woman medium, who held it to her forehead and claimed that she saw a pool of water with reddish fruit dropping into it from overhanging boughs — a good description of what is often associated with these symbols.[151]

After some more experiments, Yeats asked Russell to submit his 'waking visions', which he believed were of a higher order than those induced by symbols, to 'certain tests' to determine their nature and origin.[152] He urged him to 'examine' them and 'write them out as they occurred.'[153] That he should 'question, as Swedenborg had questioned', seemed to Yeats to be 'of the first importance'.[154] Were his visions 'so much a part of his subconscious life that they would have vanished' if they were investigated, he wondered, or 'were they like those voices that only speak, those strange sights that only show themselves for an instant, when the attention has been withdrawn; that phantasmagoria of which I had learnt something in London?'[155] Were the images his friend saw in his visions 'symbols projected by the subconscious', or were they 'physical facts?' The last question was very important for Yeats. If it were established that the images were 'physical facts', Russell would join the exalted company of Blake. Yeats knew, as an authority on mysticism has pointed out, that 'Blake's visions differed in some important respects from those of his fellow mystics. They seem to have been "corporeal", not "imaginary" in type, and were regarded by him as actual perceptions of that "real and eternal world" in which he held that it was "man's privilege to dwell"'[156]. And Yeats himself had also been deeply impressed by Mathers's claim that once he proved that an image had acted 'independently of his mind, he had proved also that neither it, nor what it had spoken, had originated there.' Proving the images of his friend's visions 'physical facts'[157] would provide further evidence for the operation of the phantasmagoria and the existence of Anima Mundi.

Russell, with the mystic's repugnance for experimenting with spiritual gifts, strenuously objected to his friend's demand with the protest that 'a vision is the personal concern of the visionary.'[158] But Yeats continued to press for some form of investigation, with the result that, in his words, their 'disputes began in earnest.'[159] This was their first major quarrel. Russell does not mention it in his writings because he believed that autobiography should trace the unfolding of the 'inner mind' and not busy itself with 'pure externalities' — a criticism he subsequently levelled at Yeats's *Reveries Over Childhood and Youth*.[160] But Yeats describes their quarrel in detail in several places, perhaps partly because it was the first time that he had felt the full force of Russell's northern stubbornness, but more because he believed that Russell's attitude would eventually prove detrimental to his painting and poetry. Before any visionary insights were incorporated into a work of art, he believed, the visions themselves should be subjected to the scrutiny of the 'analytic mind'. For instance, he pointed out in an article that some of Shelley's poems had 'an air of rootless fantasy' because of the 'too constant presence' in his poems of the beings he saw in vision, and because of his 'ignorance of their more traditional forms'.[161] And he wrote to a fellow occultist who disagreed with his emphasis on the rational: 'I hold as Blake would have held also, that the intellect must do its utmost "before inspiration is possible". It clears the rubbish from the mouth of the sybil's cave but it is not the sybil.'[162] So by chronicling the issues raised in their quarrel about Russell's attitude to his visions, Yeats believed that he was recording a significant point in his friend's imaginative development. My desire to experiment, he wrote,

seemed to him an impiety, and perhaps the turning towards [his visions] of the analytic intellect checked his gift . . . making his visions take on a form he disliked, an obviously symbolic form — there were even winged angels . . . and he became extremely angry; and my insistence on understanding symbolically what he took for literal truth increased his anger. . . . Sometimes I quarrelled with something said or done in the ordinary affairs of life which could not have been said or done, as I thought, had he not encountered the Magical Emblems and the Sick King and refused to ask questions that might have made the soil fruitful again . . . . Sometimes I broke off abruptly, afraid that he might never speak to me again.[163]

In part their quarrel arose from their different conceptions of the collective consciousness.[164] Russell in the main held the Theosophical view that all objects and events leave their images in the astral light, an omnipresent essence, as upon a photographic plate,[165] and that the act of vision merely involves seeing these images.[166] He described his own visions as at first appearing 'to have no more relation to myself than images from a street . . . one sees reflected in a glass', and though he claimed his visions became 'radiant with actuality' they never lost their pictorial quality — a point which he stresses in the 'Analytic' chapter of *The Candle of Vision*.[167] When George Moore questioned him about his visions, he refused to say whether he saw directly, or indirectly — as one sees images reflected in a mirror.[168] When Monk Gibbon quizzed him about seeing 'objectively' or 'subjectively', he retorted rather angrily: 'I don't know what you mean'.[169] And when W. Y. Evans

Wentz, who was collecting material for *The Fairy-Faith in Celtic Countries*, sent him a questionnaire which contained the query: 'Are all visions which you have had of the same character?', Russell's answer was evasive.[170]

Yeats felt that the Theosophical interpretation of visions robbed them of their absolute worth and dramatic intensity. He favoured the Cambridge Platonist Henry More's 'more precise and philosophical' theory that the collective consciousness is composed of 'forms' or spirits, who enter at all points upon this present world.[171] His own views are summarized in his assertion that:

All sounds, all colours, all forms, either because of their preordained energies or because of long association, evoke indefinable and yet precise emotions, or, as I prefer to think, call down among us certain disembodied powers, whose footsteps over our hearts we call emotions.[172]

The emphasis on correspondence, power, emotion, and evocation are all central to Yeats's idea of the collective consciousness.

Russell emphatically rejected this identification of art with magic and symbol. 'Yeats called himself a symbolist and would have made me out to be one', he told Kingsley Porter, 'but I preferred mysticism to symbolism.'[173] By practising austerities and developing his powers of concentration, Russell tried to prepare himself to receive spiritual revelations. 'As our being here becomes transparent to the Light', he wrote,

we receive more and more of the true. Intuitions begin to leap up in us every instant, and we receive, according to our capacity, vision, imagination, knowledge of past and future, illuminations about the nature of things, wisdom and poetry.[174]

The world beyond is revealed, not summoned. Like most Theosophists, Russell was hostile to the practice of evocation, holding that even when a manifestation did occur it consisted of nothing more than a transient shell composed of the basest elements of a dead person.[175] When once asked about questioning the spirits, he replied: 'The spiritualists who raise spirits at séances never get anything more than platitudes out of the mighty dead.'[176]

Yeats, however, hunted the spirits alike in adolescence and old age. In 'To Ireland in the Coming Times', where, by way of a poetic apology, he boldly declared his aims for the 'nineties, he asserted:

> For round about my Table go
> The magical powers to and fro.

In flood and fire and clay and wind,
They huddle from man's pondering mind,
Yet he who treads in austere ways
May surely meet their ancient gaze.[177]

Yeats wanted to confront and interrogate the spirits. It was characteristic of him that he should report questioning Russell in 'An Irish Visionary' if the spirit-being he saw in vision was 'the influence of some living person who thinks of us, and whose thoughts appear to us in that symbolic form?' The last two words of the question were the most important for him. It was also characteristic that after an entranced girl medium had summoned the Queen of the Fairies he should ask her 'whether she and her people were not "dramatizations of our moods"?';[178] that he should outrage the members of The Household by paying a visit to a nearby society of black magicians;[179] that he should remain a member of the Golden Dawn for over thirty years; and that his final philosophy should be communicated by automatic writing and clairaudience.

In an unpublished letter to Ernest Boyd, who was gathering material for his book, *Ireland's Literary Renaissance*, Russell expressed the opinion that Yeats mistook symbolism for mysticism, and that he was definitely not, as was commonly believed, either a 'mystic poet' or a 'mystic'.[180] These are judgments on which Yeats himself later concurred. He told Ethel Mannin towards the end of his life that he was 'not a mystic'. 'No, I am a practical man. I have seen the raising of Lazarus and the loaves and fishes and have made the usual measurements, plummet, line, spirit-level';[181] by which he probably meant that he had sought and found the miraculous, but had subjected it to intellectual scrutiny before incorporating it into his art.

Self and Soul

Despite his life-long preoccupation with Russell's visions, and despite his detailed analysis of mysticism in the *Autobiographies* and in the various editions of *A Vision*, it is clear that Yeats only partly understood the mystic temperament, even though he experienced a number of 'mystic moments' himself. For example, Section IV of 'Vacillation' describes an experience which, according to authorities such as William James and Evelyn Underhill, can definitely be characterized as mystic.

> My fiftieth year had come and gone,
> I sat, a solitary man,
> In a crowded London shop,
> An open book and empty cup
> On the marble table-top.
>
> While on the shop and street I gazed
> My body of a sudden blazed;
> And twenty minutes more or less
> It seemed, so great my happiness,
> That I was blessed and could bless.[182]

The sudden intrusion of a powerful feeling of unity with all the visible and the invisible world, the overwhelming sense of peace, and the confidence with which Yeats felt he had become a source of spiritual regeneration are the distinguishing marks of a true mystic experience. It is, however, equally important to note that most mystics would not have timed their vision ('twenty minutes more of less') they would not have described their physical surroundings; and they would have made some attempt, however faltering, to give a fuller account of the Unitive State.[183] Of course, the poem itself reminds the reader that such moments were rare, and that, at the root, Yeats knew his emotional affinities were with the antithesis of mysticism, that they took as their example 'Homer . . . and his unchristened heart.'[184]

It was undoubtedly this characteristic compulsion to pit the natural against the supernatural that lay at the centre of his quarrels with Russell about his visions. Yeats was irritated and disappointed by his friend's stubborn refusal to interrogate the spirit-beings he saw, by his persistent unwillingness to submit his visions to rigorous experiments to prove that they were not self-induced, and by his failure to search for relationships between the images he received and well-known archetypal images of human experience. This sense of disappointment lingered throughout their entire association. When he came in 1922 to introduce the section of his *Autobiographies* dealing with Russell's visions, he wrote: 'We are never satisfied with the maturity of those whom we have admired in boyhood; and because we have seen their whole circle — even the most successful life is but a segment — we remain to the end their harshest critics.'[185] His admission is, of course, more of an explanation than an apology. Nevertheless, Yeats did wonder if he had been mistaken in trying to force Russell to relate the images of his visions to traditional forms.

Certainly, I demanded of Russell some impossible things, and if I had any influence upon him — and I have little doubt that I had, for we were very intimate — it may not have been a good influence, for I thought there could be no aim for poet or artist except expression of a 'Unity of Being' . . . though I would not at the time have used that phrase.[186]

The phrase 'no aim for poet or artist' is the most telling. In the 'nineties Yeats hoped that Russell would exploit his visions for either poetry or painting. By 1922 Russell knew that he would never do either. In fact, he broke into his recollections of Russell in the *Autobiographies* to correct his past misunderstanding.

I now know that there are men who cannot possess 'Unity of Being', who must not seek it or express it — and who, so far from seeking an anti-self, a Mask that delineates a being in all things the opposite to their natural state, can but seek the suppression of the anti-self, till the natural state alone remains. These are those who must seek no image of desire, but await that which lies beyond their mind — unities not of the mind, but unities of Nature, unities of God.[187]

The only situation that would have made Russell's visions more fertile for his life, Yeats concluded, was if he had been born in a different age.

I think that Russell would not have disappointed even my hopes had he, instead of meeting as an impressionable youth with our modern subjective romanticism, met with some form of traditional belief which condemned all that romanticism admires and praises, indeed, all images of desire; for such condemnation would have turned his intellect towards the images of his vision. It might, doubtless, have embittered his life, for his strong intellect would have been driven out into the impersonal deeps where the man shudders; but it would have kept him a religious teacher, and set him, it may be, among the greatest of that species . . .[188]

These conditions belong to those 'impossible things' that Yeats admitted demanding of Russell. To speculate about what might have happened had his friend met other influences is tantamount to redrawing his personality. To require that he submit his visions to the intellect is to deny their mystical status, for the mystic believes his visionary apprehensions are intrinsically beyond the noetic. In fact, Russell subsequently exacted his revenge by taking Yeats to task for failing to analyse adequately the circumstances surrounding his spirit communications. In his review of the first edition of *A Vision* he declared that there is always

> some enchantment upon the intellect when it enters into the dream world, so that it loses the alert waking questioning habit, and it becomes dreamlike itself, for in dream we are never inquisitive, we suffer or endure or gaze in joy or terror at the pageant of which we are part. Once we are inquisitive the pageant dissolves and we wake.[189]

Since this passage was written after the paragraph where Yeats had expressed his disappointment, it should be taken as the final answer to a quarrel that had ebbed and flowed for over thirty years.

For his part, Russell seems never to have fully understood the reasons for his friend's preoccupation with the occult. The extent of his failure can be gauged by a letter he wrote on 10 June 1935, just a few weeks before he died, to Sean O'Faolain in which he offered a friendly criticism of an article about Yeats and the occult that the young writer had recently published in the *English Review*. Assuring him that he agreed with 'much of his psychological analysis', Russell nevertheless went on to offer what he obviously considered was the definitive explanation. Yeats had mainly turned to the occult, he asserted, in an attempt to resolve the conflict between his native idealism and the legacy of his father's scepticism.

> The influence of the poet's father on Yeats was very great. The poet was naturally [an] idealist. His father was sceptical and because of this early influence there are layers of faith and scepticism in Yeats's mind. I think it was to get rid of the sceptical element in himself so that he might have a whole faith that he adventured into magic and spiritualism hoping for a clear fact of experience or a sign which would enable him to have an untroubled faith.[190]

This explanation needs to be assessed point by point, beginning with perhaps the most important, the issue of scepticism. While Yeats himself acknowledged the importance of his father's stance, emphasizing in the *Autobiographies* that it was essentially his father's scepticism which caused him to weigh the question of religious belief 'perpetually with great anxiety',[191] for he was convinced that he could not live without a system of thought which in some way took account of the supernatural, and while the tension thus created between his own idealism and his father's scepticism probably led to 'layers of faith and scepticism' in his mind, Yeats did not venture into magic and spiritualism 'to get rid of the sceptical element in himself.' The intellectual rigour and 'questioning curiosity' of the sceptic were as vital to him as the acceptance and assurance of the believer. 'We prove what we must', he once said, 'and assume the rest upon hearsay'.[192] On the one hand he showed great reverence for those ancient faiths recorded in 'the book of the people', defending, for example, his own belief in the existence of the Sidhe by quoting Socrates' retort to Phaedrus: 'the common opinion is enough for me'.[193] On the other hand, he defended himself against the charge that he was credulous about the spirits by writing in the Introduction to *A Vision*: 'Some will ask whether I believe in the actual existence of my circuits of sun and moon. . . . To such a question I can but answer that if sometimes, overwhelmed by miracle as all men must be when in the midst of it, I have taken such periods literally, my reason has soon recovered.'[194] Even in his first public statement about his belief in magic, he shielded himself against criticism by saying of his account of his own evocations: 'I do not give these examples to prove my arguments, but to illustrate them.'[195] In fact, his pronouncements about his attitudes to belief give nice point to an assertion once made by his father that what distinguishes the Irish from others is that they are at once 'sceptical and credulous'.[196] Yeats was not interested in an unreserved commitment to a 'whole faith'. In contrast to Russell, who sought to bring his mind into harmony with that of the Infinite, Yeats believed in the generative power of the 'division of a mind within itself'.[197] 'Without this conflict', he once told a friend, 'we have no passion, only sentiment and thought'.[198]

Neither is it true, as Russell contended, that Yeats sought in the occult for the incontrovertible evidence that would permit him to 'have an untroubled faith'. The word 'untroubled' is singularly inappropriate. In the conclusion to his earliest essay asserting his belief in magic, Yeats said: 'I have now described that belief . . . which has set me all but unwilling among those lean and fierce minds who are at war with their time, who cannot accept the days as they pass, simply and gladly'.[199] As a poet he valued the stimulus of discord, asserting that poetry was generated by quarrels with oneself, and that poets sang 'amid . . . uncertainty'.[200] In 'The Tower' he celebrated his 'troubled heart'.[201] The more he wrote the more he seemed to delight in the energy released by trouble and conflict. Even in a poem such as 'Sailing to Byzantium', in which he pleaded to be gathered 'into the artifice of eternity', it is clear from the contraries used to construct the poem that 'artifice' is meant to emphasize that this desired 'eternity' is something which the poet himself makes, and that its order and abstraction is really a construct to be set over against the disorder and profusion of his own humanity.[202]

Towards the end of the second book of *A Vision*, Yeats declared: 'My instructors identify consciousness with conflict, not with knowledge, substitute for subject and object and their attendant logic a struggle towards harmony, towards Unity of Being. Logical and emotional conflict alike lead towards a reality which is concrete, sensuous, bodily'.[203] Of his instructors he said again: 'It was part of their purpose to affirm that all the gains of man come from conflict with the opposite of his true being'.[204] This conflict between self and anti-self is a fundamental tenet of his doctrine of the Mask. Yeats did not venture into magic and spiritualism for an untroubled faith, but for 'an image of mysterious wisdom won by toil',[205] for a system of 'metaphors for poetry' that would permit 'stylistic arrangements of experience'.[206] Magic and spiritualism gave him access to a source of vital energy for poetry.

Russell should have told Sean O'Faolain when he offered him his definitive explanation that Yeats turned mainly to the occult to command a spiritual power without incurring a commitment to an organization or a set of doctrines. From his own observation he ought to have realized that Yeats was always more interested in what he could accomplish for himself by his membership of the Golden Dawn than he was in the Golden Dawn itself. At first, Yeats was principally attracted to magic and Spiritualism as forms of spiritual enquiry that were free from the vagueness of the metaphysical speculation that he encountered in the Theosophical Society.[207] As he later explained to a friend, he felt compelled 'to lay hands upon some dynamic and substantializing force as distinguished from the Eastern quiescent and supersensualizing state of the soul — a movement downwards upon life not upwards out of life'.[208] And while Russell spent most of the time between 1890 and 1894 trying to unravel the tangled skeins of abstruse Theosophical doctrine, Yeats found that his study of Blake had so quickened his hatred of abstraction that the woolliness of 'what were called "esoteric teachings"' irritated him. [209] He was obviously thinking more of himself than Blake when he wrote in his 'Memoir' of the poet that 'the words that he needed most were those that should brace him to a mighty effort, not those that would entangle him in long meditation'.[210] Furthermore, the influence of his father's scepticism, which Russell correctly described as 'very great', made Yeats call into question the epistemology on which much esoteric teaching was based. It destroyed his confidence in the validity of 'speculation',[211] and forced him to the conclusion that 'truth cannot be discovered but may be revealed, and that if a man do not lose faith, and if he go through certain preparations, revelation will find him at the fitting moment'.[212] These preparations were not those of the mystic, who, whether he believes that the way of enlightenment is cataphatic or apophatic, renounces 'the world, the flesh, and the devil', but those of the mage, who seeks for revelation in rites, incantations, and ceremony.

Because he did not possess a visionary faculty like Russell, Yeats resorted to mediums, séances, evocations, and the planchette for supernatural revelations. The ritual, symbolism, and hierophancy associated with these activities excited his imagination. As a poet he coveted the mysterious powers of the mage, powers that had once been the prerogative of the filid, the Druids, and other ancient orders of poets.[213] What came out of a medium's mouth, the 'lightning' of an old ghost's thoughts, seemed as incontrovertible as it was powerful.[214] To be the intermediary between the supernatural and the natural was also to re-build Irish poetry on its ancient footings. As early as 1888, Yeats observed that 'poetry in Ireland has always been mysteriously connected with magic'.[215] In later years he declared:

I learned from the people themselves, before I learned it from any book, that they cannot separate the idea of an art or a craft from the idea of a cult with ancient technicalities and mysteries. They can hardly separate mere learning from witchcraft, and are fond of words and verses that keep half their secret to themselves.[216]

Thus, magic and spiritualism promised Yeats supernatural revelations and concrete, vivid experiences which could be verified on the pulse, at a time when he was striving to write a popular poetry of 'insight and knowledge'.[217]

He was also convinced that only magic gave him living access to the seminal, holistic traditions of pre-Christian Gaelic Ireland, traditions he came increasingly to see as the source of all his poetry. 'This subject matter', he wrote, 'is something I have received from the generations, part of that compact with my fellow men made in my name before I was born. I cannot break from it without breaking from some part of my own nature'.[218] The ancient traditions were important to him for a number of reasons. They provided him with that coherent social and spiritual faith which, in common with many early modernist writers, he felt his art demanded but neither his nation nor his age could give. They kept him proof against that corrosive and debilitating fragmentation of the European sensibility which he believed had been initiated by the birth of Christianity and completed by the triumph of empirical science in the sixteenth and seventeenth centuries.[219] And they enabled him to reconstitute his

Self and Soul 91

Irish identity, an identity that generations of his fellow countrymen had been compelled to deny. The significance of pitting a ritualized evocation of Pre-Christian Gaelic Ireland against the destructive and deracinating forces of the modern world can be seen in 'The Statues':

> When Pearse summoned Cuchulain to his side,
> What stalked through the Post Office? What intellect
> What calculation, number, measurement replied?
> We Irish, born into that ancient sect
> But thrown upon this filthy modern tide
> And by its formless spawning fury wrecked,
> Climb to our proper dark, that we may trace
> The lineaments of a plummet-measured face.[220]

Yeats was convinced that Ceremonial Magic provided him with an important means for recovering the lost traditions, for 'manipulating a continuous parallel between contemporaneity and antiquity'[221] that was as important for Irish life as it was for Irish literature.

From his study of Ceremonial Magic Yeats hoped to discover symbols for poetry, gain access to a source of energy, and realize a self. Through meditation and his study of mystical writings Russell hoped to hasten his union with the Universal Soul. The fact that they sought different ends was acknowledged though obviously not understood by Russell when, late in life, he thanked Yeats for sending him a copy of his latest volume, *The Winding Stair and Other Poems*.

> I like best 'the Dialogue of Self and Soul' [sic]. I am on the side of Soul. . . . and perhaps when you side with Self it is only a motion to that fusion of opposites which is the end of wisdom.[222]

It is characteristic of Russell that he should want, in true Hegelian fashion, to reveal a unity which transcended their apparent differences. It is characteristic of Yeats, who held with Blake that 'without contraries there is no progression,' that he did not agree.

CHAPTER IV

POETS AND DREAMERS
1894 — 1896

— People do not know how dangerous love songs can be, the auric egg of Russell warned occultly. The movements which work revolutions in the world are born out of the dreams and visions in a peasant's heart on the hillside.
— James Joyce

The success of Russell's first volume of poems, *Homeward: Songs by the Way*,[1] which was published in June 1894, helped to restore his literary association with Yeats. It removed the ill will created by their disagreements about literary nationalism and their quarrels about magic. It gave Russell the confidence to begin attempting to stamp his personality and aspirations on the association. And it won him standing as a poet. The publication of his poems established his poetic voice, and so partly alleviated his fear of being overwhelmed by his friend's 'formidable' influence.[2] Yeats greeted the book with enthusiasm. He both admired it and realized that it was well suited to his polemical purposes. In reaction against the prevailing taste for Young Ireland verse he had for several years been advocating a 'true' Irish poetry that was spiritual and undidactic, but he had been hampered by the lack of suitable contemporary work with which to buttress his case. For the first time Yeats was able publicly and formally to include his friend in the literary movement.

Homeward: Songs by the Way

That Yeats expressed 'surprise' and 'delight' at the publication of *Homeward: Songs by the Way* suggests he had not been keeping abreast of his friend's work since he had read his poems in manuscript in 1891.[3] From the 'bundle' he had been given for 'An Irish Visionary' he had selected only one, and though he said he had been 'haunted' by it, he had apparently not encouraged his friend to publish. In fact, Yeats does not even mention Russell's poetry either in his correspondence or in the approximately forty articles, reviews, and letters he published on poets and poetry between 1891 and 1894.[4]

In his 1891 article he had criticized Russell's poetry for being 'disorganized' and 'obscure', but he found the poems in *Homeward* 'clear in thought', 'delicate in form', and exhibiting a spontaneity which seemed to indicate that they had been written without excessive 'premeditation' or 'labour'. Speculating about the nature of this development, Yeats said in his *Autobiographies* that it was as if the poetry had 'organized itself, and grown as nervous and living as if it had, as Dante said of his own work, paled his cheek' — an effective comparison for imaging the transformation of ideas into experience and then into art.[5] Curiously, he attributed this development to the fact that Russell regularly gave a 'considerable portion' of his small salary to needy people.[6] Russell himself does not seem to have commented on this conjecture. In his own autobiography, *Song and Its Fountains*, he merely stated that around 1894 he 'began rapidly to adjust [himself] to the life about [him], to lose the old confused timidity, and to talk with easy assurance to others.'[7] But he did tell James Stephens late in life that he believed the forms of meditation he began practising in the early 'nineties helped him to organize his thoughts.[8] Doubtless his conversion to Theosophy, which gave direction to his life; the poems, articles, and stories he wrote for *The Irish Theosophist*; the companionship of The Household; and the efforts of his friend Charles Weekes, who turned publisher to secure a wider audience than the Dublin Theosophists for his poetry, increased his self-confidence and clarified his expression.[9]

As soon as Yeats received a copy of *Homeward*, he wrote enthusiastically to John O'Leary that he found it 'exceedingly wonderful', and that he intended

to organize a reception for it. It is about the best piece of poetical work done by any Irishman this good while back. It is the kind of book which inevitably lives down big histories and long novels and the like. It is full of sweetness and subtlety and may well prove to have three or four immortal pages.[10]

His reception began with two reviews which were enthusiastic, but which contained a number of misconceptions. Yeats was neither thoroughly familiar nor in sympathy with Russell's idea of himself as a poet, and his compulsion to mould contemporary poetic taste meant that he was often more polemical than analytical. 'When I reviewed a book', he later admitted, 'I had to write my own heated thoughts because I did not know how to get thoughts out of my subject.'[11]

He devoted the opening paragraph of his first review, which was printed in the *Bookman*, to registering the differences between Russell's poetry and the poetry of the day.[12] It was unlike most English poetry, he said, in that its concerns were spiritual rather than technical, and its sources were in mysticism rather than aesthetics.

> A young Englishman of literary ambition is usually busy with details of rhythm, the advantages of opposing methods, and the like, and is content to leave problems of government to the journalists, and questions of fate, free-will, [and] foreknowledge absolute, to the professors and the devils.

In beginning his review this way, Yeats may have been tilting at his fellow Rhymers for their conviction that poetry was an end in itself, or he may have been defending himself against Edwin Ellis, who had apparently laughed him out of his admiration for the early poems by asserting that they did not scan.[13] As well as differing from English poetry, *Homeward* was unlike most Irish poetry because it was speculative and non-political.

> In Ireland we go into the other extreme, and our literature has sprung generally from some movement in public affairs, and, but for the lack of education and the belief that all such matters have been settled out of hand by the Catholic Church, would, I doubt not, have sprung also from philosophical movements, for an Irishman cut adrift from his priest is exceedingly speculative.

Though eager to assert the distinctiveness of Russell's poetry, Yeats was equally anxious to give it a context. Immediately following his summary of English and Irish poetry he declared that *Homeward: Songs by the Way* was not an isolated volume, but was the work of the 'arch-visionary' of a 'little school of transcendental writers' which had been studying European magic and Oriental mysticism for about twelve years, and which had, 'in the last year or two', begun to produce 'many curious and some beautiful lyrics'. By depicting Russell as one of a school of writers, Yeats probably hoped to convince his readers that the type of poetry he had been advocating for the past seven or eight years was now conspicuously in resurgence.

His desire to establish a context for *Homeward* led him to misrepresent the history of this 'little school of transcendental writers.' He asserted that it grew out of the Dublin Hermetic Society, but this was not so, for The Household was founded in reaction to the Hermetic Society. Only Yeats himself held membership in both.[14] The suggestion that Russell's group did not have a formal title or hold an affiliation with any established organization is also false, for The Household was the registered headquarters of the Dublin branch of the Theosophical Society. Yeats may not have wanted to publicize his friend's commitment to Theosophy because he was no longer in sympathy with it himself, and because he would not have been able to claim that his friend was not a part of a contemporary movement, and such a claim was central to his contention that he himself was in the vanguard of an emerging poetic. The statement he made concluding his survey of Russell's group is also untrue. He said that its more literary-minded members had 'accumulated a set of convictions for themselves, of which a main part was . . . that the poets were uttering under the mask of phantasy, the old revelations'. In fact, this exaltation of a literary way to truth, as can be seen from the *Autobiographies* and from *Essays and Introductions*, is what Yeats himself hoped would be the guiding principle for the Hermetic Society that he had founded and Russell had refused to join.[15] It is not explicit, as he claimed, in the 'quaint' preface to *Homeward*, which if it has any literary debt, may owe something to the *Brihadâranyaka-Upanishad*, fourth adhyâya, third brâhmana, verses six to thirty-eight.[16] The preface, which he quoted in his review, is essentially a personal confession of faith in the doctrine of reincarnation.

I moved among men and places and in living I learned the truth at last. I know I am a spirit, and that I went forth from the self-ancestral to labours yet unaccomplished; but, filled ever and again with homesickness, I made these songs by the way.[17]

The confessional tone of the preface presented Yeats with an embarrassing problem. It indicated that Russell probably meant his poetry to be didactic; but didacticism had been one of the aspects of Irish poetry that Yeats had most roundly condemned in redefining the 'great tradition' of nationalist literature. In praising *Homeward* he was faced with the dilemma of justifying an attitude he had been widely known to attack. In his 1891 article he had admitted that Russell's life was characterized by 'spiritual eagerness', and that informing all his work was 'some tender homily addressed to man's fragile hopes'.[18] But in his first review of *Homeward*, written at a time when he was being forced to press his campaign for his own style of literature more vigorously following his defeat in the controversy about the New Irish Library, a project which would have readily enabled him to shape Irish taste,[19] he was mainly concerned with proving that his friend was writing the type of poetry which he was advocating, and thus was not didactic. He stressed that Russell was

> a moralist, not because he desires, like the preacher, to coerce our will, but because good and evil are a part of what he splendidly calls 'the multitudinous meditation' of the divine world in whose shadow he seeks to dwell.[20]

He argued that Russell was a true poet because he expressed his own emotional response to an idea instead of attempting to establish the validity of the idea. 'Such poetry is profoundly philosophical in the only way in which poetry can be', he declared, for 'it describes the emotions of a soul dwelling in the presence of certain ideas.' 'A.E. [would not] be angry', he added,

> with one who turned away from his ideas, for he himself knows well that all ideas fade or change in passing from one mind to another, and that what we call 'truth' is but one of our illusions, a perishing embodiment of a bodiless essence.[21]

The poems in *Homeward*, he concluded, are 'in no sense . . . the work of a preacher, but of one who utters, for the sake of beauty alone, the experience of a delicate and subtle temperament.'[22]

Russell disagreed with this assessment of his work. Firstly, he did not think that beauty should be pre-eminent. 'I deny altogether that Beauty is the *sole* end and law of poetry', he told Yeats. 'I think the true and the good, using them in the old Hermetic sense, are equally the subject of verse.'[23] He wanted his poetry to affirm the eternal verities, not merely shadow forth, however beautifully, a private vision of changing or fading ideas. And secondly, he believed that the poet should aim to instruct as well as to delight. 'I am primarily a dealer in ideas', he once explained to a friend. 'I only want my images to be like a dim tapestry behind my clear cut idea, and I don't want people to look at my tapestry and not listen to me.'[24] That the images themselves were the medium for expressing his ideas does not seem to have occurred to him.

When Yeats reviewed the second edition of *Homeward* for the May 1895 issue of the *Bookman* he reverted to the position he had adopted in 1891 and acknowledged that Russell was a didactic poet. 'Other writers may celebrate life and joy and love, or set their hearts on fame, or in the sheer delight of writing', he declared, but Russell wrote solely 'to hearten the pilgrims to the eternal city'.[25] Why Yeats abandoned the position he had so strenuously defended the year before is not clear. He may have felt, having just edited *A Book of Irish Verse*,[26] which demonstrated that there was a substantial amount of his style of poetry being written, that it was no longer necessary to align his friend's work as closely to what he himself was advocating; he may have realized that the position he had adopted in 1894 was no longer tenable; or he may have simply yielded to Russell's protests.

After the 1895 review he was again forced to retract one of his statements. Russell objected to the idea that he did not 'celebrate life and joy and love', and sent his friend a copy of an essay he had written for *The Irish Theosophist* in which he stressed that in their search for spiritual perfection believers should 'cast away the mood of the martyr' and assume 'a mood at once gay and reverent, as beseems those who are immortal'.[27] Yeats obligingly quoted from this essay when he next wrote about his friend's work. He emphasized that Russell's poetry was irradiated by a Blakean delight in joy, that he 'often [sang] of that energy "which is eternal delight"'.[28]

The essay in which he made this statement, the third in a series of four on Irish National Literature that was published in the *Bookman* between July and October 1895, contains Yeats's most enthusiastic appreciation of Russell's poetry. While he unequivocally accorded his friend first place in the literary movement, he was uncharacteristically hesitant about the reasons for his success. His admission that he was only 'nearly convinced' of his assessment may owe something to the number of times he had been obliged to retract or rework earlier judgments.

No voice in modern Ireland is to me as beautiful as his. . . . I am nearly convinced that it is because he, more than any, has a subtle rhythm, precision of phrase, an emotional relation to form and colour, and a perfect understanding that the business of poetry is not to enforce an opinion or expound an action, but to bring us into communion with the moods and passions which are the creative powers behind the universe; that though the poet may need to master many opinions, they are but the body and symbols for his art, the formula of evocation for making the invisible visible.[29]

Again the polemicist has largely replaced the literary critic. Some of the qualities that are praised are more characteristic of his own poetry than Russell's. Some of the praise is overstated. The passage clearly shows that he still refused to acknowledge the homiletic tone of much of his friend's verse, and that he still refused to close with some of the major critical issues, such as the use of Theosophical symbols. Though he now perversely reaffirms that Russell is not a didactic poet, he offers a different explanation from the one that he had advanced the year before. In 1894 he had contended that his friend was not a 'preacher' because he was inspired by beauty; the 1895 article contends that Russell does not use poetry to expound dogma but to evoke the spiritual powers, 'the moods and passions which are the creative powers behind the universe.' But the terms 'moods' and 'passions' are more appropriate for describing his own poetry, as are the comments that immediately follow this statement. The first, that a poet 'may need to master many opinions' yet should not incorporate them directly in his poems, echoes a pronouncement that he had appropriated for his own aesthetic — Goethe's aphorism that the poet must know all philosophy but should keep it out of his work.[30] The second, that the best poetry contains a 'formula of evocation for making the invisible visible', points to Ceremonial Magic and Symbolism, which again belong more to his own aesthetic than to Russell's.

Most of the other claims are overstated rather than inappropriate, and are the result of a critical stance which was more descriptive than analytical. For example, the claim that the poems reveal that Russell possessed an 'emotional relation to form and colour' needs to be qualified. While colour imagery is prolific, and is sometimes used skilfully, its cumulative effect, as Sean O'Casey noted with some wit and considerable malice, is monotonously monochromatic.

He sees but one colour . . . in the world. . . . Purple . . . There's hardly a poem of his he left bare of the word Twilight, or of the colour usually associated with that time of the day — purple mountains, lilac trees, violet skies, heliotrope clouds, and amethyst ancestral selves. . . [31]

Careful criticism from Yeats might have put more colours into Russell's palette.

The claim that Russell's style is characterized by 'precision of phrase' also needs to be qualified. Some of the poems do display 'precision' in the sense that their diction and imagery is 'carefully distinct.' For example:

> At dusk the window panes grew grey;
> The wet world vanished in the gloom;[32]

or

> Its edges foamed with amethyst and rose,
> Withers once more the old blue flower of day:[33]

But the majority of poems in *Homeward* do not display 'precision of phrase' if 'precision' is used in the sense of 'definite or exact in statement'. Many of the poems evoke a mood rather than make a statement. The most common setting, a cloud-scape, is always slightly out of focus, and is generally used to engender a feeling of awe and reverence. For example:

> When the breath of twilight blows to flame the misty skies,
> All its vaporous sapphire, violet glow and silver gleam,[34]

or

> Still as the holy of holies breathes the vast,
> Within its crystal depths the stars grow dim;[35]

The first line of the second example provides an excellent illustration of the connotations of precision which are admissible and those which are not. The diction and imagery of this line is 'carefully distinct', but it is used to evoke a mood rather than make a statement. The mood evoked is one of a shadowy sense of some felt, sacred immensity. Most of the sense of immensity is created by the archaic substantive, 'the vast', which for the literate reader carries Shakespearean and Miltonic echoes.[36] In Russell's line 'the vast' is given a human point of contact through the use of personification ('breathes'), and by the simile, 'still as the holy of holies'. The holy of holies was the small inner Sanctuary of the Jewish Temple entered only once a year, on the Day of Atonement, by the High Priest. The movement of the line from the locally sanctified to the universally sacred helps to evoke the mood, as does the pattern of soft 's' and 'h' sounds.

> Still as the holy of holies breathes the vast

The line displays 'precision of phrase' in that the diction and imagery are 'carefully distinct'; it does not display 'precision of phrase' in that it is not 'definite or exact in statement.' In fact, some of the connotations of 'statement', such as establishing limits and providing careful, detailed explanations, violate the sense of limitlessness and awe that are integral to the mystic experience which inspired the line. The world of *Homeward* is not a collection of individually-realized objects, emotions, and events to be detailed by 'precision of phrase', but a spirit-infused, harmonious whole to be evoked by the interplay of subtle, meditative rhythms, muted imagery, and sensitively modulated diction.

The one claim that Yeats made in his 1895 *Bookman* article which does withstand scrutiny is the claim that Russell's poetry is notable for its 'subtle rhythms'. Perhaps the main achievement of *Homeward: Songs by the Way*, the more so because it was a first book, is its technical maturity. All the poems have been carefully, though not mechanically, shaped on an appropriate metrical last, demonstrating that even though Russell had not elected to devote himself wholly to poetry he had nevertheless taken care to master the formal intricacies of his craft. His favourite metre is the tetrameter, with twenty-eight of the fifty-one poems in *Homeward* written in either iambic or trochaic tetrameter. In addition, one poem has been written in alternating trochaic trimeters and tetrameters, while another has been written in iambic trimeters, tetrameters and pentameters. When he uses trochaic tetrameters, Russell generally employs catalexis, and sometimes a trimetric refrain, to avoid the jogging monotony inevitably produced by acatalectic trochees. When he uses iambic tetrameter, he generally varies the length of the line by an unstressed syllable to escape a similar monotony. Sometimes, he employs an anapaest or a dactyl to vary the emerging pattern and set up a pleasing tension between the rhetorical rhythm and the metre.

The first verse of 'Mystery' provides an excellent example of his skilful use of some of these devices.

> Why does this sudden passion smite me?
> I stretch my hands, all blind to see:
> I need the lamp of the world to light me,
> Lead me and set me free.[37]

Though the basic pattern for the verse is iambic tetrameter, only one line strictly conforms. Appropriately, this is the second, a line which expresses Russell's awareness of his present limitations. He feels himself bound by his senses; the line which expresses this is likewise bound to the emerging pattern. The masterful use of the anapaest in the third line introduces the suggestion that he can escape from this bondage. A lesser poet than Russell, one who was mechanically bound to his emerging pattern, might have written the line as

> I need the lamp of life to light me,

and justified it to himself on the grounds of metrical regularity and, perhaps, a pleasing alliteration. But the feeling of expansion and lightness which the anapaest evokes in Russell's line furnishes a subtle introduction to the confidence evinced in the final line, a confidence which is engendered by the new impetus given to the verse by the falling rhythm of the final line, the hidden rhyme of 'need . . . lead', the alliteration, and a number of other assonantal and consonantal patterns. The subtleties of rhythm evident in this poem, and also in many others in *Homeward*, fully justify Yeats's commendation.

Other poems where Russell employs anapaests and dactyls with equal effect are 'The Great Breath', 'Pain', 'Truth', and 'The Veils of Maya'. Other metrical subtleties which should be mentioned include his use of trochaic heptameter and tetrameter, with a skilful inversion of the rhythmically sensitive foot, in 'By the Margin of the Great Deep'; the thematic reinforcement provided by carefully modulated dactylic dimeters in 'The Unknown God'; and the masterful use of polysyllabic words to carry the regular iambic trimeter of 'Sacrifice'.

Yeats was as interested as he was impressed by these achievements because he was himself in reaction against the popular forms of the day: the long dactylic and anapaestic lines, and the elegant and overripe alexandrines which had been popularized by Ernest Dowson and Lionel Johnson. In the mid 'nineties he tried to recapture in his poetry what he called 'wavering, meditative, organic rhythms', which he argued were superior to traditional forms because they embodied 'the imagination, that neither desires nor hates, because it has done with time, and only wishes to gaze upon some reality, some beauty.'[38] In his poems he achieved these 'wavering, meditative' rhythms by boldly counterpointing rhetorical stress and metrical stress, which had the effect of persuading his readers to pause in the flow of a line to recapture the metrical pattern. Only rarely was he too free with his rhetorical stresses:

> Beloved, let your eyes half close, and your heart beat
> Over my heart, and your hair fall over my breast.[39]

In a few poems he merely overloaded the lines with prepositions in an attempt to fill out a traditional form, as with the hexameter:

> And the flame of the blue star of twilight, hung low on the rim of the sky.[40]

But metrical and rhythmic irregularities are in general rare, and they became even less frequent with the general strengthening of his verse.

Not only could Yeats achieve a pleasing effect by varying a traditional form, saving his alexandrines for example from monotony by including additional short syllables:

> O heart the winds have shaken, the unappeasable host
> Is comelier than candles at Mother Mary's feet.[41]

but he gradually developed a characteristic use of the monosyllabic and counterpointed foot which made his poems taut, forceful, and distinctive.

> I know, although when looks meet
> I tremble to the bone,
> The more I leave the door unlatched
> The sooner love is gone,
> For love is but a skein unwound
> Between the dark and dawn.[42]

W. H. Auden, himself acclaimed as one of the most accomplished poets of this century, believed that Yeats was the only poet to bring to perfection the reassessment of English metres begun by Browning and carried forward by poets like Hopkins, Bridges, and Hardy. It was also his contention that 'Yeats released regular stanzaic poetry, whether reflective or lyrical, from iambic monotony; the Elizabethans did this originally for dramatic verse, but not for lyric or elegiac'.[43] By comparison, Russell's achievements, though notable, were on a lesser scale. The difference can be readily illustrated by comparing two poems which were published within eighteen months of each other, both written in accentual four stress metre. Russell handles this metre skilfully in his poem, 'The Last Hero', to engender a feeling of a crushed, plodding withdrawal from defeat.

> We laid him to rest with tenderness;
> Homeward we turned in the twilight's gold;
> We thought in ourselves with dumb distress—
> All the story of earth is told.[44]

The metrical devices used to shape the emotion are more conventional, and hence more limited, than those employed by Yeats in his poem, 'The Everlasting Voices':

> O sweet everlasting Voices, be still;
> Go to the guards of the heavenly fold
> And bid them wander obeying your will,
> Flame under flame, till Time be no more.[45]

Comparing the first and third lines of each poem shows that Russell has deployed his stresses in a more regular manner than Yeats. Even though he is writing accentual four stress metre, he has allowed the metre to take control. He is less skilful than Yeats in that he sometimes allows his emerging pattern to become too firmly established.[46]

Yeats himself eventually drew attention to the difference between their command of prosody when he compared their attempts to set their poems to music in his article 'Speaking to the Psaltery'.

Mr Russell found to his surprise that he did not make every poem to a different tune, and to the surprise of the musician that he did make them all to two quite definite tunes, which are, it seems, like very simple Arabic music. . . . I varied more than Mr Russell, who never forgot his two tunes, one for long and one for short lines, and I could not always speak a poem in the same way.[47]

The observation about Russell's 'two tunes' is not strictly true; though there is no doubt that Yeats did possess the finer ear, and that he did delight in constituting a much wider and subtler range of effects.

The only hesitation Yeats expressed about *Homeward: Songs by the Way* when it was published in 1894 was that it was 'not specially Irish in subject'.[48] For Russell the other-world mood, the principal subject of his poetry, was one of spiritual belief:

> I am the tender voice calling 'Away',
> Whispering between the beatings of the heart.[49]

For Yeats the other-world mood was inextricably bound up with folklore and the Irish peasant imagination:

> The host is riding from Knocknarea
> And over the grave of Clooth-na-Bare;
> Caoilte tossing his burning hair,
> And Niamh calling *Away, come away;*
> Empty your heart of its mortal dream.[50]

By 1895, however, Yeats was hopeful of a change in Russell's poetry. In January or February Russell joined the National Literary Society of Dublin, something he had refused to do when it was founded by Yeats and others in 1892.[51] This meant that Yeats was able to include two of Russell's poems, 'Our Thrones Decay', and 'The Place of Rest' in the first edition of *A Book of Irish Verse*, which was dedicated to the members of the London and Dublin Societies, and published in March 1895.⁵² In the second edition he increased the number of Russell's poems to eight.⁵³ Russell also began to write articles and poems on Irish mythology for *The Irish Theosophist*, so that by September Yeats was able to note with pleasure that 'even A.E. has begun to dig for new symbols in the stories of Fin and Oisin, and in the song of Amergin'. At last Yeats could proclaim him one of a group of Irish writers, who sought

> to bring their literary tradition to perfection, to discover fitting symbols for their emotions, or to accentuate what is at once Celtic and excellent in their nature, that they may be . . . tongues of fire uttering the evangel of the Celtic peoples.⁵⁴

In October 1895 Yeats dedicated the first section of his *Poems*, 'Crossways', to Russell, thereby acknowledging his respect for his friend's poetic achievement, and signalling what he believed was their kinship of purpose.⁵⁵

The Independent *Review*

A reverent admiration for his friend's poetry, and perhaps a feeling of indebtedness for the enthusiastic reception he had organized for his own work, inspired Russell to write a review of the 1895 *Poems*. The review, which appeared in *The Irish Weekly Independent* for 26 October 1895, is the first piece of literary criticism Russell published on Yeats, but like much of Yeats's criticism of the time it offers more insights into Russell's mind and into the state of their literary association than it does insights into its subject. It shows him still the rapt disciple, repeating in substance the caricatured stammerings of the 1888 *Evening Telegraph* sketch that he had laughed about: 'H-he envelops h-his l-listeners in a de-delicious atmosphere.' In fact, at the end of his review, Russell frankly acknowledged that what he had written was not a critical analysis but a personal response to the way his friend's poetry had affected him:

> Do I seem too much the uncritical enthusiast? Yet I hold it the business of the critic to say exactly how he is affected. Either he gets into his author's mind or he does not. And once again, after many times, I have forgotten the outside world and its cares, enfolded by the fairy mist, and seen the immortals dancing upon the mountains, and heard the enchanted voice of Neave, called forth by Eri — last and most beautiful voice of Eri, the heart and home of so many mystic races.⁵⁶

Of course, the stance of the admirer enabled him to avoid many of the critical problems raised by the 1895 volume. Instead of assessing, for instance, the merits of Yeats's extensive revisions, and their importance for his poetic development, as Ernest Rhys was to do in his review of *Poems* for *The Academy*,[57] he merely passed off the issue with a metaphor: 'Mr Yeats has collected from his early work all he wishes to be remembered . . . I cannot say so much for the wisdom of that, finding it difficult to like so well an old friend who returns with altered voice and features.'[58]

Not only has he deliberately misrepresented the extent of the revisions, but he has failed to appreciate their significance for his friend's and potentially for his own work. The 1895 *Poems* demonstrated Yeats's concern for tightening the matter and manner of his poetry. He had excluded poems which he felt did not harmonize with the general mood and atmosphere of his work, and he had rigorously pruned the poems he had included of archaisms and inversions. He had revised his syntax to approximate more closely to the syntax of common speech, and he had reshaped his diction towards the specific and the suggestive.[59] Had Russell been less anxious to protect himself from Yeats's influence, had he been less anxious to worship and more willing to learn, he might have avoided some of the faults that limit his own poetry.

Yet even toward the end of their long association he found it difficult to admit either the revisions or the process of revision. In 1925 he published an article entitled 'Yeats Rewritten', in which he used much the same simile as he had used in his 1895 review to describe the way changes in his friend's poetry affected him: 'It is as disconcerting as for a lover to find his mistress has powdered the hair or tinted the face he had come to love for its natural beauty.'[60] The simile itself belongs to his long debate with Yeats about form and content, and expresses his deeply-held prejudice that style was nothing more than ornate frippery meant to adorn the body of thought. Russell was of course too good a critic not to acknowledge that many of the revisions were improvements, but he was only prepared to allow them on psychological grounds. In his 1925 article he postulated that Yeats merely 'found other words for his thought which [were] not better words, but only temporarily [released] the artist from the ache over absolute perfection unrealised.' Yeats denied this, and chose poetry to do so:

> The friends that have it I do wrong
> When ever I remake a song,
> Should know what issue is at stake:
> It is myself that I remake.[61]

Unlike Russell, Yeats did not write poetry to disembarrass himself of divinely inspired truths; his poetry arose from his quest for a self, and was integral to his realization of that self.

Evangelism in Eire

The 1895 article on mythology in *The Irish Theosophist* which persuaded Yeats that Russell had finally found his nationality contained the seeds of two ideas that were to shape the literary association for several years. Russell proposed that the Celtic legends embodied sacred truths which could help to restore Ireland spiritually and culturally, and that the heroes and heroines of the legends were about to incarnate as guiding spirits or avatars to direct this programme of restoration. As a Theosophist he believed that these incarnations were imminent, for Madame Blavatsky had prophesied that the world would pass from a cycle of materialism into a cycle of spiritual growth some time in 1897.[62] By 1895 Russell thought he could already sense the approach of the new age. 'A new cycle is dawning and the sweetness of the morning cycle is in the air', he announced. 'We can breathe it if we will but awaken from our slumber.'[63]

Yeats shared Russell's chialistic hopes and his belief in the imminent return of the avatar, but he felt that the birth pangs of the new age would be bloody and violent. And while Russell in the main accepted the Theosophical view, Yeats drew his interpretation from Irish folklore and from the neo-Platonic tradition. Some of his poems from the mid 'nineties, for example, take their images from the same millennial strand of folklore that O'Connell had so skilfully exploited in his emancipation speeches of the 1820s and 1830s.[64] Several employ the iconography of alchemy. The recurrent images are images of clashing armies, crying winds, engulfing flame and flood, and pale frenzied creatures with tossing hair and burning eyes who, in the thrall of an erotic fever, sweep tumultuously across the heavens. The poems are full of the portents of war. Late in 1895 Yeats asked his friend and fellow member of the Golden Dawn, Florence Farr, if the 'magical armageddon' had begun, and reminded her that a world war 'would fulfill the prophets and especially a prophetic vision I had long ago'.[65] His anticipation of the coming crisis found expression in poems like 'The Secret Rose', where the persona announces

> I, too, await
> The hour of thy great wind of love and hate.
> When shall the stars be blown about the sky,
> Like the sparks blown out of a smithy, and die?
> Surely thine hour has come, thy great wind blows,
> Far-off, most secret, and inviolate Rose?[66]

The choice of a persona, the posing of rhetorical questions, the ready assimilation of the event into his own iconography, and the comparison of the impending apocalypse to a blacksmith's forge — where the homeliness of the conventional image works against the intensity and magnitude of what is being described — emphasize that for Yeats caution was as important as commitment.

Russell, on the other hand, became so fired with enthusiasm about the coming cycle that he issued a challenge to his fellow believers: 'Give me seven mystics in earnest and we will evoke the ancient spirit; we will bring back the old magic; the fires will burst forth and illuminate the land.'[67] One Sunday, while on a visit to the sea-side resort of Bray, he threw off his customary shyness, climbed on a wall by the promenade, and began to harangue the bewildered passers-by about the return of the gods.[68]

Some of the zeal for this unusual form of public evangelism was a result of his friendship with James Pryse, an American Theosophist who arrived at The Household in January or February 1895 to take charge of the printing of *The Irish Theosophist*.[69] Pryse, a shabby, unimpressive man with a strong Southern accent seemed to acquire an almost hypnotic influence over Russell; he would, for example, describe a circle around him and defy him to leave it without his permission.[70] Pryse launched him on a number of projects. He had studied Greek, and for a time he instructed Russell in the esoteric meanings of the New Testament. They collaborated on a translation of the fourth gospel into verse, which Russell abandoned when he discovered that only one of his friends could identify the source.[71] They also worked on a number of long poems in an attempt to revive Russell's poetic inspiration, which seemed to have exhausted itself after the publication of *Homeward: Songs by the Way*, but when he spoke admiringly to Yeats of the encouragement he had received he was curtly informed that Pryse's poetry was nothing but 'American jingle'.[72] Perhaps his chief contribution to Russell's development was the instruction he gave him in psychometry, a form of divination which allegedly enables an adept to reconstruct events from the past in vision.[73] The acquisition of this new form of psychic power was subsequently celebrated by Russell in one of his poems:

> our grey visitor
> Who taught me not in words, but gave to me,
> In vision on the intellectual air,
> The noble images that once were seen
> In the ritual of the holy mysteries.[74]

Towards the end of 1895 the two men embarked on an ambitious project to reconstruct psychometrically the events which had inspired some of the Irish legends. As they worked from one legendary site to the next they published their findings in *The Irish Theosophist* in a series of articles entitled 'The Enchantment of Cuchullain'.[75] In fact, what they claimed to have seen in the astral light bears a suspiciously close resemblance to O'Curry's famous account of the enchantment of Cuchullain in his *On the Manners and Customs of the Ancient Irish*, a copy of which was held by The Household library.[76]

With so many projects in hand, and with the entire membership of The Household fired by mystical fervour, Russell was eager that Yeats should join their evangelistic effort. When he heard in November 1895 that his friend was about to take rooms in Fountain Court adjoining those of Arthur Symons, the prospective editor of *The Savoy* and one of the more daring of the London dilettante, he wrote urging him to come to Ireland.

> Herewith is a copy of [*The Irish Theosophist*], and [the] first chapter of [the] astral records concerning Cuchullain. This is mine. Pryse will do the rest. . . . I think you should clear out of Arthur Symons's vicinity, and come over here. It will be much better for you morally, and as a place to get inspiration. Charlie Johnston is here, and is going to make a long stay. Weekes is going shortly to publish translations of three Upanishads, and perhaps later on another book of his own.[77]

The plea, which was probably entered unconsciously, is for a return to the Dublin schoolboy set of 1884 — Yeats, Russell, Johnston and Weekes. Somehow Russell never overcame the nostalgic longing to restore his association with Yeats to what it had been in 1884, when they had both been virginal idealists.

Thus the response Yeats received when he informed Russell that he intended to write for *The Savoy* was that of an outraged and puritanical provincial. Denouncing the magazine as 'the organ of the incubi and the succubi',[78] Russell declared:

> I never see *The Savoy* nor do I intend to touch it. I will wait until your work is published in other ways. I don't want to get allied with the currents of people with a sexual mania like [Symons . . .] or that ruck. It is all

'mud from a muddy spring', and any pure stream of thought that mingles must lose its purity. I am not a believer at all in the power of words to convince apart from the current that inspired them.[79]

This letter was accidentally read aloud at the dinner given to launch the magazine, and its vehemence, according to Yeats, 'reduced everyone [to] silence'.[80] But the outburst served only to alienate Yeats, who was equally anxious not to ally himself with the 'currents' of a group of self-righteous fanatics.

In part, Russell was deeply concerned that Yeats would lose his soul as a result of his idolatry of art. *The Savoy* had declared itself boldly for Art. 'We are not Realists, or Romanticists, or Decadents', Symons announced in his first issue. 'For us, all art is good which is good art.'[81] But Russell was not impressed. 'Don't bother too much about your art as art', he told Yeats. 'The finer essences often escape you at your artistic best. After all the soul it is which is immortal and its body is only the fashion of one day.'[82]

The bulk of his objection, however, sprang from the fact that he had a rival project in mind which he believed demanded his friend's full attention. From January to June 1896 he wrote Yeats a number of long letters in which he attempted to persuade him to collaborate with a group of mutual friends on a collection of essays that would bring the mysticism of the ancient Celts to the attention of the Irish people.[83] He was convinced that they would find a responsive audience. 'You must have noticed when here how little English or European materialism, psychology, literature, social and political theories have affected the vast mass of the people', he told him in January 1896.

> They are practically uncoloured by any of them except in one or two of the towns. Our national humanity remains with its love, mysticism, tenderness. I have been astonished at the readiness with which the ordinary transcendental thoughts are received. I do not mean technical mysticism, but that spirituality which greets instantly heroic thought. To the people throughout the country nourished upon Davis, Emmet, etc., and on their thoughts, the simplest idealism would fall like rain on a just sown field.

'If we make a determined effort', he assured him, 'we can mould the ideals of the country and foster this latent spirituality. . . . The hour has come to strike a blow. . . The Celtic Twilight is going to break into dawn. . . . Let us be hopeful, confident, defiant!'[84]

But Yeats, who had been nettled by the outrage over *The Savoy*, proved unresponsive. He was not attracted to Russell's enthusiasm for a popular revival of Celtic mysticism, with its emphasis on

Adeptship, its unfiltered vision, and its passive acceptance of a vaguely cyclical destiny. He preferred organization and ritual, and he wanted to discover a *tertium quid* between Adeptship and Art. His long silences and failure to settle details exasperated Russell to the point where he burst out in a letter sent in April 1896:

What am I to understand? Am I to tell my men to go ahead? . . . Are your fixtures definite enough for that? . . . One cannot do anything artistic or forcible if you do not know to what proportions you may enlarge certain portions of your argument. For Heaven's sake keep all of these things in your mind and do not let the enthusiasm effervesce by unsettled details.

He concluded:

We are going to do great things over here, and by degrees you will find the mystics arising everywhere. [Madame Blavatsky] prophesied concerning Ireland and so did W.Q. [Judge].[85]

Some time later that month or early the next, Russell had a vision in which he saw a procession of spirit beings pass before a sacred mountain. 'All I could make of that sequence', he wrote, 'was that some child of destiny, around whom the future of Ireland was to pivot, was born then or to be born, and that it was to be an avatar.'[86] Several days later he saw a vision of the Dactyli, semi-divine beings who were thought to have incarnated as people in the previous cycle, rising over a mystic landscape.[87] A number of fellow Theosophists reported seeing visions of ancient initiation ceremonies, and on 10 May the President of the Dublin Lodge claimed that the Master K.H., one of the two spirits who were alleged to have guided Madame Blavatsky, had appeared in vision.[88] Ten days later Russell saw a tall, archaic figure, whom he believed to be the new avatar. He wrote excitedly to Yeats:

I am not going to bother you about any derned thing this time but simply to tell you some things about the Ireland behind the veil. You remember my writing to you about the awakening of the ancient fires which I knew about. Well, it has been confirmed from other sources and we are likely to publish it. The gods have returned to Erin and have centred themselves in the sacred mountains and blow the fires through the country. They have been seen by several in vision, they will awaken the magical instinct everywhere, and the universal heart of the people will turn to the old druidic beliefs. I note through the country the increased faith in faery things.

Towards the end of his letter Russell mentioned that 'a branch of the school for the revival of the ancient mysteries' was soon to be established in Ireland.[89] This refers to a decision which had been taken at the International Theosophical Convention in New York two months before, when Claude Falls Wright, a former friend of Yeats and Russell, had proposed that a special school of the mysteries be founded to prepare initiates for the dawn of the new age. His proposal was enthusiastically received, and within days $35,000 was collected to purchase land and build temples. Some of this money was set aside for Ireland.[90]

Yeats must have read Russell's letter with excited attention, because he had just published a short prose work in *The Savoy* entitled 'Rosa Alchemica' in which he had imaginatively explored some of the consequences of attempting to restore the worship of the old gods.[91] The plot of 'Rosa Alchemica' can be briefly summarized. A narrator describes his spiritual languor and his uneasy yearning for the transcendent that have resulted from his study of alchemy, and the way his secluded reveries have been broken by the unexpected arrival of an old acquaintance called Michael Robartes. The narrator has been avoiding Robartes because he does not want to be drawn into his occult Society, The Order of the Alchemical Rose, which is dedicated to the practice of alchemy and the worship of the old gods. Again urged to accept initiation, the narrator falls into a trance where he sees a vision of some of the divinities who 'are always making and unmaking humanity'.[92] He is then swept through many worlds and beyond many beings until he passes into 'that Death which is Beauty herself'.[93] On recovering, he finds himself submissive to Robartes. His initiation takes place in a temple built by the Order near a small fishing village on the west coast of Ireland. Like Russell, Robartes believes that the time is approaching when the local people will return to the worship of the pagan deities. But he is mistaken. Some of the local fishermen, led by an aged votary, break down the doors of the temple and stone Michael Robartes and his fellow adepts to death. The narrator escapes, and thereafter takes refuge from the lure of the arcane in a pious but timid Catholicism.

At the narrative level, 'Rosa Alchemica' can be read as an implicit criticism of Russell's naive belief that there would be a popular revival of Celtic mysticism. Yeats wrote it while he was receiving letter after letter from Russell urging him to lead the campaign to restore the pagan past. But he knew from his own experience that the Catholic Church, represented in his story by the votary, would vigorously and perhaps even violently oppose any attempt to bring about a 'return to the old beliefs'.[94] It had already shown itself hostile to his own attempts, carefully outlined as early as 1892 in his Preface to *The Countess Cathleen and Various Legends and Lyrics*, to draw inspiration from both the Christian and the pre Christian cycles of legends. His mentor, John O'Leary, had warned him when he began to write that in Ireland 'a man must have upon his side the Church or the Fenians, and you will never have the Church'.[95] A violent confrontation between Paganism and Catholicism is a common theme in Yeats's work in the early 'nineties. Apart from 'Rosa Alchemica', it constitutes the plots of 'The Crucifixion of the Outcast', 'Where There is Nothing There is God', and 'The Old Men of the Twilight', and it provides the central action of *The Land of Heart's Desire*. That Russell did not feel that such a confrontation was likely can be inferred from his zeal for publishing his beliefs, and from the way that he had preached to the holiday crowds from the sea wall at Bray.[96]

'Rosa Alchemica' can also be read as an implicit criticism of Russell's view of 'the old beliefs'. The letters he wrote to Yeats in the early months of 1896 characterize them as 'our national humanity', with 'its love, mysticism, tenderness'; but Yeats knew, from his study of the occult and his research into folklore, that they also had a dark side, that they could be terrifying and destructive, drawing their energies from some matrix of primitive, fibrous darkness. The year before he wrote 'Rosa Alchemica' he had received an eerie proof of this. The main incident in his poetic play, *The Land of Heart's Desire*, involves the conflict aroused by the fairy abduction of a young bride. A year after the first performance, a similar situation was unwittingly played out in a remote corner of County Tipperary. A young woman was burned alive by her husband and relatives in the belief that her own body and mind were absent and that they were expelling a fairy changeling. The murder trial, which attracted wide publicity, was held at the Clonmel Assizes in 1895.[97] With the myopia that only religious fanaticism can bring, *The Irish Theosophist* calmly reported this horrifying event as simply another opportunity for a successful witness of the faith: 'A discussion at a local club on the witch burning at Clonmel enabled a member to show that the belief in elemental spirits never died, and that it could not so long as they existed; the much abused peasants being nearer the truth if lacking in discrimination.'[98] A comparable myopia is displayed by Michael Robartes in 'Rosa Alchemica' when he encourages the narrator, with Russell-like earnestness, to 'seek a mystical union with the multitude who govern this world and time.'[99] He is temporarily resisted with the cry: 'You would sweep me away into an indefinite world which fills me with terror.'[100]

Michael Robartes symbolizes formlessness and fanaticism. Critics have traditionally associated him with MacGregor Mathers,[101]

Yeats's mentor in the Golden Dawn, and there are several parallels, but Yeats himself told Lady Gregory when he visited her at Coole two months after he had published 'Rosa Alchemica' that Michael Robartes was based on Russell.[102] The identification is general, for the fictional character represents an attitude of mind rather than a particular person, though there are some specific similarities. He is described as having 'wild red hair, fierce eyes, sensitive, tremulous lips and rough clothes', which apart from the colour of the hair is a good account of Russell's appearance.[103] Frank O'Connor, who was a close friend, described Russell as having 'wild hair';[104] Austin Clarke called him 'a big-bearded Pan';[105] and both James Joyce[106] and James Stephens[107] immortalized his rough clothing in novels. Joseph Holloway, that inveterate chronicler of Dublin and Dubliners, noted: 'George Russell . . . his overcoat hung carelessly unbuttoned about him, and a big pipe struggled through his ample straggling beard and moustache from his well-concealed mouth. He wore a soft felt hat perched on his long unkempt hair . . .'[108] But Yeats seems to have exaggerated Russell's uncouth appearance when he spoke about him to other people. George Moore, for example, recalling his first encounter with Russell, wrote: 'He was more winning than I had imagined, for, building out of what Yeats had told me in London, I had imagined a sterner, rougher, ruder man.'[109] Robartes retained his rough appearance in Yeats's writing as late as 'The Phases of the Moon', where he is depicted walking 'the uneven road' near Thoor Ballylee with Owen Aherne.

> Their boots were soiled,
> Their Connemara cloth worn out of shape.[110]

For Yeats, who was always elegantly dressed, the rough Donegal tweed generally worn by Russell might have been a convenient symbol for formlessness and fanaticism.[111]

Michael Robartes's appearance is said to make him look 'something between a debauchee, a saint, and a peasant'.[112] What Yeats may have meant to describe by this elliptical statement is a mode of thought, a way of responding to experience, rather than a type of physical appearance. In his typology the debauchee, the saint, and the peasant share the common characteristic of not scrutinizing their experience. Like Russell in vision, they are all as 'wax to every impression of emotion'.[113] The debauchee's preoccupation with the body prevents him from submitting his experience to the test of the soul or spirit. The saint's desire 'to be nothing, to do nothing, to think nothing; but to permit the total life, expressed in its humanity, to flow in upon him and to express itself through his acts and thoughts'[114] prevents him from submitting his experience to the test of the body or flesh. And the peasant's unquestioning acceptance of local tradition and popular superstition prevents him from submitting his experience to the test of the mind or intellect. Thus, it could be argued that Yeats chose to represent Russell through Robartes as 'something between a debauchee, a saint, and a peasant' because he felt that Russell did not probe his psychic or emotional experiences with the 'analytic mind'.[115]

There are several other details in 'Rosa Alchemica' which link Robartes with Russell. Russell's spiritual diary for 1895 reveals that at that time he was intensely interested in initiation ceremonies, as is Robartes.[116] His visionary faculty always held a strong fascination for Yeats. Of the fictional personae of the 'nineties, Robartes pre-eminently possesses and retains the visionary faculty.[117] In the poems to which he gives his name, he is said to represent 'fire reflected in water', which is an excellent metaphor for Russell's passive, uncritical acceptance of his fervid visions.[118] In 'The Double Vision of Michael Robartes', he proclaims:

> Although I saw it all in the mind's eye
> There can be nothing solider till I die.[119]

The line echoes Russell's insistence on the corporeality of some of the forms he saw in vision. An incident which occurs shortly after Robartes arrives unexpectedly at the narrator's house in 'Rosa Alchemica' is similar to an incident recorded in the opening paragraph of 'An Irish Visionary'. In both, the narrator is unable to see the supernatural form which has momentarily arrested the attention of his visitor.[120] The intricate designs and Arabic inscriptions which decorate the temple of the Order of Alchemical Rose may owe something to the murals Russell painted at The Household in 1892.[121] Recalling this temple in the second edition of *A Vision*, Yeats interestingly relocates it on Howth Pier,[122] which could be a disguise for the East Pier at Kingstown where Philip Francis Little wanted Russell to establish a mystic headquarters,[123] or the sea wall at Bray, where Russell had first preached to the holiday crowds about the imminent return of the Irish gods.[124] The criticism which this later Robartes directs against Yeats's style, that he has 'substituted sound for sense and ornament for thought' is also reminiscent of much of Russell's criticism of the style of prose that Yeats was writing in the 'nineties.[125] Taken singly such details may seem trifling, but

Poets and Dreamers

their cumulative effect is to give substance to Yeats's claim that he had based Michael Robartes on Russell.

The formlessness and fanaticism which Robartes personifies is, of course, only one strain in the rich complexity of 'Rosa Alchemica'. Its fastidiously orchestrated prose and languorous irony bring into array many of the personal, aesthetic and occult forces that were threatening to overwhelm Yeats in the 'nineties.[126] The story is important for understanding his literary association with Russell because it shows how he was able to scrutinize these forces even as he experienced them. The narrator of 'Rosa Alchemica' senses a similar dichotomy as he gazes on the Western sea, which, as Yeats reminded his readers elsewhere, is a 'symbol of the drifting indefinite bitterness of life.'[127]

One part of my mind mocked this phantastic terror, but the other, the part that still lay half plunged in vision, listened to the clash of unknown armies, and shuddered at unimaginable fanaticisms, that hung in those grey leaping waves.[128]

The word 'mocked' is one that Yeats himself had used to describe the tone of the collection of stories that included 'Rosa Alchemica'. He confided to John O'Leary that they were being written in a spirit of 'fierce mockery of most Irish men and things . . .'[129] But his own attitude to the 'phantastic terror' that surrounded him was not a simple dualism; nor is 'Rosa Alchemica' itself *faux-naif*. All the complexities of the authorial consciousness seem to have been accommodated by the narrative voice. In this respect, Russell's fervid and uncritical acceptance of his chiliastic visions, which he expressed in a series of frenetic articles to *The Irish Theosophist*[130] in the summer of 1896, contrasts sharply with Yeats's scrutiny in 'Rosa Alchemica', where the measured cadences and complex irony, which constantly undercuts his elaborate self-effacement, indicate poise, distance, and conscious control.

Early in 1897 Yeats collected 'Rosa Alchemica' and a number of other stories which he believed were 'signatures',[131] or the characteristic peculiarities, 'of things invisible' into a volume entitled *The Secret Rose*.[132] He dedicated the volume to Russell, partly out of admiration for *Homeward: Songs by the Way*, and partly in recognition of what he saw was their common purpose. It may also be that he had been inspired by his friend's boldness, a more charitable term than fanaticism, to advance with greater urgency some of the 'unpopular thought' which he himself had been keeping partly concealed for several years. 'My dear AE', he wrote in the Preface:

I dedicate this book to you because, whether you think it well or ill written, you will sympathise with the sorrows and the ecstasies of its personages, perhaps even more than I do myself. Although I wrote these stories at different times and in different manners, and without any definite plan, they have but one subject, the war of spiritual with natural order; and how can I dedicate such a book to any one but to you, the one poet of modern Ireland who has moulded a spiritual ecstasy into verse?[133]

While Yeats has emphasized a fundamental affinity by stressing that Russell has 'moulded' his 'spiritual ecstasy into verse', he has also unwittingly indicated an important difference between their conceptions of the relationship between the spiritual and natural order. For Yeats, the relationship was one of conflict, a dramatic conflict between sexual love and the deep:

> I wander by the edge
> Of this desolate lake
> Where wind cries in the sedge:
> *Until the axle break
> That keeps the stars in their round,
> And hands hurl in the deep
> The banners of East and West,
> And the girdle of light is unbound,
> Your breast will not lie by the breast
> Of your beloved in sleep.*[134]

Russell saw the natural and spiritual order in harmony, the one, as Plato taught, inspiring humanity to strive for the other. For example, the stars in 'Star Teachers' are represented as being

> These myriad eyes that look on me are mine;
> Wandering beneath them I have found again
> The ancient ample moment, the divine,
>   The God-root within men.
>
> For this, for this the lights innumerable
> As symbols shine that we the true light win:
> For every star and every deep they fill
>   Are stars and deeps within.[135]

In 1897, however, both men were more interested in stressing their affinities than in defining their differences.

Russell greeted *The Secret Rose* with enthusiasm. He thought 'Rosa Alchemica' was a 'most wonderful piece of prose', its richness

Poets and Dreamers

signifying that it had been born from a wealth of profound spiritual experiences. 'A book sustained at that level throughout', he assured Yeats, 'would be one of the greatest things in literature.' He was very relieved to discover that his friend had not been affected by his association with Arthur Symons and the other contributors to *The Savoy*. 'I must forgive you for many reasons', he confided to Yeats, but 'mainly' for the Red Hanrahan stories.

Many things which I used to think were due in your work to a perverted fancy for the grotesque I see now in another way. Your visionary faculty has an insight more tender than the moralist knows of . . . [You] unveil beneath excess and passion a love for spiritual beauty expressing itself pathetically in the life of this wayward outcast. That insight is indeed an ennobling thing to impart, and I suppose just because the highest things are the most dangerous you will find a number of people, who have not got your mental balance, using your visionary revelation of a hidden spirit seeking for beauty as justification and defence of passions which have no justification, except that they are the radiations of a spirit which can find no higher outlet.[136]

It is characteristic of Russell that he should wish to impose a moral interpretation on his friend's work, and that he should be anxious that the stories might be misunderstood. It also illustrates an important feature of their early literary association. Russell's response to *The Secret Rose* and Yeats's reviews of *Homeward: Songs by the Way* demonstrate that each brought his current preoccupations to bear on what his friend had written. Though they admired one another's work, their admiration was seldom disinterested.

By dedicating *The Secret Rose* to Russell, Yeats affected a temporary reconciliation. Some of the ill will which had been created by Russell's shrill protests about Arthur Symons and *The Savoy* was removed, and the balance in their literary association was redressed. After the publication of *The Secret Rose*, Russell displayed a reluctance to recruit Yeats for Celtic evangelism and a growing desire to help him to construct rituals for 'The Castle of Heroes'.

'The Castle of Heroes'

One reason why Yeats paid scant attention to his friend's persistent pleading through 1896 to join him in preaching the return of the gods was that he was formulating his own plans for a revival of Celtic mysticism. Unlike Russell, who seems to have envisioned gathering the converted into a loose federation of Hermetic societies, Yeats wanted to found a secret cult that was exclusive, hieratic, and ritualistic. Part of an early unpublished draft of *Per Amica Silentia Lunae* clearly distinguishes between their different approaches. Yeats wrote:

Could I not found an Eleusinian Rite, which would bind into a common symbolism, a common meditation, a school of poets and men of letters, so that poetry and drama would find the religious weight they have lacked since the middle ages perhaps since ancient Greece? I did not intend it to be a revival of the pagan world, how could one ignore so many centuries, but a reconciliation, where there would be no preaching, no public interest.[137]

The holistic mythology constructed by the cult was thus to provide a solution to a personal and a national problem.

Yeats, particularly in the mid 'nineties, seems to have become obsessed by the conviction that the multiplicity of interests and opinions current in Ireland and the modern Western world had so fragmented Irish life that it had robbed Irish poets of their lingua franca, impoverishing their poetry and alienating them from their audience.[138] He looked with envy to the Greeks, the Middle Ages, and the early Renaissance, where a common symbology and a unified system of belief had united poet and audience. 'Had not Europe shared one mind and heart', he asked himself, 'until both mind and heart began to break into fragments a little before Shakespeare's birth?'[139] Perhaps an exclusive cult could evolve a mythology which would reassociate intellect and sensibility and reunite, through a common lexicon, poet and people.[140] Yeats believed that he could fuse the aesthetic, spiritual and national consciousness, and could convert Irish places of beauty and legendary significance into unifying symbols by means of a mythopoetic occultism.[141] For the myths to be pervasive he realized that he would have to draw from both the Christian and the pagan traditions. He thus sought to 'unite the radical truths of Christianity to those of a more ancient world',[142] to return Ireland, in effect, to the fifth century, when 'a man just tonsured by the Druids could learn from the nearest Christian neighbour to sign himself with the Cross without sense of incongruity.'[143] It was also his hope that the mythology which resulted from this union would make his own poetry more resonant. 'I wished by my writings and those of the school I hoped to found', he later revealed, 'to have a secret symbolical relation to these mysteries, for in that way, I thought, there will be a greater richness, a greater claim upon the love of the soul, doctrine without

Poets and Dreamers

exhortation and rhetoric.'[144] 'The Castle of Heroes' thus represents Yeats's most overt attempt to fuse Adeptship and Art.

The idea of this secret, mystical cult began to take definite shape while he was visiting Douglas Hyde at the conclusion of his summer tour of 1896 of the Aran Islands and Galway. In the middle of Lough Key, on a small, uninhabited island, he discovered an unoccupied castle in an excellent state of repair.[145] Perhaps sufficient money could be raised to buy or rent it as a Temple for his cult.

From Lough Key, Yeats went to Dublin, where he spent several days with Russell before catching the boat train to London. On his departure Russell jestingly reported to a friend that 'Willie Yeats has just come by me wrapt in a faery whirlwind, his mouth speaking great things'.[146] The humour was only a ploy to conceal his own enthusiasm. The idea of formulating myths which would re-awaken the Irish love for sacred places appealed to Russell. In a virulent attack on the Catholic Church which he published shortly after his talk with Yeats, he declared that 'a Religion must always be exotic which makes a far off land sacred rather than the earth underfoot'.[147]

His enthusiasm for the project was increased by a vision he saw in May or June 1897. He wrote excitedly to Yeats that he had obtained new information on the whereabouts of an important avatar.

(Private). The Celtic adept whom I am inclined to regard as the genius of the Renaissance in its literary and intellectual aspects lives in a little white-washed cottage. I feel convinced it is in Donegal or Sligo. There is a great log of a tree with the bark still on it a few feet from the door. It is on a gentle slope. He is middle aged, has a grey golden beard and hair (more golden than grey), face very delicate and absorbed. Eyes have a curious golden fire in them, broad forehead. . . . *Don't spread this about.*

He concluded the letter with an invitation to Yeats to join him and his fellow Theosophists when they went to look for this venerable adept in their mid-year vacation.[148]

This invitation was accepted, and in July the two men set off for Sligo, where they stayed with George Pollexfen, an uncle of Yeats's who was an amateur astrologer.[149] When he expressed interest in their plan to establish a school of the Mysteries and make contact with the forward spirits of the new age, he was invited to help them construct some of the rituals.[150] These rituals were compilations of elaborate sets of related symbols, which were used to evoke specific Celtic deities, who conducted the adepts on journeys on the astral plane.[151] The correspondence between symbol and astral experience was determined by a form of complementary clairvoyance, a pair or a group of adepts meditating on a given symbol and then describing what they saw to one another. For example, Yeats recorded in the notebook he kept on this visit:

I saw quite suddenly a tent with a wooden badly-carved idol, painted dull red; a man looking like a Red Indian was prostrate before it. The idol was seated to the left. I asked [Russell] what he saw. He saw a most august immense being, glowing with a ruddy opalescent colour, sitting on a throne to the left.[152]

The vision was considered to be the sum of these elements. From such investigations they hoped to compile a precise list of symbols and their associated visions.

While they were in Sligo, the two men received an invitation to continue their psychic investigations at Coole Park. This was to be Yeats's first extensive visit to the house where he was to spend many of his summers, and which was to figure prominently in his poetry. 'George Russell and myself will reach Gort by the train that gets there at 1.27 on Monday', he wrote to Lady Gregory on 24 July.

[Russell] has made drawings since he came here of quite a number of supernatural beings. The resemblance between the things seen by him at certain places and the things seen there at different times by a cousin of mine have been very curious. They have met however and so as we say 'may have got the things out of each other's sphere' although they did not talk about them.[153]

Though Yeats may have wished to appear sceptical to his new friend, his caution proved unnecessary. Lady Gregory was as anxious for the psychic well-being of her guests as she was for their physical comfort. The afternoon they arrived she took them to a nearby cromlech, where Russell saw a purple Druid.[154] Russell could only stay a few days because he had to return to the cashier's office at Pim's in Dublin, but he left sketches of the spirit beings he had seen. Yeats, Lady Gregory, and William Sharp, who had arrived at Coole shortly after Russell left, showed some of these sketches to Mr Saggerton and Mary Sheridan, two local seers. Both agreed that the beings they had seen at various sacred places in the district were similar to those depicted in the drawings.[155] On 4 August Yeats wrote asking for more drawings, and received sketches of 'the aureole of the Mor Rega . . . and the Dragon's crest, which is common and is worn by Nuada'.[156] Mr Saggerton recognized the figures in the drawings and, when Mary Sheridan was shown them, she 'at once

Poets and Dreamers

explained that it was a "photograph" of the fairy queen she had often seen, only that the strange girdle of fan flames was around her waist and not on her head as in the drawing.'[157] Russell was delighted to have his visionary powers corroborated, and wrote to Yeats that the success of the tests confirmed his theory that what the 'peasant seers' called 'fairy' was in fact 'the immemorial images of the ancient mystic with their crowns and initiation robes'.[158]

Yeats left Coole early in November 1897, and spent a few days in Dublin before taking the boat train to London. His visit left Russell uneasy, for he discovered that his friend had developed an enthusiasm for evoking 'bad spirits'.[159] In reporting this to Lady Gregory, he emphasized that he did 'not share Willie's enthusiasm for the shades.' 'I have done something which will delight his heart', he wrote good humouredly.

I have designed [a drawing] . . . of the Black Pig moving through lightning and storm. You know that this uncanny creature is more to W.B.Y. at present than God or love or country. He fondles it to his heart as a lover the sweetest glance of his girl. I believe in dreams he tucks this weird animal under his arm and roams through the vast.

I foresee Yeats and his black pig in many a ballad and tale of future Ireland and many a wild vision

Who is he that rides upon the storm
Who carrieth a black porker
And sheds shadowy terror and laughter
It is William Mac Yeats Bard of Gael![160]

By gently ridiculing some of his friend's occult preoccupations, Russell was perhaps covertly indicating his desire to dissociate himself from 'The Castle of Heroes'. He consistently avoided any form of psychic investigation which involved the evocation of evil spirits.

From December 1897 to the following March, Yeats wrote him a number of letters asking for more materials for the rituals, but he received only grudging replies.[161] Attributing this to a dislike for the meticulously schematic way they were proceeding, he attempted to secure his friend's full co-operation by a direct appeal through the supernatural. 'When Miss Gonne and myself were seeing visions', he informed Russell on 27 March 1898, we got a message for you which was 'number the people of God.' Does it mean anything to you? Is it an appeal to you to help in that systematization which you so dislike? Miss Gonne and myself both got a message for you, which seemed to be the same thing, but in different words. These messages at the worst are messages from one's deeper self . . .[162]

Russell, who suspected the messages came from Yeats's deeper self and not from the Immortals, dispatched a tart reply:

Do not forget your own literary work for . . . Celtic Mysteries . . . . The mysteries are here for five years (or ten more likely) in the future. Your verse universally intelligible will help you more powerfully later on than a secret propaganda now.[163]

The parenthetical remark and the labelling of Yeats's work as 'a secret propaganda' indicate that by March 1898 Russell had lost most of his enthusiasm for the project.

The remainder of their collaboration on rites for 'The Castle of Heroes' was done in a desultory fashion whenever the two men were at Coole. In September 1898 Lady Gregory took them to the old house at Balinamantane, where Mary Sheridan had seen a number of strange spirit beings. Both Yeats and Lady Gregory pressed Russell to describe the spirits to them, but as he had a strong aversion to being asked about his visions he maintained a moody silence. Yeats persisted. 'Don't you see anything', he queried? 'Oh, yes', Russell replied dismissively. 'I do, but they are a low lot.'[164]

By the Autumn of 1899, when Russell next visited Coole, Yeats had almost completed the first set of six rituals, which were called: 'Opening', 'Stone', 'Cauldron', 'Sword', 'Spear', and 'Spirit'.[165] As they had been devised to screen initiates, Yeats was anxious to ensure that the 'correct' interpretation had been assigned to the sets of symbols associated with each ritual. The two men spent some time checking the first two rituals, and when Russell returned to Dublin, he took a set of 'Cauldron' symbols with him. After conducting his own experiments he suggested some modifications to one of the symbols. 'See what you can get from it', he suggested to Yeats. 'I think I remember somewhere [Madame Blavatsky] saying this represented the first dualism (in its cosmic sense) and in the human sense it ought correspondingly to represent the last division before spiritual unity.'[166] Yeats, whose conception of such matters was always more physical, replied on 27 August 1899:

You are perhaps right about the symbol, it may be merely a symbol of ideal human marriage. The slight separation of the sun and moon permits the

Poets and Dreamers

polarity which we call sex, while it allows of the creation of an emotional unity, represented by the oval and the light it contains.[167]

Not all their collaboration, however, was conducted in this spirit of disinterested deference. For example, Lady Gregory recorded in her diary during Russell's next visit to Coole:

1 August [1900]. They had a fiery argument in the woods yesterday on the sword, whether it was the symbol of fire or air, and 'called each other all the names'; but were good friends in the evening.[168]

Whoever was arguing for 'air' must have won, for the 'Sword' ritual of Set Two opens with the Initiators instructing the candidate to 'come through the wind and the air to the gaining of the Sword.'[169]

A major source of tension in their collaboration was the difference between their commitment to the project and their powers. Russell possessed the requisite psychic expertise but was simply content to record what he saw, whether it was or was not relevant to 'The Castle of Heroes'. Yeats was fully committed to the project, but was constantly frustrated by a lack of visionary power. Often, he could not see what Russell saw. Arnold Harvey, acting as a tutor to Robert Gregory, also spent the summer of 1900 at Coole Park, and in his 'Memories of Coole' recalled an example of the difference between the two.

About a mile from Coole there is a point in the road notorious for the number of accidents which occurred there. To the rationalists the reason seemed clear. The road takes a sharp right-angled turn, and the corner is quite blind because of a high wall running along the road. In addition, a large tree stands at the very corner well out into the road. But this explanation did not satisfy the mystics, and one day Yeats and AE set off to investigate. On returning, AE produced a pastel which showed a gnome-like creature crouched at the foot of the tree, with its long arms stretched out into the road. On their approach, he said, it retreated up the tree backwards. Yeats had to admit, regretfully I thought, that he had seen nothing.[170]

Towards the end of 1900 a bitter quarrel broke out in the Golden Dawn, and MacGregor Mathers, who had worked with Yeats on the rituals since 1897, was lost as a collaborator.[171] Yeats was now forced to rely principally on Russell and William Sharp. In June 1901, for example, Russell suggested some minor alterations to two symbols.

The colour of the ring in the Nuada symbol is gold or yellow, not blue. I have tried it with the gold circle and the true figure was seen. The other symbol (Macha) only requires a very slight modification. I had it at home here and in looking at it when I came back I saw there were some little differences which I will correct when you are in Dublin. They cannot matter much as you seemed to get it all right. I have also got the symbols of some deities which I shall not tell you about until you can try them first. They bring very powerful beings.[172]

Sharp also took an active part in the project, though he was less satisfied than Russell with the progress which had been made. In July he asked Yeats if he would 'object to a complete reconstruction of the Rite'.[173] Tirelessly, Yeats set to work, notifying Lady Gregory on 13 January 1902 that he had done 'a great deal of work' on the rituals and had 'sketched them all out in their entirety'.[174] But no sooner were they completed than he put them aside for almost seven years, after which he appears to have abandoned the project.[175]

His decision to postpone work on the rituals in 1902 arose partly from his growing distaste for the fanaticism of some of his collaborators. In the previous year a series of bitter quarrels had broken up the Golden Dawn, and though he became an active leader of its successor, Stella Matutina, the intensity of the quarrels made him wary of proceeding with his own Order.[176] His changed attitude is reflected in the change of tone part way through Section II of *The Speckled Bird*, a novel he had begun towards the end of 1896, and which he took up again in the early months of 1902.[177] In Section I, which was written in 1897 and 1898, the hero plans a secret Order similar to 'The Castle of Heroes', but in Section II, which was written during the early months of 1902, the hero is suddenly made aware that some of the people who are to assist him are absurd and fanatical.[178] The sudden imposition of this realization on the hero, and the change from flaccid realism to crude satire, point unmistakably to Yeats's inability to conceal his own disappointment. Some of his spleen is vented on Russell. In one of the main episodes in Section II, a gathering of heterogeneous occultists in a drawing room situation reminiscent of Blake's *An Island in the Moon*, Russell's visions and vague mysticism are made ludicrous.

... [Russell], who had listened silently to all this discussion, said he did not know why anybody should bother their heads with such things. The only thing important was contemplation. It did not matter whether Swedenborg or the spiritualists or the followers of Harris or the Martinists or the Kaballists had got a little nearer to the truth with their theories. Everything of that kind was unimportant. One should take some text out of a religious book, it didn't matter whether it was the Bible or the Vedas or indeed very much what the text was about, only you had to take the same text and every day at the same hour for the same length of time fix all your attention upon it. At first it was very difficult. You kept thinking of something you did the day before or of some friend or something you had read, but gradually it got easier. After a time you saw flames inside your head, but you must not pay any attention to these, for you must rise into the formless. At last you got ecstasy.[179]

When one of the group confesses that his psychic powers are limited, Russell advises him to fast.

I never could see anything till I fasted. You just go without your meals for a couple of days, and you'll see the odic light quite easily. It shines about magnets and about people and it comes up from graves, and fasting is not really disagreeable except at meal-times. I've often gone quite without food for as much as three days, [and] the third day I have seen myself walking in front of myself. One has to keep walking about, otherwise one gets into a lethargy.[180]

As the novel was not published in Russell's lifetime, he remained ignorant of the attack.

The satirical portrait in *The Speckled Bird* represents Yeats's final break with Russell as a visionary. Following their estrangement in 1907, Russell took delight in telling humorous stories about Yeats's occult investigations.[181] Yeats rarely retaliated; perhaps he knew that in *The Speckled Bird* he had exacted a more lasting revenge.

Mysticism or Mystification?

The failure of Madame Blavatsky's apocalyptic prophecies and the decision to abandon 'The Castle of Heroes' affected Yeats and Russell in different ways. Three months after it became apparent that an avatar would not incarnate as prophesied, Russell seceded from the Theosophical Society; but he remained loyal to Madame Blavatsky, and in 1904 formed his own Hermetic Society to give closer study to her writings.[182] Throughout most of his life, particularly at times of crisis, he continued to look for the promised avatar. When Ireland seemed on the brink of civil war in 1912, he wondered whether the prophecy was about to be belatedly fulfilled, and in 1917, as he followed the rise of the Sinn Fein movement, he declared: 'I look everywhere in the face of youth, in the aspect of every new notability, hoping before I die to recognize the broad-browed avatar of my vision.'[183] Toward the end of his life the vision dimmed. In *The Avatars*, a futurist fantasy completed two years before his death, Russell made the avatars vanish shortly after they had incarnated. The question of whether they have been killed by the agents of the State, or whether they have been 'translated', is a type of theological problem bequeathed to the small community to whom they had appeared. The book thus charts Russell's own experience: the brevity of the avatars' appearance paralleling his own enthusiasm, and the problem left by the avatars' disappearance, his own perplexity. The transformation which the avatar undergoes, from the benign old peasant of the 1897 vision to the broad-browed militarist of the 1933 novel, also reveals the growth of his frustration at the failure of prophesied reform.

But he was not affected by the decision to discontinue work on 'The Castle of Heroes'. Though he shared Yeats's desire to unify and spiritualize the Irish imagination, he was able, as we will see in the next chapter, partially to achieve something of these aims through his contribution to the Co-operative movement. His poetry, which had only been slightly influenced by the rituals, remained largely unchanged. 'The Well of Ballykeele', for example, contains a governing symbol from one of the rituals, but the poem is very similar to others written after 1902.[184]

Yeats, on the other hand, was not affected by the failure of Madame Blavatsky's prophecy; but the decision to abandon the rituals was important for his poetry. By 1902 he had begun to realize that his quest for a unifying symbology was misconceived. The method of clairvoyance which he had hoped would yield precise results seemed only to increase the confusion. 'Image called up image in an endless procession', he recalled, 'and I could not always choose among them with any confidence.'[185] 'To that multiplicity of interest and opinion, of arts and sciences, which had driven me to conceive a Unity of Culture defined and evoked by Unity of Image, I had but added a multiplicity of images.'[186] For example, in June 1897, the first summer he began extensive work on the rituals, he wrote a poem entitled, 'He mourns for the Change that has come upon him and his Beloved, and longs for the End of the World'.

> Do you not hear me calling, white deer with no horns?
> I have been changed to a hound with one red ear;
> I have been in the Path of Stones and the Wood of Thorns,
> For somebody hid hatred and hope and desire and fear
> Under my feet that they follow you night and day.
> A man with a hazel wand came without sound;
> He changed me suddenly; I was looking another way;
> And now my calling is but the calling of a hound;

And Time and Birth and Change are hurrying by.
I would that the Boar without bristles had come from the West
And had rooted the sun and moon and stars out of the sky
And lay in the darkness, grunting, and turning to his rest.[187]

To argue that the symbols in this poem stir within the reader's mind unconscious forces, the spirits of Anima Mundi, is to indulge in unwarranted special pleading. To be told that 'a hound with one red ear following a deer with no horns' is an archetypal image for 'the desire of the man "which is for the woman", and "the desire of the woman which is for the desire of the man"', and that 'the man [with] a hazel wand may have been Aengus, Master of Love', and to discover that in the 'Sword' ritual some of these symbols are related to 'The Chase After the Ideal' does not transform this concatenation of symbols into poetry.[188] Yeats would have been much better to have followed Russell's advice: 'Your verse universally intelligible will help you more powerfully later on than a secret propaganda now'.[189] Not until *The Tower* was he able to begin to deploy his 'half-read wisdom of daemonic images' with any telling effect.[190]

The failure of his mythopoetic occultism forced Yeats to realize that he had to 'renounce the deliberate creation of a kind of Holy City in the imagination, and express the individual'.[191] This renunciation, which for several years shaped his literary association with Russell, can be charted in the exchange of the 'Celtic' for the 'Irish' mode.

CHAPTER V

CELTIC AND IRISH

1897 — 1900

> Adieu, Sweet Angus, Maeve and Fand
> Ye plumed yet skinny Shee . . .
>
> — J. M. Synge

During the 'nineties Yeats largely devoted his energies to alerting his readers to the emergence of an international Celtic revival and to fostering a literary movement in Ireland. As the decade drew to a close he began to place less emphasis on pan-Celtic propaganda and more on what he called the Irish Literary Movement. The reasons for this exchange of modes provide an excellent way of understanding the development of the literary association between the late 'eighties and the turn of the century.

Like many of his contemporaries, Yeats first used the terms 'Celtic' and 'Irish' synonymously.[1] In one of his earliest extant pieces of literary criticism, published in the *Dublin University Review* in 1886, he encouraged poets to study the 'Irish' legends for 'in them is the Celtic heart'.[2] In 1889 he wrote to John O'Leary about *The Countess Cathleen*: 'I think you will like it. It is in all things Celtic and Irish.'[3] His 1891 article on Russell, though entitled 'An Irish Visionary', laid great stress on the Celtic nature of his friend's poetry and visions. Again, in September 1895, in a series of articles on 'Irish National Literature', Yeats challenged Russell and other

> Irish writers to bring their literary tradition to perfection, to discover fitting symbols for their emotions, or to accentuate what is at once Celtic and excellent in their nature, that they may be at last tongues of fire uttering the evangel of the Celtic peoples.[4]

By yoking the term 'Irish', with its connotations of the parochial and the political, with the term 'Celtic', with its connotations of the international and the cultural, Yeats hoped to suggest that his literary movement belonged to the mainstream of European thought. From the middle of the nineteenth century the word 'Celtic' was associated with European antiquarianism, with the scholarly and speculative work of philologists, social historians and comparative mythologists such as Zeuss, Glück, Stark, Flechia, Diefenbach, Windisch, de Jubainville, O'Curry, Stokes, Rhys, O'Donovan, and Campbell. It carried connotations of an ancient culture, of a pure, seminal, pre-classical language and civilization integral to the heritage of Europe.[5] Some feeling for the force of these connotations can be gained from the way the word was exploited by the Irish Nationalist politicians in the House of Commons. When the Board of Intermediate Education was set up by an Act of Parliament in 1878 a small group interested in the Irish language petitioned that it be listed as a recognized subject. The politician who presented the petition, O'Connor Don, M.P. for Roscommon, suspecting that it might founder on anti-Catholic and anti-Nationalist prejudice, changed the word 'Irish' to 'Celtic', and the petition was granted.[6] And so a language which had been outlawed by the penal code and widely denigrated as 'gibberish' for almost one hundred and fifty years was smuggled into the Intermediate Board's programme of subjects under the respectable title of 'Celtic'. By the time Yeats came to publish, the term had been further buttressed by writers like Tennyson, who popularized the Celtic legends in poems such as 'The Voyage of Maeldune' and *The Idylls of the King*, and Matthew Arnold, whose essay 'On the Study of Celtic Literature' was so widely discussed that it prompted the founding of a Chair of Celtic Studies at Oxford University.[7] To be 'Celtic' in the early 'nineties was to be in the vanguard of literary and cultural cosmopolitanism.

That Yeats himself was aware of the popular appeal of the term can be seen from a letter he wrote to Katharine Tynan early in 1889 proposing that they ask the contributors to *Poems and Ballads of Young Ireland* to agree to represent themselves, for the sake of promoting their work through an English publisher, as a school of 'New Celtic' poets.[8] He consistently referred to himself in the articles he wrote from 1889 to 1892 for an American paper, *The Boston Pilot*, as 'The Celt in London' or 'The Celt in Ireland'.[9] The title of his 1893 collection of poems, essays and stories, *The Celtic Twilight*, gave the name, as Holbrook Jackson has shown, to one of the main literary styles of the eighteen-nineties.[10] In 'The Celtic Element in Literature' which was published in *Cosmopolis* in June 1898, Yeats went so far as to assert the pre-eminence of Celticism and the Celtic tradition over all other forms and mythological sources used by his contemporaries:

I will . . . say that literature dwindles to a mere chronicle of circumstance, or passionless fantasies, and passionless meditations, unless it is constantly flooded with the passions and beliefs of ancient times, and that of all the fountains of the passions and beliefs of ancient times in Europe, the Slavonic, the Finnish, the Scandinavian, and the Celtic, the Celtic alone has been for centuries close to the main river of European literature.[11]

This essay, and two others which were published in 1898, 'The Autumn of the Flesh' and 'A Symbolic Artist and the Coming of Symbolic Art' mark the apogee of his pan-Celtic propaganda.
Concurrent with this campaign, but as he himself came to realize antagonistic to it, were his Irish interests. These led him throughout the 'nineties to found Irish literary societies, to collect and publish Irish fairy and folklore, to formulate a theory of literary nationalism, to edit books of Irish verses and selections from Irish novelists, and to launch an Irish Literary Theatre.[12] The increased emphasis which he accorded the Irish mode grew partly out of a shift in his own sensibility, partly out of his association with Lady Gregory and Synge, and partly out of his desire to distance himself from the way Celticism had become a literary fad.[13] But the main impetus for change came from his work in the theatre, work which brought him opposition and which obliged him to change his style.
Most of this opposition came from the Irish Irelanders who, particularly after the turn of the century, began vigorously to attack the notion of 'Celticism' as 'an affectation of a mystical, aesthetical cult which is at present in favour'.[14] Perhaps the shrillest attack, and one of the most personal as far as Yeats was concerned, was mounted by Frank Hugh O'Donnell in his virulent little book *The Stage Irishman of the Pseudo-Celtic Drama*[15], published in Dublin in 1903 and London in 1904. The vigour and timing of the Irish Ireland campaign was a consequence of their own recently acquired sense of strength. Although the Gaelic League had been founded in 1893, it took nearly seven years for them to establish their first one hundred branches. In the three years following, however, the number of branches doubled almost every year until by 1904 there were some 600 branches with a total membership of 50,000 people.[16] One of their most articulate and representative spokesmen, D.P. Moran, asserted in *The Philosophy of Irish Ireland* (1903) that the 'Celt' was 'one of the most glaring frauds that the credulous Irish people ever swallowed'.[17] In the same year, a young reviewer wrote in the *United Irishman* of a poetry anthology:

[The poems] are mostly cast in the same mould. There is a constant straining after the 'Celtic note', as it is called — a misnomer if ever there was one. Sadness, retrospection, idealization, an intense sympathy with the unknown

Celtic and Irish

forces of life, a tendency to dwell on the past rather than prepare for the future, to regret and glorify that which has gone, do not alone go to form the 'Celtic note' — by which I take it, is meant the humming of the soul-strings of the Gael; for are not hope, laughter, the joy of life, the clang of battle also part of his being, and that the part which is most predominant in the fight?

And if we leave out these last named qualities, is not the same 'note' to be found in the poetry of every land to a greater or lesser degree? Therefore what is distinctly Celtic about it?[18]

Lugubriousness, as far as the Irish Irelanders were concerned, was not an emotion that would ready the troops for battle.

By 1903 these attacks had little point because Yeats himself had for the most part already exchanged the Irish for the Celtic mode, the exchange being made as much in response to the shift in his own sensibility as to the shift in expectations of his Irish audience. Having used the term 'Celtic' to establish his own literary movement, he was prepared, especially when it began to come under fire, to replace it with the term 'Irish' to distinguish his movement from the general English and European enthusiasm for pan Celticism. For example, he wrote to Lady Gregory on 24 October 1898, 'I go to Dublin sometime in January or February to work at the "Celtic Theatre", which by the way we now think should be called "The Irish Literary Theatre" as less dangerous than Celtic. What do you think?'[19] The same type of exchange, though more cautious, was taking place at the public level, as can be seen from a note he appended to some speculations about 'Celticism' in the 1902 edition of *The Celtic Twilight*. 'I wrote' this passage long ago, he assured his readers.

This sadness now seems to me a part of all peoples who preserve the moods of the ancient peoples of the world. I am not so preoccupied with the mysteries of the Race as I used to be, but leave this sentence and others like it unchanged. We once believed them, and have, it may be, not grown wiser.[20]

Yeats's exchange of the Irish for the Celtic mode, and the fact that he made this exchange in private at a different rate than he made it in public, governed the course of his literary association with Russell throughout the late 'nineties.

Celtic Propaganda

The vagueness of the term 'Celtic' often proved advantageous to Yeats. It enabled him to assemble a variety of writers and, with a set of loosely defined adjectives, demonstrate their common aspiration. Of this set of adjectives the most over-worked was 'spiritual'.[21] Yeats found it particularly useful for describing Russell's poetry which, though not 'Irish' was indisputably 'spiritual', and therefore 'Celtic'. He tried to use this critical sleight of hand to good effect in an article he contributed in December 1897 to the *Irish Homestead*, a recently established farmers' weekly with a small circulation.[22] Entitled 'Three Irish Poets', it purported to show that the work of Russell, Lionel Johnson and Nora Hopper was preeminently spiritual, and therefore quintessentially Celtic.

Yeats began his article with an announcement of an impending change in world thought: 'The influence of the Celt . . . has been a spiritual influence, and men are beginning to understand how great it has been'. As examples he cited Arthurian legend, which he said had shaped the social behaviour of Medieval Europe; Dante's *Divine Comedy*, allegedly based on Celtic legends and visions seen by Irish saints, which had transformed early Renaissance Theology; and Sir Walter Scott's revival of Celtic romance, which had 'influenced all the literature and art and much of the religion of the nineteenth century'.[23] He then gave his familiar roll call of contemporary Celts, who would presumably affect comparable changes in the social, religious, literary and artistic attitudes of the age: Lamennais, Chateaubriand, Renan, Count Villiers de l'Isle-Adam and William Morris. Having emphasized the significance of their heritage by naming their British and Continental counterparts, Yeats now brought forward his three poets, oblivious that their slight talents might not be able to bear the weight of such an elaborate and tendentious introduction, and that his largely rural audience might by now have given up in bewilderment and turned to the cattle market reports.

Two of his 'Celts', Nora Hopper and Lionel Johnson, prove unequal to his claims for them. The description of Nora Hopper as a poetess who has discovered 'many tender and beautiful meanings' in the legends has not been substantiated. The example of her work which Yeats quotes, 'Fairy Fiddler', is heavily derivative of the type of fay balladry that Allingham made famous. Her poem is patently not 'a little snatch of song that will not soon pass away'. Lionel Johnson's poem, 'Christmas and Ireland', which juxtaposes the callous indifference shown the Virgin at the time of her confinement with the brutality suffered by Ireland throughout history, more properly belongs, despite Yeats's protestations, to the Young Ireland League or the Catholic Truth Society.

Russell is the only one of the three to emerge with credit from this occasionally strained and at times coy article.

> 'A.E.' takes our ancient legends just as the story-teller of the twelfth century took the legends of the Holy Grail and shows us their spiritual meaning. For instance, we read somewhere of a certain well called 'Connla's well', and how the sacred hazel tree grew over it and dropped nuts, that were nuts of wisdom to all who eat of them; and in his dream the well seemed to fill the world, and the thoughts that came to him from the beauty of nature, seemed but its dropping berries; and he made this poem about it.
>
> > A cabin on the mountain side hid in a grassy nook,
> > With door and windows open wide where friendly stars may look;
> > The rabbits shy can patter in; the winds may enter free,
> > Who throng around the mountain throne in living ecstasy.
> > And when the sun sets dimmed in eve and purple fills the air,
> > I think the sacred hazel tree is dropping berries there,
> > From starry fruitage waved aloft where Connla's well o'erflows;
> > For sure the enchanted water runs through every wind that blows.
> > I think when night towers up aloft and shakes the trembling dew,
> > How every high and lonely thought that thrills my being through,
> > Is but a shining berry dropped down through the purple air,
> > And from the magic tree of life the fruit falls everywhere.[24]

Yeats's only comment was a lame assurance:

> To Irish people accustomed to the eloquent and argumentative poetry of *The Nation* newspaper, this new poetry will sometimes seem strange and difficult, but it is really very like the Celtic legends that influenced the world long ago.

Though Russell's is the most 'Celtic' of the three according to Yeats's criteria, it is a poor poem. The description of the cabin is marred by sentimentality. 'Starry fruitage' is infelicitous. The use of 'for sure', most likely in imitation of Tom Moore's *Irish Melodies*, is inappropriate. The description of his response, 'that thrills my being through', is trite. The metre, an old fourteener, is clumsily handled, its rather dogged progress recalling the common measure of many of the Nonconformist hymns Russell had sung as a child.[25]

Yet Yeats admired the poem. He wrote to Russell early in December 1897:

I read a poem of yours — the 'Connla's Well' [sic] — in my lecture at the Nat. Lit. Society and the *Pall Mall* called it a beautiful poem. The audience liked it greatly.[26]

Yeats included 'Connla's Well' in the enlarged edition of *A Book of Irish Verse*[27], and used it for the title and as the opening poem for *The Nuts of Knowledge*, a selection of poems made largely by himself and published at his sisters' private press.[28] Part of his admiration for the poem may have come from his interest in the subject at the time it was written. Connla's well figures prominently in the psychic experiments which he and Russell conducted in late 1897 and early 1898 during their work on the first order rituals for the 'Castle of Heroes'.[29]

It would seem then that Yeats allowed his personal taste, and perhaps his interest in the occult significance of Russell's poem, to over-rule his critical judgement. What he failed to realize was that his friend was ill served by having one of his poorer poems written up in a tendentious article for an obscure farmers' weekly. A carefully considered review elsewhere of some of the excellent poems which Russell had written since the publication of *Homeward: Songs by the Way*, such as 'Janus', 'Illusion', 'Duality', 'Star Teachers' and 'The Gift', might have secured a wider and more demanding audience for his friend's work, and encouraged him to perfect his art.

That Yeats knew of these poems and had been very impressed by some of them is evident from a letter he wrote to Russell following the publication of the volume in which they appeared, *The Earth Breath*, in August 1897. Russell had dedicated this volume to Yeats[30], who informed him:

Do you know I now think *The Earth Breath* quite your best work. There are great poems in it. It is an enormous advance in art too. 'Janus' cannot help being immortal and 'Dream Love' is [as] fine in style as a Jacobean lyric and has a far finer style than many Jacobean writers ever had. I think you will yet out-sing us all and sing in the ears of many generations to come.[31]

This letter expresses more than a passing enthusiasm, for he wrote again about a month later to report some of his friends' reactions to the poems.

Symons . . . is full of admiration. He tried to get it for review . . . but failed. In a review of Stephen Phillip's book . . . he wrote that 'a perfectly achieved poem like A.E.'s 'Janus' outweighs a whole volume like Phillips'; but the *Athenaeum* cut out the reference. Edmund Gosse, who did not like your work at first, is . . . enthusiastic . . . I feel absolutely confident of the book now. I know everything almost by heart.³²

Yeats himself reviewed *The Earth Breath* in *The Sketch* for 6 April 1898.³³ Like his *Homestead* article, his review stressed the spiritual qualities of Russell's poetry. It began with a criticism of the murals which Russell had painted at the headquarters of the Theosophical Society in the early 'nineties.

They are the work of a hand too bewildered by the multitudinous shapes and colours of visions to narrow its method to a convention, and, without a convention, there is, perhaps, no perfect spiritual art. It has sought unavailingly, despite much talent, to make of unmoving and silent paint a mirror for the wandering, exultant processions that haunt [the] margins of spiritual ecstasy . . .

But the poems in *The Earth Breath*, he argued, expressed Russell's kaleidoscopic visions more successfully, because poetry more readily accommodated shifts in subject matter and perspective: 'poetry is a more perfect mirror because poetry changes with the changing dream'. To support his contention Yeats paraphrased the poem, 'The Robing of the King'.

The poet looks at the heavens, and they become a great bird with a blue breast and wings of gold, and at the wood, and it becomes a great sheep shaking its shadowy fleece, and then bird and sheep become, through some vague wisdom floating in the rhythm and in the colour of the words, moments of divine tenderness.

Instead of offering a penetrating analysis of the poems where Russell had succeeded in capturing the 'wandering exultant processions' of sensation that 'haunt' the 'margins of spiritual ecstasy', or of the poems where he had obviously failed, Yeats merely fobbed off his readers with a generalization about the nature of mystical experience.

All things in these elaborate and subtle verses are perpetually changing, and all things are the symbols of things more unsubstantial than themselves . . . 'For every star and every deep' filled with stars 'are stars and deeps within.' It is the doctrine of all mystics, the doctrine that awakened Plotinus to his lonely and abstract joy. 'In the particular acts of human life', he wrote, 'it is not the interior soul and the true man, but the exterior shadow of the man alone, which laments and weeps, performing his part on the earth as in a more ample and extended scene, in which many shadows of souls and phantom forms appear.'

The conflict between the 'interior soul' and the 'exterior shadow', he pointed out, was a recurrent theme in *The Earth Breath*; 'All things are double, for we either choose "the shadowy beauty", and our soul weeps, or the invisible beauty that is our own "high ancestral self", and the body weeps.' Yeats concluded his review: 'Many verses in this little book have so much high thought and they sing it so sweetly and tenderly that I cannot but think them immortal verses.'

Yeats reworked most of this review into an article entitled 'The Poetry of A.E.', which he published in the Dublin *Daily Express* for 3 September 1898. Apart from substituting 'Sung on a By-way' and 'Janus' for the three verses which he had quoted from *The Earth Breath*, and writing another introduction, he largely let stand what he had published in the *Sketch*. He cited the same passage from Plotinus, though he qualified its significance for Russell's poetry by adding,

'A.E.', in *Homeward Songs by the Way* and in *The Earth Breath*, repeats over again the revelation of a spiritual world that has been the revelation of mystics in all ages, but with a richness of colour and a subtlety of rhythm that are of our age.[34]

Yeats's review of *The Earth Breath* and the two articles which he published on Russell's poetry collectively amount to little more than 'Celtic' propaganda. At best they performed the useful function of bringing Russell's poetry to the attention of the public. At worst they denied him a considered appraisal of his work on its own merits. The *Homestead* article demonstrates that Yeats was prone to publicize second-rate work if he felt it showed that the style of poetry he favoured was in resurgence. The review in *The Sketch* and the article in the *Express*, though laudably enthusiastic, are marred by his elaborate apology for the formlessness of Russell's poetry. Quoting from Plotinus may provide a rationale for the source of his friend's inspiration, and an explanation of a recurrent theme in his work, but it is irrelevant to the important issue of form. Form and content cannot be divorced. That Yeats should have ignored the formal aspects of Russell's work at a time when he was embarked on a rigorous reappraisal of his own style seems puzzling. Perhaps one explanation for this anomaly lies in the fact that in the latter years of the 'nineties Yeats's and Russell's literary association operated at both a public and a private level. While he was publicly defending the formlessness of his friend's poetry, Yeats was privately encouraging him to preserve 'the natural order of the words' in his poems, to eliminate archaisms — advice which strikes directly at the conscious antiquarianism of much 'Celtic' poetry — and to look to folklore and legend for inspiration.

'Irish' Advice

The best samples of this advice are contained in two sets of correspondence from 1898. Early in February, in response to Yeats's suggestion that he look for fresh subjects in Irish folklore and legend, Russell sent him a copy of two poems which he had recently composed.

I tried running a Mayo legend into verse . . . but it was no good as you can see.

It's a lonely road through bogland to the lake at Carrowmore
And a sleeper there lies drowsy where the water laps the shore:
Tho' the moth wings of the twilight in their purple are unfurled,
Yet his sleep is filled with gold light by the King of all the World.

There's a hand is white as silver that is fondling with his hair.
There are glimmering feet of sunshine that are dancing with him there:
And the scarlet lips that whisper him were dyed with richest red
In revels when the hazel tree its holy clusters shed.

'Come away', the red lips whisper, 'All the world is weary now;
Tis the twilight of the ages, and it's time to quit the plough —'
Oh the very sunlight's weary ere it lightens up the dew,
And its gold is changed to daylight ere it passes down to you.

Far more tender than your colleen is the heart we'll bring you near,
What's the starlight in her glances when the stars are shining here?
And who would kiss the shadow when the flower face glows above?
Tis the Beauty of all beauty that is calling for your love.

And the mountain gates of dreamland close behind his spirit's feet,
And a heart enraptured meets him, and a music far and sweet,
And a cry exultant ringing over cabin bog and shore,
Say a spirit's leaped to dreamland from the lake at Carrowmore.

I groan when I write like that. 'Beauty and loveliness have passed away.'
I began again this morning.

> What call may draw thee back again?
> Lost dove, what art, what voice may please?
> The tender touch, the kiss are vain:
> For thou wert lured away by these.
>
> Oh, must we use the iron hand
> And veil with hate the Holy Breath;
> Though alien lips give love's command,
> As though they love the call of death.

The first is undigested new matter, the second the phantom apparition of old inspirations.[35]

Yeats replied on 10 February:

I send you, as I said I would, two suggested modifications of the two little poems. In the first verse of the first poem I have changed 'King of all the World' which sounds a little commonplace to 'the masters of the world' and 'gold light' which the verse puts out of the usual accentuation, to 'music' which gives a full sound. In the second verse I have got rid of the needless passing from 'scarlet' to 'red' and of the commonplace 'richest', and in the last line of the third verse (a very fine verse) I have got rid of the strained accentuation of 'daylight' (which is accentuated as if to rhyme with 'sunlight') and of the abbreviation 'ere' which is a conventional bit of poetic diction. I have changed two lines of verse five, the first because the last part of it was out of the natural order of the words and a little clumsy I thought, and line three because you have forgotten a syllable (the first).

To which he added:

I have made one or two slight changes in the little poem too. I think they explain themselves. They were made for sound. The first line seemed harsh ('back again') and the fourth a little lacking in vitality and 'bare' seems stronger, both as sound and sense than 'use'.

Tell me what you think of these changes. I left out the last verse of the longer poem because it seemed poorer than the rest and had a very conventional ballad close. The two poems seem to me now admirable. It was just as if you had left them unfinished through despondency. I have tried to do the finishing which you could have done much better. The little thing is full of charm and verse three of the bigger thing is most beautiful.[36]

Eliminating poetic diction and archaisms, preserving the 'natural order of the words', and paying close attention to accentuation and metre were some of the forms of revision which Yeats applied with particular rigour to his own poetry from 1892 to 1899.[37]

Celtic and Irish

Russell was not as conscious or as deliberate a craftsman. He complained in an article published at the time of their correspondence: 'Mr Yeats's prodigal imagination is restrained by an artistic sense, perhaps over-developed, and we have to wait years before he lets his verse take final form in a volume.'[38] But he did follow some of his friend's advice. In the long poem, which he called 'The Gates of Dreamland' and then 'Carrowmore', he admitted all the suggestions except the substitution of 'and' for 'ere'. Instead of discarding the final verse he re-wrote it.[39] But he rejected all the revisions which Yeats suggested for the shorter poem, 'Recall'.[40]

Not all of Yeats's criticisms were delivered in as friendly a manner as his letter about 'Carrowmore' and 'Recall'. In March 1898 he read a poem that Russell had contributed to *The Internationalist*. It contained the verse:

> Glory and shadow grow one in
> The forest dense:
> Laughter and peace in the stillness
> Our spirits sense . . .[41]

Yeats promptly informed his friend that he was very sorry that he had

left that horrible — as it seems to me — Theosophical phrase about sensing a thing in the poem in *The Internationalist*. I cannot, and I know there are plenty like me, enjoy a poem in the least, if there is one such phrase in it. I might as well admire a woman with a sore on her face.

Echoing what Beardsley had said to him at the dinner to launch *The Savoy* after he had heard Russell's vehement denunciation of the new magazine as 'the organ of the incubi and the succubi',[42] he added: 'It is bad morals not to obey to the utmost the law of one's art for good writing is the way art has of being moral, and the only way.'[43]

Russell was unrepentant. He replied:

The horrible word 'sense' — you suggested I remember

> Glory and shadow grow one in
> The Hazel Brake
> Laughter and peace in the stillness
> Awake, awake.

Well, I could not get over the incorrectness of peace 'awaking', and I could not find anything better, so I had to let it go for the present. I will hunt for another word.[44]

But when he prepared his poems for *The Divine Vision*, he did revise the stanza; though he did not follow Yeats's suggestions.

> Glory and shadow grow one in
> The hazel wood:
> Laughter and peace in the stillness
> Together brood.[45]

By encouraging him to eliminate poetic diction and archaisms, and to preserve 'the natural order of the words' in his poems, Yeats was attempting to persuade Russell to join him in exchanging the 'Celtic' for the 'Irish' mode. Since the publication of Hyde's *Love Songs of Connacht*,[46] his own journey to the Aran Islands in 1896 in search of material for *The Speckled Bird*, and his association with Lady Gregory and Synge, Yeats had begun increasingly to use the English of the Irish-speaking districts as a corrective to the hushed tones of the Celtic Twilight. The characteristics of peasant speech which most impressed him — 'the naming of things that have direct personal connotation, the use of images taken from common experience, and the idioms of the spoken voice'[47] — are first evident, as a number of critics have pointed out, in the re-written versions of the Red Hanrahan stories, in 'The Folly of Being Comforted', and in 'Adam's Curse'.[48] These stories and poems provide significant landmarks in the general strengthening of his style.

Poetry and Belief

Style to Yeats was more than craftsmanship. He considered it the element in literature which corresponded to the moral element in life. 'Good writing', he had told Russell in his letter about the poem in *The Internationalist*, 'is the way art has of being moral, and the only way.' Good writing embraced the whole writer. The words he chose, the emphasis he gave them, and the stance he adopted, whether affirmative or sceptical, modern or archaistic, created a hierarchy of values in his work that was the expression of his personality. For Yeats, style, as Buffon had said, *'est de l'homme même.'*[49] It arose from the self and was integral to self-realization.

This view of style brought Yeats into conflict with Russell over two poems for the enlarged edition of *A Book of Irish Verse*. The

Celtic and Irish

first, 'Dana', a poem about the mother of the Tuatha de Danaan, contained the lines:

> I breathe
> A deeper pity than all love, myself
> Mother to all, but without hands to heal:
> Too vast and vague they know me not.[50]

Yeats disliked 'vast and vague', and suggested that it be changed, but Russell was adamant that the line stand.

> I mean to keep 'vast and vague' as it exactly expresses my very meaning, i.e. that mortals conceive of her, the mother, as something too vast and indefinite to understand her nearness to the spirit, 'whispering between the beatings of the heart.'[51]

Yeats thought it not worth arguing about, but he advised Russell to avoid the 'poetic', and not to subordinate style to doctrine.

> Let 'Dana' go in by all means, though I am a little doubtful if it is quite desirable to speak of the form of a goddess as 'vague'. The conception seems a little modern. It seems an application to a form, of a word which gets its appropriateness, such as it is, from being used about a doctrine. It is not however incorrect. I think I would myself avoid it in poetry for the same reason that I would avoid 'haunted' and because vague forms, pictures, scenes, etc. are rather a modern idea of the poetic and I would not want to call up a modern kind of picture. I avoid every kind of word that seems to me either 'poetical' or 'modern' and above all I avoid suggesting the ghostly (the vague) idea about a god, for it is a modern conception. All ancient vision was definite and precise.[52]

Russell replied:

> ... I do not think you are accurate in saying the idea of vagueness is unknown to the early mystics. In fact the earliest known writing in the world, the Vedic Hymns, are an instance of just this very vagueness. Read Colbrooke's translation of the first Vedic Hymn. If you have not got a copy of the Hymns you will find it quoted in the beginning of the first or second volume of *The Secret Doctrine*. It ends, 'He knows or perhaps even He Himself knows not.'[53]

The second poem in dispute, 'The Master Singer', contained the lines,

> A myriad lovers died for me, and in their latest yielded breath
> I woke in glory giving them immortal life though touched by death.

and ended,

> For joy of me the daystar glows, and in delight and wild desire
> The peacock twilight rays aloft its plumes and blooms of shadowy fire,
> Where in the vastness too I burn through summer nights and ages long,
> And with the fiery-footed planets shake in myriad dance and song.

Yeats recommended that the phrase 'in their latest yielded breath', be changed to 'at the yielding of their breath' for the sake of euphony; that the word 'sunlight' be substituted for the neologism 'daystar'; and that the last line, 'And with the fiery-footed planets shake in myriad dance and song', be re-written as, 'And with the fiery-footed Watchers shake in myriad dance and song.' He felt that the Theosophical term 'Watchers', the name for the guiding spirits of each incarnation, was more appropriate than the 'scientific' term 'planets', and that 'Watchers' could legitimately be described as 'fiery-footed' while 'planets' could not.

Russell replied:

I admit two of your suggestions, "sunlight" for "daystar" and "at the yielding of their breath", but cannot admit "Watchers" [for it is] too vague a term. I do not understand what you mean by "planets" being scientific, or why [it is acceptable] when you use it in

> The old planets seven
> Are gay with your mood

and elsewhere, and scientific when A.E. employs it. The mote in thine own eye, critic, first pull out. I do not think "planets" any more "scientific" than "sun" and "moon" or "stars". It only in fact becomes scientific when you limit the number as in your verse and suggest the difference between our system of planets and the stars beyond our system.[54]

Yeats justified his use of the word "planets" on contextual grounds. 'The word "seven" ', he explained to Russell, 'throws the imaginative strength back to the when the planets were gods.' By contrast "fiery-footed planets" elicited a connotation that was inappropriate to the subject of the poem and emphasized the material at the expense of the spiritual.

The planets of science are round objects, flattened a little top and bottom and quite without feet. To write of a material object being 'fiery-footed' is almost always to write from the phantasy rather than the imagination. The imaginative deals with spiritual things symbolized by natural things — with gods and not with matter. The phantasy has its place in poetry but it has a subordinate place.[55]

Russell believed that his use of the word 'planets' could be justified on contextual as well as doctrinal grounds. 'I still fail to see the difference between your use of the word "planets" and mine', he protested.

If planets to your mind are small round bodies flattened at the top you ought not to have used the word even qualifying it with the number seven. I never thought of them in that way. If I had I would not have spoken of them as 'waving in myriad dance and song', which ought to be evidence to you. I think it is rather absurd fastening on a word in this way without regard to the context. My idea I would have imagined is perfectly clear. The spirit who speaks exists in the spirits of the planets and guides their motion and song, in the sense in which the old Chaldean oracle says, 'The father moves in a circular manner comprehending omniform ideas and making a melody in the aether.' I never believed even in the existence of the planets of science you described. I think they are an illusion. The word 'planet' is as old or older in literary use than 'stars'.[56]

Yeats countered that it was pointless their arguing for Russell's defence of 'Dana' and 'The Master Singer' amply demonstrated that he was more interested in giving expression to his own interpretation of Theosophical doctrine than in composing a good poem. He himself believed that artistic harmony and not the exact expression of doctrine was the more important criterion. The poet should always measure the diction of his poem against the language of common speech, and should strive to write a poem in which the diction and the theme reinforced one another. He should not allow his belief in the idea that had inspired his poem to guide his choice of diction to the extent that he subordinated style to content. He informed Russell:

Beauty is the end and law of poetry. It exists to find the beauty in all things, philosophy, nature, passion — in what you will, and in so far as it rejects beauty it destroys its right to exist.[57]

But Yeats omitted to say that there is no absolute, universal standard by which to assess whether or not something is beautiful and to what degree it is beautiful. And he chose to pass over the way in which 'the beautiful' might or might not relate to 'the good'.[58]

Predictably, Russell addressed himself almost entirely to the issue of the relationship between art and morality.

I deny altogether that Beauty is the *sole* end and law of poetry . . . I think the true and the good using them in the old Hermetic sense are equally the subject for verse and demand an equal share in the guidance of the writer. I grant that the idea . . . which cannot be filled with beauty [is] unsuitable for verse.

He also challenged Yeats's stance on diction:

With regard to the use of words. It is quite allowable to use some which express ideas with a peculiar fitness, even if the word be . . . not beautiful . . . So in music discords are purposely introduced to heighten an after harmony for the total effect. Ideas have a beauty in themselves apart from words and in literature or art I think the aim of the writer should be to afford an avenue to the idea and make the reader forget the words or painting or sound which evoked it.[59]

Yeats retorted that he could not accept the distinction that Russell was attempting to draw between the word that expressed his idea and the most beautiful word. Didn't the general effect depend on the beauty of each detail? How could he justify the argument: 'I don't mind whether my sonata is musical or not so long as it conveys my idea?' If you want to give ideas for their own sake', he cautioned, 'write prose. In verse they are subordinate to beauty which is their soul if they are true. Isn't this obvious?'[60]

'I find nothing to agree with in your letter', Russell replied,

and see clearly that in mysticism and in our ideas we have little or nothing in common. Of course that is desirable enough, as uniformity is detestable, but you see that I must follow the law of my own being and do my work in the way I have hitherto found it possible to get my inspiration. If I held your ideas I would never write another line.[61]

The antagonism that was generated by this exchange of letters sprang from their different views about the function of poetry and the relationship between poetry and belief. Russell was more concerned with the purpose of poetry than he was with a poem qua poem. He thought that a poet should use language to transport his readers beyond the specific instance of beauty to a contemplation of the essence of Beauty, the ideal form of the Beautiful. He should choose his language not according to its rightness or decorum for a particular poem, but according to its efficacy. The most suitable language was the one which provided access to the idea, the visionary insight, or the mystical experience which had inspired the poem. The language should not attract the reader's attention to itself but should direct him to the source of its inspiration.⁶² 'I think the aim of the writer', he had informed Yeats in their exchange of letters, 'should be to afford an avenue to the idea and make the reader forget the words or painting or sound which evoked it.' Russell tended to see his readers as uncritical, willing neophytes, a group of people who unquestioningly accepted his presuppositions and the validity of his vision because they had surrendered themselves to him for spiritual instruction. Poetry, he believed, should provide an initiation into the secret doctrine.

This emphasis on function and limitation is characteristic of the mystic temperament. Because mystics believe that 'the object of their contemplation hath no image', they distinguish clearly, as Evelyn Underhill has pointed out, 'between the ineffable reality which they perceive and the image under which they describe it'.⁶³ If they choose to describe this perception through poetry it is because they are working at the extremities of language, with language at its highest pitch, not because they are poets. For Yeats to argue that Russell should use prose if he wished to write about his ideas is to misunderstand the kind of ideas that Russell felt were the subjects of his poems. These ideas were not thoughts, notions, conceptions, or hypotheses, but images and phrases which were revealed to him in vision.⁶⁴ 'All my thoughts', he wrote in one of his poems, 'are throngs of living souls.'⁶⁵ These thoughts or ideas could collectively be accorded the status of beliefs because they were derived from experiences he was sure were true. Poetry was one way he could fulfil his moral obligation to provide others access to these beliefs. To write poetry was to become an apologist, an historian of belief. 'A thousand beliefs have occupied the minds of men', he wrote, 'and probably as many more will follow, and in all of these the protean soul takes on strange graces which it is the business of the artist to record.'⁶⁶

Yeats disliked the word 'belief'. He held the opinion that belief implied 'an unknown object, a covenant attested with a name or signed with blood, and being more emotional than intellectual may pride itself on lack of proof'.⁶⁷ The appropriate stance for the poet was a temporary adoption of those ideas that were life enhancing or life sustaining and that generated poetry.⁶⁸ They needed to be held firmly enough to sense their worth and experience their force, but not so firmly that they hardened into beliefs. At times these ideas needed to be asserted, at times pitted against one another, and at times abandoned. A poet was not someone who simply recorded beliefs, an historian of the soul, but someone who discovered, evoked, unleashed emotions and ideas. His primary allegiance was not to an experience that lay beyond his poem, but to the poem itself. He needed to be able to move through the landscape of human opinion like a chameleon, at once registering the intensity of its impact without ever sacrificing his own individuality. Likewise, the process of composition should involve a partial abandonment to the emotions and ideas generated by the emerging poem, partial because the poet should submit what was being created to the scrutiny of his intellect. Throughout his life, Yeats found congenial Blake's dictum: 'I care not whether a man is good or bad, all I care is whether he is a wise man or a fool. Go put off holiness and put on intellect.'[69]

The intellect of the poet should call into question the images and ideas generated by the imagination to keep them malleable for poetry. In an essay on Blake published shortly before his argument with Russell about his theory of diction, Yeats asserted:

The limitation of his view was from the very intensity of his vision; he was a too literal realist of [the] imagination, as others are of nature; and because he believed that the figures seen by the mind's eye, when exalted by inspiration, were 'external existences', symbols of divine essences, he hated every grace of style that might obscure their lineaments.[70]

Yeats might have said the same about Russell. By failing to submit his visions to the analytic mind, by recording beliefs instead of expressing ideas and emotions, he had failed to subordinate doctrine to poetry. Yeats was also aware that a too rigorous questioning could drive a poet into the wastes of scepticism. The means of escape however was not belief, which involved submission and a loss of individual power, but an extensive knowledge of a tradition or a convention that provided an exposition of the poet's current emotional and intellectual needs. By dwelling in the presence of ideas, rather than taking those ideas to himself as beliefs, the poet was free to anastomose with what other people were thinking and with what they had thought.[71] He was able to express himself fully, to make his subjects pliable to his own distinctive style. Poetry, Yeats thought, should be 'assertion without doctrine'.[72]

Moods

Though he eschewed belief as inappropriate for the poet, Yeats

Above left: a portrait of W. B. Yeats by AE, which must date from the time that they first met. Bought at the sale of the contents of Coole Park in 1932. Above right: a portrait of Yeats by AE, dated 1903. Below: an undated pencil portrait of Yeats by his father John B. Yeats. All three pictures are in the National Gallery of Ireland.

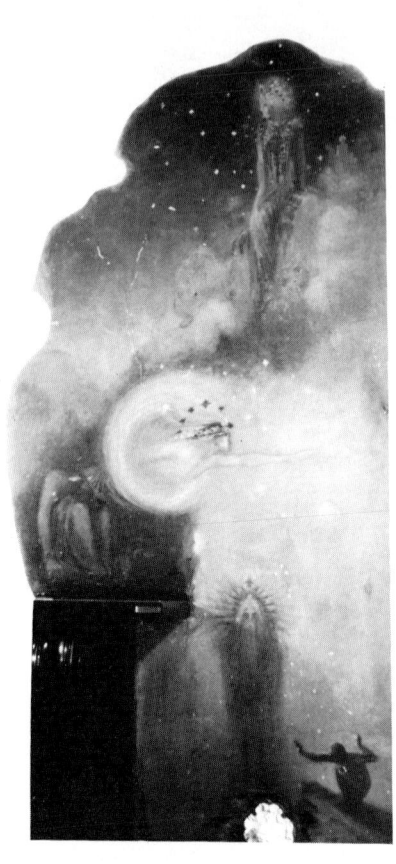

In 1892, Russell, with Yeats's help, started painting murals symbolising the journey of the pilgrim soul on the walls of The Household, 3 Upper Ely Place. These two pages show three (all about the same height) of those still extant. The artists' signatures appear below the winged figure holding the orb (above left). Photographed and reproduced by kind permission of Dr. Colm McDonnell.

AE. A pencil portrait by John B. Yeats, the elder, dated January 1898. Facing page: W. B. Yeats. A pencil and wash portrait, with white highlights, by John B. Yeats, the elder, dated 1898. Both these pictures were bought by the National Gallery of Ireland at the sale of the contents of Coole Park on 8-9 August 1932.

 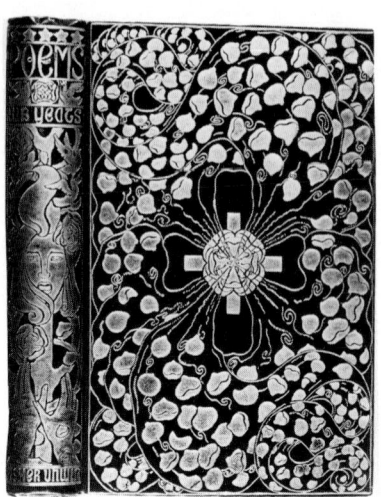

Above: the covers of Yeats's *The Secret Rose* (1897) and *Poems* (1899 and subsequent editions) by Althea Gyles. Below: the title page of AE's *The Earth Breath and Other Poems* (1897), for which AE himself composed the type.

Facing page: *Deirdre* by AE. Dress rehearsals of the completed portions of the play took place in the garden of George Coffey's house, 5 Harcourt Terrace, 2-3 January 1901. AE played the part of Naisi. Courtesy the Ulster Museum.

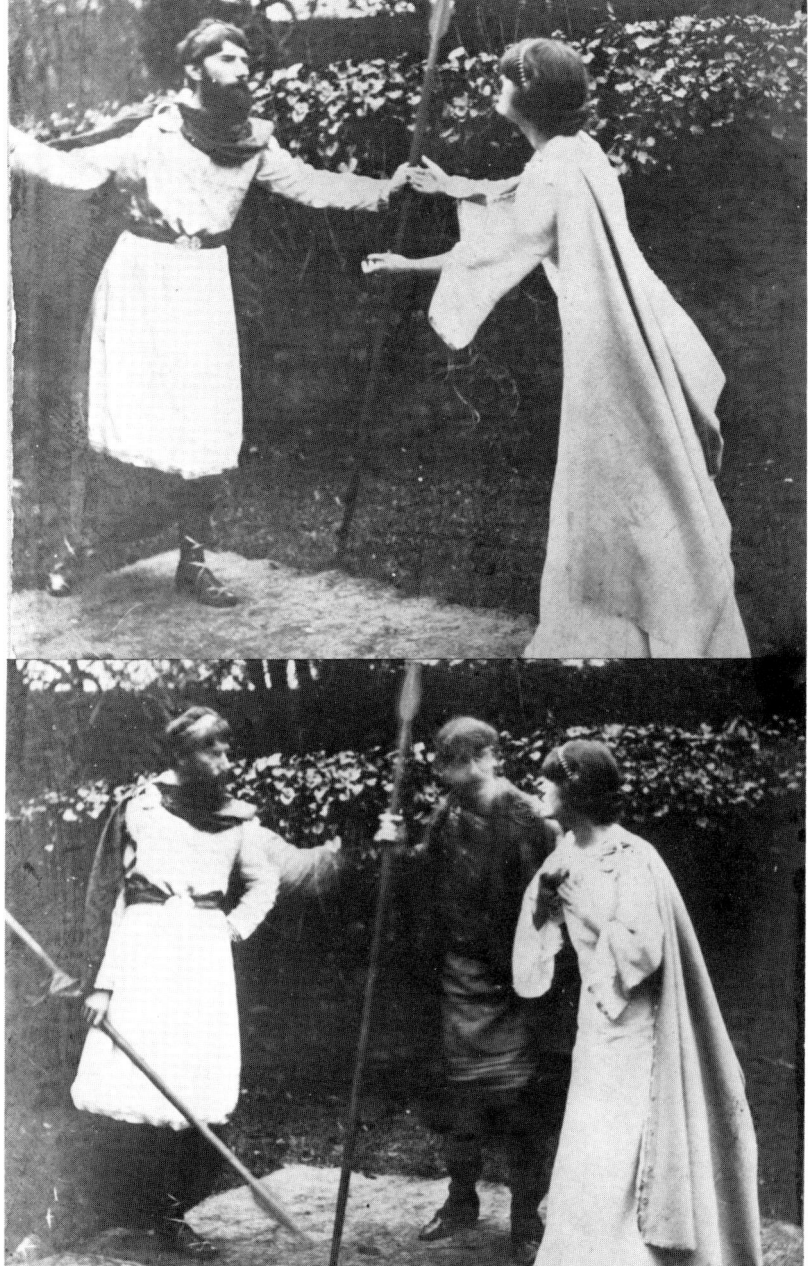

Above: a spiritual being riding a winged horse over the sea. Courtesy the Hugh Lane Municipal Galley. Below: the Serpents of Wisdom, about which AE wrote to Yeats on 19.4.1902. '. . . they are glorious beings. They were watching over my baby's cot one night, and I now understand the serpent myths.' Courtesy of the Oriel Gallery, Dublin.

Above: A mystical painting by AE, recalling passages in *The Avatars* (p. 36), 'many immortals shining . . . in majesty, each on their thrones, with calm faces turned to him', and *The Candle of Vision* (pp. 35-38), 'plumed with brilliant fires . . . They sat shining and starlike'. Courtesy the Oriel Gallery, Dublin. Below: one of a series of AE's paintings of the history of man, 'a minute philosopher, a creature less than three inches in height, sat on one of our gigantic skulls and watched the skies' (*The Candle of Vision*, p. 72). Collection Lord and Lady Dunsany.

AE also painted the walls of his office in Plunkett House, 84 Merrion Square, Dublin. The paper was removed in 1971 and given to the National Gallery of Ireland.

Coole Park. Above: a sketch by Harold Oakley of Yeats, AE and J. M. Synge fishing on Coole Lake. Facing page: A photograph of Coole Library and a pen and ink sketch by Jack B. Yeats dated 1900, showing AE, Lady Gregory, possibly her son Robert, and W. B. Yeats.

Above: AE and Yeats, quick sketches by AE in one of Lady Gregory's albums, undated. Below: portraits of Yeats and AE from *The Bookman*, January 1905.

Four portraits by John Butler Yeats. Above left: Sir Horace Plunkett. Above right: Susan Mitchell. Below left: Lady Gregory. Below right: George Moore. All in the National Gallery of Ireland.

Above: Poulnabrone Dolmen, the Burren, Co. Clare. Below: 'The Castle of Heroes', Lough Key, Co. Roscommon, where Yeats hoped to have the headquaters of his celtic mysteries order. Photos: courtesy Bord Failte.

realized that he had to incorporate beliefs in some form in his poetry. In the mid 'nineties he coined a special word to describe the content of a poem. 'Literature', he proposed, 'differs from explanatory ... writing in being wrought about a mood, or a community of moods.'[73] The term 'mood' in this special sense derives from his reading of Pater, his study of the occult, and his explication of Blake, and seems to have been developed in conjunction with his theory of the collective consciousness, or 'Anima Mundi' as he came to call it. Yeats did not believe that individual experiences were hermetically sealed within each person, and that they were private and incommunicable. He came to hold the view that everyone is linked to a universal mind which is like a vast, encompassing, undivided reservoir of experience. It was itself constantly being enriched by individual experiences, and they were themselves constantly releasing from it an enriching flood of sympathetic ideas and emotions.[74] The poet was someone who possessed the power of tapping this reservoir of experience, of calling down, as Yeats said in his essay on 'The Symbolism of Poetry', 'certain disembodied powers, whose footsteps over our hearts we call emotions'. These disembodied powers were the moods.[75] There were eternal, archetypal states of mind,[76] outlasting, as a poem published in 1893 asserts, the destruction of woods and mountains and even the decay of Time itself.[77] By describing the content of a poem in terms of an archetypal state of mind rather than an emotion, an idea, or a belief, Yeats hoped to be able to co-join the real and the ideal, the individual and the universal, the physical and the spiritual, the temporal and the eternal, and the emotional and the intellectual. It signified his intention to locate his poetry within that unified sensibility which he identified with Unity of Being.

Yeats may have been helped to achieve his concept of the mood by combining two conflicting approaches to poetry — his father's and Russell's. J. B. Yeats thought that a poem should embody 'a personality', which he defined as

a man brought into unity by a *mood*, not a static unity . . . but alive and glowing like a star, all in harmony with himself. Conscience at peace yet vigilant; spiritual and sensual desires at one; all of them in intense movement.[78]

All must be passionate, dynamic, but intellectually controlled. A poem should reveal the intellectual ordering of a poet's emotions, and it should be transparently the work of its creator. Yeats himself noticed that his father 'did not care even for a fine lyric passage unless he felt some actual man behind its elaboration of beauty'.[79]

Russell believed that poems were wrought about 'a bodiless essence' or 'formless spiritual essences', and that their origins were spiritual rather than emotional.[80] 'I think all true poetry was conceived on the Mount of Transfiguration and there is revelation in it and the mingling of heaven and earth', he wrote in *Song and Its Fountains*. 'The Mount is a symbol for that peak of soul when, gone inward into itself, it draws nigh to its own divine root, and memory and imagination are shot through and through with the radiance of another nature.'[81] Thus the poet's task was not to order his emotions, but to seek spiritual perfection.[82] 'As is our aspiration, so is our inspiration', was one of Russell's favourite maxims.[83] Poetry arose out of a search for the spirit and was itself a revelation of the spirit.

Yeats's concept of the mood fuses these two views, though it amounts to more than simply their sum. It incorporates his father's emphasis on structure, personality and emotion. As archetypal states of mind, moods at once order, contain and amplify individual emotions. Though they are evoked by personal experiences and by the symbolism of art and magic, and though they enrich each emotion with a flood of corresponding ideas and emotions from Anima Mundi, they never forfeit their particularity or submerge the emotion they are enriching. Behind the invocation of any mood there is always a specific experience belonging to an actual man.[84] The content of a Yeatsian poem is then partly emotional. It also reveals an ordering of this emotion, because the particular has become embedded in the archetypal.

Yeats incorporated Russell's emphasis on the spiritual, oracular content of poetry by elevating the mood into an apprehension of a kind of Platonic form, though he tended to represent its operation in neo-Platonic rather than Platonic terms. Moods, which are invoked by particular experiences, reveal the essences of those experiences. Like Russell, Yeats thought that the poet belonged to 'the invisible life' and delivered 'its ever new and ever ancient revelation'.[85] Access to this invisible life was obtained through the imagination, which released the poet from the clog of the mundane. Assisting the imagination was the dreaming or visionary faculty which, according to Yeats, made accessible a reality more fundamental than that experienced by an individual man feeling a particular emotion. The content of a Yeatsian poem then is partly concerned with spiritual essences; but these essences are not formless, for they take their shape from an individual's reaction to a specific experience, and they are not exclusively spiritual, for though they reverberate with the world beyond, they are firmly anchored in the physical present.

Celtic and Irish

It is also significant, though it probably owed more to his love of holistic theories than to any conscious design, that Yeats's concept of the mood brings together aspects of the 'Irish' and the 'Celtic' modes. It ensured for a time that his poems had both a spiritual and a personal content. As a number of critics have pointed out, the two modes co-exist in 'Adam's Curse'.[86] The opening lines, with their 'naming of things that have direct personal connotation, the use of images taken from common experience, and the idioms of the spoken voice', are distinctly in the 'Irish' mode.[87]

> I said: 'A line will take us hours maybe;
> Yet if it does not seem a moment's thought,
> Our stitching and unstitching has been naught.
> Better go down upon your marrow-bones
> And scrub a kitchen pavement, or break stones
> Like an old pauper, in all kinds of weather;
> For to articulate sweet sounds together
> Is to work harder than all these, and yet
> Be thought an idler by the noisy set
> Of bankers, schoolmasters, and clergymen
> The martyrs call the world.'

The closing lines, with their expression of unfulfilled desire, their spiritual yearning, and their dissatisfaction with the material world are essentially in the 'Celtic' mode.

> We sat grown quiet at the name of love;
> We saw the last embers of daylight die,
> And in the trembling blue-green of the sky
> A moon, worn as if it had been a shell
> Washed by time's waters as they rose and fell
> About the stars and broke in days and years.
>
> I had a thought for no one's but your ears:
> That you were beautiful, and that I strove
> To love you in the old high way of love;
> That it had all seemed happy, and yet we'd grown
> As weary-hearted as that hollow moon.[88]

Belief and Reincarnation

The difference between Yeats's and Russell's approach to belief and its relevance for poetry is clearly demonstrated by their attitudes to reincarnation. In his *Memoirs*, Yeats recounts a conversation which he and Russell had with Maud Gonne in the mid 'nineties. Neither of them knew at the time that she had given birth to a love child, that it had died, and that her interest in reincarnation sprang from her anxiety about the fate of the child's soul.

[Russell] had seen many visions, and some of them had contained information about matters of fact that were afterwards verified; but, though his own personal revelation was often original and very remarkable, he accepted in the main the conclusions of Theosophy. He spoke of reincarnation, and Maud Gonne asked him, 'How soon a child was reborn, and if [reborn] where?'[89]

Russell's reply, 'It may be reborn in the same family', is the answer a Theosophist would give. He may even have taken it from Sinnett's *Esoteric Buddhism*:

A child dying before it has lived long enough to begin to be responsible for its actions has generated no fresh Karma. The spiritual monad leaves that child's body in just the same state in which it entered it after its last death in Devachan . . . . A re-incarnation of the monad, therefore, may take place immediately, on the line of its old attraction.[90]

Yeats says in his *Memoirs*:

I could see that Maud Gonne was deeply impressed, and I quieted my more sceptical intelligence, as I have so often done in her presence. I remember a pang of conscience. Ought I not to say, 'The whole doctrine of the reincarnation of the soul is hypothetical. It is the most plausible of the explanations of the world, but can we say more than that?' or some like sentence?[91]

The scruple is characteristic. Though several of his early poems are fashioned around the idea of reincarnation, and though he came to use it with a 'vehemence that increased with age and with the general strengthening of his mature verse, it was never more to him than "the most plausible of the explanations of the world" '.[92] And while he felt deeply the need of 'old forms, old situations' to 'escape from scepticism' he was ever wary that his flight did not end in the arms of credulity.[93] In the later poetry, reincarnation is often presented as one of the recurrent questions of life.

Celtic and Irish

> how shall I know
> That in the blinding light beyond the grave
> We'll find so good a thing as that we have lost?
> The hourly kindness, the day's common speech,
> The habitual content of each with each
> When neither soul nor body has been crossed.[94]

In his poem 'On Woman' the uncertainty of any future life is again pitted against the certainty of this life:

> What else he give or keep
> God grant me — no, not here,
> For I am not so bold
> To hope a thing so dear
> Now I am growing old,
> But when, if the tale's true,
> The Pestle of the moon
> That pounds up all anew
> Brings me to birth again —
> To find what once I had
> And know what once I have known. . . [95]

Even in his Spenserian elegy for Robert Gregory, 'Shepherd and Goatherd', where the urge to comfort Lady Gregory might have tempted him to affirm the truth of reincarnation, Yeats presents it as a possibility, an old tale, an idea that can be found in the Indian Scriptures, the Orphic Mysteries, Irish folklore, and the writings of Thomas Taylor, Shelley, and Swedenborg.[96]

Russell, who as Yeats said, 'accepted in the main the conclusions of Theosophy', believed in reincarnation and felt it suited his expression of the world. He himself frequently claimed to be able to recall aspects of at least seven previous existences: in Chaldea, in Egypt, as a contemporary of St John the Revelator, in ninth century Spain, as a contemporary of Blake, and two previous lives in Ireland.[97] He was also convinced that by brooding on past lives he could generate material for poetry. In reply to a young Irish writer who once questioned him about the validity of the doctrine, Russell asserted:

Believe with three-quarters of the human race that you have lived before and will always live . . . [In] believing this you will have grown up in mind and will get an age into your thought. . . . [Tap] your past memories my friend, what wells up within you as imagination, and you will get stories innumerable.[98]

This simple, fervent faith contrasts sharply with the elaborate, tortuous explanation of a vision of a past life which Yeats offered in his 1901 essay on 'Magic'.

> In coming years I was to see and hear of many such visions, and though I was not to be convinced, though half convinced once or twice, that they were old lives, in an ordinary sense of the word life, I was to learn that they have almost always some quite definite relation to dominant moods and moulding events in this life. They are, perhaps, in most cases, though the vision I have but just described was not, it seems, among the cases, symbolic histories of these moods and events, or rather symbolical shadows of the impulses that have made them, messages as it were out of the ancestral being of the questioner.[99]

What this labyrinth of images and qualifications eventually leads to is not a statement about the doctrine of reincarnation but a summary of evidence giving tentative support to his own theory of the moods.

As the 1890s progressed it became increasingly apparent to Yeats that Russell's uncritical acceptance of Theosophical doctrine and his evangelical fervour were progressively harming both his life and his poetry. The more he became bound up with the back street fanatics of Dublin the less likely it seemed that he would make a worthwhile contribution to the literary movement. Yeats realized that he must somehow broaden his friend's perspectives. The opportunity to do this came from an unexpected quarter. Towards the end of 1897 he learned of a vacancy in Sir Horace Plunkett's recently established Irish Agricultural Organization Society (I.A.O.S.). The successful applicant would be required to work at the Society's Dublin headquarters and travel extensively throughout the depressed areas of the West of Ireland. He at once pressed Russell to apply, believing, as he confided to Lady Gregory, that the job would give him 'a great knowledge of Ireland and take him out of the narrow groove of Theosophical opinion'.[100]

Farmed out for Poetry

Sir Horace Plunkett's I.A.O.S. was probably the most successful and undoubtedly the most idealistic of the many schemes set up to revitalize the West of Ireland, a vast agricultural region that had been laid waste by the great potato famines of the 1840s and 1850s and progressively depopulated by large scale immigration.[101] Plunkett believed that the only way to achieve a regional revival was to begin

Celtic and Irish 153

with the individual farmer. Small farm production must be increased, distribution made more efficient, and everybody must be encouraged to adopt the principle of mutual self-help, or 'co-operation'. He was convinced that if farmers were taught how to help one another and shown how to manage their own affairs successfully, it would not only help their self-respect, which had been sapped, so it seemed to him, by decades of exploitation, neglect, coercion, eviction, and by the demagoguery of nationalist politics, but it would also generate an economic and a moral revival that would eventually reform the whole country. 'When Irishmen realize the truth of co-operation', he declared in his book, *Ireland in the New Century*,

the splendid human power of their country, so much of which now runs idly or disastrously to waste, will be utilised; and we may then look with confidence for the foundation of a fabric of Irish prosperity, framed in constructive thought, and laid enduringly in human character.[102]

The root system for this reformation was the local rural bank, a simple credit society designed to provide low interest loans to improve an individual farmer's purchasing power and marketing potential.

Plunkett first met Yeats in the autumn of 1897 after Lady Gregory had invited him to Coole Park to explain the I.A.O.S., which was then still in its infancy, to the local farmers. He noted in his diary after their first conversation: 'W. B. Yeats, a young poet, a rebel, a mystic and an ass, but really a genius in a queer way.'[103] The intimations of genius seem to have soon prevailed, for, surprisingly, Yeats was invited to address the third annual conference of the I.A.O.S., which was held in Dublin in November 1897. His speech, later printed in the Society's official newspaper, the *Irish Homestead*, was warmly received.[104] Plunkett thought it showed 'poetic fancy and real talent'; Lady Gregory wrote indulgently in her journal that he had also remarked that it was 'like a rose leaf falling among a lot of agricultural implements'.[105]

At the end of the conference Yeats learned that Plunkett was looking for someone to organize rural banks in the West. He immediately suggested Russell. For several months he had known that his friend was restless and unhappy, especially since the disbanding of The Household in February 1897. In April, for instance, he had received a ten page letter from him recounting his troubles. 'I wish I could congratulate myself upon such a steady movement to mastery over my art as you', he complained. 'I write fitfully. Then one of your "moods" comes and afflicts me and tells me it is only working in shadows I am, and all is worthless and so I lose heart in it all and get no further.' Russell was also depressed by the way he had been conscripted into the literary movement. The enthusiasm Yeats had shown for his first article on Celtic mythology, and the finality with which he had publicly announced that 'A.E.' was now one of the principal voices of the Celtic renaissance, were forcing him to betray, he felt, his true self.

I am afraid it would be a futile task to try consciously for the Celtic traditional feeling. A certain spirit of it I have but I am not a Celt inside, not for many lives. I remember vividly old America and Chaldea, and sometimes as a mountain beyond lesser heights I get glimpses of the Dedanaan days.

Perhaps the cause of this erosion of his confidence, he explained in the closing paragraph of his letter, was his changing conception of himself as a poet.

When I knew comparatively little of the invisible and my blood was hot I wrote most spiritually. Now I perceive more and feel less I feel more drawn to write of the ordinary human emotions.[106]

Yeats, who had also begun to feel the pull of the earth, the desire for contact with the soil from which, as he was to say much later in review of his own work, everything 'Antaeus-like' would grow strong, was most anxious for him to achieve his aim.[107]

But as important as helping him to regain confidence and to establish himself as an Irish writer was the urgent need to ensure that he broke with the Dublin Theosophists. Throughout 1897 Yeats viewed his friend's growing fanaticism with alarm. In January, Russell had become so incensed by the way that Cardinal Logue had prevented John Dillon, the man who had succeeded Parnell to the leadership of the Irish Parliamentary Party, from holding a political rally at Louth that he had informed his friend: 'I believe you may expect my violent death in the near future as I get more irritable, brooding over this point. I will say things in fierce print to make people's hair stand.'[108] He fulfilled his promise with a virulent pamphlet entitled *Ideals in Ireland: Priest or Hero*, in which he challenged his fellow countrymen to exchange the tyranny of Rome for the freedom of Emain Macha.[109] A little later Yeats heard via Sarah Purser that Russell intended to walk through Ireland, carrying a staff with a head like the letter 'T' in his hand, to preach the ideal paganism of the past and the imminent return of the ancient gods. Knowing that he had already offended the Church with his pamphlet, Yeats had visions of him suffering the same fate as Michael Robartes and being stoned to death by outraged Catholics.¹¹⁰ Even though the planned tour did not come off, the fanaticism burnt on unabated. In March, Russell published another pamphlet, *The Awakening of the Fires*, in which he rapturously proclaimed the near advent of the new age, adding:

What has been called the Celtic renaissance in literature is one of the least of the signs. Of far more significance is the number of strange, dreamy children one meets, whose hearts are in the elsewhere, and young people who love to brood on the past I speak of which is all the world to them.¹¹¹

In June all his anger erupted as physical violence. In one of the mêlées in the rioting that marked Queen Victoria's jubilee, Russell achieved local notoriety by counter attacking a police baton charge so effectively that he dispatched at least one policeman to hospital with a broken head.¹¹²

About October, Yeats learned that the American Theosophists were pressing Russell to give up his job as a cashier at Pim's drapery store in Dublin, and emigrate to Point Loma, California, and become a full time writer for the cause. His name had probably been brought to their attention by D.N. Dunlop, who had recently gone to America as a private secretary to Mrs Tingley, the new leader of the Theosophical Society. Informing Lady Gregory of the offer, Yeats observed: 'I am afraid that his conscience would compel him to write too much and not perhaps always in his best way. He would feel bound to be very propagandist.'¹¹³ Some alternative employment that would enrich him as a person and as a writer would have to be urgently found. Consequently, as soon as Yeats heard that Plunkett was looking for a banks organizer, he acted promptly to secure Russell for Ireland and for poetry. He at once arranged for him to be interviewed; and then spent several evenings in complex negotiations, part of the time trying to persuade the local Theosophists to release his friend from his religious duties, and part of the time trying to persuade him to accept the position. As he told Lady Gregory:

At first [Russell] refused on the ground of its being impossible for him to leave the little Dublin group of mystics for so long at a time. I brought some of the mystics to him, and they all promised to hold together and work on while he was away, and now I think it is all right. Plunkett saw Pim yesterday and Pim gave Russell a very high character. Russell sees Anderson, Plunkett's chief organizer, on Monday and will then decide finally.¹¹⁴

On the Monday, Russell was offered the post as organizer of co-operative credit societies for the Congested Districts of the West of

Ireland. He accepted, concurring fully with the aims of the I.A.O.S. and agreeing not to refer in any way to his Theosophical beliefs.[115]

After a training course lasting the first three weeks of December, he was sent to County Mayo for his first tour of duty. He spent a lonely Christmas in the isolated town of Belmullet, brooding on the way he had once more fallen victim to Yeats's powers of persuasion. In a letter to Synge he complained that the 'wild country' of the West had filled him with so much melancholy that he was unable to compose either poetry or prose.[116] To his close friend, John Eglinton, he wrote: 'I am [marooned] up here in this desolate bogland with priests as my advisers and an ardent young Parnellite to balance . . . Pity me!'[117] On 30 December he addressed the existing society in Belmullet, and then went to Aughoose, Kilmore Erris, and Ballyglass, organizing a new society in each of these towns. This completed his first tour of duty, and he returned to Dublin.

Though he had raised the number of credit societies in Ireland from three to six, and though he believed that the work he was doing was necessary and valuable, he was deeply depressed about his new job. Rebuking Yeats for persuading him to accept it, he roundly declared: 'If ever I can get a job in Dublin at the merest living wage I will take it!'[118]

In reply, Yeats pleaded with him to persevere, and challenged him to see the work as preparation for writing:

My Dear Russell,
    I feel certain that things will greatly improve with you in a month or so. I do entreat you to give this work a fair trial. It is so unlike all that you have done that it was certain to trouble your thoughts at first. Every change of life, everything that takes one out of the old habits, even a change for the better, troubles one at first. But remember always that now you are face to face with Ireland, its tragedy and its poverty, and if we would express Ireland we must know her to the heart and in all her moods. You will be a far more powerful mystic and poet and teacher because of this knowledge. This change of life will test you as a man and thinker and if you can gradually build up a strong life out of it you will be a bigger soul in all things. You are face to face with the heterogeneous, and the test of one's harmony is our power to absorb it and make it harmonious. Gradually these bars, hotels, and cottages and strange faces will become familiar, gradually you will come to see them through a mist of half humorous, half comical, half poetical, half affectionate memories and hopes.[119]

Russell, who was more encouraged by the tone than by the arguments, responded with characteristic fortitude:

Celtic and Irish

My dear Willie,
    I thank you for your very kind letter. I have made my path inevitable and I have only to go on. . . . It may be as you say that I will gradually absorb and harmonize these things and something new will come out of them. I hope so. But at present no vision, no inspiration visit me.[120]

Towards the end of January 1898 he returned to County Mayo for his second tour of duty. To his relief it proved, as his friend had predicted, more congenial than his first. He admitted to Yeats that he had 'actually enjoyed' himself,[121] while he wrote light-heartedly to Lady Gregory that he believed he had the raw materials of a mob orator hidden somewhere in himself, for he was convinced that he could at last address a crowd of several hundred people without having his heart take refuge in the toes of his boots.[122]

Throughout February he was at the I.A.O.S. headquarters in Dublin. During the month he quarrelled bitterly with Mrs Tingley, the President of the Theosophical Society, about her proposal to measure the spirituality of each member to determine their status in the movement. Russell, who was fond of quoting Thoreau's observation that in the course of a spiritual day there was 'often a little languor in the afternoons', protested, and then resigned, thus severing nine years of association with the Theosophists.[123] He also resigned his co-editorship of *The Internationalist*, the successor of *The Irish Theosophist*, in protest against the policy of his co-editor, H.A.W. Coryn, who wanted sectarian propaganda instead of the free ranging discussion of ideas which Russell favoured.[124] All the patterns of his old life were now broken up.

In April he toured Donegal, where he established several more credit banks, but his distaste for the work returned. The break with Theosophy had left him unsettled, and he was struggling to learn Irish, because he had just been pilloried by *Fainne an Lae*, the weekly bilingual newspaper of the Gaelic League, for taking a job in the Gaeltacht without any knowledge of Irish.[125] On 10 April he wrote to Yeats from the small town of Letterkenny:

I have written nothing for a long time, and have given up *The Internationalist* editorship. . . . I feel all my old yearning to tramp through America come on me, and if I get a chance, I think I will go. I seem to myself to be doing no good anyhow, and Agricultural Banks could be organized by anyone with a clear head and a capacity for smiling when he is bored. Look what you have drawn me into. I dine with [parish priests] every week. Today I dine with a Bishop. I gave evidence before a money-lending Commission; I am asked to enquire the price of pigs; I have been forced to learn the different properties of manures; I have lived in country hotels, and been a thing apart from the 'wholesome cheerful life of men', because I won't get drunk.[126]

Yeats, who was in Paris, alerted Lady Gregory, who promptly contacted Plunkett, who arranged for Russell to spend a few days in the vicinity of Coole.[127] Then Plunkett himself came down to Coole, and he and Russell set off for a tour of Galway. The diary he kept on this trip shows that he found his new employee's company very stimulating.

28. 5. 1898.   Russell a delightful companion.
29. 5. 1898.   Russell's conversation truly elevating and inspiring. He is a splendid fellow.
3. 6. 1898.   In the afternoon, Russell got, while driving, on to his own subjects, mysticism, etc. . . . He was most interesting.[128]

In the course of their long association both men formed a high regard for one another. 'I never knew a man so unwearied in helping others', Russell once told Katharine Tynan.[129] For his part, Plunkett confided to Lady Gregory: 'A.E. — the highest ideals and more practical than any of us.'[130]

Russell gradually became accustomed to his work as an organizer, as Yeats predicted he would. When it became apparent that he was not going to master Irish, another organizer was appointed, which permitted him to spend more time in Dublin helping with the production of the *Irish Homestead*.[131] The mix of journalism and short tours organizing new societies appealed to him. His quick mind, remarkable memory, Northern business acumen, obvious tolerance, woolly bonhomie, and lively sense of humour endeared him to Irish farmers. Perhaps his greatest strength as an organizer — and he became one of Plunkett's best — lay in his power to make his hearers share his dream of a rural community where the individual's self-improvement benefited all. One colleague, hearing him address a meeting of about forty farmers in County Cavan, somewhat fulsomely observed:

The audience sits tense, rapt, elevated. His dream of brotherhood descends on them. They rise to it. When he ends, there is a [release] of emotional tension, an intake of deep breath.[132]

Such occasions were not forgotten, and after 1905, when he had entirely given up field work for the editorship of the *Irish Homestead*, farmers would inevitably ask visiting I.A.O.S. officials, 'and do you know Jarge Russell?' A number of them once missed the Church service on a minor religious festival to hear Russell explain co-

Celtic and Irish

operation, and when asked by the priest to explain their absence one of them replied: 'Shure, an' wasn't we doin' just as good as to be at Mass, listen' as we was to Jarge's sermon down at Ballymascalan?' The priest who recounted the story concluded by admitting: 'And in the name of God I think they were!'[133]

At the end of 1898, after only a year's experience with the I.A.O.S., Russell drew up a plan, which was warmly received by Gerald Balfour, the Chief Secretary for Ireland, for re-settling the Congested Districts. As Yeats explained in a letter to his sister Lily:

Dublin is waking up about a number of things. Russell is doing a good part of the awakening. He is a most amazing person. He is at the moment busy over a scheme to settle the Congested Districts on a plan of his own invention. Gerald Balfour has described it as the only practical scheme yet thought of, and is going to introduce a bill — which Russell and certain solicitors and others are now consulting over — to make it possible.[134]

Eventually, Russell became one of the leading agricultural advisers of his day. He was consulted on several occasions by the British Government, and in 1934 he was invited to America to advise Roosevelt's Secretary for Agriculture, H. A. Wallace, on the best way to reconstruct the nation's primary industries in the wake of the Great Depression.[135]

Yet he did not become the Irish poet that Yeats hoped he would. In the many years that he worked for the I.A.O.S. he wrote very little poetry. The constant travelling from one part of Ireland to another as an organizer, and then the volume of copy he was obliged to produce as editor of the *Irish Homestead*, sapped his creativity and absorbed his time. 'I lead such a busy life', he complained to Yeats on a number of occasions, 'that I do not have time to dream and make myself at home in my themes.'[136]

Neither did the vivid English of the Irish speaking districts affect his poetry. Phrases and images sometimes captured his attention, but never his imagination. He often told how two men had once come to him in the small town of Crossmolina and pleaded for assistance, saying: 'The white sun in heaven does not look down on poorer people than this man and myself', but he did not use the expression in a poem.[137] Neither did he use any of the 'beautiful turns of language', such as, 'Ah, sure, your shadow is only a light at the door!', that he told Yeats in a long letter had delighted him as he travelled about the West.[138] And though he expressed on one or two occasions a qualified admiration for Synge's 'passionate, poetical speech', he generally disliked what he called 'dialect' writing. In 1915 he told the young critic Forrest Reid that he thought the

Kiltartan idiom 'distinctly boring; capable in its so limited vocabulary of expressing none save the very simplest ideas.'[139] Ten years later he repeated the same argument to the poet Thomas Sharp:

I am very dubious about dialect poetry or prose because dialect rarely has a vocabulary rich enough to enable the subtlest thoughts or feelings to be expressed . . . Yeats, who wrote his Hanrahan stories at first in rich English, afterwards turned them, with the help of Lady Gregory, into a country dialect and he had to leave out many of the subtleties, though the folk version has a beauty of its own. This means nothing except that I am greedy for beauty and wish to discover it at once and dislike having to peel off a prickly layer of strange words before I can take it in.[140]

Perhaps Russell went to the West of Ireland too late in his life to absorb the strangeness of the peasants' speech; perhaps his poetry was too ethereal to admit its earthiness and vigour; perhaps he was afraid that his ability as a poet was too fragile to bear the weight of its strong rhythms and vivid imagery. Whether one or all of these reasons is the correct explanation for his aversion to the robust English of the Gaeltacht, it is certain that Russell, in the guise of the spirit-inspired poet A.E., continued to write visionary, mystical verse about his own spiritual experiences and the doctrines of Theosophy for the rest of his life.

For his part, Yeats came to hold the opinion that his friend's diction had remained immured in the remoteness and idealism of the 'nineties:

My friend . . . seems convinced that spiritual truth requires a dead language. He writes 'dream' where other men write 'dreams', a trick he and I once shared, picked up from William Sharp perhaps when the romantic movement was in its last contortions. Renaissance Platonism had ebbed out in poetic diction, isolating certain words and phrases as if they were Platonic Ideas.[141]

Even a cursory glance at the *Collected Poems* will substantiate these criticisms; especially that Russell, though perhaps more in emulation of Yeats himself than Sharp, consistently attempted to elevate the particular to the universal by using the singular rather than the plural form of a noun. It is also worth emphasizing that many of his poems are constructed around the pairing of one of these nouns with the definite article; for example: 'the vision', 'the flame', 'the dream', 'the gleam', and 'the light'. This predilection for universalizing personal insights, for a diction purged of the energy of the everyday world, and for jewelled phrases and dream-like meditative rhythms, meant

Celtic and Irish

that Russell began, and essentially remained, a poet of the Celtic Twilight.

The obvious comparison, and it is one which Yeats himself makes in *A Vision*, is with that other writer who was for a time imprisoned in mellifluousness, and who Yeats had also encouraged to go to the West of Ireland to absorb its language — John Millington Synge. Synge filled his mind, his notebooks, and his plays with the 'strange, exciting words' he heard in Wicklow and the West.[142] In the Preface to his most famous play, he declared: 'I have used one or two words only, that I have not heard among the country people of Ireland.'[143] He was transformed by what he heard. As Yeats explains in *A Vision*, 'in Synge's early unpublished work, written before he found the dialects of Aran and of Wicklow, there is brooding melancholy and morbid self-pity', but these dialects gave him a 'passionate image which made him forgetful of himself' so that he underwent 'an aesthetic transformation, analogous to religious conversion' and became the 'audacious, joyous, ironical man we know'.[144]

Russell did not undergo the same self-transformation. He did not allow himself to come close enough to the people of the West of Ireland to be affected. Whereas Synge went to listen sympathetically to them, Russell went to preach at them. When Synge was out cycling he would sometimes pretend that his bicycle had broken down so that he could engage an oncoming traveller in conversation.[145] George Moore's memories of cycling with Russell were ones of the breathless pursuit of a determined figure who hurled himself and his machine around the roads at an alarming speed.[146] *The Aran Islands* contain a number of sketches of quiet sociability, of Synge sitting by the hearth, smoking his pipe, and occasionally playing his fiddle.[147] By contrast, in the Christmas 1897 letter written from Belmullet to his friend John Eglinton, Russell paints a picture of gloomy isolation:

I sat up until three at a party here, comprising the Priest, the doctor, the Clerk of Works, a shopkeeper, his wife, his two girls, his son (the young Parnellite) and two fellows from Cambridge. They all but myself drank whisky and sang songs and played various musical instruments and I the only child of light and the light in me turned to darkness. Pity me![148]

A month or so later he complained to Yeats: 'I have lived in country hotels, and been a thing apart from the "wholesome cheerful life of men", because I won't get drunk.'[149] But sociability does not have to be equated with drunkenness. It would seem that Russell was so self-absorbed and so consumed with his mission to improve country life that he never, as Yeats had hoped, got to know the West of Ireland in some, let alone 'all of its moods'.

Furthermore, the failure of the poet A.E. to benefit from the experiences of the man George Russell can be attributed to the failure to achieve what Yeats had set out in one of his letters of encouragement: 'You are face to face with the heterogeneous, and the test of one's harmony is our power to absorb it and make it harmonious.'[150] Russell never achieved that unity. He put neither his whole self nor an accessible self into his poetry, and the loss was great.

Indeed, he himself came to the realization that he could not achieve that unity within months of joining the I.A.O.S. He confided to Lady Gregory early in 1898: 'I find it difficult to survey Ireland and its people at once from the industrial and artistic standpoint.'[151] In June of the same year he wrote to her again:

I am afraid I will never get the 'economic peasant' out of my mind, and I will never be able to write about him or make poems on him — not for ages to come . . . W.B.Y. ought to keep clear of me . . . I am really interested more and more in this movement, and see the promise of great things for Ireland in it, and am doing what I can to understand it and the principles at the back of it. Meanwhile, literature and other things lie over. . . . Whatever I take up I must take up altogether, and I am afraid Willie would only be bored by the new dyes of my mind.[152]

Instead of trying to unify the different aspects of his experience, or allowing them to co-exist in a state of tension, Russell evolved new personae for new areas of his life. To A.E. the mystical poet, and the two 'Russells' represented by the two distinct prose styles in *The Irish Theosophist*,[153] he added, as a result of his work in the West of Ireland, the persona of 'Jarge' Russell the co-operator. It was 'Jarge' Russell who wrote clear, vigorous prose on a wide variety of contemporary subjects, and it is to the editorials of the *Irish Homestead*, to pamphlets such as *To the Masters of Dublin*, and to the columns of *The Irish Statesman* that one must turn to assess the impact of his co-operative work on his thought.[154]

In later years Yeats reproached himself for forcing Russell into the I.A.O.S.

I have since regretted an action that entangled in practical discussion a mind ripe for spiritual theory. . . . Was he a German Christian born too soon or a Swedenborg I had turned from the road before his vision clarified?[155]

He also came to realize, as he admitted in his *Autobiographies*, that the work Russell was expected to do in the I.A.O.S. was totally unsuited to making him a great writer.

Celtic and Irish

... politics, for a vision-seeking man, can be but half achievement, a choice of an almost easy kind of skill instead of that kind which is, of all those not impossible, the most difficult. Is it not certain that the Creator yawns in earthquake and thunder and other popular displays, but toils in rounding the delicate spiral of a shell?[156]

And yet, without his intervention, Russell might never have become more than the Rathgar ranter or one of the minor prophets of Point Loma. Because it is impossible to know what would have happened to him had he refused to join Plunkett's movement, it is impossible to know whether to accuse Yeats of unwarranted interference in his friend's life. The expectations of friends can be sources equally of suffering or inspiration. What is certain is that working for the I.A.O.S. did lift Russell out of 'the narrow groove of Theosophical opinion', and though he did not write plays like Synge's, or produce adaptations of the legends like Lady Gregory's, it did enable him to exercise an important influence in that wider Irish renaissance which accompanied the literary revival.[157]

The 'Express' Controversy

The apogee of Yeats's pan-Celtic propaganda was marked by a controversy about the relationship between literature and life that broke out in the columns of the Dublin *Daily Express* in the latter months of 1898. The controversy arose out of an article by John Eglinton entitled 'What Should be the Subjects of a National Drama' which appeared in the 18 September issue of the paper. Having heard about the plans for an Irish Literary Theatre and the types of plays that were to be staged, he wished to protest against their irrelevance. He presented his article as an Arnoldian plea to dramatists to write plays that contained critical appraisals of contemporary Irish life, but it was essentially an attack on Yeats's idea of the Celtic poet as symbolist and visionary, as one who drew his inspiration from folklore and legend.[158] Yeats was in London at the time, so Russell wrote to alert him of the challenge. He offered to support him, though he thought it might be advisable for him to write under a pseudonym to avoid the appearance of conspiracy.[159] Yeats did not immediately compose a full length reply, but merely appended a postscript to an article he was about to send to the *Express* in which he pointed out that the national literature of several major European countries had drawn its inspiration from the very sources which Eglinton had disparaged.[160]

Eglinton, eager for a full debate, replied with a long article entitled 'National Drama and Contemporary Life'. He allowed that a type of national drama might be constructed by an 'aesthetic' poet rendering the Celtic legends *sub specie temporis nostri*, but he argued that the most meaningful expression of Nationality could only come from the 'philosophical' poets, who wrote about the daily life of the country.[161]

Russell was disappointed that Yeats had not at first entered the lists in full armour. 'I think you ought to write and do up John Eglinton', he encouraged. 'A complete answer to his points will only make him have a greater respect for your ideas.'[162]

Yeats's 'complete' answer, 'John Eglinton and Spiritual Art' was published in the 29 October issue of the *Daily Express*. While he welcomed the opportunity to broaden the discussion beyond drama, he took issue with Eglinton's definitions. Instead of dividing literature between the 'aesthetic' and the 'philosophic', a classification, Yeats said, that multiplied misconceptions, he should have followed the younger Hallam's essay on Tennyson and divided literature between the 'aesthetic', *après* Keats and Shelley and the 'popular', *après* Wordsworth.[163] To have done so would have kept him from confusing 'philosophical' — the literature of ideas with 'popular' — the literature of social criticism. The latter would always secure a wide audience because a mix of anecdote and maxim always appealed to 'dull temperaments'. The poetry of the 'aesthetic' school on the other hand could only attract a select audience, for, being the expression of the most refined sensibilities of the age, it was beyond the ordinary person who possessed neither the 'patient sympathy [nor] the exaltation of feeling needful for its understanding'. It was a mistake to accuse the 'aesthetic' poets of not being in contact with life, for they, and not the 'philosophic' poets, who merely discussed ideas, were sensitive to the rhythms of man's thought. And it was equally a mistake to emphasize content apart from form. The two were inseparable, the 'spirituality' and 'nationality' of art being dependent on its artistry. The ultimate criteria for poetry were the 'volume and intensity of its passion for beauty, and . . . the perfection of its workmanship'.[164]

Russell, who congratulated Yeats on his 'excellent' reply, was delighted to see his friends locked in combat. 'I have been the subject of controversy with both of you, and now I will slip out and let you two come crash. If I join in, I will do as the lawyer in the fable, eat the oyster and leave he disputants the shell'.[165]

In his rejoinder Eglinton fastened once more on Yeats's choice of subject matter, arguing that it belonged to the 'fancy' rather than the 'imagination'. A work like Milton's *Samson*, which embodied the thought of the writer's own era was 'imaginative'; a work like Fergson's *Congal*, which simply retold an ancient legend, was merely 'fanciful'. He also rejected Yeats's criticisms of his definitions, and censured him for attempting to elevate the 'poetry of art and artifice' above the 'poetry of thought'. 'Art which only interest itself in life and humanity for the sake of art', he concluded, 'may achieve the occult triumphs of the symbolist school, but humanity will return its indifference in kind, and leave it to the dignity and consolation of unpopularity.'[166]

Yeats though Eglinton's adoption of a defensive stance meant that he was tiring. Russell agreed, and told him that he had just written something 'defining' their position which he believed would affec a reconiliation.[167]

In the introduction to his article, 'Literary Ideals in Ireland', published on 12 November, Russell blandly announced that Yeats's and Eglinton's differences were far less significant than their common desire to reveal 'the presence of the spirit.' Having made his conciliatory gesture, he then proceeded to attack Eglinton. The pertinent criterion for evaluating the fitness of legend for literature was not relevance to contemporary life, but the power of suggestion. As the raw material of legend passed from historical fact to remembered tale, from 'things which the eye can see and the ear can hear' to principles and ideas which 'the heart ponders over', it became more 'spiritual' and hence more suitable for literature. Furthermore, the accusation that Yeats wished to divorce literature from life demonstrated that Eglinton had misunderstood his argument. What Yeats meant was that the poet should free himself from the clog of mundaneness which the unenlightened called 'real life'. While it was important, as Eglinton had argued, to assert the primacy of the 'normal human consciousness', it was more important, as Yeats had argued, to assert the primacy of the spiritually elevating.[168] Russell's article patently fails to reconcile Yeats's and Eglinton's positions. Poetry as oracular statement and poetry as a 'criticism of life' cannot be logically subsumed under the title 'spiritual'. Neither does the division of 'life' into higher and lower reconcile the idea that literature performs an essentially social function, in that it enables everyone to understand life, with the elitist view that literature is for a coterie for whom it provides a heightened awareness of the Infinite. In fact, his attempt at conciliation merely provoked a quarrel with Eglinton. 'We argued on Saturday evening up to 2.00 a.m.', he informed Yeats, 'and he went off in a slight huff . . . I expect he will, if he can, go for me.'[169]

But Eglinton was prevented from 'going for' Russell by the intervention of the Irish author William Larminie, who entered the controversy on 19 November with an article entitled, 'Legends as Material for Literature'. He took issue with Yeats for his elitism, arguing that poetry was not written with conspicuous success by coteries. He qualified Russell's assertion that poetry was a 'spiritual activity' by pointing out that it was one thing to say what was good for the soul and another to say what was good for literature. And he attacked both Yeats and Russell for their defence of Symbolism, which he dismissed as an attempt to substitute verbal magic for ideas.[170]

Yeats began his reply, 'The Autumn of the Flesh', not with an argument, but, as was often his way, with a grandiose flourish: 'Our thoughts and emotions are often but spray flung up from hidden tides that follow a moon no eye can see.' Despite what Larminie had alleged, the tide of 'popular' literature was on the ebb, and the tide of 'aesthetic' literature was rising; Browning and Tennyson, for example, were yielding to Rossetti and Bridges. 'The new poets', he asserted, putting aside Kipling for his lack of 'seriousness', and conveniently forgetting Housman and Hardy, 'speak out of some personal or spiritual passion in words and types and metaphors that draw one's imagination as far as possible from the complexities of modern life.'

In the wake of this selective analysis of contemporary literature is a polemical survey of world literature, which Yeats represents as having been in decline for the last four thousand years. Since the *Kalevala*, all poetry, including the works of Homer, Virgil, Dante, Shakespeare, Goethe, Wordsworth, and Browning, has been a betrayal of the golden age, of the purity of the primitive priest-poet, because poets have successively yielded to the temptation to assume the role of 'critic' and 'interpreter of things as they are'. Yet he believed he could sense a change:

I see, indeed, in the arts of every country those faint lights and faint colours and faint outlines and faint energies which many call 'the decadence', and which I, because I believe that the arts lie dreaming of things to come, prefer to call the autumn of the flesh.

The change, he asserted, had been captured in a line of poetry by 'an Irish poet whose rhythms are like the cry of a sea-bird in autumn twilight'.

The very sunlight's weary, and it's time to quit the plough.[171]

The line, heavily revised by Yeats, is from 'Carrowmore', one of the poems Russell had sent to him for criticism. Finally, Yeats took issue with Larminie for attacking Symbolism by arguing that the *Symbolistes* were now in quest of the very essence of life. The work of Mallarmeé and others suggested that the poetry of the future would be a 'poetry of disembodied essences', 'a more and more arduous search for an almost disembodied ecstasy'.[172]

Russell was astonished to find himself represented as the epitome of decadence. Though he had twice cautioned Yeats not to oppose him in print, 'so as not to make a division in the camp', he brushed aside his own advice and published a stern rejoinder. His article, 'Nationality and Cosmopolitanism in Literature', which was published on 10 December 1898, brought what had become known as the *Express* controversy to a close. It was not true, he asserted, that literature had to follow the inexorable sequence that Yeats had outlined and only gain a spiritual character after the bodily passions had exhausted themselves. It was also open to question whether the Decadents, who espoused this idea, were capable of experiencing or giving expression to a genuine spiritual insight.

The mood in which their work is conceived, a sad and distempered emotion through which no new joy quivers, seems too often to tell rather of exhausted vitality than of the ecstasy of a new life. However much, too, their art refines itself, choosing even rarer and more exquisite forms of expression, underneath it all an intuition seems to disclose only the old wolfish lust hiding beneath the golden fleece of the spirit.

Decadence could only be deleterious to the Irish writer, for he needed all his spiritual strength to fulfil his sacred duty of forging in the smithy of his soul the conscience of his race.

In fact, arguing about the relative merits of the 'philosophic', 'aesthetic', 'popular', and 'symbolist' schools was itself irrelevant. Instead of debating these 'cosmopolitan' issues, Yeats, Eglinton, and Larminie should have tried to construct guidelines for a national literature that would meet Irish needs. The essential difference between a cosmopolitan and a national literature was one of function.

A literature loosely held together by some emotional characteristics common to the writers, however great it may be, does not fulfil the purpose of a literature or art created by a number of men who have a common aim in building up an overwhelming ideal — who create, in a sense, a soul for their country.

Of course, Irish writers would not so much have to create a soul for their country as evoke it, for Ireland had been and would remain a holy land. Yeats, he said, had realized this, for he had written,

> And still the thoughts of Ireland brood,
> Upon her holy quietude.[173]

The best way to evoke the spirit of Ireland was to write about those legendary heroes who embodied the qualities which the nation appeared to lack. If a writer felt that the nation was deficient in heroism, for example, he should write about the heroic exploits of the Fianna. Irish writers would be well advised to emulate Whitman, who had attempted to 'elevate and harmonize the incongruous human elements' in his native country by 'upholding a common ideal', 'a stock personality'.

'I have written at some length', he concluded,

on the two paths which lie before us, for we have arrived at a parting of ways. One path leads, and has already led many Irishmen ... to obliterate all nationality from their work. The other path winds spirally upwards to a mountain top of our own, which may be in the future the Meru to which many worshippers will turn.[174]

Russell's article greatly impressed Yeats. A fortnight after it was published he told his sister that Russell had 'begun to write very fine prose.'[175] Later that month, in an essay on Althea Gyles entitled 'A Symbolic Artist and the Coming of Symbolic Art', he retracted one of the main arguments that he had advanced in 'The Autumn of the Flesh'. He now doubted that the Decadents could express spiritual truths: 'Once or twice an artist has been touched by a visionary energy amid his weariness and bitterness, but it has passed away.'[176] Later in the same essay he wrote of Russell, Fiona MacLeod and Althea Gyles: 'These persons are of very different degrees and qualities of power, but their work is always energetic, always the contrary of what is called 'decadent'.'[177]

'A Symbolic Artist and the Coming of Symbolic Art' contains Yeats's warmest public praise of Russell.

I do not believe I could easily exaggerate the direct and indirect influences which 'A.E.' (Mr George Russell), the most subtle and spiritual poet of his generation, and a visionary who may find room beside Swedenborg and Blake, has had in shaping to a definite conviction the vague spirituality of young Irish men and women of letters.[178]

Celtic and Irish

This essay, and the articles Yeats and Russell contributed to the *Express* controversy, mark an important point in their respective imaginative developments.

The controversy enabled Russell to formulate a theory of national literature before the literary movement gathered momentum with the contributions made by Synge and Lady Gregory. From 1898 he began increasingly to see himself as an Irish Whitman, as one who was forging the soul of his country. This shift in his conception of himself as a poet is noticeable as one moves from the narrow Theosophical world of *Homeward: Songs by the Way* and *The Earth Breath* to the wider perspectives of *The Nuts of Knowledge* and *The Divine Vision and Other Poems*. These last two volumes include poems about mythological figures, and poems in which Russell has related his own visions to events and characters from the legends, as in 'A Farewell'.

I will enter the heart of the hills where the gods of the old world are gone.
And will war like the bright Hound of Ulla with princes of earth and of
    sky.[179]

The first line could have been written before 1898, but not the second. *The Divine Vision and Other Poems*, perhaps in imitation of *The Wind Among the Reeds*, has an appendix explaining the references and allusions to Celtic mythology. Russell's desire to present the heroes and heroines of the legends as national ideals eventually led him (as will be seen in the next chapter) to write his play *Deirdre* to protest the denigration of the heroes in Yeats's and Moore's *Diarmuid and Grania*.

Yeats's contributions to the *Express* controversy and his essay, 'A Symbolic Artist and the Coming of Symbolic Art', marked the climax of his pan Celtic propaganda. After 1898 he gradually abandoned the Celtic for the Irish mode. The change is evident as one moves from the dream-burdened poetry 'of longing and complaint' of *The Wind Among the Reeds*, where the beloved is merely a vague sensuous presence with 'passion-dimmed eyes and long heavy hair'[180] to the more realistic poetry of 'insight and knowledge'[181] of *In The Seven Woods*, as in 'The Folly of Being Comforted'.

> One that is ever kind said yesterday:
> 'Your well-beloved's hair has threads of grey,
> And little shadows come about her eyes;
> Time can but make it easier to be wise
> Though now it seem impossible, and so
> All that you need is patience.'

> Heart cries, 'No
> I have not a crumb of comfort, not a grain.
> Time can but make her beauty over again:
> Because of that great nobleness of hers
> The fire that stirs about her, when she stirs,
> Burns but more clearly. O she had not these ways
> When all the wild summer was in her gaze.'
>
> O heart! O heart! if she'd but turn her head,
> You'd know the folly of being comforted.[182]

The bold appropriation of maxims, the heightening of the rhythms and idioms of natural speech and the counterpointing of conversation and lament are all new tones in Yeats's poetic voice.

A good index of the change from the Celtic to the Irish mode is provided by Yeats's reassessment of 'The Autumn of the Flesh'. His next essay, 'A Symbolic Artist and the Coming of Symbolic Art', with its disavowal of decadence, was the first of several retractions made over a number of years. In 1903 he wrote to Russell:

I am no longer in much sympathy with an essay like 'The Autumn of the Body',[182a] not that I think that essay untrue. 'But I think I mistook for a permanent phase of the world what was only a preparation. The close of the last century was full of a strange desire to get out of form to get to some kind of disembodied beauty and now it seems to me the contrary impulse has come. I feel about me an impulse to create form, to carry the realization of beauty as far as possible.[183]

The following year, after he had read *New Songs*, a selection of young poets' work which Russell had made, and it became apparent to him that his friend was loath to relinquish the Celtic mode, he wrote to him:

Some of the poems I will probably underrate . . . because the dominant mood in many of them is one I have fought in myself and put down. In . . . some of my [early] lyric verse . . . there is an exaggeration of sentiment . . . which I have come to think unmanly. . . . I have been fighting the prevailing decadence for years, and have but just got it under foot in my own heart — it is sentiment and sentimental sadness, a womanish introspection. . . . We possess nothing but the will and we must never let the children of vague desire breathe upon it nor the waters of sentiment rust the terrible mirror of its blade. . . . Let us have no emotions, however abstract, in which there is not an athletic joy.[184]

This 'impulse to create form' and the urge to write about emotions which had been hardened by 'athletic joy' spelled the end of

Celticism. In part, both aims reflect Yeats's reading of Nietzsche, who eschewed sentimentality, demanded hardness and opposed passivity with 'astringent joy', with 'gaiety transfiguring all that dread'.[185] In part they reflect the influence of Synge, who wrote: 'On the stage one must have reality, and one must have joy . . . the rich joy found only in what is superb and wild in reality.'[186] And in part they reflect Yeats's own work for the Theatre, and his contributions to such magazines as *Beltaine*, *Samhain*, and *The Arrow*, which 'rang down the curtain', he said, 'so far as I was concerned on what was called "The Celtic Movement" — An "Irish Movement" took its place.'[187]

CHAPTER VI

PLAYS AND CONTROVERSIES: ACT I

1898 — 1902

'The trouble about literary movements in any country is this, that there are only two or three writers of genius and they hate each other because they see different eternities.'

— AE

The long campaign which Yeats fought to establish his own professional theatre in Dublin brought most of his literary associations with Russell to an end. The Theatre with its 'management of men' and plays that seemed as though they had to be 'set up in fifty ways'[1] became the place where their views of life and literature clashed most strongly. This chapter will examine some of the origins of that antagonism, and the following will plot in detail the rising action of the various quarrels that eventually provoked them to break with one another.

At root, most of the quarrels sprang from a conflict of aims. Russell, who only gradually became interested in drama, wanted a small, amateur theatre that would encourage local talent and that would provide sixpence-worth of wholesome, informative, Irish entertainment. Yeats also enjoyed working with amateurs, but had more exacting standards and a much higher aim: he wanted a fully professional theatre that would be the equal of the best experimental theatres in England, Norway, France, and Germany.[2]

The difference between these aims explains the difference between the two men's commitment to drama. Russell was never deeply engaged in either writing or producing plays, even though he was a prominent and active member of several theatre societies. Most of his time in the early nineteen hundreds was taken up with I.A.O.S. business, business that became more and more pressing with the rapid expansion of the co-operative movement, and with his appointment in 1905 to the editorship of the *Irish Homestead*. What must have been a common occurrence for him at this time has been skilfully captured by James Joyce in *Ulysses*. At about two thirty in the afternoon of 16 June 1904, at the height of a discussion between Stephen Dedalus, Russell, John Eglinton, and Richard Best on the relationship between life and art in Shakespeare's *Hamlet*, the 'tall figure in bearded homespun', who is Russell, rises from the shadows, and unveiling his 'co-operative watch' remarks, 'I am afraid I am due at the *Homestead*.'³ For six days in every week, year after year, that 'co-operative watch' must have brought hundreds of conversations about plays and playwrights to an abrupt end. Recalling one of his earliest discussions with Russell, George Moore wrote somewhat testily in *Salve*: 'A.E. took out his watch, and said that he must be getting back to his office. "Damn that office!" I answered. It seemed to me that all my life was on my lips that afternoon, and I begged him to stay. He said he couldn't, and bade me good-bye quickly.'⁴ At times, it seems, even Russell himself regretted the tyranny of his daily routine. In January 1904, when the theatre movement was rapidly gaining momentum, he tried to justify his small output to his close friend Charles Weekes with the rueful observation: 'I would . . . like to write plays, but the Lord with infinite duration to bestow on his creatures has given me only one hour out of every twenty-four lest the tower of Babel might grow up to the heavens.'⁵ Of course, it was George Russell and not the Almighty who chose to put agricultural economics before drama, and who chose to represent the egoism of the dramatist as the egotism of Nimrod.

In fact, despite his protestations about what he would like to have done, Russell's initial involvement with the theatre was so much a matter of coincidence that it could be said he became a dramatist by default. His one major play, *Deirdre*, was mainly taken up as a protest against what he believed was Yeats's and Moore's denigration of one of his favourite episodes from Irish legend. It was not the work of an avid theatre-goer who had been offended by an amateur theatrical, for he was openly cheerful about the fact that he had been to the theatre only once in his life before he attempted his play.⁶ What is more, *Deirdre* would probably never have been completed if the first two acts hadn't been seen by a group of young actors and producers who strenuously encouraged him to finish it, in the belief that it was the type of drama Dublin audiences should see performed. When it was produced it was well received, but Russell's enthusiasm for writing plays soon waned. On being pressed by Joseph Holloway just two years after his theatrical debut for information about his next play, he is said to have replied emphatically: 'There will never be a next.'⁷ It is not surprising that, with his time for drama restricted and only one production to his credit, Russell's understanding of the theatre remained limited. Essentially, the theatre for him was an extension of the Victorian drawing room. It was a place where young people went to enjoy and improve themselves. Similarly, a play meant either a social comedy, a *tableau vivant*, or a verse drama based on Celtic mythology.

By contrast, Yeats's passion for the theatre was intense, and reached back to his childhood. As a boy he built model theatres, imitated performances he had seen of great actors like Henry Irving, and spent long afternoons playing the imagined life of one of a cast of literary heroes whose principals were Hamlet, Alastor, and Manfred.[8] While at High School he wrote dramas with grandiose titles like *Vivien and Time*, *Love and Death*, and *The Epic of the Forest*.[9] When he began his literary career in London, he decided to shun office work of all sorts and try to support himself from his own writing. This gave him much more time than Russell ever had to mix with playwrights, actors, actresses, set designers and producers, and go as often as he could afford to experimental and literary theatres. As early as 1894 he made his debut as a playwright with *The Land of Heart's Desire*, a one act play in blank verse that ran for six weeks at the Avenue Theatre in a double bill with George Bernard Shaw's *Arms and the Man*.[10] Three years later, as a result of the generous solicitude of Lady Gregory, he was able to devote whole summers entirely to the writing of plays.

Even if he had been given the same opportunities as Yeats, Russell might not have exploited them in the same way, for in terms of temperament and self-expression the theatre was not important to him. His prolonged and earnest search for mystic calm, for self-abnegation, and his preoccupation with the grass-root practicalities of the Co-operative movement in one way or another considerably lessened his desire to turn to the stage for self-expression. For Yeats, however, the histrionic was a central, if not a dominant, aspect of his personality.[11] Throughout his entire life and work, it occupied a pre-eminent place in his aesthetic as the doctrine of the Mask. It informed his belief that 'if a man is to write lyric poetry he must be shaped by nature and art to some one out of half a dozen traditional poses, and be lover or saint, sage or sensualist, or mere mocker of all life.'[12] It coloured the tone of everything he wrote. Even his early poetry, much of which has been characterized as remote and diffuse, reveals in close study a personality with a deep affinity for the theatre — as evidenced by the variety of stances he adopted in 'Crossways'; by his careful deployment of ordered, declamatory phrasing; and by his tacit conviction that the most appropriate point of contact for a writer and his audience is in the dramatization of a mood or role. Similarly, a measure of his life-long attraction to arcane cults like The Hermetic Order of the Golden

Dawn was partly due to the sonorous theatricality of their rituals. The theatre for Yeats was integral to his artistic development and central to his self-expression.

In the event, the specific argument that eventually divided the two men — a dispute about the terms of an actress's contract — was as much due to their differences in manner as to their differences in temperament. Russell was more approachable and more hospitable than Yeats. He mixed freely with the members of the Theatre Society, who were for the most part working class, and who either felt daunted by the middle and upper class world of Yeats and Lady Gregory or resentful when Yeats tactlessly insisted on referring to them in public as 'shopgirls' and 'clerks.'[13] To encourage them and set them at their ease, Russell would unfailingly press everyone from leading lady to theatre-hand to come to his Sunday evenings at Rathgar Terrace, where they would be plied with weak tea, armfuls of books, seemingly endless conversation, home-made scones, and a mixture of gentle criticism and woolly enthusiasm.[14] Yeats was neither as familiar nor as accessible. For most of the early years of the theatre movement he restricted his visits to Dublin to a fortnight either side of a performance; his Coole and London addresses stamped him as an outsider in Dublin circles; and his distant manner and penchant for oracular statement, often interpreted as dogmatism (which it frequently was), made him appear forbidding and dictatorial. A measure of the relative accessibility of both men can be taken from the memoirs of Maire nic Shiubhlaigh, one of the original members of the first Theatre society.

We had many visitors to rehearsals. Yeats would come in, discuss technicalities with the Fays, and sit back in the shadows, watching. Yeats seemed to be always in the shadows. Occasionally his voice would make itself heard during lulls in the hammering, as he made suggestions. He looked strangely out of place with his flowing cravat, loose clothes and unruly poet's hair beside us in our work-a-day attire.
One could never claim to have known Yeats well. Unlike A.E., whose manner was benevolent, his attitude was haughty. A.E. muffled in his great tweed coat, peering pleasantly through a tangle of spectacles and beard, was always ready to talk with us, listen to our theories. Yeats, on the other hand, appeared to give only half his attention. In conversation, one got the impression that he looked through and beyond you towards another world.[15]

The reaction of this talented young actress is typical of many who worked in the theatre.

In terms of the theatre as a stimulus to creativity, however, the differences between the two men went far beyond merely making people feel either comfortable or uncomfortable. As Frank O'Connor, a writer who became closely associated with the theatre in the late 'thirties, has pointed out in his autobiography:

Once, when I was talking with Yeats about *The Saint and Mary Kate*, which I was writing at the time, he said wistfully, 'I wish you would write that as a play for me.' Had he been George Russell I probably would have tried to, for I realized a great editor like Russell would have handled the situation so differently. 'My dear boy, that is a play, not a novel. Now the first date available is November 10th, which means that we have to start rehearsals not later than October 15th, so if you can let me have a script within the next month I can guarantee you a production.'[16]

This enveloping friendliness and interest, and the guarantee of some form of publication was what constantly distinguished Russell's patronage from Yeats's.

The complexity of a relationship with Yeats has been perceptively described by Sir Maurice Bowra in his *Memories*. His assessment is particularly valuable because Bowra was an Oxford don who was not easily awed and was not under any obligation to underwrite Dublin opinion. From his brief, but apparently close, friendship, he observed that:

Yeats was not in the least 'cosy'. His genius for words was an obstacle between you and easy intimacy. They turned everything into a high occasion and encouraged you to ask for more of the same kind. He claimed, truthfully enough, that he was a shy man, and that also in company he adopted a mask which was not his real self, but this was not quite true. Rather, he made the most of his thoughts and feelings by adapting them to a public world, but the magnificent choice of words was the rough material from which he made his poetry.[17]

Such a manner did not make for relaxed working relations with an amateur theatre society composed of talented, ambitious, and strong willed young people. It was characteristic of the two men that on Sunday evenings the front door of Russell's small house was always left encouragingly ajar; access to Yeats's Monday evening soirées in Merrion Square, when he held them, was by invitation only.[18]

The opinions that Yeats and Russell formed of one another through their work in the theatre were precisely summed up by Yeats in the first draft of his autobiography: 'I seem to him harsh, hypercritical, overbearing even, and he seems to encourage in all the arts the spirit of the amateur.'[19]

The word 'encourage' in this statement implies an important distinction. While some of Russell's popularity was undoubtedly due to his affability, some of it was due to the fact that he never fully formulated his ideas about the theatre. Beyond a number of satirical pieces, a social comedy, and the one three-act play he wrote, his own aspirations as a dramatist were short-lived. Demanding little, he offended few. It was easier for him than it was for Yeats to be less exacting, less combative, and less discriminating with his praise, because he was less concerned about the evolution of a distinctive theatrical style. The complexity and idiosyncrasy of Yeats's ideas about stage-craft and his compulsive search for perfection inevitably bred tension, and this tension was not always counterbalanced with praise. Sometimes his personal dissatisfaction with his inability to achieve a particular effect communicated itself, without his being aware of it, to the producers and actors and actresses, who in turn became dissatisfied with what they were doing.[20] Sometimes his obvious intolerance with sub-standard work made him careless of the feelings of its creator.[21] George Moore observed from working with Yeats in their attempt to improve Edward Martyn's play, *The Tale of a Town*: 'Yeats is no longer capable of understanding anything but the literary valuelessness of Edward's play. The man behind the play is ignored.'[22]

There can be no doubt that under Russell the Theatre would have been happier and perhaps more popular with Dublin audiences, but it would not have been as professional nor would it have acquired an international reputation. As Willie Fay, who was responsible for stage-craft and voice training in the first theatre company, once protested with characteristic petulance to Yeats:

Russell may be reliable on creameries, but he hasn't the ghost of an idea about the managing of any business as far as I can see. . . . If [he] had from the start impressed these friends of his that there is nothing to be got in this world without plenty of hard work, instead of listening to all their little squabbles, it would have helped us more materially than all his drafting of rules.[23]

Yeats did have business sense; and he did work extremely hard. In spite of periodic upheavals, he made the theatre successful because he brought to it all the restless energy and concentrated intellect that he applied to his own poetry. 'He could give', as Frank O'Connor said, 'things that I think now [are] . . . worth while — admiration, tolerance and absolute loyalty, but he was as pitiless with others as he was with himself.'[24] In charting the ebb and flow of friendship through their work in the theatre it is important to remember that while the theatre was merely a passing enthusiasm for Russell, it was an integral part of Yeats's imaginative development.

The Irish Literary Theatre

The Theatre became a shaping force in their association with the launching of The Irish Literary Theatre in May 1899. Founded by Yeats, Edward Martyn, and Lady Gregory, who were alternately advised and embarrassed by George Moore, it was designed to offer the Dublin public a more substantial and national fare than that offered by the local theatres and visiting French and English companies. Russell was not able to assist with preparations for the first season, comprising performances of Martyn's *The Heather Field* and Yeats's *The Countess Cathleen*, because the rehearsals were carried out in London.[25] Even though he wrote a favourable review of Martyn's play for the Dublin *Daily Express*,[26] and a warm, column-length notice of Yeats's for the *Irish Homestead*,[27] and delivered at a special meeting of the National Literary Society a spirited defence of Yeats against Frank Hugh O'Donnell's attacks on the orthodoxy of *The Countess Cathleen*,[28] he was not wholly enthusiastic about his friends' controversial venture. When Sir Horace Plunkett, in the role of proprietor of the *Daily Express*, honoured the two dramatists with a dinner at the Shelbourne Hotel to celebrate the success of the opening night, Russell did not accept the invitation to dine, but merely stopped by on his way home from work and listened to the speeches.[29] His restraint must have seemed odd to Plunkett, whose eager support for the project had provoked one wit into protesting to the *United Irishman*: 'Will the Union of butter and poesy endure? I hope not. I prefer poetry unbuttered and sniff suspiciously at butter idealized. I do not want Mr Plunkett to wrap me up my pound of butter in the book of *The Countess Cathleen*. I prefer the old flag with its harp to the new one with its churn.'[30]

Russell's reluctance to take part in the Shelbourne Hotel celebrations was symbolic of his attitude to his friend's growing preoccupation with the Theatre. At first he made light of the issue by publishing in the *Homestead* a lame parody of *The Countess Cathleen* entitled *The Countess of the Wheel*. Two cyclists, who have been pursued by sowlths, phookas, thivishes, and all manner of demons, take refuge in a country pub near Ballygoose (a thin disguise for Ballyglass where Russell had the previous year collected folklore for Yeats?) only to have their bicycles stolen by the sidhe. They discuss the theft with the maid, and then leave to rouse the local constabulary, who are reported to be drunk. The parody, which is artless and derogatory, was Russell's sole comment on the first season of The Irish Literary Theatre.[31]

When he saw that Yeats was devoting most of his time to preparations for the second season, scheduled for February 1900, his expressions of disapproval became more insistent. This irritated Yeats, and by June of that year the two men were quarrelling openly.

Most of Russell's disapproval sprang from his conviction that The Irish Literary Theatre was robbing Yeats of valuable time for poetry. He believed his friend was pre-eminently a lyric poet, and a lyric poet who had reached a critical point in his imaginative development. Though *The Wind Among the Reeds* had been awarded the *Academy* prize for the best book of poetry for 1899, and though he had written to Yeats: 'I confess that many of my old objections to verses, which I have mentioned to you, have melted away [;] there are more perfect poems in it than any previous book of lyrics of yours'[32], Russell soon realized that the volume represented a mature harvest rather than the breaking of new ground. In an article written two years after the publication of *The Wind Among the Reeds*, he argued that the land of his friend's verse was not 'The Land of the Living Heart', but 'Ildathach', 'The Many-Coloured Land', by which he meant that Yeats was no longer drawing his inspiration from Nature and experience but from the recondite and arcane, that he was not concerned with the pursuit of fresh truth but with concealment by decoration. In the same article he declared his dissatisfaction with the increasing abstruseness of his friend's work:

I . . . would rather roam in the bee-loud glade than under the boughs of beryl and chrysoberyl, where I am put to school to learn the significance of every jewel. I like that natural affinity which a prodigal beauty suggests more than that revealed in esoteric hieroglyphs, even though the writing be in precious stones.

As well, he registered his impatience with his friend's evasiveness, and his hope for a change: 'I am interested more in life than in the shadows of life, and as Ildathach grows fainter I await eagerly the revelation of the real nature of one who has built so many mansions in the heavens.'[33] Thus, Russell greeted the news of fresh scenarios for The Irish Literary Theatre with growing impatience. When, for example, Yeats began revising *Diarmuid and Grania*, Russell wrote to Lady Gregory advising her to make him pay for his meals with a fixed quantity of verse: 'Treat him as the Balearic slingers did their children. No work, no breakfast.'³⁴ When she told him she thought the play was finished, he wrote to Yeats: 'I hope now that this is done that you will go back to your own work.'³⁵ For every play Yeats wrote, Russell would have preferred a volume of lyrics.

Some of his disapproval, however, stemmed from his fear that several of the friendships which Yeats had formed through his work in the Theatre would rob him of his soul. In particular, he was deeply suspicious of George Moore, not so much of Moore as a person, for until he came to Ireland in 1899 they had not met, but of Moore as the latest incarnation of London decadence. Russell's fear that Yeats would be led astray by a London dilettante was as perennial as it was Irish. For example, when Yeats had first announced his intention of contributing to *The Savoy*, he had vehemently denounced him for allying himself with 'the currents of people with a sexual mania like Beardsley, Symons or that ruck'³⁶, even though he had not met either man, and promptly approved of Symons as soon as they were introduced.³⁷ But Moore appeared to represent a greater threat than Beardsley or Symons because he was suspect on patriotic as well as moral grounds. Moore's *Parnell and his Island* contained passages that were pointedly contemptuous of the peasantry; his *Confessions of a Young Man* branded him a libertine; the realistic detail of *A Mummer's Wife* argued a close acquaintance with some of the sordid aspects of the theatrical world.³⁸ Russell was thus deeply disturbed when he discovered that Yeats and Moore had become good friends, and that Yeats considered Moore's assistance vital to the success of The Irish Literary Theatre.

The first major dispute about Moore involved Yeats's rewriting of *The Shadowy Waters* in the summer and autumn of 1899. The original scenario of this play held considerable sentimental value for Russell because it was one of the projects which he had discussed with Yeats in the early 'eighties, when they were students together in Dublin.³⁹ But the play had never been satisfactorily completed, and when Yeats came to start work on it at the end of May 1899, two weeks after the final performance of *The Countess Cathleen*, he realized, from the experience he had recently gained in the theatre, that several of the key ideas would have to be changed. He set to work, planning to have it published and put into rehearsal by the late autumn, an aim that seemed feasible considering his circumstances: Lady Gregory had invited him to Coole for an extended stay and was willing to protect his health and his time; George Moore, who had given him considerable assistance with the writing and staging of *The Countess Cathleen*, was staying nearby as a house guest of Edward Martyn.[40]

In *Ave*, Moore has given a playfully ironic, though apparently accurate, account of the advice he gave Yeats, and from this, and the evidence of the manuscripts, it is possible to locate precisely the revisions Russell disliked.[41] Originally, the play recounted an imagined episode from the Prehistory of Ireland involving the struggle between the Fomorians, the gods of 'night and death and cold', and the tribes of Danu, the gods of 'light and life and warmth.'[42] A mythical hero called Forgael has the Fomorians in a Prospero-like thraldom, and yet he is compelled to supply them with human sacrifices. Driven by their blood-lust, he captures a galley which contains a beautiful princess, Dectora, and though he slaughters her lover and the crew of the galley, he spares her in the hope that her love will release him from the Fomorians and from the burdensome belief that the world as he knows it has no distinct reality but merely consists of delusive appearances emanating from himself. To win Dectora's love, he casts a magic spell over her, only to find the love so evoked is simply an echo of his own desire. And so he abandons her and goes off alone to the Infinite.[43]

As a result of the numerous revisions Yeats had attempted between this 1883 version and his working draft of 1899, the fabric of the play had become unmanageably encrusted with abstruse symbolism drawn randomly from the Kabbalah, the Golden Dawn, Blake, and from his own symbol-induced visions. In addition, the plot and some of the characterization had become confused because Yeats was uncertain about the exact nature of Forgael's and Dectora's love. When Moore heard the most recent version for the first time in the early autumn of 1899, he confessed himself utterly bewildered. In despair of ever disentangling the meaning from the mythology, he proposed scrapping the Fomorians and their Danaan counterparts; changing the crew of Forgael's ship into a band of pirates, with Forgael as their leader; and closing the action by having Forgael abandon Dectora to his drunken crew. Surprisingly, Yeats agreed to the first two suggestions; and though he thought the third indecorous, he followed it to the point of making Dectora momentarily attracted to the drunken pirates before she sails away with Forgael into the unknown.[44]

The immediate benefit of Moore's advice was to have the stage cleared of the Fomorians. This gave the crew of Forgael's ship a more meaningful role, and it dismantled some of the unnecessary mythological scaffolding that had been obscuring rather than supporting the action.

When Russell learned about the changes in late September, he immediately suspected Moore, and thought the worst. 'I am very sorry you are changing *The Shadowy Waters*', he wrote to Yeats.

> I swore at Moore when I heard it. I suppose he is the fiend who suggested alterations. I would like to strangle him. . . . Tell Moore . . . his time would be better spent in putting some art into his own stories.[45]

Yeats did not disclose the extent of Moore's influence in his reply, but he assured Russell that while he regretted the loss of the Fomorians, the change in the ending, and some of the impressiveness of the original setting, he felt that the poetry of the new version was richer and that it would be easier to stage. He boasted that 'the new *Shadowy Waters* could be acted on two big tables in a drawing room; not that this will please you who don't much like acting at all I think.'[46]

The new version, which was first published in *The North American Review* in May 1900, and later in the same year as a book, did not please Russell, though not all his objections had to do with the advice that Moore had given. In the course of a long conversation early in 1901 he told George Roberts, a young printer who had become interested in the theatre, that the new version was marred by illogicalities in the plot, a considerable loss of dramatic intensity, and an obscure symbolism that was as meaningless as it was arbitrary.[47] These criticisms, while harsh, are perceptive.

Many of the illogicalities in the plot are a result of Moore's suggestions. They seem to have arisen from the incompatibility of the old mythological structure with the new naturalistic setting, and to be the inevitable consequence of one writer's inability to assimilate another's ideas. For example, even though the Fomorians have been removed from the stage, they have still been retained, albeit ambiguously, as part of the mythological schema. At times they are represented as faintly hovering in the wings of the stage, at the periphery, as it were, of the protagonists' consciousness, while at other times they seem to impinge directly on the action. Moore's advice about the ending also created problems, particularly as Yeats had already changed his mind a number of times about the nature of Forgael's and Dectora's love, with the result that several important scenes were somewhat muddled. Instead of completely recasting his protagonists' characters when he was finally persuaded to change their love from one that was merely self-reflective to one that was ultimately fulfilling, he simply lumped together their initial solipsism with their final accord. The result is that an important sequence in the plot founders on a contradiction. In some parts of the play Forgael and Dectora seem to suspect that they will only be imprisoned by their love, while in other parts they seem confident that love is their only key to freedom.[48]

In his final assessment of the play in later life, Russell perceptively attributed Yeats's willingness to change the ending, and his failure to see the consequences of this for the plot, to the fact that at the time he made the change he was deeply in love with Maud Gonne. 'I think', he wrote in *Song and Its Fountains*, 'when the poet came himself to love, the thought of that lonely journey to the Everliving grew alien to his mood.'[49] Russell's explanation becomes even more plausible when it is realized that the ending was changed shortly after Yeats had achieved his self-styled 'spiritual marriage' with Maud Gonne following his experiments in astral projection;[50] and that in several manuscripts Dectora's decision to fly with Forgael in part results from her crushing some apple blossom, a flower closely linked in Yeats's mind with Maud Gonne, and, in particular, with his first conversation with her.[51]

Russell's second criticism — that the play had lost most of its dramatic intensity — can only partly be blamed on Moore. An unfortunate consequence of his advice to Yeats to banish the Fomorians, alter the setting and change the protagonists' love from frustration to fulfilment was a considerable loss of potential for struggle and conflict, two elements vital to any drama. Furthermore, his advice that the ending be changed had the effect of removing some of the distinctions that had been drawn in the early drafts between Forgael's and Dectora's characters. The hero and the heroine of the 1900 version are too similar. For example, both their quests are dream-inspired, a parallel that runs counter to the symbolism of the play, which clearly indicates that Dectora, until she is won over, is supposed to represent everything that Forgael is not.[52]

In terms of the whole play, however, it would be grossly unjust to blame Moore for all the loss of dramatic intensity. Most was due to Yeats's own theories of poetic drama, theories informed by his admiration for the misty stillnesses of the plays of Maeterlinck, Villiers de l'Isle-Adam, and Robert Bridges.[53] He spoke variously of the composition of *The Shadowy Waters* as being inspired by a 'strange desire to get out of form, to get to some kind of disembodied beauty',[54] and as being a search for 'a kind of grave ecstasy',[55] a 'trying for a more remote wisdom or peace',[56] an attempt to write a play that was 'almost religious', that was 'more a ritual than a human story.'[57] At the time he was revising it, he declared that the principal criterion for a great work of art was to be found in 'the volume and intensity of its passion for beauty.'[58] Yet the 1900 version is dreamily passionless, and decorative rather than beautiful. Throughout the whole play the action is constantly arrested by dream, and the dialogue inevitably drifts into reverie. All the characters speak with the same cadences and the same profusion of metaphors.[59] Everything seems to be elaborate, allusive, exquisite, strained, and above all, static. The final effect, as Russell justifiably complained to Roberts, is that of a 'Burne-Jones [painting], with drapery placed in position merely for effect and flowers stuck up where the decorative scheme needed them without considering whether thing[s] could grow there or not'.[60] In particular, he reserved his scorn for the final scene, where Dectora says to Forgael,

> Bend lower, that I may cover you with my hair,
> For we will gaze upon this world no longer.[61]

Russell argued that while such extravagant gestures might have been strikingly pictorial they were not dramatically effective, for they were symbolic gestures rather than characteristic actions, and they appeared ludicrous when they were staged. In his opinion, the entire play had taken on the enervated atmosphere of a 'London drawing room at the end of the season',[62] an opinion Yeats himself partly accommodated in milder language when he spoke of the 1900 version as being marred by a 'continual insistence upon certain moments of strained lyricism'.[63]

Finally, Russell believed that Yeats's compulsion to write poetic drama had led him to add ornament for its own sake, and to employ a symbolism that was as meaningless as it was arbitrary. He told Roberts:

Yeats has no philosophical basis for his [play], except an arbitrary system which he has from the 'Rosicrucian cult' which is . . . only to be understood by initiates. . . . The gods to Yeats are merely symbols, which he frequently uses in a . . . fanciful way. . . . Because [love] changes from a mortal world into an immortal, [it] does not [automatically] change from sexual to spiritual. It can only do so by sacrifice and experience; Yeats may intend 'chrysoberyl' and 'beryl' etc. as symbols for self sacrifice and heroism — but they are only symbols to him because someone has said they are.[64]

Yeats himself subsequently acknowledged the truth of this criticism. In 1906, in a review of the play's history to that point, he admitted that 'the plot had been so often re-arranged and was so overgrown with symbolical ideas that [it] was obscure and vague.'[65]

The Shadowy Waters was revised several times between 1900 and 1904, extensively in 1905, and again in 1906 and 1907, but Russell remained critical. As he pointed out in 1932, Yeats's strenuous attempts to improve the play were misguided, for each revision only took him further away from 'the noble imaginative logic of its first conception.'[66] Most modern critics have disagreed, in the main seeing each revision as an improvement, but Sidnell, Mayhew and Clark, at the conclusion of what must surely be the definitive study of the evolution of the play, support Russell. After examining all the extant manuscripts, they declared:

It was in part the theatre and Moore's technical and conventional competence that bedevilled the work; and in part the destructive temper of Yeats (particularly in the years between the versions of 1900 and 1906) with regard to his early work. A poem might have survived the destructive mood, but when that was allied to the pressing needs of a practical theatre, the work had to be dismembered and sewn together as a rather grotesque fairy-tale.[67]

It seems, then, Russell was at least partly justified in 'swearing' at Moore when he heard, late in 1899, that he was 'helping' Yeats with *The Shadowy Waters*.

The second major conflict between Yeats and Russell over Moore involved politics. Yeats and Moore, who seem to have shared prejudices rather than policies, were drawn together by their mutual abhorrence of the Boer War. When Queen Victoria's visit to Dublin was announced early in 1900, ostensibly to acknowledge the heroism of Irish troops in the Transvaal but more likely as an effort to increase recruitment for her failing army, both men entered strong public protests. Moore, who shortly after this was to sell his London flat and move to Dublin to register his disgust with English attitudes, wrote a number of inflammatory letters to the English and Irish press in which he caricatured the Queen as a 'recruiting-sergeant', 'with the "shilling" between her forefinger and thumb and a bag of shillings at her girdle'.[68] He was openly supported by Yeats, who published two letters and an article.[69] What perhaps was not well known was that Yeats had been asked to organize a protest by John O'Leary, and that he had gone to considerable lengths to think of something that would prevent a recurrence of the rioting that had followed the 1897 protest against the Queen's Jubilee in which an old woman had been killed, about two hundred people wounded, and over two thousand pounds worth of damage done.[70] And, from a thinly veiled reference in Lady Gregory's autobiography, it seems that even

Russell had been caught up in the violence of 1897 to the extent of sending at least one policeman to hospital with a broken head.[71] In an effort to prevent another outbreak of rioting, Yeats proposed in his first letter that a giant meeting under the chairmanship of John O'Leary be called at the Rotunda on the day the Queen left Windsor for Dublin. He shrewdly pointed out that the date of her departure happened to coincide with the centenary of the passing of The Act of Union. Instead of simply protesting about the visit of a Queen, he wrote, it would be more fitting for loyal Irishmen to protest peaceably against an entire century of English domination.[72] In his second letter, Yeats quoted the French politician Mirabeau — 'the silence of the people is the lesson of kings' — and urged his fellow countrymen to remember this when they greeted the Queen.[73] The article, which he wrote for the *United Irishman* and entitled 'Noble and Ignoble Loyalties', was directed at those who had cheered the Queen, reminding them that her three previous visits, in 1849, 1853, and 1861, had 'commonly foreshadowed a fierce and sudden shaking of English power in Ireland', and asking them to contrast the ignoble 'self-applauding egotism' of loyalty to Queen Victoria with the noble, enduring self-sacrifice of loyalty to Kathleen ny Hoolihan.[74]

Though he was himself anti-royalist and pro-Boer, Russell responded to what Yeats had written with some very patronizing advice:

My dear Yeats,
    I have read your article in *United Irishman* and think it splendid. I wish you had written it first and not written the other two letters on the Queen's visit which were poor. I think as a literary man you should only enter a political discussion when you have some principle to declare, as in *United Irishman* article.[75]

This rebuke could only have irritated Yeats. He had been careful to ensure that his letters and his article complemented one another, and he had been careful to gauge his tone. After all, he had been in the forefront of a number of important political movements for almost a decade, actively combating the type of nationalist demagoguery he was now being accused of practising.[76]

The next rebuke from Russell, advising Yeats to complete the novel he had begun in 1896 instead of accompanying Moore on a lecture tour of America about the Boer War, provoked an angry outburst.[77] Though Russell did not know, Yeats had already confided to Lady Gregory that the idea of an American tour might be 'the mounting tide or a folly', and had placed the decision about whether he should go entirely in her hands. 'I shall wait your advice with eagerness', he told her, 'for my own dislike of the bother upsets my judgement, but that dislike is only indolence after all'.[78] Lady Gregory gently advised him that he would be much better employed publishing 'one or two more books', since his output for the year had been very low.[79] 'I am certainly much relieved to be out of this American business', he replied.

I shall be glad if [Moore] himself goes less because of any harm he may do to the Anglo-American alliance than because he will help to make our extremists think about the foundations of life and letters, which they certainly do not at present. To transmute the anti-English passion into a passion of hatred against the vulgarity of materialism whereon England founds her worst life and whole life that she sends us has always been a dream of mine, and Moore may help to make that transmutation. I think with you that I must keep from mixing my aim with his more than I can help, but I must do my best to make him do that work.[80]

Having arrived at this decision, it is not surprising that Yeats was extremely irritated to get a patronizing letter from Russell strongly urging him to separate himself from Moore and admonishing him to complete all his unfinished work. Yeats replied indignantly to Lady Gregory:

I shall certainly not go to America with Moore. The reason you gave was quite final. Russell's reasons do not influence me. Russell has the defects of his qualities and where a moral dislike or disapproval of anybody comes in, his judgement ceases to be dispassionate. His letter irritated me a little. He has bemoralized me as long as I can remember, and nobody likes, or, as I agree with Goethe in thinking, is benefited by being bemoralized. The attitude of bemoralization is not the attitude of understanding.

To Russell's accusations that he was lazy and that he had begun more projects than he had completed, Yeats replied with some heat:

There is of course a good deal of truth in what he says about my indolence, [but] there is also a characteristic exaggeration; and there was no truth at all about what he said to you some time ago about its being better for me morally to finish the novel or something of that kind. He himself has again and again begun things and never finished them, while I, since I was seventeen, have never begun a story or poem or essay of any kind that I have not finished.[81]

Yeats concluded his letter with a detailed comparison of himself with Russell:

He and I are the opposite of one another. I think I understand people easily and easily sympathize with all kinds of characters and easily forgive all kinds of defects and vices. I have the defect of this quality. Apart from opinions, which I judge too sternly, I scarcely judge people at all and am altogether too lax in my attitude towards conduct. He understands nobody but himself and so must always be either condemning or worshipping. He is a good judge of right and wrong so long as they can be judged apart from people, so long as they are merely actions to be weighed by the moral sense . . . . When he speaks of any action connected with a man like either Moore or Symons he is liable to be equally wrong because of his condemnation of the man. His moral enthusiasm is with him an active inspiration but it makes him understand ideas and not human nature.[82]

Yeats returned again and again in descriptions of Russell in his published and unpublished writings to the idea that his friend's 'moral enthusiasm' or 'religious genius' limited his understanding and his powers of discrimination. In the rough draft of his *Autobiography*, which he began in 1915, Yeats wrote of Russell and himself:

He has the religious genius, and it is the essence of that genius that all souls are equal in its eyes. Queen or apple woman, it is all one, seeing that none can be more than an immortal soul. Whereas I have been concerned with men's capacities, with all [that] divides man from man.[83]

In 1921, when he wrote *The Trembling of the Veil*, Yeats was even more caustic about Russell's inability to distinguish between people of different merit, alleging that the only criterion he appeared to employ was familiarity with people or with their works.

. . . [he] has come to see all human life as a mythological system, where, though all cats are griffins, the more dangerous griffins are only found among politicians he has not spoken to, or among authors he has but glanced at; while those men and women who bring him their confessions and listen to his advice carry but the snowiest of swan's plumage.[84]

For his assessment of Russell in the 1925 and 1937 editions of *A Vision*, where he is placed with Newman, Luther, Calvin, and George Herbert at phase 25, Yeats returned to the idea he had expressed in his *Autobiography* a decade earlier that Russell's 'moral enthusiasm' was for him 'an active inspiration.' The man of phase 25 'has but one overwhelming passion, to make all men good.'[85] He seeks to achieve this by mastering 'the multitude . . ., by imposing upon it a spiritual norm.'[86] 'His object is to limit and bind, to make men better, by making it impossible that they should be otherwise, to so arrange prohibitions and habits that men may be naturally good, as they are naturally black, or white, or yellow.'[87] This preoccupation with making men good, Yeats considered, made it impossible for Russell to be impartial or discerning. Obsessed by what men might become, he could not see them for what they were.

This welter of criticism, though it is remorselessly harsh, is not altogether without foundation. Russell's treatment of Symons, and then of Moore, to a degree substantiates the charges. Solely on the basis of rumour, he had denounced both men with a vehemence approaching hysteria, and yet once he had been introduced to them, had talked with them, and to some extent been flattered by them, he was eager to be a friend. But the very vigour and seemingly stark precision of Yeats's analysis indicates that perhaps he was striking out at something for reasons he himself did not fully understand. Monk Gibbon, who knew both men well, has observed:

Yeats was quite definitely jealous of the affection which A.E. inspired. . . . I think it would be absolutely wrong to suggest that Yeats was anything but a friend of A.E., but I do think that there was this unconscious or subconscious jealousy that made him take it out on A.E. a little bit.[88]

Casting Russell in the role of an insinuating salvationist may have been the most effective way Yeats had of denting the image of the astute and genial A.E.

The quarrel between Yeats and Russell over Moore and the lecture tour of America in June 1900 was resolved, to the amusement of many, by Moore plying Russell with some judicious flattery. Himself an acknowledged master of style, Moore had for some time been an admirer of Russell's prose, and when he heard that he was preparing a volume of his mystical stories for publication in America he sent his congratulations, assured him that the stories were as good as those Yeats had collected in *The Secret Rose*, and generously offered to write a preface for the volume.[89] This offer effectively dispelled Russell's suspicions about Moore's morality, and the two men became close friends, especially when Russell found Moore a charming house in the centre of Dublin after he had sold his London flat.

Russell made his customary attempt to convert his new friend to mysticism. 'I think that he wished to be convinced of survival after death', he later told Joseph Hone, 'but he asked for evidence that would pass in a police court, and it was no use applying the Socratic argument and appealing to an inner sense.'[90] The maieutic method having failed, Russell decided, as he told Yeats, to 'drive Irish mythology and idealism' into Moore by taking him late in 1900 on a cycling tour of some of the pre-Christian sacred places near

Drogheda, to the north of Dublin.[91] Moore's account of the tour in *Salve* is misdated and probably distorted by the whimsical humour which constantly undercuts the narration, but a letter he wrote to Lady Cunard on his return to Dublin reveals that he was in fact genuinely impressed by Russell's beliefs.[92] And it could be that one piece of information he gave about the heroine of *Evelyn Innes*, a novel he was revising at the time, provides more of an insight into his own state of mind than that of his character's. Midway through the novel, the narrator informs the reader that Evelyn's attempts at affecting the tired hedonist are to be interpreted as her longing 'to take refuge in an emotionally sympathetic morality.'[93] Perhaps the same interpretation could be applied to Moore's attraction to Russell.

The influence Russell exerted on Moore at that time, and the way he gradually replaced Yeats in Moore's affections, can be detected in the earliest revisions of *Evelyn Innes*. The novel is about a beautiful young English Catholic who is torn between her love for Sir Owen Asher, a wealthy aristocrat who has made it possible for her to become a famous opera singer, and Ulick Dean, a young Celtic musician who is a close friend of her father's. Sir Owen gives her titillating novels and Darwin, Spencer and Huxley to read, and she becomes his mistress, but Ulick, by his eloquent conversations about the Celtic gods and Blake's mysticism, convinces her that her present life of sensuous ease and celebrated wealth is empty. After a long retreat in a convent she has helped to save from financial ruin, she renounces her career and the possibility of a life with either of the two men, and takes the veil. In the first edition, published in 1898, Ulick Dean was modelled on Yeats. In appearance, he was described as having

a smooth young face, the colour of old ivory . . . with flat, slightly hollow cheeks, a long chin. It was clean shaven, and a heavy lock of black hair was always falling over his eyes. It was his eyes that gave its sombre ecstatic character to his face. They were large, dark, deeply set, singularly shaped, and they seemed to smoulder like fires in caves, leaping and sinking out of the darkness. He was a tall, thin young man, and he wore a black jacket and a large, blue necktie, tied with the ends hanging loosely over his coat.[94]

For the 1901 edition, Ulick was remodelled on Russell. From being a rather remote and mysterious character, he becomes more accessible, engaging, and consequently, more fully realized. When Evelyn first sees him, she admires

his tall thin figure. The wide grey eyes were full of quiet resolve, and they and the soft brown beard carried the likeness back through the ages. . . .

Plays and Controversies: Act I

He was dressed in an old grey suit of clothes, and she could not think him in any other, and he wore a loose necktie and a soft felt hat, and she liked him in it.[95]

In the 1898 edition, Ulick speaks at length about his membership of a secret society called The College of Adepts and Rosicrucians.

The College of Adepts, she learned, was the antithesis of the monastery. The monastery is passive spirituality, the College of Adepts is active spirituality; the monastery abases itself before God, the Adepts seek to become as Gods. 'There is a spiritual stream', he said, 'that flows behind the circumstance of history, and they claim that all religions are but vulgarizations of their doctrine. The Adept, by conquering passion and ignorance, attains a mastery over change, and so prolongs his life beyond any human limit.'[96]

This passage and others characteristic of Yeats were removed from the 1901 edition and replaced with descriptions reminiscent of the meetings Russell used to hold in his rooms in Dawson Chambers.

. . . the door was ajar, she pushed it open and she saw Ulick seated at a small wooden table. The light of the paraffin lamp fell on his face. There were many others in the room, but she could not distinguish their faces. Ulick got up to receive her, and he pointed to a chair in the corner of the room where she might sit, and in a few words he told her they had been discussing the five senses and had now come to the last, the sense of permeability. . . . The scene was for all time, a young man teaching philosophy. His listeners were poor clerks and seamstresses, men and women weary of the brutality of daily life, glad to forget the world for a while, glad to rest for a while in a dream of beyond the world.[97]

Ulick's views on Shakespeare, Blake, and Shelley,[98] suggestive of Yeats rather than Russell, were also reworked, as were his claims for hypnotism.[99] Instead, he was depicted as a pantheist who constantly but persuasively speculates on the divinity of the earth.[100] In the 1901 edition, Evelyn and Ulick even go to Ireland together and, as incongruous as this may seem for a famous opera singer, bicycle to the sacred places where Russell had taken Moore.[101]

During the short time they were friends, Yeats, Moore, and Russell contributed essays to *Ideals in Ireland*, a small volume edited by Lady Gregory and published early in 1901. The book was meant to announce the new Ireland, but it amounted to little more than a collection of personal preoccupations. Moore entered a plea for the creation of a bi-lingual Ireland, with Gaelic as the native literary medium and English as the *lingua franca*.[102] Yeats entered a plea for the tradition of pagan and peasant Ireland, elevating it above the Nationalist tradition, which he accused of merely encouraging a strenuous rhetoric and a narrow patriotism, and above the middle class tradition, which he condemned as being selfish, materialistic, and Anglophile. The pre-Christian tradition, he asserted, which had been preserved by the peasantry and was currently being expressed by the small coterie of writers who comprised the Literary Movement, embodied all that was quintessentially Irish.[103] Russell challenged the Irish people to commune with their National Being, the guiding spirit which he believed had come into existence with Ireland herself, and which had spoken and could still speak to all Irishmen through their ancient legends. He assured his readers that:

The seeds which are sown at the beginning of a race bear their flowers and fruits towards its close; and those antique names which already begin to stir us with their power, Angus, Lu, Deirdre, Finn, Ossian, and the rest, will be found to be each one the symbol of enduring qualities, and their story a trumpet through which will be blown the music of an eternal joy, the sentiment of an inexorable justice, the melting power of beauty in sorrow, the wisdom of age, and the longings of the spirit.[104]

Having emphasized the spiritual importance and sanctity of the legends, Russell was indignant when Yeats and Moore read the first act of their *Diarmuid and Grania* to him in the early months of 1901.[105] The play, which was intended for the final season of The Irish Literary Theatre, was a modern rendering of the Fenian saga of 'The Pursuit of Diarmuid and Grania'.[106] The saga tells of Diarmuid, a handsome young warrior who unknowingly causes Grania, daughter of the High King, to fall in love with him on the eve of her being given in marriage to the High King's elderly captain, Finn MacCoole. Diarmuid and Grania elope, and are pursued by Finn, who eventually succeeds in getting Diarmuid mortally wounded by a wild boar and in regaining the love of the fickle Grania. In their attempt to modernize the legend, Yeats and Moore were guilty of a number of infelicities. When Diarmuid and Grania first meet, for example, she says to him:

The wedding feast is spread and I shall be wedded and bedded before dawn if someone does not carry me away.[107]

These, and similar lines, the characterization of Diarmuid and Grania, the portrayal of the Fianna, and even the choice of legend provoked widespread criticism when the play was first performed

Plays and Controversies: Act I

in Dublin on 21 October 1901. Of course, in their open, if somewhat prurient, acknowledgement of the frank sexuality of the legends, Moore and Yeats were in fact much closer to the spirit of the past than either their fellow countrymen's prudery or their insistence on an hygienic history would admit. The Irish press, at first enthusiastic, quickly became almost unanimous in its condemnation: *The Freeman's Journal* thought Grania had been turned into a 'sister to Evelyn Innes';[108] *The Evening Herald* though she had been made into 'an embryo Mrs Tanqueray,B.C.';[109] and *The Fortnightly Review* wondered why 'Mr Moore and Mr Yeats had gone to Irish legend to find . . . the plot of an average French novel'.[110]

The production of *Diarmuid and Grania* brought the three year experiment of The Irish Literary Theatre to a close. It also marked the end of Yeats's and Moore's literary association. Their collaboration, as a contemporary man of letters, Stephen Gwynn, remarked at the time, had been 'unfortunate for both men', and when Moore made an extravagant proposal to establish a clerical censorship for the Theatre during an interview he gave *The Freeman's Journal*[111] in November 1901, Yeats moved quickly to dissociate himself publicly from the idea and from Moore, and to emphasize that The Irish Literary Theatre had passed out of existence.[112]

While Yeats was severing his connections with Moore, Russell was unwittingly preparing the way for Yeats and himself to work together in the Theatre. Russell, who was eminently Victorian in his prudishness, had been deeply offended by *Diarmuid and Grania*, and as a protest had begun a play of his own based on one of the elopements, the legend of Deirdre. The first of the *Tri Thruaighe na Scealasgheachta,* or the Three Most Sorrowful Tales of Ireland, the legend of Deirdre is a story from the *Tain* about a beautiful girl who, like Grania, persuades one of the Fianna to carry her off so she can avoid being given in marriage to an older man.[113] Russell may have hoped that the similarities between the two stories would enable him to demonstrate as clearly as possible to Yeats and Moore the correct way to dramatize the legends. The first act of his play was published in *The All-Ireland Review* in July, and the second in two instalments in October and November. Early in December 1901 Russell was approached by a group of young amateur actors, all avid critics of The Irish Literary Theatre, and asked to complete the play and allow them to produce it.[114] Controversial, and in many ways unsuccessful, The Irish Literary Theatre had nevertheless aroused sufficient interest in Irish drama to ensure its continuing development.

Enter the Fays

The amateur group which approached Russell at the end of 1901 and urged him to complete his *Deirdre* was led by the Fay brothers, two enthusiastic young Irish actors and producers who at that time were only vaguely known to Yeats and Russell. Their work together in 1902 laid the foundation for Irish national drama.

The Fay brothers, one an electrician and the other an accountant's clerk, had been acting with various fit-up companies and their own groups since 1891, but it was only towards the end of the 'nineties that they began to take an interest in plays on Irish subjects.[115] Early in 1901 W.G. Fay, the younger and more outgoing of the two brothers, was asked to conduct drama classes for Inginidhe-na-hEireann, the women's branch of the Cumann na nGaedheal which Maud Gonne had founded to promote Irish culture.[116] In August, drawing from the drama class and from his own company, the Ormonde Dramatic Society, he staged the first play in Irish ever produced in Dublin, P. T. Mac Fhionnlaoich's *Eilis agus an Bhean Déirce*, and two *tableaux vivants* by the poetess Alice Milligan, *The Harp that Once* and *The Deliverance of Red Hugh*.[117] Yeats, Lady Gregory, and Russell were in the audience and were impressed, Yeats afterwards complimenting Fay on the 'grave acting' of his company.[118] Encouraged by this success, the company reassembled as W. G. Fay's Irish National Dramatic Society, but though there was much enthusiasm there were only a few plays that were suitable for the new Society to produce.[119] Fay confided to James Cousins, whose interest in drama had been aroused by The Irish Literary Theatre, that the only plays which seemed to be available to amateur groups were those by Boucicault and similar dramatists.[120] Cousins, who had come down from Belfast to be near Russell because he greatly admired his work, showed Willie Fay a copy of the latest issue of *The Celtic Christmas*, which contained the first act of *Deirdre*, and offered to introduce him formally to the author.[121] Russell was at first reluctant to give them his play, which was unfinished, but Fay persuaded him to set aside two or three days to write a final act, and to allow them to put the two acts which had been published in *The All-Ireland Review* into rehearsal.[122] These began in December 1901.[123] On 2 and 3 January 1902, before the final act was available, a private performance of the first two acts was given in George Coffey's garden to celebrate his son's twelfth birthday. Maud Gonne was invited to attend, and she was so impressed by the play that she offered to sponsor Fay's production through Inginidhe-na-hEireann.[124] When the final act was completed at the end of February, it was realized that *Deirdre* would be too short for a full programme.[125] Fay suggested adding musical items, but Russell and Maud Gonne decided to ask Yeats for permission to stage *Kathleen ni Houlihan*, a one act play he had recently written in collaboration with Lady Gregory.[126] At first Yeats hesitated, for he did not want his play to be associated with Russell's. He confided to Lady Gregory: '*Deirdre* rather embarrasses me. I do not believe in it at all.'[127] But Lady Gregory did not share his doubts, and when Maud Gonne offered to play the title role, Yeats at once gave his consent. Russell welcomed the decision, and wrote to him in London:

> I am very glad that you are giving the Fays your play! The Fay people are developing an enthusiasm which will carry them far. . . The plays will be produced Easter week. Please send over your copy as soon as possible. I hope you will be here when they produce it because I am sure there are great possibilities of creating a public interest . . .[128]

Deirdre and *Kathleen ni Houlihan* were performed by the Fays' company at the Hall of St Teresa's Total Abstinence Association, Clarendon Street, on 2, 3, and 4 April 1902.[129] Yeats, who had come to Dublin only a few days before the opening night, attended all but one of the performances.

St Teresa's Hall, which seated about 300 people, was not well equipped. There were no dressing rooms, and the stage had hardly any wings, so Yeats's play was presented second because it was the simpler production and therefore required less time to set up.[130] As the story of a 1798 Kilalla family whose eldest son, on the eve of marrying into wealth, abandons all to follow the mystical figure of Ireland, who comes to him in the form of an old woman, but leads him away as 'a young girl with the walk of a queen', *Kathleen ni Houlihan* captured the admiration of all those who had been estranged by *Diarmuid and Grania*. The critics were unanimous in their praise; the nationalists were fired by its intensely patriotic theme.[131]

Russell's *Deirdre* was not quite as warmly received, though many felt the play successfully captured what they believed was the atmosphere of the legend. The production, however, provoked considerable comment. It seems to have been heavily influenced by Lugné-Poe's famous production of Maeterlinck's *Pélleas and Mélisande* at the Opéra Comique in 1895. That Frank Fay knew of this production and grasped the significance of the staging for the meaning of the play can be readily seen from a letter he wrote to Joseph Holloway,[132] and from a review of a Dublin production he wrote for the *United Irishman* on 1 September 1900.[133] In Lugné-Poe's production the play had been staged behind a thin gauze, there were no footlights, the scenery was decorative and symbolic rather than realistic, and the actors, having dispensed with as much business as possible, posed and chanted their lines.[134] *Deirdre* was also presented behind a thin gauze, on which Willie Fay played a green arc, thus giving the stage a ghostly, mist-like appearance — an effect that was variously received by the critics, and eventually imitated by Yeats for the third scene of the 1912 version of *The Countess Cathleen*.[135]

Some of the critics thought that the scenery and the costumes, which had been designed by Russell and Willie Fay, harmonized well with the atmosphere created by the lighting, but Yeats, who had begun formulating his ideas on scenery in a debate about the staging of *The Countess Cathleen* with George Moore and William Archer in the *Daily Chronicle* in 1899, and who had recently found an ally for these ideas in the English set-designer Gordon Craig, thought that the scenery was too realistic. He wrote in the *United Irishman* for 26 April:

The scenery of a play as remote from real life as *Deirdre* should, I think, be decorative rather than naturalistic. A wood, for instance, should be little more than a pattern made with painted boughs. It should not try to make one believe that the actors are in a real wood, for the imagination will do that far better, but it should decorate the stage. It should be a mass of deep colour, in harmony with the colours in the costumes of the players.[136]

This approach to scenery was subsequently adopted with success by both The Irish National Dramatic Company and The Abbey.[137]

The acting in *Deirdre*, apparently a blend of Lugné-Poe's and Frank Fay's methods, also provoked considerable comment.[138] George Moore, who looked in on one of the early rehearsals and who was unaware of the French precedent, warned Yeats that the acting was 'the silliest' he had ever seen.[139] At first Yeats himself so detested the play that he was unable to form an opinion. He admitted to Lady Gregory after the opening night:

I hated *Deirdre*. In fact I did not remain in the theatre because I was so nervous about it. I still hate it, but I suppose Moore is the only person who shares my opinion. When I saw it in rehearsal I thought it superficial and sentimental, as I thought it when it first came out in [*All*]-*Ireland Review*.[140]

But the enthusiasm which the plays aroused prompted Yeats to sit

Plays and Controversies: Act I

through the second and third performances. In later years, when he came to reflect on his various reactions to *Deirdre*, he admitted finding it very difficult to disentangle his feelings about Russell from his literary judgement of his work. 'A.E. himself, then as always, I loved and hated, and when I read or saw his play, I distrusted my judgement, fearing it mere jealousy, or some sort of party dislike.'[141] By the final performance however, he had begun to find some merit in the play. He wrote to Lady Gregory:

Strange to say I like *Deirdre*. It is thin and faint but it has its effect of wall decoration. The absence of character is like the absence of individual expression in wall decoration. It was acted with great simplicity. The actors kept very quiet, often merely posing and speaking. The result was curiously dreamlike and gentle.[142]

Yeats was sufficiently impressed by the method employed in *Deirdre*, which accorded closely with his own theory of acting, to write an article praising it. He contrasted the 'grave and simple' acting of Fay's company with that of most amateur companies, where the actors, in an attempt to 'copy at every moment the surface of life' moved restlessly about the stage intruding on one another's performances and preventing the evocation of any 'beautiful emotions' in the audience.[143] In fact, these criticisms could equally be made of most of the professional companies of the day. Though he did not allude to it in his article, Yeats may have carried in his mind the Benson Company's poor performances in *Diarmuid and Grania*, which, as that compulsive Dublin theatre-goer Joseph Holloway had noted in his private journal alternated erratically between the 'jaunty' and the 'limp';[144] and which Frank Fay had criticized in public as 'execrable' and 'vulgar'.[45] In the production of Russell's play, Yeats said:

The actors moved about very little, they often did no more than pose in some statuesque way and speak; and there were moments when it seemed as if some painting upon a wall, some rhythmic procession along the walls of a temple had begun to move before me with a dim, magical life. Perhaps I was stirred so deeply because my imagination ignored, half-unconsciously, errors of execution, and saw this art of decorative acting as it will be when long experience may have changed a method into a tradition, and made Mr Fay's company, in very truth, a National company, a chief expression of Irish imagination.[146]

Apart from the production, the play itself provoked considerable discussion. Broadly speaking, the critics concentrated on tone and interpretation, the drama critic of *The Freeman's Journal* offering the best summary of opinion on both issues. On the one hand, he praised the tone of the play:

In *Deirdre*, to a greater extent, perhaps, than in any other drama of the kind by a modern writer, the heroic past of Ireland stands revealed. A.E. has the power of imaginative creation to a very high degree, and his figures move with a dignity and a beauty which accord well with our ideals. The language, too, is throughout of the loftiest beauty, and some of the speeches are perfect little poems in prose.

On the other hand, he felt that Russell's interpretation had depersonalized the legend and had robbed it of some of its dramatic intensity.[147]

There are several versions of the legend of Deirdre, but basically it describes the origin of the internecine wars which destroyed the kingdom of Ulster. Although the Druids have prophesied that Deirdre's great beauty will lead to wars between Fergus, the sons of Usna, and Conchubar, High King of Ulster, the King refuses to have Deirdre killed when she is born. Instead, he places her in the care of Lavercam, an old woman, and banishes them, intending to marry Deirdre and make her his queen when she comes of age. In the oldest versions Deirdre sees a raven drinking blood spilled on the snow, and demands to have a husband whose hair is as black as the raven, cheeks as red as the blood, and skin as white as the snow. When she sees Naisi, the eldest of the sons of Usna, whose beauty matches this image, she seizes him by the ears and shames him into carrying her off to Alba, or Scotland. In later versions, Naisi accidentally sees her, falls in love, and persuades her to flee with him to Alba. In most of the versions they remain there for seven years, when Naisi, who longs to be united with his fellow warriors of the Fianna, is persuaded by Fergus to return to Ulster, where he and his brothers are treacherously killed. Broken by their murder and the King's treachery, Deirdre commits suicide. The death of these young people, who had placed themselves in his trust, so enrages Fergus that he burns Emain Macha and ravages Ulster.

As with the transmission of much folk literature, the legend of Deirdre was adapted by each generation to reflect its own view of life and literature. Apart from rearranging various episodes and introducing new ones, the most significant changes that were made between the earliest version recorded in *The Book of Leinster* and the late medieval version recorded in the Glenn Masam manuscript were changes to the characters of Lavercam and Deirdre. In *The Book of Leinster*, Lavercam is represented as being one of those most dreaded of ancient peoples — a female satirist. And though she is the King's 'conversation-woman', meaning the royal woman of lamentation or professional keener, he stands in awe of her. He would like to separate her from Deirdre, whom she has taken into her care, but he is afraid of her lacerating wit and her formidable magic powers. By the late medieval period this terrible magician has been transformed into a fond and foolish old nurse. Even though she is afraid of the King, she cannot resist the wilful entreaties of her charge, and so is brought without much difficulty to consent to the lovers' meeting.[148] An equally marked change is made to the character of Deirdre. In *The Book of Leinster*, she is represented as wilful, vigorous, sexually aggressive, and possessed of a violent but brittle pride. With each version her character is softened, until, by the late medieval period, she has become a wan maiden, a sentimental Lydia Languish who sighs and sobs for *la grande amour*. Thus, in terms of tone, content, and character, the general movement of the process of revision is from the barbaric, energetic, and vigorously sexual, to the romantic, heroic, and tragic.[149]

Russell's *Deirdre* continues, and in some areas accelerates, this line of development. He selected the translations he had to work from, for he could not read Gaelic, on the basis of tone and content rather than dramatic effectiveness. 'Drama', he declared, 'was the vehicle through which divine ideas, which are beyond the sphere even of heroic life and passion, [are] expressed.'[150] From the internal evidence of his play it seems that Russell borrowed from Theophilus O'Flanagan's bowdlerized translation of the oldest version, and extensively from Whitley Stokes' and Eleanor Hull's translations of the medieval manuscripts.[151] Wishing to emphasize further the spiritual and mystical rather than the human aspects of the legend, he flattened and idealized the characters of most of the participants. But he carried the process too far, reducing his major characters to stock figures and introducing some serious inconsistencies into their personalities and into the plot. Russell's Lavercam, for example, is not simply a fond and foolish old nurse; she is, in imitation of Eleanor Hull's translation, a 'dear foster mother',[152] a title that seems inconsistent with her readiness to surrender Deirdre to what she knows will be certain tragedy, her elaborate scheming to secure the return of Deirdre and Naisi, and her final vehement denunciation of the King. She is too much a mixture of the bitter and the sweet. And though she is reported to be very wise, she has not prepared any plan whatsoever for diverting the King's anger when he discovers on Deirdre's return, as he surely must, that she has deceived him about Deirdre's alleged loss of beauty.

For her part, Russell's Deirdre is little more than a conventional nineteenth century ingénue, and her implicit trust in Lavercam detracts from both their characters. Too often throughout the play she is merely a convenient foil for the dialogue and for set pieces of ornamental prose. Naisi, in the role of handsome prince, is for the most part simply another conventional figure. Fearless, loyal, able in battle, and intensely patriotic, he is the ideal lover for Deirdre, and yet he does not appear to experience any tension between his love for her and his desire, which is contrary to her wishes, to return to the Fianna. At the conclusion of Act II, for example, he summarily dismisses her dream-inspired predictions of their death as mere womanly fears that would tempt him and his brothers to cowardice. This lack of tension between Naisi's love for Deirdre and his view of himself as a hero removes the basis for one of the most important and potentially one of the most dramatic scenes in the play.

Of the major characters, Conchubar, or Concobar, as Russell spelt it, is the least satisfactory. Russell has attempted to transform him from a bitter, treacherous, lustful old man into a law-giver, a King who sometimes tempers his anger with Solomon-like justice, but the transformation has only been partly effected, and this gives rise to a serious inconsistency. At times Concobar expresses the loftiest sentiments, and appears to be the champion of the law; at other times, and for no apparent reason, he seems to be the baffled victim of passion and jealously, so bent on revenge that he flouts the law.[153] The authorial key to his character, Naisi's passing observation to Deirdre, and to the audience watching the play, that Concobar 'is a wise king, though moody and passionate',[154] is not sufficiently worked into the delineation of the King's character to provide a convincing explanation for his behaviour. The rapid alternation between justice and revenge also weakens the plot. In both the ancient and late medieval recensions of the legend the relentless bitterness of Conchubar serves effectively to accentuate the pathos surrounding the deaths of the young lovers, to demonstrate more fully the reasons for the treachery, and to play off the inflexibility of human passion against the inexorability of fate. Russell's Concobar, on the other hand, merely seems bewildered by what has happened, and his justification for his treachery — 'the death of Naisi was only the fulfilling of the law'[155] — sounds hollow and unconvincing.

Yeats's final assessment of the play, a single sentence in *Dramatis Personae*, accurately sums up some of its strengths and weaknesses, and provides a clue to understanding the cast of mind that wrote it: 'It was well constructed . . . but all its male characters resembled

Lord Tennyson's King Arthur.'[156] In Russell's *Deirdre*, as in Tennyson's epic, there is the same attempt to use legend for didactic purposes, to use the past to admonish and inspire the present. There is the same strained idealism, the insistence that every character should be at least six feet tall. And there is, as Sir Maurice Bowra rightly said of Tennyson's work, the same 'hysterical purity'.[157] Russell's heroine is sexless to a nicety. To emphasize that her premonitions of doom come from seership rather than sex, he has her say to Naisi: 'You remember when we fled that night; as I lay by your side — thou wert yet strange to me — I heard voices speaking out of the air. . . .'[158] The parenthetical disclaimer is unnecessary. Not only is it distressingly coy in its attempt to prevent what in any case would be an untenable interpretation — sex does not produce clairaudience — but also, and perhaps more importantly, it aptly reflects that nineteenth century preoccupation with using archaisms, circumlocution, and euphemisms to at once admit and then immediately repress sexuality. In short, Russell wrote a Victorian work, as Yeats rightly claimed, of 'poetic rather than dramatic merit'.[159] *Deirdre* is not really a play; it is a blend of the lyric sequence and the tableau vivant.

And yet, despite its limitations, *Deirdre* was very popular with the members of the Theatre Society. The actress who played Lavercam, Maire nic Shiubhlaigh, spoke for many when she said, 'If there were any [faults] I did not notice them'.[160] The play was as Yeats confirmed in *Dramatis Personae*, 'admired by everybody'.[161] In a letter to Joseph Holloway dated 6 November 1902, shortly before the Society gave its first season of plays in its own theatre in Camden Street, Frank Fay wrote: '*Deirdre* is, I think, wondrously beautiful and I think if it were put to a vote, we would all say we prefer to act it than anything else we have'.[162] Even though the Society at that time had a limited repertoire, the compliment is still high praise, for Frank Fay was an experienced actor and critic.

Soon after Russell's play had been produced, Yeats decided to write a play on the Deirdre legend.[163] While for Russell she had been 'a symbol of eternal beauty',[164] for Yeats she was 'the Irish Helen, and Naisi her Paris, and Concobar her Menelaus'.[165] Characteristically, in search of passion, conflict, and energy, what he was vividly to call in his play, 'the tumult of the limbs',[166] he returned to the earliest version of the legend recorded in *The Book of Leinster*. But instead of dramatizing the whole legend as Russell had done, he chose to construct a one act play in blank verse which began *in medias res* — with the return of Deirdre and Naisi, or Naoise, as he spelt it in his text, to Ulster under the protection of Fergus. This choice of beginning may have been influenced by Sir Samuel Ferguson's epic poem in *The Lays of the Red Branch*;[167] or it may have been an attempt to avoid one of the mistaken assumptions underlying Russell's work, that the legend as recorded could simply be used as a scenario. In a note on his own play, Yeats explained: 'I have selected certain things which seem to be characteristic of the tale as well as in themselves dramatic, and I have separated these from much that needed an epic form or a more elaborate treatment.'[168] In terms of characters he omitted Lavercam, and Naoise's brothers, Ainnle and Ardan; in terms of setting he isolated Deirdre, Naoise, and Fergus in the King's guest house; and in terms of plot he concentrated on the events leading up to Deirdre's deception of Conchubar and her death.

For the opening scene Yeats used three women musicians, wandering story-tellers, to provide the necessary background. They briefly recount the details of Deirdre's birth, upbringing, love-affair, flight, and exile. This form of introduction enabled Yeats to solve successfully two of the problems which had defeated Russell. It enabled him to establish effectively and economically the distance of the action from the present, and, without ponderous self-assertion on their part, the heroic stature of the protagonists. It also enabled him to emphasize that his play was essentially a re-telling of the legend of Deirdre. In effect, the theatre is turned into a West of Ireland cottage, the musicians fulfilling their roles as seanchai so effectively that they appear to speak the legend into existence.

In the opening scene the musicians tell as much of the story as they know, surmise what will happen from their own experience and from their knowledge of similar stories, and then, with the audience, watch the protagonists complete the story from within the story itself. The opening scene is thus a brilliant device for establishing the course of the action of the folk tale, and for subordinating interest in the plot to interest in the characters. The question left with the audience as a result of the musicians' speculations is not what will happen, but, when will the various characters themselves realize the type of story they are enacting, and how will they react to their discovery. As Peter Ure has perceptively argued, the source of dramatic tension in the play is each character's level of awareness and his individual reaction to the story's conclusion.[169]

Of the principal characters, Fergus and Naoise are least aware of what is going to happen. Both firmly believe, a response which blinds them to what is taking place, that Conchubar will not break faith. And Conchubar, though he appears to be in control of events for much of the play, is in the end himself deceived. His consuming passion for Deirdre blinds him to the intensity of her hatred for him. Deirdre is the only character who is alert to what is happening throughout the play, and who changes to meet the changing situation. With the audience, she suspects that the musicians are correct. Her story will have a tragic end. But she cannot acquiesce in this. In view of the musicians and the audience, who are both condemned to watch, she uses silence, passion and cunning in a vain attempt to change the end of her own story.

Yeats's Deirdre is a more complex and a more tragic figure than Russell's Deirdre. She is confused and fearful as well as dignified and courageous. She also displays greater passion, cunning, and intelligence. Nor does she merely accept her great beauty. The thought of what it has caused so troubles her at one point that she even threatens to disfigure herself.[170] Yeats further increases the scope of her character by delaying the point at which she assumes her tragic dignity. Russell has Lavercam warn Naisi early in the first act that the beautiful woman to whom he is talking is the Deirdre of the prophecies. Yeats moves her acceptance of her tragic role to the meeting between herself and Conchubar, which is much nearer to the close of the action. He splendidly contrives to have her agree to go to Conchubar if he pardons Naoise, but behind her back, while she is speaking on his behalf, Naoise is gagged, bound, taken away, and killed. It is this act of treachery which rouses her to assume her fated role. She challenges Conchubar to permit her to lay out Naoise's body, and then she commits suicide. Her suicide takes place behind a small curtain in the centre of the stage, and is revealed when Conchubar draws the curtain to boast to Fergus of his conquest of her. In a closing speech in which he once again assumes the command of his court, Conchubar acknowledges her greatness and reasserts his dominance.

> Howl, if you will; but I, being King, did right
> In choosing her most fitting to be Queen,
> And letting no boy lover take the sway.[171]

This is a more effective ending than Russell's because the recognition of what Deirdre has done, and the human passions that have motivated her actions, come from her greatest enemy.

Although Yeats's is undoubtedly the better play, Russell's *Deirdre* appealed strongly to contemporary taste and was very popular with the members of the Irish National Dramatic Society. It was revived several times, and many felt, even after Yeats, Synge, O'Kelly and others had written their versions, that Russell's was the only one to capture what they considered to be the spirit of the legend.[172]

Much Ado About Where There is Nothing

With the Theatre successfully launched, Yeats, and to a lesser extent Russell, began casting around for subjects for new plays. On 19 April 1902, a little over a fortnight after the first performances of *Deirdre* and *Kathleen ni Houlihan*, Russell informed Yeats that he had begun working on the second story in the *Tri Thruaighe na Scealasgheachta*.

I have decided to take the legend of the Children of Lir for a dramatic subject and am brooding over certain structural difficulties just now, but I expect they will come out all right. I would weave in a whole lot of druidism into it, and I could get a fine end.[173]

However, the structural difficulties proved too great, and after a month's work he abandoned the subject, though he did eventually use parts of it for a fine lyric poem.[174] Towards the end of May, he wrote again to Yeats that he was planning a tragedy on an episode from the life of his favourite legendary hero, Cuchulain.[175] In July he began work on a scenario on Cuchulain's and Ferdiad's fight at the ford, an episode he had already asserted in his article 'The Dramatic Treatment of Legend' would make a fine play.[176] But once again he encountered problems, so he decided to abandon the idea of writing about a legendary subject and develop instead a topic he had been turning over in his mind since the end of April.

At that time he had mentioned to Lady Gregory that he was thinking of writing a comedy based on one of his friends, an eccentric Roman Catholic visionary called Philip Francis Little.[177] Russell had known him since his Art School days, and must have been sufficiently sympathetic with his freakish behaviour for Little to suggest that they jointly renounce the world and form a small mystic community. To a somewhat startled Russell, he had declared: 'There is an overturned truck on the East Pier of Kingstown. We two shall live there, and we shall teach the people, and we shall be known by the name of "The Wonderers". The people may jeer at us, but they will get tired of jeering at us sooner than we shall get tired of doing good to them.' But 'The Wonderers' did not become even a nine-day wonder for Russell unfortunately smiled at the proposal and was promptly denounced as unfit. In fact, the jeremiad seems to have figured prominently in Little's idea of what was good for

Plays and Controversies: Act I

people. On one occasion he stopped Russell in the middle of a crowded street, and for the sake of his soul called down the wrath of God on him, rounding off with the prophecy: 'There shall be a great fire hereafter and great rejoicing [at] your burning'. On another occasion, he startled a group of pious church-goers by bursting into their midst and haranguing them about the immodesty of their dress. Eventually, his relatives, who were frequent targets, allegedly became so tired of his outbursts that they clubbed together and paid him a living wage of three pounds a week to stay away from them. And yet Russell appears to have been prepared to indulge if not endorse his behaviour. According to him, Little was 'born, perhaps, out of his due era. Seven hundred years ago he might have been a great preacher or saint, or in the Elizabethan period his imagination might have run riot magnificently at a time when mighty mouthfuls of words were listened to with equal mind by mighty men and adventurers.'[178] Exactly how Russell proposed to depict all this on the stage is not clear, but he made the mistake of talking about it at some length to both Moore and Yeats.

There are a number of conflicting accounts about what followed. It seems that Moore felt that he could work Russell's anecdotes about this anarchic visionary into a good novel, though whether or not he told Russell or sought his permission is not clear.[179] Yeats, on the other hand, thought the idea of writing a play was sound, but he doubted Russell's ability to do justice to the subject.[180] Some time late in April 1902, Yeats visited Moore at his home in Ely Place, and for twenty minutes or half an hour they walked in the garden and discussed Russell's idea. They agreed to collaborate on a play and a scenario was drafted. A copy, bearing the date 3 July, has been found among Moore's correspondence.[181] Yeats later claimed that he did most of the preliminary work, and that Moore's contribution was limited to the suggesting of prurient details, such as giving the protagonist a brother who seduces the housemaid, but this conflicts with the evidence of the extant manuscripts.[182] In the meantime, the project was put aside for the summer; Moore continued to write the short stories he eventually collected in *The Untilled Field*, and Yeats returned to London to prepare two works for publication — a revised and enlarged edition of *The Celtic Twilight*, and a volume of essays entitled *Ideas of Good and Evil*.[183]

While he was still in London, Yeats received a formal invitation from Frederick Ryan, the Secretary of the newly constituted Irish National Theatre Society, requesting him to be their inaugural President. The invitation was dated 10 August 1902. Though he did not know it at the time, he was their second choice. At first they had unanimously agreed to ask Russell, who was more popular and more accessible, but he had pleaded lack of time and ignorance of the theatre and had persuaded them, with some difficulty, to ask Yeats.[184] Delighted, though not unaware of the difficulties he might encounter, Yeats accepted.

When he next met Moore, on 31 August 1902 at the Galway Feis which Lady Gregory had organized to honour the poet Raftery, Yeats explained that they could no longer collaborate on a play because he was now officially associated with the Theatre Society whereas Moore was not. Joseph Hone, who wrote both men's biographies, called this reason 'a slender pretext', but this is unnecessarily harsh.[185] It might well have been that Yeats was using a scrap of bureaucracy to distance himself from his one-time collaborator because he knew that the Fays did not like working with Moore. For the sake of both the new Society and himself, he would have been anxious to keep his working relationship with the Fays on the best possible footing. At first, Moore himself appears to have accepted the explanation with good grace, though when he returned to Dublin he obviously had second thoughts, for he wired Yeats at Coole: 'I have written a novel on that scenario we composed together. Will get an injunction if you use it'.[186] Suspecting this was only a bluff, Yeats contacted Russell, who dutifully assured him that Moore had not written a novel, but warned him that he had begun work on a play.[187] Yeats promptly retired to the writing-room at Coole where, with the help of Lady Gregory and Douglas Hyde, he composed in a fortnight a five act tragedy which he called *Where There is Nothing*.[188]

Though some critics have argued that there is only a 'slight resemblance' between Moore's and Yeats's play, McFate and Doherty have convincingly demonstrated that in substance the two works are very similar. The five act scenario that Moore drafted tells of a University Professor who, overcome by a sense of futility, renounces his career and denounces civilization. He takes to the road, meets a tinker, and persuades him to exchange clothes. At a gathering of the tinkers he gets everyone drunk on free porter. A short time later he founds a religious community, similar to the one that Philip Francis Little wanted to found with Russell, but this does not satisfy him, so he leaves the community and joins the peasantry. He then marries the dirtiest girl in the village, promising to turn over all his property to her and her relatives. After a series of adventures, he becomes a hermit living in the ruins of a monastery. The neighbouring monks accuse him of attempting to revive the ancient Celtic religion. They turn the villagers against him, and he is killed.[189]

Plays and Controversies: Act I

The plot of Yeats's play is very similar. His protagonist, Paul Ruttledge, is a West of Ireland squire who has become obsessed with the notion that his own life and the lives of his fellow landowners is fraudulent. When a tinker comes to his house, he changes clothes with him, abandons his property to his brother, and joins the tinkers wandering the roads. To celebrate his marriage to one of them, he distributes free porter to the surrounding countryside. Everyone gets drunk. When the local magistrates come to arrest him, he seizes them, and with the help of the tinkers puts each magistrate on trial to determine whether or not he is the Christian he professes to be. The hard life of the tinkers eventually breaks his health. He enters a monastery where, as one who performs miracles and sees visions, he continues to preach his doctrine of anarchy. He tells his fellow monks: 'We must destroy everything that has Law and Number, for where there is nothing, there is God.'[190] The Superior of the Order drives Paul and his followers from the monastery, and they take up residence among some 'ecclesiastical ruins'.[191] The local villagers are angry that unfrocked monks should be living among them, so they surround them and kill Paul.

Though he had written his play in great haste, Yeats proceeded cautiously with its publication. He did not want to give Moore even the slightest pretext for litigation. He consulted his lawyer friend John Quinn about the American copyright, and he wrote again to Russell, from whom he had kept the details of his own progress, about the seriousness of Moore's threat.[192] Russell replied that he was confident Moore could not achieve anything by an injunction. They could counter-attack if there was a court case, he suggested lightheartedly, with an annotated compilation of the plagiarisms in Moore's work. There would be such a long list that the amount of borrowing would effectively make nonsense of his allegations against Yeats.[193] Meanwhile, Yeats had arranged with the *United Irishman* to publish his play, a tactic further calculated to increase Moore's discomfort, for he knew that Moore would not dare proceed against a Nationalist newspaper for fear of getting the windows in his house broken.[194] On 4 October, he sent Lady Gregory a progress report:

All is arranged with the *United Irishman* and Moore has no suspicion. I have not told Russell my plan but have told him things generally. He has seen Moore. Moore blustered and then Russell said, 'Yeats will not lack money to fight it. His friends will give him any amount', on which Moore got plaintive and after a little seemed inclined to give way.[195]

Once he had completed negotiations with the *United Irishman* and had secured the American copyright, Yeats wrote exultantly to Russell: 'Many thanks for note about Moore. Of course I will publish play. Tell Moore to write his story and be hanged.'[196]

Both Russell and Moore were confounded by the speed at which Yeats had worked. Austin Clarke, who was acquainted with all three men, was of the opinion that Russell was so 'disturbed by this display of rustic cunning' that his friendship with Yeats 'gradually dwindled'.[197] This is not the case. The extant correspondence clearly indicates that Russell consistently played the role of the unruffled mediator, and that Moore was the one who was piqued. As soon as the play was published, Moore went round to the Fays and told them that he would immediately take out an injunction if they produced it. 'You will, are you quite sure you will', Frank Fay is said to have replied. 'Then, I'm a made man. I'll never have to advertize if you'll only take out the injunction.'[198] Finding himself thwarted on all sides, Moore turned to Russell, who eventually dissuaded him from brandishing the law. With characteristic magnanimity, Russell offered to circulate a version of what had happened that would not be to the detriment of any of the parties. 'I am glad that the matter seems to be clearing up', he told Yeats.[199]

But the matter was never 'cleared up'. The well-known vignettes of Yeats which Moore used to spice the narrative of *Hail and Farewell* attest to the persistence of his resentment. Within the three volumes Yeats is variously described as 'a Finnish sorcerer',[200] 'a subaltern soul',[201] ' a monk of literature, an inquisitor, a Torquemada'.[202] He is said to look like 'a rook',[203] 'a crane',[204] 'a Bible reader',[205] or 'a great umbrella forgotten by some picnic party'.[206] Above all

> he is the type of the literary fop, and the most complete that has ever appeared in literature[207] . . . a man of excessive appearance . . . a long black cloak drooping from his shoulders, a soft black sombrero on his head, a voluminous black silk tie flowing from his collar, loose black trousers dragging untidily over his long, heavy feet. . . .[208]

And though Yeats protested a number of times at Moore's puckish malice,[209] the tenacity of his own dislike found corrosive expression in the variety of explanations he appended to successive versions of *Where There is Nothing*; in his description of Moore in *The Cat and The Moon* as 'the old lecher' who 'does be telling over all the sins he committed, or maybe never committed at all';[210] and in the various crusty passages about him in the *Autobiographies*. All Moore's behaviour is said to be characteristic of the typical 'peasant sinner'.[211] He is depicted as a man who 'had gone to Paris straight from his father's racing stables, from a house where there was no culture . . . acquired copious inaccurate French, sat among art students, young writers about to become famous, in some cafe; a man carved out of a turnip, looking out of astonished eyes'. As far as Yeats was concerned, Moore could be summed up as someone who 'spoke badly and much in a foreign tongue, read nothing, and was never to attain the discipline of style'.[212]

And yet, in spite of his intense dislike for the man, Yeats came to realize that he had grievously wronged him. 'Had I abandoned my plot and made him write the novel', he admitted in the *Autobiographies*,

he might have put beside *Muslin* and *The Lake* a third masterpiece, but I was young, vain, self-righteous, and bent on proving myself a man of action. *Where There is Nothing* is a bad play . . . I soon came to my senses, refused a distinguished Frenchman permission to translate it, and in later years with Lady Gregory's help turned it into *The Unicorn from the Stars*.[213]

The literary criticism and the self-analysis are as accurate as they are damning.

Russell, for his part, sided with one and then with the other several times throughout his life. He tried for a number of years to reconcile the two men, but was unsuccessful, his most conspicuous failure being an attempt in 1905 to secure Moore an honorary membership of the Irish National Theatre Society.[214] When Russell resigned from the Theatre in 1906 after quarrelling with Yeats, he became close friends with Moore, and visited him regularly every Saturday night for over seven years at the Dublin house he had found for him, but with the publication of *Vale*, which contained some snide remarks about Violet Russell, the friendship between Russell and Moore cooled.[215] By that time he had become reconciled with Yeats.[216] Russell's final assessment of his association with the two men is contained in *The Avatars*, a fanciful exploration published in 1933 of some of the principal figures and leading ideas of the literary renaissance. Moore is caricatured as a story-teller with a 'subtly insinuating, self-caressing voice' and a leprous imagination who enrages the small band of initiates by announcing that he plans to write up the visitation of the avatars as a popular love story.[217] Yeats is depicted as the hero Aodh, the name recalling a *persona* Yeats had himself adopted in *The Wind Among the Reeds*. In *The Avatars*, Aodh is one of the god-beings filled with the divine wisdom of the new age.

CHAPTER VII

PLAYS AND CONTROVERSIES: ACT II

1902 — 1908

'To Yeats, Russell was as much mob as man' — Frank O'Connor

The years following the controversy about *Where There is Nothing* were pockmarked with disputes. Most of them were provoked by the clash between Russell's desire to be one of a small amateur group that encouraged local writers and Yeats's need to be in command of a fully professional theatre. When they came to describe what had happened, both men coined short phrases that vividly displayed their reactions to one another's attitudes. For Russell, the disputes were caused by 'wire pulling and bickering',[1] a phrase that points to his distaste both for Yeats's treatment of young writers and his constant scheming to achieve his ends. For Yeats, the disputes were caused by 'sapping and mining',[2] an expression that emphasizes his distrust of Russell, and his belief that his friend was in fact the leader of a band of saboteurs.

Throughout 1903 and 1904 the differences between the two men were increasingly drawn into focus by the loose organization of the Theatre Society and the heterogeneous nature of its membership. During these years, the Society was unmanageable because it was too diffuse and too democratic. In the main it consisted of an executive with very loosely defined powers, and an assorted membership who seem to have had no rights other than an informal vote on whether or not they wanted to produce a particular play.

This lack of a formal selection procedure encouraged lobbying, and often led to confrontations between the various groups of people who had been attracted to the Society. Towards the end of the first year, tensions began to develop between three main factions: the ardent Nationalists, led by Maud Gonne and Arthur Griffith, who did not think it possible to have a valid art without a pervasive nationalism and who preferred to subordinate drama to politics; the majority of young working class members, who wanted a small amateur theatre as a haven for local talent and who regarded Russell as their leader; and Yeats, Lady Gregory, Synge, and the Fays, who were devoted to the theatre and who wanted to forge a National company that would express their own distinctive ideas and methods.

The first confrontation was between the Nationalists and those who wanted a professional theatre, and it involved Lady Gregory's *Twenty-Five*, a slight, sentimental, one-act play about a returned emigrant who deliberately loses all the money he has earned in America to the man who is married to his former sweetheart in order to save them from eviction.³ The play was due to go into rehearsal in September 1902, but Maud Gonne, exercising what she believed was one of her executive rights,⁴ vetoed it on the flimsy grounds that representing a young man earning a large sum of money in America might encourage emigration. To what extent she was motivated by her jealousy of Lady Gregory's hold over Yeats is a matter for speculation. To replace *Twenty-Five*, the Nationalists suggested *The Saxon Shillin'* by the young writer Padraic Colum, a stridently anti-British recruiting play which had recently been awarded first prize in a drama competition sponsored by Cumann na nGaedheal.⁵

The Saxon Shillin' exploits the tension between that deep-rooted Irish loyalty to 'the hearth' and the oath of allegiance to the English king. As a new recruit, Hugh Kearney finds himself seconded to the detachment that has been ordered to evict his orphaned sisters from the family cottage. Hugh offers to pay the rents, but his sisters will not accept his English money. In a rage of remorse, he barricades himself in the cottage to defend it against the eviction, only to be shot by his own sergeant.⁶ Colum's play was put into rehearsal in December 1902, but some people thought that the main situation, the eviction, was too difficult to stage and that the ending was too melodramatic, so Willie Fay pressed for extensive revisions. Maud Gonne and Arthur Griffith then accused Fay of terrorizing Colum and of using a trumped up literary criticism to avoid a clash with the Castle.⁷ Tempers flared, and it seemed that the Society would break up. When Russell heard about the quarrels he called two meetings and, drawing from his experience with the Co-operative Society organizing local credit banks, formulated a set of rules. It was largely at his suggestion that a system of voting rights for all members was introduced. While the nomination of plays was for the most part retained as the prerogative of the executive, ratification and casting were, in future, to be decided by a three-quarter vote of the membership. Shortly after the second meeting, he wrote to Yeats in London:

There was a rebellion going on which was natural among voluntary workers at the way in which plays were accepted or rejected without their consent, so I drew up and got them to pass the only rules which were possible under the circumstances. I think you got a copy of them. I knew you would not like them, but if they were not passed I do not think there would be a Theatre Society.[8]

Yeats, who was very annoyed by the superior tone of this letter and by the way Russell had misrepresented him before the entire Society, replied:

Of course I have no objection to a regular constitution being drawn up for the theatre. It was you who objected. I foretold when I saw you last Autumn that you would have disputes of precisely this nature, if you had not a regular constitution and rules. I remember saying to you that I would prefer a committee of selection and when you objected to this, saying that if the whole company were to choose the plays I should like that fact embodied in a definite constitution. Both you and Miss Gonne said that things were going on so nicely that I ought to leave them alone. Why do you say that I asked for a veto? I wrote to you from Galway proposing precisely that arrangement which is now embodied in the rules for the submitting of plays to the Presidents and Vice Presidents. I have still the letter in which you replied saying that you approved of my proposal and would submit it to the Fays. When I got to Dublin I found that you and some others thought that I had asked for a veto. I contradicted this at the time and have been contradicting it ever since. I cannot think how the idea arose. I certainly disapprove of a democracy in artistic matters, but a veto is certainly not the form of government I would propose. I said to you once that the absence of all arrangements for the selection of plays might force upon me an informal veto; in the sense that I should have to make the dropping of very bad plays a necessity — or go. But this was certainly not proposing a veto.[9]

As soon as the rules had been ratified, Yeats managed to persuade Colum to withdraw *The Saxon Shillin'*, Lady Gregory to halve the amount of money earned in America by the hero of her play, and the whole Society to recommence rehearsing *Twenty-Five*.[10] Lady Gregory's play was then advertised as the supporting play for *The Hour Glass*, a one act morality play Yeats had written which was almost ready for production.

Early in March, Russell went down to the Camden Street theatre to watch the rehearsals. The play portrays the dilemma of a reputedly wise agnostic who is suddenly confronted by an angel and told that if he can find, within the next hour, a single believer among all those he has influenced he can go to Heaven, but that if not he will be condemned to Hell. Having detected what he thought were two flaws in the play, Russell wrote to Yeats, who was in London, to offer some suggestions. In the first place he felt that some parts of the speech that the Wise Man makes just before the Angel enters, where

Plays and Controversies: Act II   213

he boasts of his success in overthrowing the 'hosts of foolishness' with the 'seven sciences', were out of keeping with his character. In this speech, the Wise Man exclaims: 'But, Rhetoric and Dialectic, that have been born out of the light star and out of the amorous star, you have been my spearman and my catapult!'[11] Russell objected:

> Of course in astrology the planets are gods, [but] when he speaks of the 'amorous star' he speaks of the spiritual power which it symbolises. I do not think it is logical to disbelieve in God and the angels and to believe in the divine influence of the planets. I think he should be sceptic [sic] of these things also and tell how men before he came believed in love coming from the 'amorous star' but that now it is simply a comely presence and the promise of bodily beauty which awakens love.[12]

Yeats did not change the speech. As the reply he wrote has been lost, his reasons for retaining the speech can only be conjectured. He may have pointed out that the Wise Man's allusions to the origins of the seven sciences were a display of learning rather than a statement of belief. He may also have directed Russell to Dante's *Paradiso*, his acknowledged source for these allusions, indicating that in canto VIII, for example, the 'amorous star' signifies both the reigning deity and the philosophy attributed to her, and that a person may believe one without necessarily believing the other.[13]

Russell's second objection involved a small item of stage business that immediately followed the Angel's departure. 'It [is] a little difficult to understand', he explained to Yeats in his letter,

> why the Wise Man remains lamenting in his room though there are crowds without. He has only a few moments to find his believer and [yet] he sends messengers and remains himself. It is a little hard to believe and is not quite convincing as I saw it. Could you invent some reason for his remaining? This point is not observable when reading but is to my mind noticeable when it is acted.[14]

Realizing that Russell was correct, Yeats rewrote the speech and made the Wise Man cry out:

> O, look out of the door and tell me if there is anybody there in the street. I cannot leave this glass; somebody might shake it! Then the sand would fall more quickly.[15]

In his effort to correct one mistake, Yeats unfortunately committed another; no matter how vigorously an hour glass is shaken the sand cannot be made to 'fall more quickly.' Furthermore, the new speech did not solve the problem of inconsistencies within the Wise Man's character that Russell had first drawn to his friend's attention. In what was otherwise a laudatory review, the drama critic of the *United Irishman* correctly pointed out that

The Wise Man's collapse is inevitable, perhaps, after his other-world visitor, but it weakens his character. When alone, he has no flashes of that questioning, critical intellect that challenged the visions of the saints and martyrs. We have to take Mr Yeats's word for it that his Wise Man was a sceptical thinker; the man himself does nothing to drive the fact home to us.[16]

Apart from minor criticism about structure and staging, *The Hour Glass* and *Twenty-Five* were well received by the critics and the public when they were first produced at the Molesworth Hall in Dublin on 14 March 1903.[17] Joseph Holloway perceptively noted in his diary: 'I think the evening was the turning point of the career of The Irish National Theatre Company, and has placed them on the wave of success.'[18] And if perhaps Holloway's dating of their success can be disputed, the fact that it had been achieved cannot. The two plays were again performed, with three others, when the Society played at the Queen's Gate Hall, South Kensington on 2 May 1903, at the invitation of the Irish Literary Society of London.[19] Several influential English drama critics, including Arthur Walkley and William Archer, wrote long, enthusiastic notices, which helped the reputation and the morale of the Society. On their return to Dublin, Russell wrote to Yeats, who was again in London:

I am delighted they did so well from all accounts. I am sure it was an immense relief to you. Had you frightened the London critics, or was it genuine appreciation, or was it due to the union of hearts . . .?[20]

Regrettably, the good will generated by the Dublin and London triumphs of March and May was very short-lived.

By June 1903 the Society was embroiled in bitter argument, Yeats and the Fays clashing with Russell and some of the more moderate Nationalists over the plays of James Cousins. Cousins, who, it will be remembered, had introduced the Fays to Russell, and so tended to see himself as one of the founding fathers of the Theatre, was a prolific writer and a useful actor. His first two plays, *The Sleep of the King*,[21] and *The Racing Lug*,[22] billed with two of Yeats's plays, had been performed in October and November in Dublin and Belfast with moderate acclaim.[23] But Yeats disliked him intensely, and took no trouble to conceal the fact. Towards the end of

December 1902 he told Frank Fay that he considered Cousins was 'hopeless' and that the sooner he had him 'as an enemy the better'.[24] The same month he blocked the production of his third play, a two act farce entitled *Sold*, which he informed Fay was 'rubbish and vulgar rubbish',[25] even though the play had been welcomed by Fay and put into rehearsal.[26] Subtitled 'A Comedy of County Down Life', *Sold* unashamedly employs all the tricks of popular farce. Faced with foreclosure, a farmer's wife persuades her husband to feign death after he has signed over the farm to a local pedlar, who happens to be one of the wife's former lovers. When the two bailiffs come, the pedlar tells them that as first mortgagee he is just about to sell the farm and is willing to discuss favourable terms. One of the bailiffs also happens to be a former lover, and when the pedlar and the other bailiff leave to finalize the settlement, he proposes marriage. Act II takes place in a Belfast solicitor's office. By a variety of complicated intrigues the farmer's wife manages to foil a detective; outwit the solicitor; play off the pedlar, the love-sick bailiff, and the alleged second mortgagee; and secure a receipt for 'payment' of her debt. Their farm cleared, she 'restores' her husband to life. While this jumble of thrilling events may make racy reading, it is, as Yeats rightly claimed, execrable theatre.[27]

Thinking that *Sold* had only been temporarily put aside, Cousins promptly submitted a fourth play, a three act heroic drama in prose entitled *The Sword of Dermot*.[28] This was also blocked by Yeats, even though Russell and Maud Gonne spoke on Cousins's behalf and the National Literary Society and Cumann na nGaedheal sponsored productions starring Dudley Digges and Maire T. Quinn, two of the best players in The Irish National Theatre Society.[29] In the meantime, despite Cousins's ability to secure the necessary three-quarter vote of the membership, Yeats persistently and successfully thwarted every attempt to produce *Sold*.[30] By June 1903, it was evident to everyone that as a result of this impasse the democratic procedures which Russell had set up the previous February were no longer workable. At a meeting of the Society on 2 June, Russell finally acceded to Yeats's long-expressed wish for a standard selection procedure and proposed that a reading committee be formed.[31] The motion was carried unanimously, with Yeats, Russell, Colum, and the Fays being elected.[32] Cousins promptly submitted *Sold*, which split the new committee, Russell and Colum being prepared to vote for it, while Yeats and the Fays were adamantly opposed.[33] At first Yeats refused to discuss the matter with Russell, but after some weeks he wrote him a brief letter in which he pointed out various flaws in the play, emphasizing that even if these were remedied he would still vote against it for he did not think that Cousins's work had any merit.

> His unfamiliarity with the writing of farce has made him deal with [the main situation] in a spirit of winking vulgarity. He would not have done this if conventional stage [situations] had not destroyed his own sense of what befits a writer. . . . Cousins has no originality as a writer — so far as I can judge. His material is always old, his sentiments always conventional, and I see nothing for our committee but firmness from the first. Every encouragement we give him as a writer will only bring trouble on us in the future.[34]

The correspondence between Yeats and Russell over Cousins was prevented from becoming more acrimonious by Cousins's resignation from the Theatre Society.[35]

Though Russell and Cousins were not particularly close friends, Russell considered him a valuable link with the moderate Nationalists and a promising young writer. He must also have been swayed by Cousins's outspoken admiration for his poetry, and his obvious receptiveness to his spiritual teachings, even though Cousins did not officially join the Theosophical Society until 1908.[36] It was therefore difficult for Russell to accept the public and ruthless way Yeats had treated his young friend, particularly when at that time Yeats was vigorously promoting another young writer who was, and was to remain, largely unknown to him, and whose work was anathema to the Nationalists — J. M. Synge.[37] All Russell knew of this silent man was a brief acquaintance through one or two casual meetings, and the fact that he had written slightingly of him in *L'Européen* the previous May in his article 'Le Mouvement Intellectuel Irlandais':

> A part M. Yeats, nous avons un poète, M. George Russell, dont l'imagination extraordinaire n'arrive pas toujours à s'exprimer dans une forme pleinement satisfaisante. Dans les deux volumes qu'il a déjà publiés, on trouve quelques petits poèmes à peu près parfaits, à côté de beaucoup de pièces sans valeur.[38]

[Apart from Mr Yeats, we have a poet, Mr George Russell, whose extraordinary imagination doesn't always find expression in a fully satisfactory form. In the two volumes he has so far published, one finds a number of near perfect poems alongside many worthless ones.]

The first of Synge's plays to be performed, *The Shadow of the Glen*, was produced with Yeats's *The King's Threshold* at the

Molesworth Hall on 8, 9 and 10 October 1903.[39] During the opening performance there were disturbances in the theatre, prompted largely by attacks in the *Independent* and the *United Irishman* which alleged that Synge's play was a 'slur on Irish womanhood', 'a Lie', and a 'perversion of the Society's avowed aims'.[40] Yeats answered these and other attacks in stentorian tones in a curtain speech on the final night, and in three vigorous and scornful articles: 'An Irish National Theatre', 'The Theatre, the Pulpit and the Newspapers', and 'The Irish National Theatre and Three Sorts of Ignorance.'[41] His championing of Synge made him many enemies, and caused a rift in the Theatre Society; Maud Gonne, Dudley Digges, Maire T. Quinn, and several others resigned in protest, and openly aligned themselves with the Cumann na nGaedheal Theatre Company, which was continuing to rehearse Cousins's plays.[42] Throughout the controversy Russell remained conspicuously silent, an attitude he was to adopt again four years later, to Yeats's intense annoyance, for the *Playboy* controversy.

It would seem that Russell's silence on both occasions was due to the fact that he agreed with the opposition. For example, in common with Maud Gonne, he thought that 'it is for the many; for the people, that Irish writers must write'.[43] He would have also agreed with James Connolly's assertion that 'the artist is the teacher, a prophet and a leader of his people'.[44] And like most of the 1903 secessionists, he believed that the theatre should actively shape Irish morality and Irish opinion. Perhaps the most eloquent exponent of this view, though he was only marginally associated with the theatre, was Thomas Kettle, a young University College graduate and friend of James Joyce. As a rejoinder to Yeats's defence of Synge, Kettle submitted a closely-argued article to the *United Irishman* entitled 'Mr Yeats and the Freedom of the Theatre' in which, by giving expression to his own objections, he articulated the hitherto unpublicized fears of Russell, the moderate Nationalists, and some of the younger members of the Theatre Society.

Mr Yeats . . . seems to think that the whole duty of a dramatist is fulfilled when he has expanded some mood of his private experience into a self-consistent person, and sent him journeying through a world, contact with which unfolds a picture of his mind. Whether the event and issue of this contact be good or bad, the dramatist is not concerned; his interest is purely psychological; he explains conduct but does not estimate it. This is a clear and workable conception of drama, and it certainly makes the writer's task easier. But it also impoverishes his function beyond the consent of anyone who is in earnest with life. . . . I expect by laying bare the idea of this and that, by constructing a story in which the line of causation is clear and unbroken, [the dramatist] will manifest the essential nullity of evil, the necessary triumph of good. But Mr Yeats would reject such 'moral' drama.[45]

The debate was further complicated for Russell by a private quarrel with Yeats about art and morality involving a volume of poems to be published by Dun Emer, his sisters' new press. With the poems ready to print, an argument broke out over the adjective 'big' in a line from the poem 'A Memory':

> How God was a big kind brother

Russell protested that the word was essential to the message of the poem and to those following it in the sequence; Yeats countered that the line was inartistic. Both remained 'stiff-necked', until Yeats suggested that Russell make a new selection from all his poetry rather than insist on the original arrangement. To prevent further embarrassment he agreed — though he observed wryly to a friend that if Yeats did not allow his sisters to print 'anything which is not on the level of a sacred book' the output of their press would be very small. Having carried the day, Yeats was expansive, and when *The Nuts of Knowledge* appeared in December he described it as 'perfectly charming', better than his own recently published *In the Seven Woods*, and certain to 'advance the fame of the press'.[46]

At the same time, some of the tension that had resulted from their disagreements about art and morality in the theatre was removed by the success of Padraic Colum, a young working class writer who was one of Russell's protégés and who was friendly with the moderate Nationalists.[47] Colum's *Broken Soil* was produced with *The Hour Glass* and *The Pot of Broth* on 3, 4, and 5 December 1903 at the Molesworth Hall.[48] The programme was specifically designed to win back the support of some of those alienated by Synge's play. Colum was a close friend of Arthur Griffith, the editor and proprietor of the *United Irishman*, and he was admired by most of the young people in Inginidhe-na-hEireann and Cumann na nGaedheal. His play, a three-act tragedy about a wandering fiddler and his daughter, who are torn between their desire to wander the roads and their wish to remain in the quiet seclusion of a small farm, displayed a sympathetic insight into the Irish peasant character that accorded well with the Nationalists' rigid construct of the ideal peasant and that was free from the astringent realism which had proved so offensive in Synge's work.[49] The season was a success; audiences were enthusiastic, and most of the reviews of *Broken Soil* were long and pleasant, a striking contrast to those of *The Shadow of the Glen* staged two months before.[50]

Yeats was in America on a lecture tour when the programme was compiled and *Broken Soil* was staged. As he had blocked the initial production of Colum's *The Saxon Shillin'* two years before, and had rejected the first draft of *Broken Soil*, he was as relieved as Russell was proud of its success.[51] On Christmas day he wrote to his sister Lily:

Colum's success has overjoyed me. I was more nervous about that play than anything else, for my position would have been impossible if I had had to snuff out the work of young men belonging to the company. It would have always seemed that I did so from jealousy or some motive of that sort. Now, however, one can push on Colum and keep one's snuffers for the next.[52]

What Yeats did not know was that even as he wrote his 'snuffers' were temporarily being made less effective. Heartened by the success of Colum's plays, some of the members of the Theatre Society persuaded Russell to revise the rules to limit further the powers of the President and the Vice-Presidents and to give the actors more control.[53] Russell did not tell Yeats about this when he wrote to him, but he could not resist boasting about Colum's success, particularly as Yeats had not been as readily persuaded of the young dramatist's potential as he had. 'Colum's play', he assured him,

interested a great many people. It acted much better than I thought it would. There are certain passages which were extraordinarily moving and original which affected everyone. I feel more and more convinced that the boy has a great faculty.[54]

At the same time, he confided to John Quinn: 'I don't know whether Colum will ever write better or as well as Yeats or Synge but he is the hope of the Theatre as far as the public are concerned.'[55] A little later, about a month before Yeats was due to return to Ireland, Russell admitted to Quinn:

I will be very glad to see W.B.Y. again. I am always fighting with him, but if I hadn't him to fight with it would make a great gap in my life. He is, after all, save O'Grady, the only real live soul I meet in this country. The others are all active in dreams or are sub-human and concerned in Gaelic Leagues or Leagues of some kind or other.[56]

His admission was unhappily prophetic; within weeks of Yeats's return the two men had a bitter quarrel which created a gap in both their lives.

The quarrel involved a plan to produce Russell's *Deirdre* and a number of other Irish plays at a vast international trade fair to be held in the summer of 1904 at St Louis, Missouri. While Yeats was still in America the Theatre Society was approached by Mr Rearden, one of the thirty commissioners representing the Louisiana Purchase Exposition from St Louis, Missouri, and asked if they would perform the best of their repertoire at the Exposition.[57] At first they were eager to go, but when they realized that they would all have to give up their jobs and form themselves into a professional company because they would have to stay in America for several months, they all, with the exception of P.J. Kelly, refused the St Louis offer.[58] Rearden then approached several former members, of whom Dudley Digges, C. Caulfield, Maire T. Quinn, and Elizabeth Young agreed to go.[59] Rearden and Digges asked if they could produce *Deirdre*, and Russell, though at first reluctant, gave them permission. When Yeats heard about the arrangement he wrote to Russell and asked him to withdraw the permission because he was planning to take the Theatre Society on a tour of America himself, and he did not want them to be confused with Digges's group. Russell replied that he could not go back on his word, but that he had asked Rearden to print 'performance by permission of Irish National Theatre Society' on all the advertising for *Deirdre*, a precaution he believed would prevent the confusion that Yeats wanted to avoid. 'If you wished to be good-natured', he added, you could

let them have one or two plays like *The Hour Glass*. . . . But you have more knowledge of U.S.A. than I, and can judge best. For small plays it is likely the performances will be quite as good as the National Theatre Society could give, Digges, Miss Young and Kelly being quite as good as any remaining here. I doubt altogether their power to do the big plays competently but I dare say *The Pot of Broth*, *Cathleen ni Houlihan* and *The Hour Glass* would be done well enough, especially as both Digges and Kelly have been in them already and so has Caulfield in *Cathleen*.[60]

Yeats retorted that it was not a matter of whether he was prepared to be good-natured; it was a matter of protecting the interests of their own Theatre Society. As an American tour was the only way the Society could make a substantial sum of money, it would be foolish to put their future in jeopardy by giving their plays to incompetent actors who had persistently proved their disloyalty to the Society. Furthermore, he told Russell, even though he was a Vice-President, he was not entitled to give permission for performances of *Deirdre* without the Society's consent, for the play belonged to

Plays and Controversies: Act II 221

the Society. By giving Rearden and Digges *Deirdre* he had acted illegally and had been disloyal.[61]

Russell was furious. 'You say', he wrote,

> that the only chance of the Company making money is by an American tour. If that is so I think the company had better dissolve at once for I would lose all interest in it if it was to live only for America and by America. I have no interest in its work outside Ireland and if it is hopeless to expect success by touring in Ireland, with occasional tours in England, then it is in my opinion useless to continue taking any interest in it. With this I think the Company would agree.

Neither, in his opinion, would an American tour enhance the society's reputation.

> You have had a triumphal procession through America and no one in Ireland except a few friends to whom cuttings were sent has heard of it. There was only one short paragraph so far as I know in Irish papers and so far as you are concerned you have no more influence here for all your work than you had before. Your own knowledge of the little effect your great reputation elsewhere has here ought to have taught you this. You and the Company will only be known by what you actually do over here by personal work here, and I think the Company realize this well enough.

To the accusations that he had been disloyal and acted illegally Russell replied:

> I have quite as much interest in the Company as you have, and in my own way have worked quite as much as you have to preserve it here, settling to the best of my ability rows which threatened its existence, but if they were to assume the right to control the disposal of what I could write outside these islands I would withdraw from them at once.

'I am sorry to have to write all this and be in continual disagreement with you on matters of policy', he concluded, 'but I hope having expressed myself that you will not urge the matter further for I believe I would simply lose my temper'.[62]

Yeats stubbornly refused to yield, so Russell resigned from the Society. 'I know you will be considerably relieved by my taking this step and that you have wished it for a long time', he told Yeats. 'I do not think you will find my letter to the Secretary written in any spirit of vexation.'[63] For what it is worth, this is so. In contrast to the belligerent parochialism of his correspondence with Yeats, his letter of resignation was tendered in the spirit of injured nobility.

In withdrawing I do so with the least ill will and with the hope that my personal friendship and the goodwill which has existed between myself and the members may remain unbroken. . . . I believe in resigning I have acted for the interests of the Society. Mr Yeats has more power to aid the Society than I have. His literary work in the future is likely to be altogether dramatic in form and I could not feel justified in opposing any course which he took, as I believe to a great extent the success of the Society is bound up with the future of his work.

In essence, as Russell pointed out in his letter, he and Yeats were at variance because they held different views about the function of literature.

Mr Yeats does not seem to think that his plays have, I will not say any dramatic significance, but that they lose most of their significance if separated from a special form of artistic presentation. To a certain extent I agree with him but I have never concerned myself so much with these things for my own part, and have written always to express art in abstract ideas [sic] which I think of importance, than to help in the creation of beautiful arts which I recognize of equal importance, but which do not interest me quite to the same extent. And regarding my literary work, small as it is, as the vehicle for ideas which I believe to have a certain human value, I am not disposed to restrict their circulation in any way: for I feel that if I did I would be acting contrary to my own intuitions of what was right.[64]

Yeats accepted Russell's resignation and his flurry of accusation and protest with measured calm, a stance which it was perhaps easier for him to maintain when he discovered that the Society were solidly behind him rather than Russell. The letter he wrote in reply, which indirectly answers many of the objections Russell had at one time or another raised to his work in the Theatre, is a masterful blend of conciliation and attack. He began with a promise of new beginnings, a brief apology, and some elaborate praise:

. . . Please do nothing at present. When we start in [the] Autumn in the Abbey we will make our next appeal to the public. . . . Please forgive me for giving expression to some of my general exasperation . . . and making *Deirdre* the scapegoat. I was foolish enough to quote a phrase of Lady Gregory's which must have annoyed you, but when you think of it remember that she, like myself, puts your best poetry above any spiritual poetry written in our time and your best prose among the loftiest in the world.

Yeats then took up the description of their different attitudes to literature which Russell had given in his letter of resignation, and showed that in his opinion they were further apart than Russell had indicated:

> I myself sometimes give unbridled expression to my dislikes, moved perhaps by my knowledge of the strength of my likings and my loyalty to them. I am nothing but an artist and my life is in written words and they get the most of my loves and hates, and so too I am reckless in mere speech that is not written. You are the other side of the penny, for you are admirably careful in speech, having set life before art, too much before it as I think for one who is, in spite of himself perhaps, an artist. It is the careless printed word that remains after one's death to mar many people it may be, while the careless spoken word troubles an ear or two at the most. That is I think the root of all our differences.[65]

The use of the adverb in the ironic self-effacement of 'I am nothing but an artist' anticipates the famous lines from 'Ego Dominus Tuus':

> The rhetorician would deceive his neighbours,
> The sentimentalist himself; while art
> Is but a vision of reality.[66]

In these lines semantics is made to work against grammar, and the claims of art are absolutely affirmed by being apparently qualified. The paragraph as a whole anticipates the distinctions between the 'saint' and the 'artist' that Yeats drew in his *Autobiographies*,[67] and it anticipates 'The Choice':

> The intellect of man is forced to choose
> Perfection of the life, or of the work,
> And if it take the second must refuse
> A heavenly mansion, raging in the dark.
> When all that story's finished, what's the news?
> In luck or out the toil has left its mark:
> That old perplexity an empty purse,
> Or the day's vanity, the night's remorse.[68]

The realization that both 'artist' and 'saint' are vulnerable to mundaneness gives strength to what would otherwise be merely a glib antithesis.

In some respects Russell was relieved to be offered an olive branch, even if it was sprinkled with salt. Within three months of his resignation, the Irish newspapers began to feature detailed accounts of the failure not only of the Irish players but also of the entire

Irish Section at the Louisiana Purchase Exposition at St Louis, Missouri.[69] For his part, Yeats shrewdly realized that Russell, who was popular and influential and who had acquired a vast fund of experience in organizing small societies through his work with the I.A.O.S., could play a key role in re-organizing the amateur Theatre group into a professional company.[70]

The finance necessary for this change was made available early in 1904 by Miss Annie Horniman, a wealthy Englishwoman who had been taking an interest in the Theatre Society for several years.[71] On 9 April Yeats wrote to Russell:

I send you the enclosed offer from Miss Horniman. You need do nothing about it except hold your tongue absolutely. We must not let the slightest rumour get out until we have secured the patent . . .[72]

The following month the contract between Miss Horniman and the Society was signed, and work was begun converting an old building in the centre of the city into a small theatre. The patent was secured in August, and on 27 December 1904 The Abbey Theatre opened with performances of Yeats's *On Baile's Strand*, a revival of *Cathleen ni Houlihan*, and Lady Gregory's *Spreading the News*.[73]

Possessing their own theatre meant that the Society was able to stage many more plays than when they had been forced to hire the Molesworth Hall or The Antient Concert Rooms. In January 1905 they produced Synge's *The Well of the Saints*, which aroused widespread controversy and threatened the unity of the Society, as did all the early productions of Synge's plays.[74] Lady Gregory's *Kincora* was produced in March, William Boyle's *The Building Fund* in April, and Padraic Colum's *The Land* in June.[75] The staging of so many new plays, with revivals now and then, created pressures which threatened the organizational structure of what was still essentially an amateur group. By the summer of 1905 it was evident that the Society would either have to disband or turn professional.[76]

The major problem was how to keep the Society intact and yet dismantle the unworkably democratic machinery which Russell had erected in 1903, when all members had been given voting rights, and in 1904, when power had been effectively transferred from the executive to the actors.[77] Yeats knew that Russell was the only person with the necessary tact and knowledge to effect the change, but he also knew that Russell was anxious to resign, the move to The Abbey having clearly signalled the end of his dreams of an amateur theatre.[78] He was thus greatly relieved to receive a letter from Frank Fay in mid July outlining a plan which he and Russell had worked out. On 3 August Yeats wrote to Russell urging him to develop their scheme:

Fay has written to me about his conversation with you upon the Theatre. I think the scheme he sketches out with you seems to be a workable basis. I wish you would go into it more fully with him and make a clear draft. Anything that you and he agreed on would, I have no doubt, be acceptable to Lady Gregory and myself, and it would be far more likely to pass than if I had a hand in it.[79]

Yeats's last statement is only half true and was essentially a sop to secure Russell's co-operation. Months before he wrote his letter Yeats had a very clear idea of what he wanted; he and Lady Gregory, and to a degree, Synge, wanted the Society turned into a Limited Company with themselves absolutely in control as Directors.

The delicate negotiations to achieve this end occupied most of the autumn and winter of 1905, during which Yeats wrote Russell about a dozen long letters. First he convinced him of the need to disenfranchise some of the nominal members of the original Society. 'Every ineffective or unnecessary member', he impressed on Russell,

is like flesh where there should be muscle. I am greatly obliged to you for taking so much trouble in a matter where you are not vitally interested. You have so much influence over several of our members that nobody else can set things right.[80]

Then Yeats proceeded to get the membership of the Reading Committee restricted to himself, Lady Gregory, Synge and Colum. He suggested Colum because he knew he was popular, he felt that he would prove amenable, and he hoped that by giving him a place on the Reading Committee he would forestall Russell's plan to have Colum made one of the Directors.[81] Once he had obtained the Reading Committee he wanted, Yeats persuaded Russell to re-organize the Business Committee, and when Russell accused him of bullying one of the existing members Yeats retorted with the wry observation: 'Yes, of course I have no tact, and bully people. That is why I am leaving the whole matter to you. I can only threaten the body, but you can put the soul in uncomfortable places.'[82]

Towards the end of September, when the Articles of Association were about to be drawn up, Yeats went to Dublin to ensure that absolute power was given to the Directors. On his arrival he wrote to Lady Gregory: 'The controversy will be [about] the absolute majority proposal . . . We must leave as much as possible with Russell who now advocates everything we insisted upon in our correspondence with him.'[83] In November a general meeting was called and the Articles of Association were passed, making the Irish National Theatre Society a limited company managed by a Board of Directors who were empowered to 'appoint and remove stage manager, business manager and all other employees, fix their salaries and arrange their duties.'[84] Yeats, Lady Gregory and Synge were appointed Directors. By working through Russell, Yeats had obtained exactly what he wanted. But their break with one another was imminent.

By 21 December all the actors and actresses had signed their contracts with the new Society except Mary Walker (Maire Nic Shiubhlaigh), who refused because she wanted extra money. A compromise was worked out, and she gave her word that she would sign the contract, but when it was drawn up and presented to her, she again refused to sign.[85] Her reticence was partly due to her disappointment at not being made the leading actress of the company; partly due to her loyalty to her brother Frank, who felt the terms of his contract were a calculated insult; and partly due to her allegiance to a faction headed by George Roberts, who alleged that the aims of the new company were a betrayal of true nationalism. Yeats decided to sue Moira Walker on the grounds that her indecision and subsequent breach of contract had prevented the company from going on tour. He explained to Russell:

The reason why I think it is necessary to make a public example is that we must get our people to understand that the old vague fluctuating incoherent Dublin way is over as far as we are concerned; and that the management of the new company is not going to be trifled with.[86]

Even though the lawsuit was dropped almost immediately, the attitude Yeats had adopted gave Russell his long awaited excuse to resign. He wrote Yeats a very long letter, the last for over seven years:

I heard you wrote to Miss Walker but [I] have not seen her or spoken to her about the matter. . . . I told Roberts . . . that she would have no ground unless you on your side had broken . . . some understanding. . . . You may be acting in the best way, but I am inclined to think it unwise considering the very insecure hold you have on the old society. . . . Of course if you are prepared to let the old society go you can act regardless of any irritation you may arouse. I think if you do you will lose Dublin completely. . . . There is probably not one of the younger people of whom you have not said some stinging and contemptuous remark. They may have been justified.

But if you wish to lead a movement you can only do so by silence on points which irritate you or by kindly suggestions to the people. A man without followers can do nothing and you have few or no friends in Dublin. Their irritation leads them to tear to pieces everything you write until they persuade themselves that it has no merit at all. . . . [You] must not take this letter as written in [a] spirit of antagonism. I have had no particular reason to support you and many good reasons to fight you if I wished to do so. But I have always recognized your genius as a poet, and have always fought for you there where I could. I have felt for some years past that the old friendship between [us has] worn very thin. But at least you are one of the few people in Ireland who have done something and are still trying to do something, and I do not wish to fight you unless your track of action interferes with my own, and a question of principle arises. I have always tried to avoid any friction, and have decided that as I did not wish to write plays myself I should not interfere with you who did. I have no doubt I have been represented as always thwarting your views but as a matter of fact I have lost a great deal of my influence among the young men by defending you. . . .

[Of] course I do not deny that I have laughed at most of your dogmas, and have never disguised my opinion that in trying to write plays you are deflecting a genius which is essentially lyrical and narrative from its best manifestation and that your want of logical constructive power unfitted you for dramatic writing, at least for the stage. . . . As a poet you could and would exercise an immense influence on your contemporaries, as a dramatist you lose influence. The few dozen people who come to the Abbey Theatre are a poor compensation for the thousands who would read another *Wind Among the Reeds* or another *Usheen* or work like that. However, as you have begun it and tied the Theatre around your neck you must go on with it, and my advice to you is let Miss Walker alone and do as little as you can to irritate those who are against you, or you will find that a man with no friends and many active enemies may for all his genius have less influence on his time than some person of one-half his abilities. This is my advice.[87]

Yeats was entirely unrepentant. He replied by return post:

My dear Russell,

Many thanks for your letter, which I understand as it was meant. My sister will tell you whether I got Miss Walker's consent by 'threatening' or the like as she and she only was present. I was indignant when I found Miss Walker wavering after having wasted a week of our time but not till then. As for the more general questions. I desire the love of a very few people, my equals or my superiors. The love of the rest would be a bond and an intrusion. These others will in time come to know that I am a fairly strong and capable man and that I have gathered the strong and capable about me, and all who love work better than idle talk will support me. It is a long fight but that is the sport of it. The antagonism, which is sometimes between you and me, comes from the fact that though you are strong and capable yourself you gather the weak and not very capable about you, and that I feel they are a danger to all good work. It is I think because you desire love. Besides you have the religious genius to which all souls are equal. In all work except that of salvation that spirit is a hindrance.

I know quite well — I knew when Synge wrote his first play — I will never have the support of the clubs. I am trying for the general public — the only question with me (and it is one I have argued with Synge and Lady Gregory) is whether I should attack the clubs openly.[88]

Though Russell was deeply offended by the imperious tone of this letter he felt he should attempt a reconciliation. He soon discovered that his feelings were shared by Yeats's sisters and father. While the sisters provided a safe haven for Moira Walker at their embroidery workshop at Gurteen Dhas, Russell and J. B. Yeats approached Lady Gregory to see if she would be willing to ask Yeats to moderate his stance or offer some form of compromise. But she was equally adamant that the discontent about the aims of the new theatre and the quibbling over contracts should be dealt with firmly. On 11 January 1906 she sent J. B. Yeats her reply with instructions that he show it to Russell.

I am quite ready to open peace negotiations ... if any responsible person on the other side will say what they would have us do. Ed. Martyn says Roberts told him he and his friends had struck because we were 'Not National enough, did not have sixpenny seats or enough plays by Irish authors.' Now what does that mean?[89]

She accused them both of maligning Yeats when he wasn't present to defend himself: 'Neither you nor Mr Russell need give me a list of Willie's crimes. He is not so near being sainted that the "devil's advocate" need thunder out the case against him.'[90] And instead of administering the requested admonition to him, she took Moira Walker aside when she came up to Dublin in March. 'I don't know what you said,' J. B. Yeats exclaimed, 'but she is a new girl!'[91] With a measure of harmony restored it was decided to use the annual general meeting of the new society announced for 24 May 1906 to discuss grievances and formally ratify the constitution. Yeats and Lady Gregory set to work and by rallying their forces and skilfully deploying the voting rights of the new organization convincingly achieved all their aims.[92] The dissidents withdrew, and two days later founded their own company along the lines of the former National Theatre Society. They called it Cluithcheori-na-hEireann (The Theatre of Ireland), elected Edward Martyn President, and voted in a board of officers which included Padraic Colum, James Cousins, Patrick H. Pearse, and Thomas Kettle. Moira Walker was acknowledged as leading lady. Russell gave the new company his blessing and the right to perform *Deirdre*, a decision that signalled the end of nearly a decade's work with Yeats in the Theatre.[93]

The relationship between the two men was further strained a few months later by a quarrel over a second volume of Russell's poems for Dun Emer. Without consulting her brother, who was still acting as literary adviser to the press, Lollie asked Russell to prepare a selection that would complement *The Nuts of Knowledge*. He told her that he thought she was 'taking a risk', but drew up a list on the condition that there would be 'no correspondence with [W.B.Y.] on it. He likes the poems I like least', he cautioned her, 'and I am sure that we could not agree'.[94] With fair copy prepared and the edition ready for the press Yeats discovered what was going on and promptly vetoed the entire selection on the grounds that the poems were beneath his own standard of excellence. Lollie replied that she would print them anyway. Yeats retorted that to do so would damage his reputation as well as theirs because it was known that he was her literary adviser. A full scale family row broke out in which neither side yielded. Yeats withdrew temporarily; Russell's book, whose title *By Still Waters* contradicted all the circumstances surrounding its publication, was set in type and advertised as being ready for sale by 14 December 1906.[95]

The quarrels about Mary Walker and the row over his poems affected Russell deeply. He was weary of Yeats's imperiousness and his truculence. The more he reviewed that last three to four years of their twenty-two year old association — the years when it seemed to him that their friendship had 'worn thin' — the less it appeared that continuing it would help him to achieve his dream, a dream of a popular literary movement that would stimulate young writers to express themselves and encourage ordinary Irish men and women to better their lives because they had been inspired with a reverent pride for their heroic past.

Rather than confront Yeats with another lengthy account of their differences, Russell decided to distance himself from him. He continued to be polite on the one or two occasions that they met and to talk with studied casualness about day to day events, but he formed a stubborn resolve to withdraw all his support. He would no longer hold a brief for either his conduct or his plans. If Yeats wanted to continue to fight for a particular type of literary movement he would have to rely on his remaining allies or fight alone.

It did not take Yeats long to discover the true measure of this resolve. On 26 January 1907 Synge's *The Playboy of the Western World* opened at the Abbey. The spontaneous and organized rowdyism which greeted it are now a well-known part of literary history, as is Yeats's throwing open the Abbey on 5 February for a public debate on the freedom of the Theatre. What perhaps is not well-known is that Yeats initially persuaded Russell to chair the debate, maybe in the hope that his presence would either neutralize or win over the support of the younger writers and that his reputation for fair play would guarantee an open confrontation between the supporters of the theatre and the disgruntled Nationalists, whom Yeats believed he could convincingly rout. In the event, as he recorded in a draft of his *Autobiographies*, Russell himself, who had promised to take the chair, 'refused by a subterfuge and joined the others in the gallery.'[96] The victim of a conflict between memory and resolve, Russell found himself unable to refuse Yeats in private, but even more unable to support him in public. Lady Gregory wrote to Synge, who had stayed away from the meeting:

> No one came to support us. Russell (AE) was in the gallery we heard afterwards but did not come forward or speak. Colum 'had a rehearsal' and didn't speak or come. T.W. Russell didn't turn up. We had hardly anyone to speak on our side.[97]

To take a seat in the gallery among Synge's enemies was an act of inexcusable treachery.[98]

And what is more, as if to call attention to their opposition, Russell broke his silence just four days after the debate by publishing a vitriolic attack on Yeats and Synge in Arthur Griffith's *Sinn Fein*. Taking his cue from a challenge Yeats had thrown out to the audience at the height of the debate — 'the author of *Kathleen ni Houlihan* addresses you' — he framed his attack as a parody of the very play which Yeats had called to his self-defence. He called it *Britannia Rule-the-Wave* and gave it a cast of four: the Chief Poet of Ireland (Yeats), The Chief Actor of Ireland (Synge), an Old Lady (Britain), and a scene shifter. In the opening scene he pilloried Yeats for using the police to keep the theatre open for the advertised run of the play by drawing a parallel between his tactics and those employed by Queen Victoria for her Jubilee Parade through Dublin in 1901.

> Old Lady: Oh, I have had a hard time of it. They have hissed me through the streets. I have had a very hard time of it.

Chief Poet of Ireland: And what did they hiss you for, ma'am. Was it the play or the acting?
Old Lady: Oh, it was my beautiful play. There were miles and miles of soldiers in my play, and miles of policemen, but it never got a fair hearing.
Chief Poet of Ireland: We are just like that, we never got a fair hearing.[99]

The comparison, of course, is wickedly unjust because Yeats had vigorously opposed the Jubilee visit, so vigorously it will be remembered that Russell had rebuked him for demeaning himself.

Russell also used his parody to ridicule Yeats's pronouncements on the laureateship, his claim to have descended from the Duke of Ormonde, his conviction that Ireland needed an aristocracy of taste, and his view that art was the prerogative of a cultured minority. Echoing the title poem of *In the Seven Woods* (1905) he had his 'Chief Poet of Ireland' murmur to himself: "New Commonness upon the throne!" I must re-write that, it was an appeal to the gallery. It was bad art.'[100]

The crudeness of this attack prevented an early reconciliation while its malice ensured that Russell became the focal point of an anti-Yeats clique. Its members would gather periodically at his house to vie with one another for the sharpness of their jibes. One of the worst attacks from this time was an article entitled 'Dramatic Rivalry' which appeared anonymously in *Sinn Fein* on 8 May 1909.[101] Beginning, 'Mr Yeats, you have been a fool', it castigated him for his treatment of Mary Walker in particular and the rest of the Theatre of Ireland group in general, and urged him to make peace with them for the good of the entire literary movement. It soon became known that the author of the attack was Susan Mitchell, the sharp-witted secretary who worked for Russell at the I.A.O.S. The Yeats family knew her well. Yeats's father had taken her in as a boarder when they had lived in London in the 'eighties and 'nineties. He was dismayed by her treachery. He informed one of his daughters that he was sure Susan Mitchell had been used by Russell and George Moore; and he wrote to his son:

Russell thinks G. Moore a great man because, being from the North, he admires noblemen and he thinks Moore a sort of real nobleman, and because he is a successful writer of novels. He also admires Moore because Moore really has a poor opinion of Russell. Russell must either boss or be bossed. And then Russell is lonely. He has no friends, and he is exasperated against things, and so likes to walk into the black puddle of the Moore cesspool, and to throw mud or to get others to do it.[102]

Yet J. B. Yeats realized that Russell had cause for these outbursts of malice. 'You have offended [his] vanity, I fancy, more than once', he reminded his son, 'and though there is a Real Russell, [who] is magnanimous, one must not forget that Russell is a prophet and the centre of a circle, and therefore intensely self-appreciative.'[103]

For his part, Russell came to see that he was mistaken, and that the methods Yeats had used to build his professional theatre, while they might at the time have seemed self-centred and autocratic, did achieve results. The Theatre of Ireland, which openly professed to strive 'first for a national ideal; secondly for a theatrical',[104] began to decline after 1912 when its members became more interested in the Irish Volunteer movement than in rehearsing plays. On 9 January 1926 Russell admitted in an article in *The Irish Statesman*:

> We hope that the notice for sale attached to the premises of the Royal Hibernian Academy which was burnt in 1916, during Easter Week, means that the Academy has at last, after overlong deliberation, decided to build new premises and has found a site. It was assumed that the old site was out of the way, though in a side street as a matter of fact, it was in the heart of the city, and near to the centre of the tram system, and could be reached with little difficulty from any part of Dublin. But it may be that a site in some street more frequented by the wealthy might bring that shy creature Art more directly under the notice of those who can afford to purchase pictures. The Abbey Theatre has made itself fashionable enough, though it was only a stone's throw from the premises of the Academy. The real truth, we suspect, is that the same quality of brain and imagination was not at the service of one as it was at the service of the other. The Abbey had some sound autocratic direction, and the Academy had a council without an autocrat who knew what he wanted, as Sir Hugh Lane knew what he wanted, or as Mr Yeats or Lady Gregory knew what they wanted. It might be the best policy to get an autocrat of artistic distinction if one is available, one who will not mind the rage he creates, but who will excite the imagination of the people about Irish art, who will exclude ruthlessly the exhibition of feebleness and incompetence as Whistler did during his brief and famous Presidency of the Royal Society of British Artists, even if the outcome of a similar autocracy here was to result in a split in which the Hibernians went out and the artists remained.[105]

This is a telling admission; but it was too much and too late.

For his part, Yeats came to realize that Russell's attacks, though sometimes spiteful, were fundamentally well-intentioned in that they grew out of his anxiety for his art. Writing to his father on 10 October 1909, he declared:

> I am still reading Balzac. I have only four or five of the forty volumes left

to read. How he hates a vague man — there is a certain poet in one of his books, Canalis by name, who is Russell without Russell's honest heart.[106]

Though he was often irritated by the vagueness, especially when it took the form of a woolly benevolence that sheltered inferior art, Yeats was always vulnerable to the goodwill and integrity that were Russell's 'honest heart'.

CONCLUSION

'BUT FRIENDSHIP NEVER ENDS'

'I must face all my associations, merely stating at the outset that my hatred has won the right to call itself friendship.'—
                        Yeats of Russell's *Song and Its Fountains*

'One of [Russell's] favourite quotations was a phrase from *The Three Musketeers*—'I perceive if we do not kill one another we shall be great friends!'   —Frank O'Connor

    The bitter quarrels about forming the Theatre Society into a professional company and the controversy over *The Playboy* brought the first phase of Yeats's and Russell's literary association to an end, and caused a coolness to settle on their friendship. For about five years their relations with one another were polite but strained. The rekindling of their mutual regard and their patronage of the younger writers who were attracted to the literary movement is a separate story and will be told elsewhere.

    For Yeats, the break with Russell was one episode in a long-standing quarrel with nationalist Dublin, with what he was contemptuously to call 'the daily spite of this unmannerly town'.[1] Beginning with his battles in the theatre, it was to continue until the Easter Uprising of 1916, when the heroism of some of the nationalists he most despised moved him to declare that his view of them was 'all changed, changed utterly'.[2] Throughout this time, for what he was to categorize in his *Autobiographies* as his *Estrangement* and describe in one of his poems as 'fifteen many-times-troubled years',[3] he was both besieger and besieged. On the one front he fought the nationalists over the freedom of the Theatre and the integrity of Synge's plays, while on another he declared war on the Establishment. He defied the Castle when they banned George Bernard Shaw's *The Showing Up of Blanco Posnet*, and he attacked the Dublin Corporation and the National Gallery over the Lane Bequest. The Ireland of his poems from this time is a 'blind bitter land',[4] a 'fool-driven land',[5] peopled by myopic niggards who have betrayed their heritage.

> What need you, being come to sense.
> But fumble in a greasy till
> And add the halfpence to the pence
> And prayer to shivering prayer, until
> You have dried the marrow from the bone?
> For men were born to pray and save:
> Romantic Ireland's dead and gone,
> It's with O'Leary in the grave.[6]

In part this truculence was the result of attacks on Yeats and his friends, but it was also in part deliberately assumed as a necessary element in the new aesthetic he had begun to forge for himself in the nineteen-hundreds. Having shed 'youth's dreamy load',[7] he also felt the need to slough off the softness of his middle years. He wanted to write poetry that was shaped by conflict and hardened by contempt, that took its stance from Nietzsche, Synge and Castiglione. Coupled with this was an urge to protect the literary movement against the timid morality of the emerging Catholic middle class and what seemed to him to be the well-intentioned but etiolating mediocrity of Russell and his friends.[8]

Set over against this truculence, and yet in its own way equally preventing an early reconciliation of the two men, was Russell's temporary indifference to the literary movement. He felt he had more important work to do than to trade criticisms with Yeats. Between his appointment to the editorship of the *Irish Homestead* in 1905 and the outbreak of the First World War, when agricultural production was reorganized, he poured all of his considerable energies into the co-operative movement. The titles of his principal new publications from this time, *The Building Up of a Rural Civilization* (1910) and *Co-operation and Nationality* (1912), clearly indicate the focus of his attention. These years were also among the most difficult for the co-operative movement. Following the defeat of the Labour Party in the 1906 General Election, Plunkett was forced to resign his post in the Department of Agriculture, with the result that he was no longer able to oversee the system of subsidies he had arranged for operating the I.A.O.S. His successor, T. W. Russell, who believed that co-operation was merely a cover for a 'conspiracy of conniving landlords, gentry, clergy and industrialists',[9] gradually phased out the subsidies, so that from '1909 to 1913 the I.A.O.S. was dependent entirely on its own resources and was kept going only through the generosity of Plunkett and his friends'.[10] One of his most valuable allies was Russell, who week after week produced his fifteen columns of journalism for the *Homestead* and who relished attacking his namesake from the Department, especially when, as was generally the case, he was in a position of moral superiority.[11]

His defence of co-operation mired him in politics and took a heavy toll on his energies and time. Even his reconciliation with Yeats was brought about by politics rather than literature. They both supported the Irish Transport and General Workers Union in their fight with a cartel of some 400 employers led by William Martin Murphy who locked out their 24,000 employees for almost five months. At the height of the struggle, Russell wrote to his old friend:

> *Irish Homestead*
> [5 November 1913]
>
> My dear Yeats,
> Please let me congratulate you on your speech at the Peace Meeting and above all on your article in *The Irish Worker*. I have differed from you in many things but I felt all my old friendship and affection surging up as I read what you said. It falls on us to make a fight for social and intellectual freedom. I have a long battle before me and the Church is raging against me over Ireland and is trying to make my continuance in the co-operative movement an impossibility, and I am glad to see that you, Gwynn, Seamus [sic] O'Sullivan, Stephens are all on the same side in life. Please accept my assurance of my deep regard.
>
> Yours sincerely,
> AE.[12]

Yeats accepted the offer and the friendship was restored.

In the main it was the 'deep regard' which they felt for one another that carried their literary association through almost a quarter of a century. It was deep because it reached back to the time when they were art students in Dublin and enthusiastically admired one another's genius. Russell immediately came under the spell of Yeats's poetry, and remained enchanted all his life; Yeats was fascinated by Russell's visionary powers and continually won over by his goodness and integrity. 'I constantly quarrelled with him', he once confided to a friend, 'but he never bore malice'.[13] Their regard for one another was also deep because it was founded on a sense of common purpose, an urge to create, whether through poetry, prose, drama, oratory, arcane religion or better farming, a new conception of what it meant to be Irish. As Yeats once explained to Lady Dorothy Wellesley: 'AE was my oldest friend — we began our work together.'[14] The conviction that they were working together, which was celebrated in the several dedications they addressed to one another and made public through their collaboration on a wide range of issues, consistently proved stronger than any single quarrel that threatened to divide them. Not that their ambitions for Ireland were identical; but there was sufficient common ground to sustain a long and rich association. Finally, their regard for one another was as deep as it was because each, in spite of the influence exerted by the other, preserved his own integrity. Their individuality drew them together while ensuring their separateness. Russell always remained a little in awe of Yeats. Yeats found himself unable to incorporate Russell into his symbology to the same extent as he had Synge and Lady Gregory.

And yet Russell felt he had only maintained his individuality within the association at a cost to his personal imaginative development. His self-induced 'dread that a nature more formidable and powerful' than his own would lead him away from his own 'will and centre' caused him to limit himself too severely. Hedged in by his anxiety about the distorting effect of Yeats's influence, he found himself unable to give the full range of his interests free and rewarding play. Had he, for example, begun to write poetry while in the company of a less forceful personality he might have been less concerned to assert the distinctiveness of his voice and more at ease with a variety of subjects and stances. As the early friend of Yeats, Russell too readily became AE. His failure as a poet to advance beyond the delicate verse of *Homeward: Songs by the Way*, his sedulous yet indiscriminate encouragement of younger writers, and his unquestioning preoccupation with the spiritual life owed much to his dread that he would be overwhelmed by Yeats's influence.

The other major effect on his life, his entanglement with the practicalities of co-operation, for which Yeats openly admitted culpability, would probably have taken place, though perhaps for some other end, even if the two men had never met. True mystics are hard-headed people who willingly put their spirituality to the service of others. Yeats's introducing him to Plunkett and persuading him to accept a post with the I.A.O.S. might have prevented Russell from emigrating to America, but the same ability and force that took him from Pim's to Plunkett House would have also taken him from Point Loma to Washington. Though it is possible to argue that his association with Yeats changed the whole course of his life, no man goes out to meet what is not in some measure already a part of himself.

Yeats saw Russell as a generous friend and ally: in their youth as a fellow Romantic who gave him unstinted encouragement and who was also in revolt against the drabness of Victorian actuality; in their middle years as a Celt and fellow-believer in the world of

Fairy; and in their old age as an equally prominent citizen of the Republic which they had in part helped to create.

Yet in the end, as Yeats himself realized, some types of friendship resist exhaustive analysis and defy complete description.

> but friendship never ends;
> And what if mind seem changed,
> And it seem changed with the mind,
> When thoughts rise up unbid
> On generous things that he did
> And I grow half contented to be blind![15]

While there was an antagonism that bound Yeats and Russell together as dear friends there was also a friendship that overcame all the antagonism.

NOTES

CHAPTER I: ALLIES IN REVOLT

1. Metropolitan School of Art, Index Register. W.B. Yeats, *Autobiographies* (1955; rpt. London: Macmillan, 1970) p. 80. Hereafter Yeats, *Autobiographies*. The Art Schools were not called The Metropolitan School of Art until 1887.
2. James Stephens, *The Charwoman's Daughter* (1912; rpt. Dublin and London: Scepter, 1966), p. 27.
3. Sir William Orpen, *Stories of Old Ireland and Myself* (London: Williams and Norgate, 1924), p. 79.
4. Yeats, *Autobiographies*, pp. 240-241. George Moore, *Salve* (London: Heinemann, 1912), pp. 29-30. Hereafter Moore, *Salve*.
5. Alan Denson, *John Hughes: A Documentary Biography, With Letters* (Kendal, 1969), pp. 34-38. Henry Summerfield, *That Myriad-Minded Man: A Biography of George William Russell 'A.E.' 1867-1935* (Gerrards Cross: Colin Smythe, 1975), p. 4. Hereafter Summerfield, *Russell*.
6. Yeats, *Autobiographies*, pp. 240-241. Moore, *Salve*, pp. 29-30.
7. Frank O'Connor, 'Two Friends: Yeats and AE'. *Yale Review*, XXIX, 1939, p. 68. 'He produced abundantly, effortlessly, and yet seemed to find no real delight in his work because picture, essay, poem, created without the anguish of the artist, left an unsatisfied creative urge, and he can never have known the utter emptiness of the artist who exhausts himself in one supreme effort. . . .' Hereafter O'Connor, 'Two Friends'.
8. Yeats, *Autobiographies*, pp. 240-241.
9. Ibid., p. 115. William M. Murphy, *Prodigal Father: The Life of John Butler Yeats (1839-1922)* (New York: Cornell University Press, 1978), p. 78. Hereafter Murphy, *Prodigal Father*. Cf. Oscar Wilde, 'The Decay of Lying', in G.F. Maine, ed., *The Works of Oscar Wilde* (London: Collins, 1949), p. 916. 'The popular cry of our time is "Let us return to Life and Nature; they will recreate Art for us. . . ."'
10. Murphy, *Prodigal Father*, pp. 81-82.
11. Ibid., p. 81.
12. Ibid., p. 79. For Yeats's and Russell's opinions of art training in Dublin see *Report of the Committee of Inquiry into the Work Carried on by The Royal Hibernian Academy and The Metropolitan School of Art, Dublin* (Dublin: H.M.S.O., 1906), pp. 60-61.
13. Clifford Bax, *Inland Far: A Book of Thoughts and Impressions* (London: Lovat Dickinson, 1933), p. 41. 'When I had risen to go, I paused for a moment to look closely at four or five little pictures, visionary in subject and like enamel in the brilliance of their colour. "I did them", said Yeats, "when I was at the Art School in Dublin."'
14. Joseph Hone, *W. B. Yeats* (1943; rpt. Harmondsworth: Penguin, 1971), p. 42. Hereafter Hone, *Yeats*. Cf. *The Irish Book Lover*, V, 214, where Yeats is reported saying: 'When I was 20 the romantic movement was dying away. You saw it in your clothes, you heard it in your accents. I alone made a protest in the form of loose neck-ties.'

15 Peter Alt and Russell K. Alspach, eds., *The Variorum Edition of The Poems of W.B. Yeats* (1956; rpt. New York: Macmillan, 1973), p. 65. Hereafter Yeats, *Poems*.
16 Ibid., p. 66.
17 Ibid., p. 73.
18 Ibid., p. 65.
19 Ibid., p. 87.
20 A.E., 'Literature and Life. The Youth of a Poet', *The Irish Statesman*, 17 October 1925, pp. 176-177.
21 O'Connor, 'Two Friends', p. 66.
22 Allan Wade, ed., *The Letters of W. B. Yeats* (London: Rupert Hart-Davis, 1954), pp. 389-390. Yeats to Lady Gregory, 12 December 1902. Hereafter Yeats, *Letters*. The poems were reprinted in *The Irish Homestead* Christmas Number for 1901 and for 1902.
23 Yeats, *Poems*, p. 751.
24 Ibid., p. 708.
25 Ibid., p. 708.
26 O'Connor, 'Two Friends', p. 66.
27 W. B. Yeats, *Essays and Introductions* (1961; rpt. London: Macmillan, 1971), p. 413. Hereafter Yeats, *Essays and Introductions*.
28 A.E., *The Candle of Vision* (London: Macmillan, 1918), p. 16. Hereafter A.E., *The Candle of Vision*.
29 Alan Denson, ed., *Letters from AE* (London: Abelard-Schuman, 1961), p. 280. Hereafter Russell, *Letters*. George Moore, *Ave* (London: Heinemann, 1911), pp. 157-158. Hereafter Moore, *Ave*.
30 A.E., *The Candle of Vision*, p. 4.
31 Ibid., p. 75.
32 Ibid., p. 4.
33 Ibid., pp. 5-6.
34 A.E., *Song and Its Fountains* (London: Macmillan, 1932), p. 15. Hereafter A.E., *Song and Its Fountains*.
35 Yeats, *Essays and Introductions*, p. 413.
36 Yeats, *Autobiographies*, p. 78.
37 George Mills Harper and Walter K. Hood, eds., *A Critical Edition of Yeats's A Vision (1925)* (London: Macmillan, 1978), pp. xi-xxvi. Hereafter Yeats, *A Vision* (A).
38 Yeats, *Autobiographies*, p. 242.
39 Yeats, *Essays and Introductions*, p. 412. Cf. Monk Gibbon, *The Masterpiece and the Man: Yeats as I Knew Him* (New York: Macmillan, 1959), p. 53. Hereafter, Gibbon, *Yeats*.
40 Sir William Orpen, *Stories of Old Ireland and Myself*, p. 24. Moore, *Salve*, p. 29 is incorrect.
41 Yeats, *Autobiographies*, p. 243.
42 Yeats, *Essays and Introductions*, p. 413.
43 'A.Se.', 'Theosophy', in *Encyclopedia Britannica: A Dictionary of Arts, Sciences, and General Literature*, 9th ed. (Edinburgh: Adam and Charles Black, 1888), XXIII, pp. 278-279.
44 A. P. Sinnett, *The Occult World* (London: Trübner, 1881), pp. 49 ff.
45 Ibid., p. 87. See also H. P. Blavatsky, *Isis Unveiled: A Master-Key to the Mysteries of Ancient and Modern Science and Theology*, 6th ed. (New York: Bouton; London: Quaritch, 1901), lv: 'We believe in no Magic which transcends; the scope and capacity of the human mind, nor in "miracle", whether divine or diabolical, if such imply a transgression of the laws of nature instituted from

all eternity. Nevertheless, we accept ... that the human heart has not yet fully uttered itself, and that we have never attained or even understood the extent of its powers.' Hereafter Blavatsky, *Isis Unveiled*.

46 Bryan Wilson, *Religious Sects* (London: Weidenfeld and Nicolson, 1970), pp. 157-158.
47 H. P. Blavatsky, *The Secret Doctrine: The Synthesis of Science, Religion and Philosophy* (London: The Theosophical Pub. Co., 1888), I, pp. 231-232. Hereafter Blavatsky, *The Secret Doctrine*.
48 A. P. Sinnett, *Esoteric Buddhism*, 7th ed. (New York: Houghton, Mifflin, 1887), pp. 99-102.
49 Murphy, *Prodigal Father*, p. 137. Ernest A. Boyd, *Ireland's Literary Renaissance* (Dublin: Maunsel, 1916), p. 213 says that Yeats first heard about Sinnett's books from Prof. Edward Dowden. Hereafter Boyd, *Literary Renaissance*.
50 Richard Ellmann, *Yeats: The Man and the Masks*. 2nd ed. (1949: London: Macmillan, 1969), p. 63. Hereafter Ellmann, *Man and Masks*.
51 National Library of Ireland, MS.9967-9969, 'Letters from George William Russell (AE), Selected, Transcribed and Edited by Alan Denson'. Hereafter Denson, MS followed by call number, letter number, name of addressee, and date. Denson, MS.9967, 7, to C. C. Coates, n.d. Blavatsky later wrote in *The Secret Doctrine*, I, p. 160: 'Esoteric Buddhism ... is an excellent book, and has done still more excellent work. But this does not alter the fact that it contains some mistaken notions, and that it has led many Theosophists and lay-readers to form an erroneous conception of the Secret Eastern Doctrines. Moreover, it seems, perhaps, a little too materialistic.' See also G. W. Russell, *The Irish Statesman*, III, 504.
52 Denson, MS.9967, 5, to C.C. Coates, n.d. Cf. Moore, *Ave*, p. 159. See also Denson MS.9967, 5, 8, 10, 22.
53 Ibid., 5, to C.C. Coates, n.d.
54 Monk Gibbon, ed., *The Living Torch A.E.* (New York: Macmillan, 1938), p. 45. Hereafter Gibbon, ed., *Living Torch*.
55 Yeats, *Autobiographies*, pp. 90-91. Yeats says that Johnston was vexed by his 'lack of zeal.'
56 Quoted in A. N. Jeffares, *W. B. Yeats: Man and Poet*, 2nd ed. (London: Routledge and Kegan Paul, 1962), p. 59. Hereafter Jeffares, *Man and Poet*.
57 Yeats, *Autobiographies*, p. 26.
58 Ibid., pp. 60, 79, 115-116.
59 W. B. Yeats, *A Vision*, 2nd ed. (1937; rpt. London: Macmillan, 1969), p. 8. Hereafter Yeats, *A Vision* (B).
60 A.E., 'Some Characters of the Irish Literary Movement', unpublished lecture quoted in Monk Gibbon, 'The Early Years of George Russell (AE) and His Connection with the Theosophical Movement', Diss. Dublin, 1947-1948, p. 67. Hereafter Gibbon, *Thesis*. See also Yeats, *Essays and Introductions*, p. 101. '[I] remember the time when, as my nurse used to tell me, herons built their nests in old men's beards.'
61 H. B. Bachchan, *W. B. Yeats and Occultism* (Delhi: Motilal Banarsidass, 1965), pp. 66-68. Hereafter Bachchan.
62 Yeats, *Poems*, p. 74. See also Bachchan, pp. 63-69; Fahmy F. Farag, 'Oriental Mysticism in W. B. Yeats', Diss., Edinburgh, 1960, p. 63. Hereafter Farag, *Thesis*.
63 Yeats, *Letters*, p. 211, to John O'Leary, 23 July 1892.
64 Ibid., p. 63, to Katharine Tynan, 14 March [1888].
65 Quoted in *The United Irishman: A National Weekly Review*, p. 5, col. 3, 5 April 1902. Hereafter *The United Irishman*.

66 Jeffares, *Man and Poet*, pp. 24, 38-39; Summerfield, *Russell*, p. 10.
67 John Eglinton, *A Memoir of AE: George William Russell* (London: Macmillan, 1937), p. 10. Hereafter Eglinton, *Memoir*.
68 Hone, *Yeats*, pp. 46-47.
69 George Mills Harper, ed., *Yeats and The Occult* (London: Macmillan, 1976), p. 12. Hereafter Harper, ed., *Yeats and The Occult*.
70 Hone, *Yeats*, p. 46.
71 Summerfield, *Russell*, p. 10.
72 Gibbon, *Thesis*, p. 48.
73 Russell, *Letters*, p. 3, to C. C. Coates, n.d. See also Ellmann, *Man and Masks*, p. 48; Yeats, *Letters*, pp. 117-118.
74 Denson, MS.9967, 7, to C.C. Coates, n.d.
75 Gibbon, *Thesis*, p. 48. The mushroom theme appeared in one of Russell's Ely Place frescoes. See John P. Frayne and Colton Johnson eds., *Uncollected Prose by W. B. Yeats: Reviews, Articles and Other Miscellaneous Prose 1897-1939* (London: Macmillan, 1975), p. 111. Hereafter Yeats, *Uncollected Prose*, II.
76 Denson, MS.9967, 7, to C. C. Coates, n.d.
77 Ellmann, *Man and Masks*, p. 42.
78 John Symonds, *Madame Blavatsky Medium and Magician* (London: Odhams, 1959), pp. 177-179. The Hermetic Lodge of the Theosophical Society was formed on 9 April 1884.
79 Yeats, *Letters*, pp. 591-592, to Ernest Boyd, 20 January 1915. Cf. W. B. Yeats, *Mythologies* (London: Macmillan, 1959), p. 12, where Yeats wrote of Russell when he was 26 years old that he seemed 'scarce more than a boy'. Hereafter Yeats, *Mythologies*.
80 Denson MS.9967, 5, to C.C. Coates, n.d.
81 John P. Frayne, ed., *Uncollected Prose by W. B. Yeats: First Reviews and Articles. 1886-1896* (London: Macmillan, 1970), p. 337. Hereafter Yeats, *Uncollected Prose*, I. See also Yeats, *Letters*, pp. 344-345, to Lady Gregory, 2 June, 1900.
82 Summerfield, *Russell*, p. 22. Yeats, *Autobiographies*, p. 468. Russell lent a copy of *Light on the Path* to one of his fellow students at the art schools, who returned it with the witty comment: 'You will drift into a penumbra'. For Russell's analysis of *Light on the Path* see Denson MS.9967, 3 and 8. Mabel Collins was expelled from the Theosophical Society in 1889. See Allan Wade, ed., *Some Letters from W. B. Yeats to John O'Leary and His Sister: From Originals in the Berg Collection* (New York: New York Public Library, 1953), p. 8, to John O'Leary, 7 May 1889. Hereafter Wade, ed., *Letters to O'Leary*.
83 Denson, MS.9967, 17, to C. C. Coates, n.d.
84 Richard Ellmann, *The Identity of Yeats*, 2nd ed. (1964; rpt. London: Faber and Faber, 1968), p. 55. Hereafter Ellmann, *Identity*.
85 Yeats, *Poems*, p. 147.
86 Ellmann, *Man and Masks*, p. 19.
87 Quoted in Louis MacNeice, *The Poetry of W. B. Yeats*, 2nd ed. (1967; rpt. London: Faber and Faber, 1970), p. 84. Hereafter MacNeice, *Yeats*.
88 Yeats, *Letters*, p. 31, to Frederick Gregg, n.d.
89 Yeats, *Autobiographies*, p. 90.
90 Yeats, *Essays and Introductions*, p. 65.
91 Ellmann, *Man and Masks*, pp. 63-64, 305-306. See also Anon., *Dublin University Review*, I, August 1885, p. 66.
92 Ibid. p. 64.
93 Anon., *The Irish Theosophist*, III, 81, 15 February 1895, gives an explanation of the study method favoured by the Theosophists. 'Each Branch forms itself

into sections for the purpose of studying a certain subject. ... When the study is completed the sections compare notes, and produce, subsequently, a general statement of decisions on which they can all agree.'
94 Denson MS.9967, 8, to C. C. Coates. 31 October 1887.
95 Summerfield, *Russell*, p. 292.
96 Russell, *Letters*, pp. 6-9, to H. P. Blavatsky, 6 November 1888.
97 J. Hastings, ed., *The Encyclopedia of Religion and Ethics* (Edinburgh: T. T. Clark, 1920), XI, pp. 185-189. Buchchan, pp. 18-72. Francis V. Catalina, *A Study of the Self Concept of Sankhya-Yoga Philosophy* (Delhi: Munshiran Manoharal, 1968), pp. 1-55.
98 W. B. Yeats, 'The Way of Wisdom', *The Speaker*, 14 April 1900, p. 40.
99 Yeats, *Autobiographies*, pp. 91-92.
100 Farag, *Thesis*, pp. 57-64. The poems Farag lists are: 'Kanva on Himself', 'The Priest and the Fairy', 'Fergus and the Druid', 'Mohini Chatterjee', and 'The Indian upon God'. Bachchan, pp. 24-62 adds 'The Song of the Happy Shepherd', and 'Anashuya and Vijaya' to this list, and argues that 'Ephemera', 'He thinks of his Past Greatness when a Part of the Constellations of Heaven', 'The Three Hermits', 'Meditations in Time of Civil War', 'All Souls' Night', and 'At Algeciras — A Meditation upon Death' contain passages which reveal the influence of the philosophy of Sankara. Yeats told T. Sturge Moore that he 'believed [Sankara] until Blake drove it out of [his] head'. Ursula Bridge, ed., *W. B. Yeats and T. Sturge Moore: Their Correspondence, 1901-1937* (London: Routledge and Kegan Paul, 1953), pp. 67-69. Hereafter Yeats, *Correspondence with Moore*.
101 Mohini M. Chatterjee, 'The Common Sense of Theosophy', *Dublin University Review*, I, 396. See also Denis Donoghue, ed., *Memoirs: Autobiography First Draft. Journal* (London: Macmillan, 1972), p. 282. Hereafter Yeats, *Memoirs*.
102 Summerfield, *Russell*, p. 16. Moore, *Salve*, p. 30 is misleading. For Moore's encounter with Mohini see *Ave*, pp. 244-245.
103 Owen Thomas, ed., *Walden and Civil Disobedience* (New York: Norton, 1966), p. 197.
104 Denson, MS.9967, 7, to C. C. Coates, n.d.
105 Denson, MS.9969, 480, to Sean O'Faolain, [? April/May 1929].
106 Ibid., 547, to Sean O'Faolain, 22 April 1932.
107 Denson, MS.9967, 93, to T. B. Mosher, 26 October 1901.
108 Ibid., 146, to Clifford Bax, 4 July 1905.
109 Unpublished letter to Charles Weekes in writer's possession, 14 December 1926. See also Grace E. Jameson, 'Mysticism in AE, and Yeats in Relation to Oriental and American Thought', Diss., Ohio State, 1932, pp. 46-47; Russell, *Song and Its Fountains*, p. 76.
110 F. Max Müller, trans., *The Upanisads*, 2 pts. (1879; New York: Dover, 1962) I, p. 80. Hereafter Müller, *Upanisads*.
111 Denson, MS.9968, 251, to Edward MacLysaght, [November 1914]: 'I have often carried pictures in my head for years and things remembered from boyhood come sometimes to find expression in my poetry. I remember when 10 years old seeing the smoke rising straight high up in the air from villages in County Sligo and I noticed how far up the pillars of smoke broke and mingled.'
112 A.E., *Homeward: Songs by the Way*, 4th ed. (1894; London and New York: John Lane, 1908), p. 25. Hereafter A.E., *Homeward*.
113 Müller, *Upanisads*, II, p. 178. A.E., *Homeward*, p. 51.
114 Ibid., II, pp. 19, 163-165. A.E., *Homeward*, p. 42.
115 Ibid., II, p. 36. A.E., *Homeward*, p. 35.

116 Ibid., II, pp. 12, 13. A.E., *Homeward*, p. 61.
117 Ibid., I, p. 132; II, p. 86.
118 Ibid., I, pp. xxiii-xxvi, II, p. 283.
119 Ibid., II, p. 251.
120 Ibid., I, p. 148. A.E., *Homeward*, p. 63.
121 Ibid., I, pp. 210, 260, 278, 284; II, 20. A.E., *Homeward*, p. 64.
122 Yeats, *Uncollected Prose*, I, p. 380.
123 Benjamin Jowett, trans., *The Dialogues of Plato*. 4 vols. (1871; rpt., London; Sphere Books, 1970), II, pp. 263-265.
124 A.E., *Homeward*, p. 31.
125 W. B. Yeats, ed., *The Oxford Book of Modern Verse* (Oxford: The Clarendon Press, 1936), p. xl.
126 Bachchan, pp. 36-42 has argued that Yeats's play, *Where There is Nothing* (later *The Unicorn from the Stars*), shows the influence of Sankara. He and F. A. C. Wilson have also pointed out that *The Herne's Egg* reveals a debt to the *Upanishads*. Bachchan, pp. 185-206; F. A. C. Wilson, *W. B. Yeats and Tradition* (1958; rpt. London: Methuen, 1968), pp. 95-96.
127 Shree Purohit Swami and W. B. Yeats, trans., *The Ten Principal Upanishads* (1937; rpt. London: Faber and Faber, 1971), p. 9. Hereafter Yeats, trans., *Upanishads*. See Hone, pp. 462-463. Yeats's assertion that he had 'fed upon the philosophy of *The Upanishads* all [his] life' is an exaggeration.
128 Ibid., pp. 7-8. Cf. Müller's apology in his Preface. Müller *Upanisads*, I, p. xxviii: 'If therefore the reader finds some of these translations rather rugged . . . let him feel sure that the translator has had to deal with a choice of evils, and that when the choice lay between sacrificing idiom or truth, he has chosen the smaller evil of the two.' See also Dorothy Wellesley, ed., *Letters on Poetry from W. B. Yeats to Dorothy Wellesley*, (London: Oxford University Press, 1940), p. 65. Hereafter Yeats, *Letters to Dorothy Wellesley*.
129 Denson, MS.9967, 8, to C. C. Coates, 31 October 1887.
130 Yeats, *Poems*, p. 66.
131 Yeats, *Essays and Introductions*, pp. 429, 513-514.
132 W. B. Yeats, *Wheels and Butterflies* (London: Macmillan, 1934), p. 136.
133 Horace Reynolds, ed., *Letters to the New Island: by William Butler Yeats* (1940; rpt. London: Oxford University Press, 1970), p. 204. Hereafter Yeats, *New Island*. See also Yeats, *Poems*, pp. 610-611.
134 E. J. Ellis and W. B. Yeats, ed., *The Works of William Blake, Poetic, Symbolic, and Critical*. 3 vols. (1893; rpt. New York: A.M.S., 1973), I, p. 235. Hereafter Yeats, ed., *Blake*.
135 Yeats, *Essays and Introductions*, p. 179.
136 Ibid., pp. 513-517.

CHAPTER II: BREAKING THE SPELL

1 Herbert Howarth, in *The Irish Writers 1880-1940: Literature under Parnell's Star* (London: Rockliff, 1958), p. 168, points out that 'A.E. . . . suffered from a fear . . . that his growth might be touched and altered by another person. . . . He became the hater of everything that appears to change the inner man, including alcohol, and physical love, and great poverty, and great wealth, and magisterial authority, and ecclesiastical authority. . . . His type is anxious for

the inner self as if it were frail, and develops it strongly in reaction to the fear.' Hereafter Howarth, *Irish Writers*. See also Yeats, *Letters to Dorothy Wellesley*, p. 13.

2 Richard J. Finneran, George Mills Harper, William M. Murphy, eds., *Letters to W. B. Yeats*. 2 vols. (London: Macmillan, 1977), II, pp. 573-574, to W. B. Yeats, 14 June 1935. Hereafter Finneran, ed., *Letters to Yeats*.
3 Katharine Tynan, *Memories* (London: Nash and Grayson, 1924), p. 276; Katharine Tynan, *Twenty-five Years; Reminiscences* (London: Smith, Elder, 1913), pp. 140-143. Hereafter Tynan, *Twenty-five Years*. See also Yeats, *Uncollected Prose*, I, p. 21.
4 Dominic Daly, *The Young Douglas Hyde* (Dublin: Irish University Press, 1974), p. 55. Hereafter Daly, *Hyde*.
5 Ibid., p. 69.
6 Quoted in Murphy, *Prodigal Father*, p. 140.
7 Hone, *Yeats*, p. 46.
8 On Russell's stuttering see A.E., *Song and Its Fountains*, pp. 51, 52, 119.
9 Murphy, *Prodigal Father*, pp. 140-144.
10 Daly, *Hyde*, p. 92.
11 Ibid., p. 88.
12 Ibid., pp. 57, 87, 88, 92.
13 Yeats, *Uncollected Prose*, I, pp. 115-119.
14 Yeats, *Essays and Introductions*, p. 510.
15 Yeats, *Letters*, p. 37.
16 John O'Leary, *Recollections of Fenians and Fenianism*. 2 vols. (Shannon: Irish University Press), 1969, II, p. 25. Hereafter O'Leary, *Recollections*.
17 Russell, *Letters*, pp. 5-6, to Katharine Tynan, [December 1887].
18 Daly, *Hyde*, p. 88.
19 Colin Meir, *The Ballads and Songs of W. B. Yeats: The Anglo-Irish Heritage in Subject and Style* (London: Macmillan, 1974), p. 1. Hereafter Meir, *Ballads and Songs*.
20 Yeats, *New Island*, p. 75.
21 Yeats, *Uncollected Prose*, I, pp. 241-242.
22 Ibid., p. 21. Murphy, *Prodigal Father*, p. 146.
23 Yeats, *Poems*, p. 844. Yeats, *Autobiographies*, p. 153. Yeats, *Essays and Introductions*, pp. 3-12, 510-511.
24 Yeats, *Uncollected Prose*, I, pp. 147-162.
25 Wade, ed., *Letters to O'Leary*, p. 41. Only 275 copies of the first issue were sold, involving Yeats in a loss of about ten shillings.
26 Yeats, *Uncollected Prose*, I, p. 162.
27 Yeats, *Essays and Introductions*, p. 510.
28 Yeats, *Uncollected Prose*, I, p. 326.
29 See Samuel Hynes, 'Yeats and the Poets of the Thirties' in R. J. Porter and J. D. Brophy, eds., *Modern Irish Literature: Essays in Honour of William York Tindall* (New York: Iona College Press, 1972), pp. 1-22. Cf Yeats's approach to the legends. Yeats, *Letters*, p. 98, to Katharine Tynan, 21 December [1888]: 'I do not mean that we should not go to old ballads and poems for inspiration, but we should search them for new methods of expressing ourselves.'
30 Yeats, *New Island*, p. 157.
31 Yeats, *Essays and Introductions*, p. 256.
32 Ibid., p. 256. Yeats, *Uncollected Prose*, I, pp. 215-216. Note Yeats, *Letters*, p. 139, to Katharine Tynan [circa 10 October 1889]: 'Much may depend in the future on Ireland now developing writers who know how to formulate in clear

expressions the vague feelings now abroad — to formulate them for Ireland's, not for England's, use.'
33 Yeats, *Autobiographies*, p. 102.
34 Yeats, *Uncollected Prose*, I, p. 159.
35 Ibid., pp. 161-162.
36 Yeats, *New Island*, pp. 168-173.
37 Yeats, *Uncollected Prose*, I, p. 363. Yeats, *Essays and Introductions*, p. 256.
38 Ibid., p. 105. See Philip L. Marcus, *Yeats and the Beginning of the Irish Renaissance* (Ithaca and London: Cornell University Press, 1970), pp. 10-11. Hereafter cited as Marcus. In the late 'eighties Yeats tried to follow Davis, but after 1892, when he saw Davis's influence was stronger than he had supposed, he began to attack Young Ireland.
39 Yeats, *Uncollected Prose*, I, pp. 359-364, 366-373, 375-382, 382-387, and W. B. Yeats, ed., *A Book of Irish Verse* (London: Methuen, 1895). Hereafter Yeats, ed., *Irish Verse* (A). W. B. Yeats, ed., *A Book of Irish Verse* (London: Methuen, 1900). Hereafter Yeats, ed., *Irish Verse* (B).
40 Yeats, *Essays and Introductions*, p. x. See also Yeats, *Uncollected Prose*, II, p. 509.
41 Marcus, p. 67.
42 A.E., *Imaginations and Reveries* (Dublin: Maunsel, 1915), p. ix. Hereafter A.E., *Imaginations and Reveries*. Cf. Yeats, *Autobiographies*, p. 240: 'Russell . . . refused to join my National Literary Society, because the party of Harp and Pepperpot had set limits to discussion . . .'
43 Denson, MS.9967, 125, to Stephen Gwynn, [May 1903].
44 A.E., *Imaginations and Reveries*, pp. ix-x. Cf. Yeats, *Letters*, p. 767, to Sean O'Faolain, 15 August [1929]: 'The origins of a poet are not in that which he has cast off because it is not himself, but in his own mind and in the past of literature.'
45 G.W. Russell, 'The Art of John Hughes', *New Ireland Review*, September 1898, pp. 162-165.
46 A.E., *Song and Its Fountains*, p. 99.
47 Finneran, ed., *Letters to Yeats*, II, p. 574, to W. B. Yeats, 14 June 1935. Cf. A.E., *Song and Its Fountains*, p. 94: 'Everyone . . . has some particular work to do, and to desert that and attempt the work of others, however estimable, is full of danger.'
48 See Gibbon, ed., *Living Torch*, pp. 257-258; and Dorothy M. Hoare, *The Works of Morris and of Yeats in Relation to Early Saga Literature* (Cambridge: University Press, 1937), p. 101. 'Yet A.E., who was perhaps the social mainspring of the movement, does not essentially belong to it.'
49 Denson, MS.9969, 610, to Van Wyck Brooks, 29 May 1934.
50 O'Connor, 'Two Friends', p. 66.
51 Daly, *Hyde*, pp. 92, 208.
52 Denson, MS.9967, 10, to C.C. Coates, n.d.
53 Colin Smythe, ed., *Lady Gregory. Seventy Years: The Autobiography* (Gerrards Cross: Colin Smythe, 1974) p. 311. Hereafter Gregory, *Seventy Years*.
54 Yeats, *Uncollected Prose*, II, p. 111.
55 A.E., 'Literature and Life. The Youth of a Poet', *The Irish Statesman*, 17 October 1925, pp. 176-177.
56 Yeats, trans., *Upanishads*, p. 7.
57 See Yeats, *Memoirs*, p. 19.
58 Ellmann, *Man and Masks*, p. 21. See also Yeats, *Letters*, pp. 535-536, to J. B. Yeats, 10 October 1909: 'I agree with what you wrote about Russell. I think he has set his ideal in so vague and remote a heaven that he takes the thoughts

Notes to pages 30–34

of his followers off the technique of life, or leaves only their poorer thoughts for it. No one has ever come to anything under his influence. The poets he gathers begin with a little fire but grow worse and worse.'

59 Yeats, *Autobiographies*, p. 576.
60 Denson, MS.9967, 131, to John Quinn, [24 January 1904].
61 Denson, MS.9969, 479, to W. B. Yeats, 30 April 1929.
62 Quoted in T. R. Henn, *The Lonely Tower: Studies in the Poetry of W. B. Yeats*, 2nd ed. (London: Methuen, 1965), p. 36. Hereafter Henn, *Lonely Tower*.
63 Yeats, *Autobiographies*, p. 242.
64 Evelyn Underhill, *Mysticism: A Study in the Nature and Development of Man's Spiritual Consciousness*, 12th ed. rev. (1911; London: Methuen, 1962), p. 220. Hereafter Underhill, *Mysticism*.
65 Underhill, *Mysticism*, p. 200. Note also p. 375: 'The essence of the mystic life consists in the remaking of the personality . . .'
66 Denson, MS.9967, 4, to C.C. Coates, n.d. See also Katharine Tynan, *Collected Poems* (London: Macmillan, 1930), p. vii.
67 Denson, MS.9968, 389, to Cecil French, 29 June 1922.
68 A.E, 'Literature and Life. The Youth of a Poet', *The Irish Statesman*, 17 October 1925, pp. 176-177.
69 Denson, MS.9967, 118, to W. B. Yeats, 22 December 1902.
70 Finneran, ed., *Letters to Yeats*, II, pp. 573-572, to W. B. Yeats, 14 June 1935.
71 See 'Reviews', *Irish Homestead*, XXVI, 954, 27 December 1919.
72 Russell, *Letters*, pp. 5-6, to Katharine Tynan [late December 1887].
73 Cf. C. C. Abbott, ed., *The Correspondence of Gerard Manley Hopkins and Richard Watson Dixon* (1935; 2nd imp., London: Oxford University Press, 1970), p. 14, Hopkins to Dixon, 5 October 1878: 'Tou ask, do I write verse myself. What I had written I burnt before I became a Jesuit and resolved to write no more, as not belonging to my profession . . .'
74 Denson, MS.9967, 4, to C. C. Coates, n.d.
75 Ibid., 3, to C. C. Coates, n.d.
76 Ibid., 17, to C. C. Coates, n.d. See Sinnett, *Esoteric Buddhism*, p. 54: ' "The adept", says an occult aphorism, "becomes: he is not made".'
77 Summerfield, *Russell*, p. 29.
78 Moore, *Salve*, p. 30; Eglinton, *Memoir*, p. 59. Russell's work is commended in two of the major reports on the Metropolitan School of Art. See *Science and Art Department, Metropolitan School of Art, Dublin, Annual Report and Distribution of Prizes* (Dublin: Alex Thom, 10 February 1887), 'Report for Academic Year October 1885 to July 1886', p. 15: 'Geo. W. Russell. Drawing from Life, Fair'; p. 20, listed as one of 32 'allowed to attend for free study in the Royal Hibernian Academy' as a student who had 'shown a marked ability for art pursuits'. See also *Thirty-Seventh Report of the Science and Art Department of the Committee of the Council on Education* (London: HMSO Cmd. 6056, 1890), 'For the session of 15 months ending 31 December 1889', pp. 334-345: 'Prize £2.00, to G. W. Russell for the best painting from the living model'.
79 Gregory, *Seventy Years*, p. 311.
80 Yeats, *Autobiographies*, p. 246.
81 Ibid., pp. 246-247 and Yeats, *Letters to Dorothy Wellesley*, p. 13, to Dorothy Wellesley, 26 July [1935]: 'A.E. was my oldest friend. . . . He had no passions, but as a young man had to struggle against his senses. He gave up writing poetry for a time because it stirred his senses. He wanted always to be free.'
82 Summerfield, *Russell*, p. 21.

83 Denson, MS.9967, 5, to C. C. Coates, n.d.
84 A.E., *Song and Its Fountains*, p. 17.
85 Denson, MS.9967, 3, to C. C. Coates, n.d.
86 Yeats, *New Island*, p. 174. Cf. Richard Ellmann, *James Joyce* (New York: Oxford University Press, 1959), p. 520, Joyce to Arthur Power: 'You are an Irishman and you must write in your own tradition. . . . For myself, I always write about Dublin because if I can get to the heart of Dublin I can get to the heart of all the cities of the world. In the particular is contained the universal.'
87 Note Yeats, *Letters*, p. 99, to Katharine Tynan, 21 December [1888]: 'We both of us need to substitute more and more the landscapes of nature for the landscapes of art. . . . We should make poems on the familiar landscapes we love, not the strange and rare and glittering scenes we wonder at. . . .'
88 Ibid., p. 120, to Katharine Tynan, 21 March [1889]: 'All poetry should have a local habitation when at all possible.' Cf. Yeats, *Essays and Introductions*, p. 5: 'I had a conviction, which indeed I have still, that one's verses should hold, as in a mirror, the colours of one's own climate and scenery in their right proportion.' See also Forrest Reid, *W. B. Yeats: A Critical Study* (London: Secker; New York: Dodd Mead, 1915), p. 25. Lennox Robinson, 'William Butler Yeats: Personality', in A. Norman Jeffares and K. G. W. Cross, eds., *In Excited Reverie: A Centenary Tribute to William Butler Yeats 1865-1939* (London: Macmillan, 1965), pp. 22-23. Hereafter Jeffares, ed., *In Excited Reverie*. See also Moore, *Ave*, p. 109; Yeats, *Essays and Introductions*, p. 189.
89 Robin Flower, *The Irish Tradition* (1947; rpt. London: Oxford University Press, 1978), pp. 50-51.
90 Yeats, *Poems*, p. 88.
91 Denson, MS.9967, 89, to William Byrne, [August 1901].
92 Gibbon, Letter to present writer, 24 February 1976. Cf. Joseph Ronsley, *Yeats's Autobiography: Life as Symbolic Pattern* (Cambridge: Harvard University Press; London: Oxford University Press, 1968), p. 2, quotes a lecture by Yeats entitled 'Friends of my Youth': 'Above all it is necessary that the lyric poet's life should be known that we should understand that his poetry is no rootless flower but the speech of a man.'
93 Denson, MS.9968, 396, to Monk Gibbon, 24 January 1923.
94 Monk Gibbon, *The Seals* (London: Jonathan Cape, 1935). See dust jacket.
95 Yeats, *Poems*, p. 576.
96 Yeats, *Letters*, pp. 146-147, to John O'Leary, [26 December 1889]. The book was never completed.
97 W. B. Yeats, *Reveries Over Childhood and Youth* (Dublin: The Cuala Press, 1915), p. 120.
98 See Jeffares, *Man and Poet*, p. 40.
99 Murphy, *Prodigal Father*, p. 154. Note Sean O'Faolain, 'A.E. and W.B.', *Virginia Quarterly Review*, XV, I (Winter 1939), pp. 46-47: 'A.E. did not have a father who put things endlessly to the question, fraying them away and away while insisting, in a typical Yeatsian manner, that no artist should have any opinions; a man sociable with his equals, anti-social with the masses; mischievous of mind, complex . . .'
100 Yeats, *Memoirs*, p. 31.
101 National Library of Ireland, MS. 15, 534. G. W. Russell to T. E. Russell, 26 July [1884].
102 Denson, MS.9967, 36, to W.B. Yeats, [February 1896].
103 Murphy, *Prodigal Father*, p. 154.
104 Yeats, *Memoirs*, p. 21; Richard Ellmann, *Eminent Domain* (New York: Oxford University Press), p. 10.

Notes to pages 40-43

105 Yeats, *Autobiographies*, p. 140; Murphy, *Prodigal Father*, pp. 154-157.
106 Ibid., p. 128.
107 Ibid., p. 153. Yeats, *Letters*, p. 167, to Katharine Tynan, [March 1891].
108 Yeats, *Letters*, p. 59, to Katharine Tynan, 12 February [1888]; Ibid., p. 137, to Ernest Rhys, [September 1889].
109 Yeats, *Autobiographies*, pp. 182-188.
110 See George Mills Harper, *Yeats's Golden Dawn* (London: Macmillan, 1974), pp. 6, 314-316.
111 Yeats, *New Island*, p. 143.
112 Yeats, *Letters*, pp. 218-220, to the Editor of *The Bookman*, published November 1892.
113 Yeats, *Autobiographies*, p. 121. Josephine Johnson, *Florence Farr: George Bernard Shaw's New Woman* (Gerrards Cross: Colin Smythe, 1975) pp. 35-42.
114 Yeats, *Memoirs*, p. 40.
115 Ibid., pp. 72, 85-87.
116 For example, Yeats, *Letters*, p. 138, 10 October 1889, to Katharine Tynan: '. . . I shall sell but not yet. Many things, my own and others, have to grow first.' Ibid., p. 165, to Katharine Tynan, 5 March [1891]: 'If I can get *Sherman* and my play, *The Countess Cathleen*, together with "Blake" published this year I should be well in evidence.'
117 Sean O'Faolain, *The Irish* (Harmondsworth; Penguin, 1972) pp. 131-132.
118 Eglinton, *Memoir*, pp. 184-188.
119 O'Connor, 'Two Friends', p. 75.
120 Yeats, *Letters*, p. 80, to Katharine Tynan, 25 July [1888].
121 See Daly, *Hyde*, p. 129; Yeats, *Autobiographies*, p. 218; Anon, *Irish Theosophist*, III, 86, 15 February 1895.
122 Yeats, *Letters*, pp. 111-112, to George Russell, 8 February [1889].
123 A.E., *Imaginations and Reveries*, p. 24.
124 Yeats, *Autobiographies*, p. 193.
125 Yeats, *Poems*, p. 845.
126 Yeats, *Autobiographies*, p. 114.
127 Yeats, *Poems*, p. 844.
128 Ibid., p. 138.
129 For example, D.S. Savage, 'The Aestheticism of W. B. Yeats', in *The Personal Principle: Studies in Modern Poetry* (London: Routledge and Kegan Paul, 1944), pp. 67-91.
130 MacNeice, *Yeats*, pp. 33-45, 61.
131 Austin Clarke, *The Celtic Twilight and the 'Nineties* (Dublin: The Three Candles, the Tower Series of Anglo-Irish Studies, No. 1., n.d.).
132 Yeats, *Autobiographies*, p. 190.
133 Quoted in Howarth, *Irish Writers*, p. 114.
134 Walter Pater, *The Renaissance*, 6th ed. (1873; rpt. London: Macmillan, 1907), p. 238.
135 Quoted in Ellmann, *Man and Masks*, p. 241. Note comment which Yeats makes in his review of Sophie Bryant's *Celtic Ireland* in the *Scots Observer* 4 January 1890 which may reflect his personal life: 'In the history one sees Ireland ever struggling vainly to attain some kind of unity.' Yeats, *Uncollected Prose*, I, 163.
136 Yeats, *Autobiographies*, p. 247.
137 A.E., *Song and Its Fountains*, pp. 9-11.
138 See Yeats, *Letters*, p. 165, to Katharine Tynan, 5 March 1891: 'If *Sherman* gets printed I shall be greatly pleased. There is more of myself in it than in anything I have done.'
139 Yeats, *Essays and Introductions*, p. 4.

140 See Richard Le Gallienne, ed., *The Poems of Arthur Henry Hallam, Together with his Essay on the Lyrical Poems of Alfred Tennyson* (London: Elkin Matthews and John Lane; New York: Macmillan, 1893). See also C.M. Bowra, *Memories 1898-1939* (London: Weidenfeld and Nicolson, 1966), pp. 240-241: 'There was however one book that influenced me very greatly. . . . It was the younger Hallam's essay on Tennyson [edited by Le Gallienne]. It was only the first half of the essay which influenced me. . . .' Hereafter Le Gallienne, ed., *Hallam*.

141 Reprinted in Walter Pater, *Appreciations*, 3rd. ed. (1889; rpt. London: Macmillan, 1907).

142 See Alex Preminger, ed., *Princeton Encyclopedia of Poetry and Poetics*, enlarged ed.(1965; London: Macmillan, 1975), pp. 814-817. Hereafter *Princeton Encyclopedia*.

143 Le Gallienne, ed., *Hallam*, p. 94.

144 Pater, *Appreciations*, p. 29.

145 Ibid., p. 35.

146 Russell, *Letters*, pp. 109-110, to George Moore, [6 April 1916.]

147 A.E., *Song and Its Fountains*, p. 58.

148 A.E., 'Literature and Life. The Youth of a Poet,' *The Irish Statesman*, 17 October 1925, p. 177.

149 Quoted in *Princeton Encyclopedia*, p. 814.

150 Ibid., p. 814.

151 George Moore, *Vale* (London: Heinemann, 1914) pp. 165-166.

152 Yeats, *Autobiographies*, p. 87.

153 Yeats, *Letters*, p. 145, to Katharine Tynan, [26 December 1889]; O'Connor, 'Two Friends', p. 66.

154 Murphy, *Prodigal Father*, p. 182.

155 Quoted in Ellmann, *Man and Masks*, pp. 88-89.

156 Yeats, *Memoirs*, p. 35.

157 L. A. G. Strong, 'William Butler Yeats', in Stephen Gwynn, ed., *Scattering Branches: Tributes to the Memory of W. B. Yeats* (London: Macmillan, 1940), p. 192. Hereafter Strong, 'Yeats'.

158 Russell, *Letters*, pp. 109-110, to George Moore, [6 April 1916].

159 Strong, 'Yeats', pp. 195-196.

160 Ibid., pp. 195-196. Virginia Moore, *The Unicorn: William Butler Yeats's Search for Reality* (1954; New York: Octagon, 1973), p. 241. Hereafter Moore, *The Unicorn*.

161 Yeats, *Autobiographies*, p. 138.

162 Ellmann, *Eminent Domain*, p. 16.

163 MacNeice, *Yeats*, pp. 38-39.

164 Ellmann, *Eminent Domain*, p. 16.

165 Yeats, *Autobiographies*, p. 272.

166 Ellmann, *Man and Masks*, p. 229.

167 Yeats, *Autobiographies*, p. 138.

168 Yeats, *Mythologies*, p. 335.

169 Yeats, *Autobiographies*, p. 274; Yeats, *A Vision* (A), p. 18; Yeats, *A Vision* (B), p. 94.

170 Yeats, *A Vision* (B), pp. 232-233; Yeats, *Mythologies*, p. 366; Yeats, *Autobiographies*, p. 379. See also Harper, ed., *Yeats and The Occult*, p. 85; Blavatsky, *Secret Doctrine*, II, pp. 270-271; and R.D.P. Taylor, 'The Doctrine of the Daimon in the Works of AE (George Russell) and W. B. Yeats', Diss., Manchester, 1963.

171 A.E., *Selected Poems* (London: Macmillan, 1935), pp. 160-161. Yeats included this poem in his *Oxford Book of Modern Verse*.

Notes to pages 47–54

172 Yeats, *Mythologies*, p. 336.
173 Yeats, *Autobiographies*, pp. 246-249, 457.

CHAPTER III: SELF AND SOUL

1 Underhill, *Mysticism*, p. 151.
2 Ibid., p. 71.
3 A.E. Waite, trans., Eliphas Levi, *Transcendental Magic: Its Doctrine and Ritual* (1896; Rider: London, 1972), p. 113. Hereafter Levi, *Transcendental Magic*.
4 Quoted in Blavatsky, *Isis Unveiled*, I, p. 507.
5 Underhill, *Mysticism*, p. 71.
6 Levi, *Transcendental Magic*, p. 29.
7 Ibid., pp. 93-94.
8 Ibid., pp. 56-57.
9 Stephen MacKenna, trans., *Plotinus: The Enneads*, 3rd. ed. (1927-1930; London: Faber and Faber, 1962), p. 624. [vi, 9, 10].
10 See Underhill, *Mysticism*, p. 189.
11 Ibid., p. 286.
12 Levi, *Transcendental Magic*, p. 317.
13 See Robert Hogan and Michael O'Neill, eds., *Joseph Holloway's Abbey Theatre: A Selection from his Unpublished Journal, 'Impressions of a Dublin Playgoer'* (Carbondale and Edwardsville: Southern Illinois University Press, 1967), pp. 201-202. Hereafter Holloway, *Diaries*. Murphy, *Prodigal Father*, p. 495.
14 Edward Dowden, *The Life of Percy Bysshe Shelley*, 2 vols. (London: Kegan Paul, Trench, 1886), I, pp. 30 ff.
15 Quoted in Gibbon, *Thesis*, p. 67.
16 Edith Young, *Inside Out* (London: Routledge and Kegan Paul, 1971), p. 7. Austin Clarke, *A Penny in the Clouds: More Memories of Ireland and England* (London: Routledge and Kegan Paul, 1968), p. 43. Hereafter Clarke, *Penny in the Clouds*.
17 Mary Colum, *Life and the Dream* (London: Macmillan, 1947), pp. 165-166. Hereafter Colum, *Life and Dream*. Frank O'Connor, *A Short History of Irish Literature: A Backward Look* (1967; New York: Capricorn Books, 1968), p. 165. Hereafter O'Connor, *Backward Look*. Gregory, *Seventy Years*, p. 384.
18 Lucy Kingsley Porter, ed., *AE's Letters to Mínanlábáin* (New York: Macmillan, 1937), p. 54, Russell to Porter, [23 August 1932]. Hereafter Porter, ed., *Letters to Mínanlábáin*. Forrest Reid, *Private Road* (London: Faber and Faber, 1940), pp. 130-131. Clifford Bax, *Some I Knew Well* (London: Phoenix House, 1951), p. 88.
19 Yeats, *Poems*, p. 336.
20 Yeats, *Memoirs*, p. 210.
21 See Denson, *Bibliography*, p. 113.
22 See for example, Hone, *Yeats*, pp. 73-74.
23 Denson, MS.9967, 3, to C. C. Coates, n.d; 5, to C. C. Coates, February, 1887; Yeats, *Autobiographies*, p. 90.
24 Ibid., 2, to C. C. Coates, n.d.
25 Ibid., 3, to C. C. Coates, n.d.
26 Ibid., 5, to C. C. Coates, n.d.
27 Ibid., 10, to C. C. Coates, n.d.
28 Yeats, *Autobiographies*, pp. 103-105. Tynan, *Twenty-five Years*, pp. 144, 208. George Mills Harper, *Yeats's Golden Dawn* (London: Macmillan, 1974), p. 7.

Hereafter Harper, *Golden Dawn*. This event was parodied by Edward Martyn in his five act satire, *The Dream Physician*.
29 Denson, MS.9967, 3, to C. C. Coates, n.d.
30 Russell, *Letters*, pp. 6-9, to H.P. Blavatsky, 6 November 1888, and [December 1888].
31 Yeats, *Letters*, p. 59, to Katharine Tynan, 12 February [1888].
32 Ibid., p.125, to John O'Leary, 7 May [1889].
33 Monk Gibbon, 'AE. The Years of Mystery', *Dublin Magazine*, XXXI, 21. Hereafter Gibbon, 'Years of Mystery'. Reid, *Yeats*, p. 109. The conjecture about Yeats's involvement is the present writer's.
34 Quoted in Russell, *Letters*, p. 8.
35 Dennis Wheatley, ed., *Studies in Occultism: H.P. Blavatsky* (London: Sphere Books, 1974), p. 16. A selection of articles from *Lucifer* from 1887 to 1891. Hereafter Blavatsky, *Lucifer*.
36 Yeats, *Autobiographies*, p. 173.
37 Gibbon, 'Years of Mystery', p. 20.
38 Gibbon, *Yeats*, p. 55.
39 Denson, MS.9967, 17, to C. C. Coates, [February 1891].
40 Summerfield, *Russell*, p. 28.
41 Ellmann, *Man and Masks*, p. 67.
42 Yeats, *Letters*, p. 125, to John O'Leary, 7 May [1889].
43 Denson, MS.9969, 698, to Sean O'Faolain, 10 June 1935.
44 Russell, *Letters*. pp. xxxi-xxxii.
45 Yeats, *Memoirs*, p. 24. For Yeats's opinions of Madame Blavatsky see Yeats, *Uncollected Prose*, I, pp. 298-302; Yeats, *Autobiographies*, pp. 181-182.
46 Harper, *Golden Dawn*, p. 8. Note Yeats, *Blake*, I, p. 24: 'It is possible that [Blake] received initiation into an order of Christian Kabbalists then established in London, and known as "The Hermetic Students of the Golden Dawn".'
47 Yeats, *Memoirs*, p. 27. See Gibbon, *Yeats*, p. 61.
48 Harper, *Golden Dawn*, pp. 49, 69-88, 91-99, 259-268; Harper, ed.,*Yeats and The Occult*, p. 285.
49 Mary Catherine Flannery, *Yeats and Magic: The Earlier Works* (Gerrards Cross: Colin Smythe, 1977), p. 114. Hereafter Flannery, *Yeats and Magic*.
50 Hone, *Yeats*, p. 73.
51 Yeats, *Letters*, pp. 260-263, to W. T. Horton, 13 April 1896, 30 April 1896, 5 May 1896, n.d. Yeats, *A Vision* (A), p. xv.
52 Gibbon, *Thesis*, p. 81.
53 Russell, *Letters*, p. xxxii.
54 Summerfield, *Russell*, p. 34.
55 Anon., *The Irish Theosophist*, III, 86. Darrell Figgis, *AE (George W. Russell): A Study of A Man and A Nation* (Dublin and London: Maunsel, 1916), p. 26. Hereafter Figgis, *AE*. Hone, *Yeats*, p. 47, and Yeats, *Autobiographies*, p. 249 are misleading.
56 Yeats, *Autobiographies*, p. 249.
57 Ibid., p. 242.
58 Yeats, *Memoirs*, p. 130; Yeats, *Autobiographies*, p. 249; Eglinton, *Memoir*, p. 19: 'Individuals are nothing to me, except in so far as they are manifestations of the divine life.'
59 A.E., *Selected Poems*, p. 147.
60 Yeats, *Autobiographies*, p. 236; Summerfield, *Russell*, p. 33.
61 Ibid., pp. 236-237; Summerfield, *Russell*, p. 34.
62 Summerfield, *Russell*, pp. 33-37; Eglinton, *Memoir*, pp. 16-17; Monk Gibbon, 'AE and 'The Household', *Dublin Magazine*, XXXIII, 23-31.

63 Denson MS.9967, 17, to C. C. Coates, February 1891. Yeats, *Letters*, pp. 160, 181, 183-184; Yeats, *Memoirs*, p. 54.
64 Denson MS.9967, 5, to C. C. Coates, n.d. See also Yeats, *Letters*, p. 118, to Katharine Tynan, 21 March 1889: 'I notice by your letter that you see Russell now and then. Tell him to write to me. Tell him myself and a friend are writing a book on Blake and perhaps he will send me a letter with some Blake criticisms.' See also Alan Denson, *Printed Writings by George W. Russell (AE): A Bibliography* (Evanston: Northwestern University Press, 1961), pp. 173-174. Hereafter Denson, *Bibliography*.
65 Yeats, *Blake*, I, p. 331.
66 Yeats, *Letters*, p. 184, to George Russell, [November 1891].
67 Maud Gonne, 'Yeats and Ireland', in Stephen Gwynn, ed., *Scattering Branches; Tributes to the Memory of W. B. Yeats* (London: Macmillan, 1940), p. 19.
68 Yeats, *Blake*, I, p. 20.
69 Yeats, *Letters*, p. 182, to George Russell, [15 November 1891]. Yeats, *Uncollected Prose*, I, pp. 198-202.
70 Yeats, *Uncollected Prose*, I, p. 199. Summerfield, *Russell*, p. 66. Yeats, *Letters*, pp. 154-155, to Katharine Tynan, 1 July [1890]. Ella Young, *Flowering Dusk: Things Remembered Accurately and Inaccurately* (New York and Toronto: Longmans, Green, 1945), p. 90. Hereafter Ella Young, *Flowering Dusk*.
71 See Douglas Hyde, *Beside the Fire* (London: David Nutt, 1890), pp. xxxiv-xxxvi, and Hyde's contribution to W.Y. Evans-Wentz, *The Fairy-Faith in Celtic Countries* (1911; rpt. Gerrards Cross: Colin Smythe, 1977), p. 23. Hereafter Evans-Wentz, *Fairy-Faith*. See also Yeats, *Uncollected Prose*, I, 186-190. Padraic Colum, *The Road Round Ireland* (New York: Macmillan, 1926), p. 309: 'Folk stories are differentiated from literature by the fact that they are not about private happenings, but about things and characters that a community knows about and has an abiding interest in.'
72 Curtis Bradford, *Yeats at Work* (Carbondale: Southern Illinois University Press, 1965), p. 311. *The Celtic Twilight* was reviewed anonymously in *The Irish Homestead*, VI, 588-589, 8 September 1900: 'There are many other things told of the 'visionary', who is quite the most wonderful person in the book.'
73 Denson, MS.9967, 4, to C.C. Coates, n.d.
74 Gregory, *Seventy Years*, p. 311.
75 Summerfield, *Russell*, p. 37.
76 Wade, *Bibliography*, pp. 25-28.
77 Yeats, *The Celtic Twilight* (London: A.H. Bullen, 1902), p. 18.
78 Added when Yeats was revising the essay for the 1893 edition of *The Celtic Twilight*.
79 Yeats, *Poems*, p. 261.
80 See Yeats, *Uncollected Prose*, I, p. 302.
81 Yeats, *The Celtic Twilight* (London: A.H. Bullen, 1902), p. 15.
82 See William Daniels, 'Yeats's "Old Pensioner" and his "Visionary": 1880-1925.', *Irish University Review*, I, 2, 1971, pp. 178-188. Hereafter Daniels, 'Yeats's Visionary'.
83 R. H. Super, ed., *The Complete Prose Works of Matthew Arnold* (Ann Arbor: The University of Michigan Press, 1962), III, p. 343.
84 W. G. Hutchinson, trans., *The Poetry of the Celtic Races and Other Studies by Ernest Renan* (London: Walter Scott, 1896), pp. 9, 53.
85 Yeats, *Autobiographies*, p. 243.
86 Ibid., p. 244; Yeats, *Mythologies*, p. 11.
87 Daniels dates the encounter between Russell and the old man some time between 1 August and 15 November 1890.

88 A.E., 'The Sunset of Fantasy', *Dublin Magazinne*, XIII, I, 10-11. Hereafter A.E., 'Sunset of Fantasy.' Yeats, *Autobiographies*, p. 249.
89 A.E., *The Avatars: A Futurist Fantasy* (London: Macmillan, 1933), p. 58. Hereafter A.E., *Avatars*.
90 Yeats, *Poems*, pp. 131-132.
91 Ibid., p. 799. Yeats, *Letters*, p. 158, to W.E. Henley, November [1890]. A.E., 'Sunset of Fantasy', p. 11. 'I remember every word: "Over those hills I wandered forty years ago. Nobody but myself knows what happened under the thorn tree forty years ago. The fret is on me. The fret is on me. God speaking out of his darkness says I have and I have not. I possess the heavens. I do not possess the world. Abroad if you meet an Irishman he will give you the bit and the sup. But if you come back to your own country after being away forty years it is not the potato and bit of salt you get, but only 'who's that ould fella?' The fret is on me. The fret is on me!" '
92 Price, ed., *J. M. Synge: Collected Works*. 4 vols. (London: Oxford University Press, 1966), II, pp. 195, 202-203.
93 See Daniels, 'Yeats's Visionary', pp. 187-188.
94 Yeats, *Poems,* pp. 456-457.
95 Ibid., pp. 518-519.
96 Yeats, *Essays and Introductions*, p. 51.
97 Yeats, *Uncollected Prose*, I, pp. 201-202.
98 Yeats, *Poems*, pp. 3, 10, 61, 63, 100, 105-111, 140-141, 174-175.
99 Yeats, *Essays and Introductions*, p. 513.
100 *The Concise Oxford Dictionary*, 6th. ed. (Oxford: Clarendon Press, 1976), p. 827.
101 R. H. Super, ed., *The Complete Prose Works of Matthew Arnold* (Ann Arbor: The University of Michigan Press, 1962), VI, p. 283. John Todhunter, *A Study of Shelley* (London: Kegan Paul, 1880), p. 80. Standish O'Grady, *History of Ireland: Critical and Philosophical*, 2 vols. (Dublin: E. Ponsonby, 1881), I, p. 44. Blavatsky, *The Secret Doctrine*, I, p. 388.
102 Harold Bloom, *Yeats* (London: Oxford University Press, 1970), pp. 38-51. Moore, *The Unicorn*, p. 146. Robert O'Driscoll, *Symbolism and Some Implications of the Symbolic Approach: W.B. Yeats during the Eighteen-Nineties* (Dublin: The Dolmen Press, 1971), p. 10.
103 Yeats, *Essays and Introductions*, p. 293.
104 Yeats, *Blake*, I, p. 327.
105 Yeats, *Essays and Introductions*, p. 87.
106 Denis Donoghue, *Yeats* (London: Fontana, 1971), p. 71.
107 Quoted in Moore, *The Unicorn*, p. 241.
108 Yeats, *Essays and Introductions*, p. 159.
109 An early draft of this poem is contained in a letter Russell wrote to Carrie Rea circa February 1891, part of which expresses his disappointment that she is not going to study in Dublin. The poem was originally entitled 'To a Spiritual Woman' and seems to have been addressed to Miss Rea. Denson, MS.9967, 17, to C. C. Coates, [February 1891].
110 See Yeats, *Letters*, p. 179, to W. E. Henley, 4 September [1891]. 'My visionary by the by showed me your 'God in the Garden' poem and called it one of your best things. He is a reader of your verse and in all ways one of the few true students of poetry I know.' Compare Russell's 'Frolic' with Henley's 'Echoes'. See also Gregory, *Seventy Years*, p. 326.
111 Yeats, *The Celtic Twilight* (London: Lawrence and Bullen, 1893), p. 20.
112 See Daniels, 'Yeats's Visionary', pp. 186-187.

Notes to pages 72–79

113 Yeats, *Letters*, pp. 231-232, to John O'Leary, 26 June [1904].
114 Yeats, *Poems*, p. 101. See also harper, ed., *Yeats and The Occult*, p. 82. Cf. Denson MS. 9969, 574, to Sean O'Faolain, 11 April 1933: 'I have gone into so many byways of thought which were once highways that I have "learned to speak a tongue men do not know." You remember Yeats's prayer to be saved from that?' Cf. Yeats, *Correspondence with Moore*, p. 149: My dreams and much psychic phenomena force me into a certain little trodden way but I must not go too far from the main European track . . .'
115 John Unterecker, *A Reader's Guide to William Butler Yeats* (London: Thames and Hudson, 1969), p. 77. Hereafter Unterecker, *Reader's Guide*.
116 Quoted in Ellmann, *Identity*, p. 72.
117 See A.E., *Collected Poems* (London: Macmillan, 1913), p. 72. The last verse was changed for A.E., *Collected Poems* (London: Macmillan, 1926), p. 72, and *Selected Poems*, p. 14. In *Song and Its Fountains*, pp. 27-29, Russell gives a detailed account of the vision which inspired this poem.
118 A.E., *Homeward*, pp. 18, 19, 29, 59.
119 Quoted in Ellmann, *Identity*, p. 72.
120 Summerfield, *Russell*, pp. 33, 49. Yeats, *Memoirs*, p. 33. Yeats, *Autobiographies*, p. 254. Note unpub., lettr., Yeats to Lady Gregory, [15 June 1898]: 'Russell told [me] some four or five months ago that he was in love only once in his life and then for only "five minutes". It was a girl at Pim's shop whom he has never seen since.'
121 Quoted in Ellmann, *Identity*, p. 72. See also Ellmann, *Identity*, p. 312.
122 Gibbon, ed., *Living Torch*, p. 105. Jowett calls the dialogue *The Symposium*; Taylor calls it *The Banquet*. See also Denson, *Bibliography*, pp. 180-181.
123 A.E., *Homeward*, p. 18.
124 Ellmann, *Identity*, p. 73. Yeats later regretted the final stanza.
125 Yeats, *Poems*, pp. 111-112. For Russell's criticisms of the poem see Forrest Reid, *Private Road*, p. 137 and A.N. Jeffares, *A Commentary on the Collected Poems of W. B. Yeats* (London: Macmillan, 1971), pp. 30-31. Hereafter Jeffares, *Commentary*. See also Jeffares, *Man and Poet*, p. 308.
126 Yeats, *Essays and Introductions*, p. 509.
127 Douglas Hyde, ed., *Songs Ascribed to Raftery* (1903; rpt. Shannon: Irish University Press, 1973), p. 321.
128 See Declan Kiberd, *Synge and the Irish Language* (London: Macmillan, 1979), pp. 140-143.
129 Yeats, *Poems*, p. 808.
130 Quoted in Gibbon, *Thesis*, p. 67.
131 James H. Cousins, *New Ways in English Literature* (Madras: Ganesh and Co., n.d. [1917]), pp. 52-53.
132 Denson, MS.9967, 80, to W. B. Yeats, [May 1900].
133 Yeats, *Essays and Introductions*, p. 80: '[Shelley] could hardly have helped perceiving that an image that has transcended [a] particular time and place becomes a symbol, passes beyond death, as it were, and becomes a living soul.'
134 James Joyce, *A Portrait of the Artist as a Young Man* (1916; rpt. Harmondsworth: Penguin, 1969), p. 213.
135 William H. O'Donnell, ed., *The Speckled Bird* by W. B. Yeats, 2 vols. (Dublin: Cuala Press, 1973), I, p. 40. Hereafter Yeats, *Speckled Bird*.
136 A.E., *Candle of Vision*, p. 58; A.E., *Song and Its Fountains*, p. 41.
137 Quoted in Harper, *Golden Dawn*, p. 265.
138 Yeats, *Essays and Introductions*, pp. 148-149; 49.
139 Yeats, *The Secret Rose* (London: Lawrence and Bullen, 1897), pp. 142-143.

140 Yeats, *Memoirs*, p. 27.
141 Ibid., p. 27, and Yeats, *Autobiographies*, pp. 185-186.
142 See Levi, *Transcendental Magic*, pp. 233 ff.
143 Yeats, *Mythologies*, pp. 54-56, 100. See also Yeats, *Letters*, p. 214, to Edward Garnett, [October, 1892].
144 Yeats, *Letters*, p. 255, to Olivia Shakespear, 7 April [1895].
145 Yeats, *Essays and Introductions*, pp. 35-36. See also Yeats, *Mythologies*, pp. 157-164; Harper, *Golden Dawn*, p. 101.
146 Yeats, *Mythologies*, p. 277.
147 Yeats, *Speckled Bird*, I, 42-48.
148 Yeats, *Poems*, p. 808.
149 Bachchan, p. 102.
150 Reid, *Yeats*, p. 189.
151 Summerfield, *Russell*, p. 41.
152 Yeats, *Memoirs*, pp. 130-131.
153 Yeats, *Autobiographies*, p. 243.
154 Yeats, *Essays and Introductions*, p. 414. Yeats also compares Russell and Swedenborg in his Introduction to Lady Gregory, *Visions and Beliefs in the West of Ireland* (1920; rpt. New York: Oxford University Press, 1970) pp. 20, 345. Hereafter Gregory, *Visions and Beliefs*.
155 Yeats, *Autobiographies*, p. 243.
156 Underhill, *Mysticism*, pp. 279-280.
157 Quoted in Strong, 'Yeats', p. 207.
158 Moore, *Salve*, p. 37. See also Underhill, *Mysticism*, pp. 267-271, 353-357.
159 Yeats, *Essays and Introductions*, p. 413.
160 Russell, *Letters*, p. 110, to George Moore, [6 April 1916].
161 Yeats, *Essays and Introductions*, p. 74.
162 Yeats, *Letters*, p. 262, to W. T. Horton, 5 May 1896.
163 Yeats, *Memoirs*, pp. 130-131; Yeats, *Essays and Introductions*, pp. 413-414; Yeats, *A Vision* (B), p. 176.
164 Henn, *Lonely Tower*, p. 152 is incorrect. See A.E., *Avatars*, pp. 21-22, 64.
165 Gregory, *Visions and Beliefs*, pp. 349-350.
166 A.E., *The Candle of Vision*, pp. 39-40, 58. Gregory, *Seventy Years*, pp. 383-384. See also Blavatsky, *Lucifer*, p. 93: 'Now what is a medium? The term medium, when not applied simply to things and objects, is supposed to be a person through whom the action of another person or being is either manifested or transmitted. Spiritualists believing in communications with disembodied spirits, and that these can manifest through, or impress sensitives to transmit "messages" from them, regard mediumship as a blessing and a great privilege. We Theosophists, on the other hand, who do not believe in the "communion of spirits" as Spiritualists do, regard the gift as one of the most dangerous of abnormal nervous diseases. A medium is simply one in whose personal *Ego*, or terrestrial mind (psyche), the percentage of "astral" light so preponderates as to impregnate with it his whole physical constitution. Every organ and cell thereby is attuned, so to speak, and subjected to an enormous and abnormal tension. The mind is ever on the plane of, and quite immersed in, that deceptive light whose soul is divine, but whose body — the light waves on the lower planes, infernal; for they are but the black and disfigured reflections of the earth's memories.'
167 Ibid., p. 28.
168 Moore, *Salve*, p. 36.
169 Gibbon, *Yeats*, p. 55.
170 Evans-Wentz, *Fairy-Faith*, pp. 59 ff. See also A.E., *The Irish Statesman*, 5 October 1926, p. 96: 'I myself have had experience of clairvoyance in dream. That is

Notes to pages 83–89

I have seen people and places at a distance, and have afterwards verified the truth of the vision. But in dream also I see persons who, I feel sure, are self-created, created by the same power of the psyche transcendental to both the waking and dreaming consciousness.' Arnold Harvey, 'Memories of Coole', *Irish Times*, 23 November 1959, p. 5: 'A.E. . . . showed us a pastel sketch . . . dotted with those enchanting genii which, according to him, invisibly peopled the world of nature, sub-human, flame-like beings, who moved under a collective impulse as birds move. He firmly believed that they had an objective reality, and were not merely creatures of the imagination, but, on being questioned closely on the subject he admitted he could see them equally well with his eyes shut.'

171 Yeats, *Autobiographies*, p. 262. Gregory, *Visions and Beliefs*, p. 350.
172 Yeats, *Essays and Introductions*, pp. 156-157. See also Underhill, *Mysticism*, pp. 154-157.
173 Porter, ed., *Letters to Mínanlábáin*, p. 37, to Kingsley Porter, 5 January 1932. See also Yeats, *Memoirs*, pp. 283-286.
174 A.E., *Song and Its Fountains*, pp. 66-67.
175 Summerfield, *Russell*, p. 41. Blavatsky, *Lucifer*, p. 28.
176 Russell, *Irish Homestead*, XVII, 790, 24 September 1910.
177 Yeats, *Poems*, pp. 138-139.
178 Yeats, *Mythologies*, p. 56.
179 Ibid., pp. 37-40. See also Curtis Bradford, *Yeats at Work* (Carbondale: Southern Illinois University Press, 1965), pp. 362-364. Hereafter Bradford, *Yeats at Work*.
180 Quoted in Summerfield, *Russell*, p. 40.
181 Quoted in Hone, *Yeats*, p. 467.
182 Yeats, *Poems*, p. 501.
183 See Underhill, *Mysticism*, p. 246.
184 Yeats, *Poems*, p. 503.
185 Yeats, *Autobiographies*, p. 246.
186 Ibid., p. 246.
187 Ibid., p. 247.
188 Ibid., pp. 248-249.
189 A.E., 'A Packet for Ezra Pound', *The Irish Statesman*, 7 September 1925, p. 11.
190 Denson, MS.9969, 698, to Sean O'Faolain, 10 June 1935.
191 Yeats, *Autobiographies*, pp. 25-26.
192 Yeats, *Essays and Introductions*, p. 448.
193 W. B. Yeats, ed., *Fairy and Folk Tales of Ireland* [*Fairy and Folk Tales of the Irish Peasantry, & Irish Fairy Tales*] (Gerrards Cross: Colin Smythe, 1973), p. 8. Hereafter Yeats, ed., *Fairy and Folk Tales*.
194 Yeats, *A Vision* (B), pp. 24-25.
195 Yeats, *Essays and Introductions*, p. 48.
196 J. B. Yeats, *Essays Irish and American* (Dublin: Talbot Press, 1918), p. 30.
197 Yeats, *Essays and Introductions*, p. 321.
198 Yeats, *Letters to Dorothy Wellesley*, p. 94, to Dorothy Wellesley, 5 August [1936].
199 Yeats, *Essays and Introductions*, pp. 50-51.
200 Yeats, *Mythologies*, p. 331.
201 Yeats, *Poems*, p. 409.
202 See Maurice Bowra, *The Heritage of Symbolism* (London and Toronto: Macmillan, 1943, 1951), p. 210.
203 Yeats, *A Vision* (B), p. 214.
204 Ibid., p. 13.

205 Yeats, *Poems*, p. 373.
206 Yeats, *A Vision* (B), pp. 8, 25.
207 See Yeats, *Memoirs*, p. 27.
208 Clifford Bax, ed., *Florence Farr, Bernard Shaw, W. B. Yeats: Letters* (London: Home and Van Thal, 1946), p. 56, W. B. Yeats to Florence Farr, n.d.
209 Yeats, *Autobiographies*, p. 181. See also Yeats, *Essays and Introductions*, pp. 292-293, and *A Vision* (A), p. 129: 'Having the concrete mind of a poet, I am unhappy when I find myself among abstract things, and yet I need them to set my experience in order.'
210 Yeats, *Blake*, I, p. 23.
211 Yeats, *A Vision* (B), p. 12.
212 Yeats, *A Vision* (A), p. x.
213 See Douglas Hyde, *A Literary History of Ireland* (London: T. Fisher Unwin, 1901), pp. 82-93. Hereafter Hyde, *Literary History*.
214 Yeats, *Poems*, pp. 439, 600. See also Yeats, *Essays and Introductions*, p. 65: 'The imagination has some way of lighting on the truth that the reason has not.'
215 Yeats, ed., *Fairy and Folk Tales*, p. 5.
216 Yeats, *Essays and Introductions*, p. 10.
217 Yeats, *Letters*, p. 63, to Katharine Tynan, 14 March [1888].
218 Yeats, *Essays and Introductions*, p. viii.
219 For example, see Yeats, *Autobiographies*, pp. 189-194.
220 Yeats, *Poems*, pp. 610-611.
221 T. S. Eliot, 'Ulysses, Order and Myth', in Richard Ellmann and Charles Feidelson, Jr., eds., *The Modern Tradition* (New York: Oxford University Press, 1965), p. 681. Note comment made by George Moore in his novel *Evelyn Innes* (London: T. Fisher Unwin, 1898), p. 339: 'But did [Yeats] really believe in Angus and Lir and the Great Mother Dana? Perhaps he merely believed that as a man of genius it was his business to enrol himself in the original instincts and traditions of his race.'
222 Denson MS.9969, 595, to W. B. Yeats, 11 October 1933.

CHAPTER IV: POETS AND DREAMERS

1 The title was changed twice. First the colon was dropped, making an adjective of *Homeward*, and then *Homeward* and *Songs* were separated by a comma.
2 Finneran, ed., *Letters to Yeats*, II, p. 574, George W. Russell to W. B. Yeats, 14 June 1935.
3 Yeats, *Uncollected Prose*, I, p. 380.
4 In 1893, however, he included one of Russell's more recent poems in the revised version of 'An Irish Visionary' which he prepared for *The Celtic Twilight*.
5 Yeats, *Autobiographies*, p. 241.
6 Ibid., p. 242; Gregory, *Seventy Years*, p. 311.
7 A.E., *Song and Its Fountains*, p. 52.
8 L. Frankenberg, ed., *James, Seamus and Jacques: Unpublished Writings of James Stephens* (London: Macmillan, 1964), pp. 118-119. Hereafter Frankenberg, ed., *Stephens*.
9 Vide, Yeats, *Essays and Introductions*, p. 317. Russell was a regular contributor to *The Irish Theosophist* from October 1892.

10 Yeats, *Letters*, pp. 231-232, to John O'Leary, 26 June [1894].
11 Yeats, *Uncollected Prose*, II, p. 509.
12 Yeats, *Uncollected Prose*, I, pp. 336-339.
13 Yeats, *Autobiographies*, p. 241. Yeats, *Memoirs*, p. 30. Yeats, *Uncollected Prose*, I, p. 248.
14 See *Irish Theosophist*, III, 79, 15 February 1895.
15 See Yeats, *Autobiographies*, p. 90 and Yeats, *Essays and Introductions*, p. 65. The present writer has been unable to locate any reference to this idea in either Russell's published or unpublished writings.
16 Müller, *Upanisads*, II, p. 163-173.
17 A.E., *Homeward*, p. 8, reads: 'places,'; 'went forth in old time from'; 'Self-ancestral'; 'but filled'; 'homesickness I made'.
18 Yeats, 'An Irish Visionary', *National Observer*, 3 October 1891.
19 Marcus, pp. 79-103.
20 Yeats, *Uncollected Prose*, I, p. 337.
21 See Yeats, *Essays and Introductions*, p. 341.
22 See Moore, *Salve*, p. 357.
23 Denson, MS.9967, 80, to W. B. Yeats, n.d.
24 Quoted in Summerfield, *Russell*, p. 57.
25 Yeats, *Uncollected Prose*, I, p. 357.
26 *A Book of Irish Verse* was published in March 1895.
27 A.E., *Irish Theosophist*, III, 191, 15 August 1895.
28 Yeats, *Uncollected Prose*, I, p. 381.
29 Ibid., p. 380.
30 See Ellmann, *Identity*, p. 216.
31 Sean O'Casey, *Inishfallen, Fare Thee Well* (London: Pan Books, 1971), p. 197. See also Holbrook Jackson, *The Eighteen Nineties: A Review of Art and Ideas at the Close of the Nineteenth Century* (Harmondsworth: Penguin, 1939), pp. 140-142. Hereafter Jackson, *Eighteen Nineties*.
32 A.E., *Homeward*, p. 18.
33 Ibid., p. 24.
34 Ibid., p. 14.
35 Ibid., p. 27.
36 *The Oxford English Dictionary* (Melbourne: Oxford University Press, 1933), XII, pp. 60-61.
37 A.E., *Homeward*, p. 21.
38 Yeats, *Essays and Introductions*, p. 163. Note Austin Clarke, *Poetry in Modern Ireland*, 2nd ed. (Dublin Mercier Press, [1961], p. 16: 'When I first discovered for myself the Celtic Twilight, as a young student, and read the poems of that period, much was quite incomprehensible to me. I groped through a mist of blurred meanings, stumbled over lines in which every accent seemed to be in the wrong place. It was all quite unlike English poetry and quite unlike that Gaelic poetry which Dr Douglas Hyde declaimed for us in class. . . .' Hereafter Clarke, *Poetry in Modern Ireland*.
39 Yeats, *Poems*, p. 154. See Harvey Gross, *Sound and Form in Modern Poetry: A Study of Prosody from Thomas Hardy to Robert Lowell* (Ann Arbor: University of Michigan Press, 1964), p. 48. Hereafter Gross, *Sound and Form*.
40 Ibid., p. 122.
41 Ibid., p. 147. See also MacNeice, *Yeats*, p. 67.
42 Ibid., p. 511.
43 Quoted in James Hall and Martin Steinmann, eds., *The Permanence of Yeats* (New York: Collier Books, 1961), pp. 313-314. Hereafter Hall and Steinmann, eds., *Permanence of Yeats*.

44 A.E., *Homeward*, p. 40.
45 Yeats, *Poems*, p. 141.
46 Note Reid, *Yeats*, p. 89: '[Yeats's] prosody is based upon what Bridges has called "the natural speech stress" rather than on that which is ordered by the "numeration of syllables", and a strict regularity of accent. . . In other words, the rhythm is governed by "true speech-stresses", never, or very rarely, imposing, for the sake of the metre, a false accent, which is not in the "natural speech-intonation".'
47 Yeats, *Essays and Introductions*, p. 15.
48 Yeats, *Letters*, p. 250, to the Editor of the *Daily Express* (Dublin), published 27 February 1895. Yeats, *Uncollected Prose*, I, p. 387.
49 A.E., *Collected Poems*, p. 37.
50 Yeats, *Poems*, p. 140.
51 Denson, *Bibliography*, p. 28. See also Yeats, *Autobiographies*, p. 240. Russell was a member of the Publications Committee of the National Literary Society from 1901 to 1904. See Figgis, *AE*, pp. 27-28.
52 Marcus, p. 289.
53 Ibid., p. 289.
54 Yeats, *Uncollected Prose*, I, p. 382.
55 Note Yeats's subsequent assessments of the importance of *Homeward: Songs by the Way*. W. B. Yeats, *Pages From a Diary Written in 1930* (Dublin: Cuala, 1944), pp. 49-50: 'The Movement began with AE's little verses made out of the Upanishads.' Russell K. Alspach, ed., *The Variorum Edition of the Plays of W. B. Yeats* (London: Macmillan, 1965), p. 568. Hereafter Yeats, *Plays*.
56 A.E., 'The Poetry of William B. Yeats', *Irish Weekly Independent*, 26 October 1895, p. 9.
57 Quoted in A. N. Jeffares, ed., *W. B. Yeats: The Critical Heritage* (London: Routledge and Kegan Paul, 1977), pp. 91-94. Hereafter Jeffares, ed., *Critical Heritage*.
58 A.E., 'The Poetry of William B. Yeats', *Irish Weekly Independent*, 26 October 1895, p. 9.
59 See Thomas Parkinson, *W. B. Yeats Self-Critic: A Study of His Early Verse and the Later Poetry: Two Volumes in One* (Berkeley and Los Angeles: University of California Press, 1971), pp. 32-46. Hereafter Parkinson, *Self-Critic*.
60 A.E., 'The Youth of a Poet', *The Irish Statesman*, 17 October 1925, p. 177. See also Moore, *Vale*, pp. 164-166.
61 Yeats, *Poems*, p. 778.
62 Blavatsky, *Isis Unveiled*, I, p. 247. See also Blavatsky, *The Secret Doctrine*, II, p. 74: 'In *Isis Unveiled* we wrote what we now repeat: "We are at the bottom of a cycle and evidently in a transitory state".'
63 A.E., 'The Legends of Ancient Eire', *Irish Theosophist*, III, 103.
64 See Gearóid O'Tuathaigh, *Ireland Before the Famine, 1798-1848*: Gill History of Ireland, Vol. 9 (Dublin: Gill and Macmillan, 1972), p. 68.
65 Yeats, *Letters*, p. 259, to Florence Farr, [December 1895]. Ellmann, *Man and Masks*, pp. 100-101.
66 Yeats, *Poems*, p. 170. Cf. Russell, *Homeward*, pp. 37-38.
67 A.E., *Irish Theosophist*, III, 226.
68 Summerfield, *Russell*, p. 60.
69 Anon., *Irish Theosophist*, III, 88.
70 Eglinton, *Memoir*, p. 34.
71 Summerfield, *Russell*, p. 61
72 Eglinton, *Memoir*, p. 34.
73 See A.E., *The Candle of Vision*, pp. 57-58, 150-151; Ella Young, *Flowering Dusk*,

pp. 87-88; Yeats, *Autobiographies*, p. 237.
74 A.E., *Selected Poems*, p. 147. See also Abinash Chandra Bose, *Three Mystic Poets: A Study of W. B. Yeats, AE and Rabindranath Tagore* (Kolhapur: School and College Bookstall, 1945), p. 68. Hereafter Bose, *Three Mystic Poets*.
75 A.E., and J. M. Pryse, 'The Enchantment of Cuchullain', *Irish Theosophist*, IV, 32-35, 50-54, 72-75, 83-89, 101-108.
76 W. K. Sullivan, ed., Eugene O'Curry, *On the Manners and Customs of the Ancient Irish: A Series of Lectures*, (London and Edinburgh: Williams and Norgate, 1873), II, 195-198. Denson, *Bibliography*, p. 178.
77 Russell, *Letters*, p. 16, to W. B. Yeats, [? November 1895].
78 Yeats, *Memoirs*, p. 91.
79 W. B. Yeats, ed., *Some Passages From the Letters of AE to W. B. Yeats* (Dublin: The Cuala Press, 1936), p. 4. Hereafter Yeats, ed., *Some Passages*.
80 Yeats, *Memoirs*, p. 91; Yeats, *Autobiographies*, pp. 328-329.
81 Quoted in Jackson, *Eighteen Nineties*, p. 49.
82 Denson, MS.9967, 36, to W. B. Yeats, [? February 1896]. See also Joseph Hone, *W. B. Yeats: Irishmen of To-day Series* (Dublin: Maunsel, 1917), p. 19. Hereafter Hone, *Yeats: Irishmen of To-Day*.
83 See Denson, MS. 9967, 37, 41, 43, 44; Russell, *Letters*, pp. 17-18, to W. B. Yeats, 2 June 1896. Denson's conjectural dating of Nos. 41, 43, and 44 is incorrect. The correct sequence is: No. 43. February/March, 1986; No. 44, April 1896; and No. 41, April-June, 1896.
84 Denson, MS. 9967, 43, to W. B. Yeats, [February/March, 1896]. The alleged spiritual purity of the Irish race has frequently been a rallying point for nationalist movements. See Patrick O'Farrell, *England and Ireland Since 1800* (London: Oxford University Press, 1975), pp. 55, 56, 111 ff.; and O'Faolain, *The Irish*, pp. 81-84.
85 Denson, MS.9967, 41, to W. B. Yeats, [? April 1896].
86 A.E., *The Candle of Vision*, p. 100.
87 Summerfield, *Russell*, p. 75.
88 Ibid., pp. 69-70.
89 Russell, *Letters*, pp. 17-18, to W. B. Yeats, 2 June 1896.
90 Anon., *Irish Theosophist*, IV, 161. Clifford Bax, *Some I knew Well*, p. 80, has claimed: 'One friend of A.E., Daniel Dunlop, an engineer, tells how members of the community intensified their study during the summer holidays by living in a tower on the coast of Ireland where all could read *The Secret Doctrine* and practise meditation.' The present writer has not been able to locate the tower or substantiate the claim.
91 First published in *The Savoy*, April 1896, pp. 56-70. See Marcus, p. 49 where *Rosa Alchemica* is listed by Yeats as describing 'contemporary' events.
92 Philip L. Marcus, Warwick Gould, and Michael J. Sidnell, eds., *The Secret Rose, Stories by Yeats: A Variorum Edition* (London and Ithaca: Cornell University Press, 1981), p. 133. Hereafter Yeats, *Secret Rose*.
93 Ibid., p. 136.
94 See Hone, *Yeats*, p. 92.
95 Yeats, *Autobiographies*, p. 209.
96 See also Yeats, *Essays and Introductions*, p. 474.
97 Quoted in Clarke, *Poetry in Modern Ireland*, p. 18.
98 Anon, *Irish Theosophist*, III, 128, 15 April 1895.
99 Yeats, *Secret Rose*, p. 132.
100 Ibid., p. 134.
101 For example, Laurence W. Fennelly, 'W. B. Yeats and S. L. MacGregor Mathers', in Harper, ed., *Yeats and The Occult*, pp. 305 ff. See also MacNeice, *Yeats*,

p. 47; Ellmann, *Man and Masks*, pp. 267-268; and Jeffares, *Man and Poet*, p. 112.
102   Gregory, *Seventy Years*, p. 311.
103   Yeats, *Secret Rose*, p. 130. For a description of Mathers's appearance see Yeats, *Autobiographies*, pp. 182-184, and Ella Young, *Flowering Dusk*, p. 105: 'a tall, square shouldered man, with a strong clean-cut face, dark hair, and strange steel-blue eyes'.
104   Frank O'Connor, *My Father's Son* (1968; rpt. London: Pan Books, 1971), p. 26. Hereafter O'Connor, *My Father's Son*.
105   Austin Clarke, *Collected Poems* (Dublin: Dolmen, 1974), p. 402.
106   James Joyce, *Ulysses* (1922; rpt. Harmondsworth: Penguin, 1969), pp. 165, 191, 474-475.
107   Stephens, *The Charwoman's Daughter*, p. 27.
108   Holloway, *Diaries*, p. 132, entry for 11 December 1909.
109   Moore, *Ave*, p. 158.
110   Yeats, *Poems*, p. 372. Russell generally wore Donegal tweed. Summerfield, p. 130. Robartes was changed when Yeats wrote the Introduction to the first edition of *A Vision*. See Yeats, *A Vision* (A), p. xv; Michael J. Sidnell, 'Mr Yeats, Michael Robartes and Their Circle', in Harper, ed., *Yeats and The Occult*, pp. 231 ff.
111   O'Connor, *My Father's Son*, p. 30 compares the two men's appearances. See also Gwynn, ed., *Scattering Branches*, pp. 195-196.
112   Yeats, *Secret Rose*, p. 130.
113   Yeats, *A Vision* (A), p. 64.
114   Ibid., pp. 113-114; Yeats, *Autobiographies*, pp. 247-248.
115   Yeats, *Poems*, p. 353.
116   Summerfield, *Russell*, p. 69.
117   See Arnold Goldman, 'Yeats, Spiritualism, and Psychical Research', in Harper, ed., *Yeats and The Occult*, p. 126.
118   Yeats, *Poems*, p. 803. See also Yeats, *Mythologies*, p. 80; Ellmann, *Identity*, p. 301; and Yeats, *Essays and Introductions*, pp. 265, 284.
119   Yeats, *Poems*, p. 383.
120   Yeats, *Secret Rose*, p. 132. Cf. Yeats, *Mythologies*, p. 11.
121   Ella Young, *Flowering Dusk*, pp. 29, 30, 32.
122   Yeats, *A Vision* (B), pp. 54-55.
123   Gibbon, ed., *Living Torch*, pp. 154-155.
124   Eglinton, *A Memoir*, pp. 41-42.
125   See for example, A.E., 'A Poet of Shadows', *Imaginations and Reveries*, pp. 24-28.
126   See Ellmann, *Man and Masks*, pp. 79-84.
127   Yeats, *Poems*, p. 808.
128   Yeats, *Secret Rose*, p. 138.
129   Yeats, *Letters*, p. 235, to John O'Leary, [? Autumn 1894].
130   For example *Irish Theosophist*, IV, 120, 15 March 1896: 'The air seems to be alive with plans and ideas relative to the awakening of mystic fires to two ancient lands on this side of the Atlantic. Ireland is one of them! An archaic name thereof was Moira. Forward spirits are roused with an enthusiasm untrammelled by the limitations (however diaphanous) of any particular association — theosophical or otherwise.
131   Yeats, *Letters*, p. 255, to Olivia Shakespear, 7 April [1895].
132   The book was published in April 1897. Wade, *Bibliography*, p. 38.
133   Yeats, *Secret Rose*, p. 233.
134   Yeats, *Poems*, p. 165. The echo of Keats's 'La Belle Dame sans Merci' ('The sedge is withered from the lake') is perhaps not unintentional as the poem was addressed to Maud Gonne. The poem was first published in *The Dome*, May 1898.

Notes to pages 116–121

135 A.E., *The Earth Breath and Other Poems* (London: John Lane, 1897), p. 89. Hereafter A.E., *Earth Breath*.
136 Russell, *Letters*, pp. 18-23, to W. B. Yeats, 3 April 1897.
137 Quoted in Ellmann, *Identity*, p. 305. See also Levi, *Transcendental Magic*, p. 271: 'We must insist, however, upon one reflection, namely, that the intellectual and social chaos in the midst of which we are perishing has been caused by the neglect of initiation, its ordeals and its mysteries.'
138 Yeats, *Autobiographies*, pp. 189-195, 263, 269.
139 Ibid, p. 191. Yeats anticipated T. S. Eliot's 'dissociation of sensibility.' See Ellmann, *Identity*, p. 24.
140 Ibid, p. 254.
141 Yeats, *Memoirs*, p. 124.
142 Ibid., p. 124.
143 Yeats, *Essays and Introductions*, p. 514. Yeats also hoped that work on the rituals of 'The Castle of Heroes' would bring him closer to Maud Gonne. See Yeats, *Memoirs*, pp. 123-126. This desire was partly realized through their two 'spiritual marriages'. See Moore, *The Unicorn*, pp. 37-39, 197-204.
144 Yeats, *Memoirs*, p. 124.
145 Ibid., pp. 123-125; Yeats, *Autobiographies*, pp. 253-255.
146 Denson MS.9967, 42, to William Sharp [? September 1896]; Elizabeth A. Sharp, *William Sharp: A Memoir by His Wife* (London: Heinemann, 1910), pp. 272-277. Hereafter Sharp, *Memoir*. One of the 'great things' was a plan to steal the Lia Fail (known in Britain as the Stone of Scone) — the ancient stone housed under the coronation throne in Westminster Abbey. See Ella Young, *Flowering Dusk*, pp. 190-191; O'Connor, *Backward Look*, p. 166.
147 A.E., 'Priest or Hero?', *Irish Theosophist*, V, 127-131, 15 April 1897. Subsequently issued as a pamphlet entitled, *Ideals in Ireland: Priest or Hero?*
148 Denson, MS.9967, 50, to W. B. Yeats, [? June 1897]. See Gregory, *Seventy Years*, p. 385; Russell, *Avatars*, pp. 4-5.
149 See J. B. Yeats, *Letters to His Son W. B. Yeats and Others 1869-1922* (London: Faber and Faber, 1944 and New York: Dutton, 1946), p. 36, to Sarah Purser, 7 July 1897: 'I don't know where Willie is or what he is doing. The last I heard of him was that he and Russell have gone West (Sligo or thereabouts) to find a new god.' Hereafter J. B. Yeats, *Letters to His Son*.
150 Yeats, *Autobiographies*, pp. 255-263.
151 See Moore, *The Unicorn*, pp. 63-66.
152 Yeats, *Autobiographies*, p. 259; Yeats, *Memoirs*, p. 131.
153 Yeats, *Letters*, p. 287, to Lady Gregory, [24 July 1897]. See also Yeats, *Letters*, pp. 324-325, and Yeats, *Memoirs*, p. 125, for Yeats's and Russell's shared vision of Aengus. Yeats says: 'The forms became very continuous in my thoughts, and when A.E. came to stay at Coole he asked who was the white jester he had seen about the corridors. It was a form I associated with the God Aengus.' Yeats refers again to this incident in his essay 'The Queen and the Fool', in the enlarged edition of *The Celtic Twilight* (1902) where he writes of 'a truly great seer who saw a white fool in a visionary garden'.
154 Gregory, *Seventy Years*, p. 312.
155 Gregory, *Visions and Beliefs*, pp. 57, 64, 355, 357; Yeats, *Uncollected Prose*, II, pp. 106, 223-226.
156 Denson, MS.9967, 51, to W. B. Yeats [? August 1897].
157 Sharp, *Memoir*, pp. 287-289.
158 Denson, MS.9967, 52, to W. B. Yeats, 9 August 1897.
159 Gregory, *Seventy Years*, pp. 327-328. Cf. Yeats, *Uncollected Prose*, II, 26; and Moore, *The Unicorn*, p. 74. In a rough draft of one of the 'stone' rituals the

First officer tells the candidate: 'The region of the shades must be passed through, for amongst the shades man sees at last the true significance and the unmateriality of matter.'

160 Manuscript letter in the possession of the Robert W. Woodruff Library, Emory University. See also Moore, *Salve*, pp. 82-83.

161 National Library of Ireland, MS. 15,600, 12, 22, 23. Yeats, *Letters*, pp. 294-295, to George Russell, 22 January [1898]. Russell may have also wished to withdraw because he found the type of clairvoyance used to construct the rituals exhausting. He appears to have suffered a form of nervous breakdown toward the end of 1897. [Summerfield, *Russell*, p. 84.]. William Sharp also suffered a nervous collapse after the summer of 1897. [Moore, *The Unicorn*, p. 62]. Maud Gonne said she withdrew partly because she found the method used to construct the rituals was 'much too fatiguing'. [Moore, *The Unicorn*, pp. 71-72].

162 Yeats, *Letters*, pp. 296-297, to George Russell, [? February 1898] and 27 March [1898]. The command to 'number the people of God' might be an echo of a Biblical expression. See for example, 2 Samuel 24:2, and 1 Chronicles 21:2.

163 Russell, *Letters*, pp. 29-30, to W. B. Yeats, 30 August 1898.

164 Gregory, *Seventy Years*, p. 312. For Mary Sheridan's vision see Gregory, *Visions and Beliefs*, pp. 52, 53, 348-351.

165 Moore, *The Unicorn*, p. 73. The 'Spear' was sometimes called the 'Wand', and the 'Spirit', the 'Globe' or 'The Mountain of God'. For the occult significance of these symbols see Levi, *Transcendental Magic*, pp. 258-273.

166 Denson, MS.9967, 72, to W. B. Yeats, 4 September 1899. Gregory, *Seventy Years*, p. 343.

167 Yeats, *Letters*, pp. 324-325, to George Russell, 27 August [1899].

168 Gregory, *Seventy Years*, p. 384.

169 Moore, *The Unicorn*, p. 78.

170 Arnold Harvey, 'Memories of Coole', *Irish Times*, 23 November 1959, p. 5. Gregory, *Seventy Years*, p. 384.

171 Ellmann, *Man and Masks*, p. 128; Harper, *Golden Dawn*, pp. 19-35.

172 Denson, MS.9967, 88, to W. B. Yeats, [? June 1901]; Gregory, *Seventy Years*, p. 399.

173 Finneran, ed., *Letters to Yeats*, I, p. 84, William Sharp to W. B. Yeats, 26 July 1901.

174 Yeats, *Letters*, pp. 363-364, to Lady Gregory, 13 January 1902.

175 Moore, *The Unicorn*, p. 202.

176 Harper, *Golden Dawn*, pp. 94-121.

177 Ibid., p. 110.

178 Yeats, *Speckled Bird*, I, pp. 80ff; II, pp. 9-10. The drawing room sequence begins on p. 14.

179 Ibid., II, pp. 17-18. See also A.E., *The Candle of Vision*, pp. 137-142; Yeats, *Plays*, pp. 1127, 1135; Summerfield, *Russell*, pp. 45-47; Müller, *Upanisads*, II, 322; and Frankenberg, ed., *Stephens*, pp. 111-112: 'I asked what had happened to make him quit. And he answered very simply that he found himself turning into power. That is, he was turning into fire. He was already a pillar of flame about twenty feet high, and he could hear himself as a rushing roar like the dreadful grumbling of half a Niagara — and he switched himself off in sheer terror lest he should in another second be just one calcinated cinder which someone might carry away with a tongs.'

180 Ibid., II, p. 19.

181 For example, Gregory, *Seventy Years*, p. 384.

182 Summerfield, *Russell*, pp. 92-93. The conjecture about the relationship between his resignation and his disappointment is the present writer's.

183 A.E., *The Candle of Vision*, p. 101.

184 The poem was first published in *The Irish Theosophist*, V, 225, 15 September 1897. See also Moore, *The Unicorn*, pp. 68-69; National Library of Ireland, MS.15,600, 23, W. B. Yeats to G. W. Russell, [? 26 November 1897]; Yeats, *Letters*, pp. 293-294, to Dorothea Hunter, 1 January 1898.
185 Yeats, *Autobiographies*, p. 270.
186 Ibid., p. 269.
187 Yeats, *Poems*, p. 153.
188 Ibid., pp. 153, 806-807.
189 Russell, *Letters*, pp. 29-30, to W. B. Yeats, 30 August 1898.
190 Yeats, *Poems*, p. 427.
191 Yeats, *Autobiographies*, pp. 493-494.

CHAPTER V: CELTIC AND IRISH

1 Marcus, pp. 1-2.
2 Yeats, *Uncollected Prose*, I, p. 104.
3 Yeats, *Letters*, p. 125, to John O'Leary, 7 May [1889].
4 Yeats, *Uncollected Prose*, I, p. 382.
5 W.K.S., 'Celtic Literature,' *Encyclopedia Britannica*, 10th ed., V, pp. 297-328.
6 Tomás Ó Fiaich, 'The Great Controversy' in Seán Ó Tuama, ed., *The Gaelic League Idea: The Thomas Davis Lectures, R.T.E, 1968-1969* (Dublin and Cork: Mercier Press, 1972), pp. 65-66. Hereafter Seán Ó Tuama, ed., *The Gaelic League Idea*.
7 A. L. Rowse, *Oxford in the History of England* (New York: G. P. Putnam's Sons, 1975), pp. 202-203.
8 Yeats, *Letters*, p. 102, to Katharine Tynan, 24 January [1889].
9 See Yeats, *New Island*, pp. 69-159.
10 Jackson, *Eighteen Nineties*, pp. 147-156.
11 Yeats, *Essays and Introductions*, p. 185. Note that in a report of a lecture on the Celt given by Count Plunkett, Yeats claimed 'to have something to do with the word as now used'. See *Daily Express* (Dublin) 8 May 1899, p. 5.
12 See Yeats, *Uncollected Prose*, II, p. 455. John S. Kelly, 'The Fall of Parnell and The Rise of Irish Literature, An Investigation', in P. J. Drudy, ed., *Anglo-Irish Studies*, II (Chalfont St. Giles: Alpha Academic Books, 1976), pp. 1-23.
13 See for example Lord Castletown's lecture 'Our Celtic Inheritance' and the proposal to hold a Pan-Celtic Congress in 1900 reported in *Daily Express* (Dublin), 14 March 1899, p. 6. See also Anon, *United Irishman*, 30 May p. 1; Mary Colum, *Life and the Dream* (London: Macmillan, 1947), pp. 105-109.
14 Sean Ó Diotcain, 'The Poets of the United Irishman', *United Irishman*, 30 May 1903, p. 3.
15 F. Hugh O'Donnell, *The Stage Irishman of the Pseudo-Celtic Drama* (London: John Long, 1904). See also Yeats, *Memoirs*, p. 116.
16 Breandán S. Mac Aodh, 'Was this a Social Revolution?', in Seán Ó Tuama, ed., *The Gaelic League Idea*, p. 21.
17 D. P. Moran, *The Philosophy of Irish Ireland* (Dublin: James Duffy, 1903), p. 22.
18 Sean Ó Diotcain, 'The Poets of the United Irishman', *United Irishman*, 30 May 1903, p. 3.
19 Unpub. lettr., Yeats to Lady Gregory, 24 October [1893].
20 W. B. Yeats, *The Celtic Twilight* (London: A. H. Bullen, 1902), p. 15.
21 Yeats, *Uncollected Prose*, I, pp. 108, 364; II, pp. 56, 70, 115-116, 133. James Flannery, *W. B. Yeats and The Idea of a Theatre: The Early Abbey Theatre in*

Theory and Practice (New haven and London: Yale University Press, 1976), pp. 213-214. Hereafter Flannery, *Idea of a Theatre*, Anon., *Daily Express* (Dublin), 8 May 1899, p. 5.
22 Ibid., II, pp. 70-73.
23 See W. B. Yeats, 'The Literary Movement in Ireland', in Lady Gregory, ed., *Ideals in Ireland* (1901; rpt. New York: Lemma, 1973), p. 98. Hereafter Gregory, ed., *Ideals in Ireland*.
24 There are several misquotations: rabbits, rabbit; hazel tree, Hazel Tree; well, Well; water runs, waters run.
25 See O'Connor, 'Two Friends', p. 67.
26 National Library of Ireland, MS.15,600, 23, W. B. Yeats to G. W. Russell, [? December 1897]. The *Pall Mall Gazette*, 7 December 1897, p. 12 carries a report entitled 'The Celtic Movement' summarizing Yeats's address to the Irish Literary Society on 4 December. The only reference to A.E. is as follows: 'This belief in the presence everywhere of something which the eye cannot always see . . . the Celts alone among civilized people retain; and out of it there arises that "curious troubled ecstasy" in the contemplation of nature which is the distinguishing mark of the Celt. To illustrate his point Mr Yeats referred to the work of Miss Fiona Macleod, to a story of Miss Nora Hopper, and to some beautiful lines by A.E., a young Irish poet, to whom, as Mr Yeats exquisitely said, "all beautiful places are haunted".'
27 Yeats, ed., *Irish Verse* (B), p. 255. All the misquotations except 'well, Well' have been corrected.
28 A.E., *The Nuts of Knowledge, Lyrical Poems Old and New* (Dublin: Dun Emer, 1903), p. 3. Hereafter A.E., *Nuts of Knowledge*.
29 See Denson, MS.9967, 52, 72, 73; Yeats, *Letters*, pp. 293-294, 296; *The Irish Theosophist*, V, 12, 221, 225; Yeats, *Uncollected Prose*, II, pp. 227-228; Ellmann, *Man and Masks*, p. 127; Moore, *The Unicorn*, pp. 68-69; F.A.C. Wilson, *Yeats's Iconography* (1960; London: Methuen, 1969), pp. 39-40. Hereafter Wilson, *Yeats's Iconography*.
30 The dedication simply reads, 'To W. B. Yeats'. See also Denson, MS.9967, 47, 1 February 1897: 'I think you will like the shorter poems but the rather longer things I think not. I am sorry for it is dedicated to you.'
31 Yeats, *Letters*, pp. 294-295, to George Russell, 22 January [1898].
32 Ibid., p. 296, to George Russell, [? February 1898]. Note unpub. lettr., Yeats to Lady Gregory, 7 April 1898: 'I send you my review of Russell (I have sent him a copy also). . . . My review . . . is a little spoiled by their taking out "Janus" which I had quoted before the last sentence. I liked it when I wrote it, but do not know that I like it much now. I find that review length is a bad length for me — I can do little with it.'
33 Yeats, *Uncollected Prose*, II, pp. 111-113.
34 Ibid., p. 122.
35 Russell, *Letters*, pp. 24-26, to W. B. Yeats, 1 February 1898. Denson has printed the final versions of the poems. For original versions see Russell MSS., Manuscripts Department, Lilly Library, Indiana University, Bloomington, Indiana.
36 Unpub. lettr., Yeats to Russell, n.d. See also Yeats, *Letters*, p. 296, to George Russell, [? February 1898].
37 See Parkinson, *Self-Critic*, pp. 1-50; Ellmann, *Identity*, pp. 116-145.
38 Russell, 'Our Contributors', *A Celtic Christmas, The Irish Homestead*, December 1897, p. 28.
39 First published in *The Internationalist*, IV, 104.
40 First published in A.E., *The Divine Vision and Other Poems* (London and New

York: Macmillan, 1904), p. 67. Hereafter A.E., *The Divine Vision*.
41 First published in *The Internationalist*, I, 107, 15 March 1898.
42 Yeats, *Memoirs*, p. 91.
43 Unpub. lettr., Yeats to Russell, 7 April 1898.
44 Yeats, ed., *Some Passages*, p. 11, G. W. Russell to W. B. Yeats, [10 April 1898].
45 A.E., *The Divine Vision*, p. 20.
46 For Yeats's review see Yeats, *Uncollected Prose*, I, pp. 292-295.
47 Meir, *Ballads and Songs*, p. 77.
48 Ibid., pp. 69-71, 77; Ellmann, *Man and Masks*, pp. 154-155; Parkinson, *Self-Critic*, p. 91; T. S. Eliot, *On Poetry and Poets*, (1957; rpt. London: Faber and Faber, 1969), p. 256.
49 Quoted in G. W. Turner, *Stylistics* (Harmondsworth: Penguin, 1973), pp. 22-23.
50 Denson, MS.9967, 71, to W. B. Yeats, [? September/November 1899].
51 Ibid., 9967, 79, to W. B. Yeats, [circa May 1900].
52 Yeats, *Letters*, pp. 342-344, to George Russell, [circa May 1900].
53 Denson, MS.9967, 80, to W. B. Yeats, [late May 1900].
54 Ibid., 9967, 78, to W. B. Yeats, [late May 1900]. See also Joyce, *Ulysses*, p. 184.
55 Yeats, *Letters*, pp. 342-344, to George Russell, [circa May 1900]. See also Denson, MS.9968, 354, J. B. Yeats to John Quinn, 19 January 1920: 'I have an old prejudice against mystical poetry; it is of the fancy rather than the imagination.'
56 Denson, MS.9967, 80, to W. B. Yeats, [late May 1900].
57 Yeats, *Letters*, pp. 342-344, to George Russell, [circa May 1900].
58 See Wayne C. Booth, *The Rhetoric of Fiction* (1961; rpt. Chicago and London: The University of Chicago Press, 1973), p. 388.
59 Denson, MS.9967, 80, to W. B. Yeats, [late May 1900].
60 Yeats, *Letters*, p. 342-344, to George Russell [circa May 1900]. Cf. Henry Nicolas, *Mallarmé et le Symbolisme* (Paris: Libraire Larousse, 1966), p. 120; Mallarmé to Degas: 'Ce n'est point avec des idées qu' on fait des sonnets, Degas, c'est avec des mots.'
61 Denson, MS.9967, 80, to W. B. Yeats, [late May 1900]. Note, however, Denson MS.9968, 390, to A. de Blacam, 8 July 1922: 'I think Irish writers have influenced each other but little . . . except that there was a general tendency to write carefully which grew up around Yeats, who was a great theorist.' See also Gibbon, ed., *Living Torch*, pp. 20, 263.
62 See Padraic Colum, *The Road Round Ireland* (New York: Macmillan, 1926), pp. 364-365.
63 Underhill, *Mysticism*, p. 79.
64 Ibid., pp. 37-38: 'To the great mystic, the "problem of the Absolute" presents itself in terms of life, not in terms of dialectic. . . . He achieves a solution, not by the dubious processes of thought, but by direct perception.'
65 A.E., *Homeward*, p. 26.
66 Russell, *Letters*, p. 11, to Edward Dowden, 6 August 1894.
67 Quoted in Ellmann, *Identity*, p. 239.
68 Ellmann, *Identity*, pp. 91-98.
69 Yeats, *Essays and Introductions*, p. 137.
70 Ibid., pp. 119-120.
71 Note Yeats's assessment of *Homeward: Songs by the Way*, in Yeats, *Uncollected Prose*, I, p. 338: 'Such poetry is profoundly philosophical in the only way in which poetry can be; it describes the emotions of a soul dwelling in the presence of certain ideas.'
72 Ellmann, *Identity*, pp. 39-61.
73 Yeats, *Uncollected Prose*, I, p. 367. See also James Joyce, *A Portrait of the Artist*

as a Young Man (1916); rpt. Harmondsworth: Penguin, 1969), p. 214. Hereafter Joyce, *A Portrait*.
74 Yeats, *Essays and Introductions*, p. 28. See also Yeats, ed., *Blake*, I, pp. 243-244.
75 Ibid., p. 157.
76 See Yeats, *Memoirs*, p. 169: 'Truth is a state of mind and not a thought nor a remembered syllogism nor an opinion.'
77 Yeats, *Poems*, p. 142. See also Jeffares, *Commentary*, pp. 52-55.
78 Quoted in Ellmann, *Man and Masks*, pp. 15, 20.
79 Yeats, *Autobiographies*, p. 65.
80 A.E., *Imaginations and Reveries*, p. 54; Yeats, *Uncollected Prose*, I, p. 338; Joyce, *Ulysses*, p. 185; Richard Ellmann, *Ulysses on the Liffey* (London: Faber and Faber, 1972), p. 14.
81 A.E., *Song and Its Fountains*, p. 86.
82 O'Connor, 'Two Friends', pp. 64-65; Joyce, *Ulysses*, p. 185.
83 Probably first used by Russell in *Irish Theosophist*, III, 190, 15 August 1895. See also A.E., *Song and Its Fountains*, p. 87; O'Connor, *My Father's Son*, pp. 77-78.
84 See Ellmann, *Identity*, p. 57.
85 Yeats, *Uncollected Prose*, I, p. 367.
86 See for example, Ellmann, *Man and Masks*, pp. 154-156.
87 Meir, *Ballads and Songs*, p. 77.
88 Yeats, *Poems*, pp. 204-206.
89 Yeats, *Memoirs*, p. 48.
90 Sinnett, *Esoteric Buddhism*, pp. 186-187. Cf. Yeats, *A Vision* (A), pp. xxiv-xxvi regarding reincarnation and his own children and Yeats *A Vision* (B), p. 236: 'There are stories Asiatic and European of those who die in childhood being reborn almost at once.'
91 Yeats, *Memoirs*, p. 48. See also p. 133, and Richard Ellmann, *Golden Codgers: Biographical Speculations* (London: Oxford University Press, 1973), pp. 107-108. Hereafter Ellmann, *Golden Codgers*.
92 Ellmann, *Identity*, p. 48.
93 Quoted in Ellmann, *Identity*, p. 240.
94 Yeats, *Poems*, p. 258.
95 Ibid., p. 346.
96 Ibid., pp. 338-343. See Jeffares, *Commentary*, pp. 172-177.
97 Arnold Harvey, 'Memories of Coole', *Irish Times*, 23 November 1959, p. 5; Bax, *Some I Knew Well*, p. 93.
98 Denson, MS.9969, 626, to Joseph O'Neill, 4 October 1934.
99 Yeats, *Essays and Introductions*, pp. 35-36.
100 Yeats, *Letters*, p. 291, to Lady Gregory, 17 November [1897].
101 F.S.L. Lyons, *Ireland Since the Famine*, 2nd ed. (London: Collins, 1973), p. 216, has argued that the Co-Operative Movement did not make a substantial contribution to Irish life. 'Yet although Plunkett had clearly established something with an element of permanency about it, the results in his own life-time were less spectacular than he might have looked for. "Beyond effectively reorganizing the dairying industry," it has been said, [co-operation] made little impact on the economic or social life of the country.' For the opposite point of view see Patrick Bolger, *The Irish Co-Operative Movement, Its History and Development* (Dublin: Institute of Public Administration, 1977). Hereafter Bolger, *Irish Co-Operative Movement*.
102 Horace Plunkett, *Ireland in the New Century: With an Epilogue in Answer to Some Critics*, 3rd ed. (London: John Murray, 1905), p. 291. James Joyce, *Finnegans Wake*, 3rd ed. (London: Faber and Faber, 1964), p. 36 has parodied

Notes to pages 153–158

the idealism of the Co-operative Movement: '... and creamery establishments which for the honours of our mewmew mutual daughters, credit me, I am woowoo willing to take my stand, sir, upon the monument, that sign of our ruru redemption, any hygienic day ...'

103 Plunkett, *Diaries*, 10 September 1897, Plunkett House, Broad Street, Oxford, used by permission. Hereafter Plunkett, *Diaries*. See also entry for 21 March 1897, and Gregory, *Seventy Years*, p. 314.
104 *Irish Homestead*, III, 742, 6 November 1897.
105 Gregory, *Seventy Years*, p. 314.
106 Russell, *Letters*, pp. 18-23, to W. B. Yeats, 3 April 1897.
107 Yeats, *Poems*, p. 603.
108 Denson, MS.9967, 47, to W. B. Yeats, 1 February 1897.
109 A.E., *Irish Theosophist*, V, 127-131, 15 April 1897; 148-152, 15 May 1897.
110 Yeats, *Essays and Introductions*, pp. 474-475. This passage is slightly misleading: about eight months elapsed between Yeats's hearing about Russell's evangelistic tour and his bringing him to Plunkett. NB. 'He was not as strange as he seems in memory; such ideas were in other Irish minds; I had made a map of ancient Ireland with the sacred places marked upon it in red ink, and Standish O'Grady had announced in his weekly Review that Slieve-na-mon would yet be more famous than Olympus.'
111 A.E., *Irish Theosophist*, V, 85-86, 15 February 1897.
112 Gregory, *Seventy Years*, p. 310; Yeats, *Memoirs*, p. 112.
113 Yeats, *Letters*, pp. 290-291, to Lady Gregory, 17 November 1897.
114 Ibid. p. 291. See also Plunkett, *Diaries*, 19 November 1897.
115 Summerfield, *Russell*, p. 88. According to Moore, *Salve*, p. 85, Russell stipulated 'that he should not receive more than £3 per week. No man's work, according to him, was worth more.'
116 Russell, *Letters*, p. 23, to J. M. Synge, 25 December 1897. Doubtless some of Russell's depression was due to his mother's death on 9 October 1897.
117 Ibid., pp. 23-24, to W. K. Magee, 25 December 1897.
118 Quoted in Summerfield, *Russell*, p. 91.
119 Yeats, *Letters*, pp. 294-295, to G. W. Russell, 22 January 1898.
120 Russell, *Letters*, pp. 24-26, to W. B. Yeats, 1 February 1898.
121 Unpub. lettr., Yeats to Lady Gregory, 11 March 1898.
122 Quoted in Gregory, *Seventy Years*, p. 325.
123 Summerfield, *Russell*, pp. 92-93. See also Russell, *Letters*, pp. 28-29, [10 April 1898]. May 1900 Russell had founded a Hermetic Society (not to be confused with its namesake of 1885) for the dissatisfied members of the Dublin Lodge of the Theosophical Society. The Hermetic Society met weekly in a room in Dawson Chambers. Denson MS.9967, 79, to W. B. Yeats, [May 1900]. See Joyce, *Ulysses*, pp. 191-192.
124 Ibid., p. 92.
125 See Peter Kuch, 'Mananaan Mac Lir as Monoglot – George Russell and the Irish Language', in Declan Kiberd, ed., *The Crane Bag*, vol. 5, No. 2, 1981, pp. 49-58.
126 Russell, *Letters*, pp. 28-29, to W. B. Yeats, [10 April 1898].
127 Unpub. lettr., Yeats to Lady Gregory, [11 March 1898]; 18 May [1898]; 25 April [1898]. Gregory, *Seventy Years*, p. 323.
128 Plunkett, *Diaries*, 28 May 1898, 29 May 1898, 3 June 1898.
129 Russell, *Letters*, pp. 36-38, to Katharine Tynan, 19 December 1901.
130 Gregory, *Seventy Years*, p. 323. See also Plunkett, *Ireland in the New Century*, p. 200.
131 The Dublin appointment also enabled him to get married. See Yeats, *Letters*,

pp. 299-300, to Lady Gregory, [14 June 1898]: 'I have just heard a piece of information at which I am not very pleased though I have half expected it. Russell has married Miss North. An aerial theosophic marriage. It came off a day or two ago and the bride is off to Mullingar by herself. Mrs Russell is a person who sees visions and is well-bred and pleasant enough; but I suppose I would never think anybody quite good enough for Russell. She has, as I have noticed, been in love with him for some years. He has got into the habit of looking after her. She is consumptive and has some literary power. I imagine you will like her.'

132 Summerfield, *Russell*, p. 101.
133 Ibid., pp. 101-102.
134 Yeats, *Letters*, pp. 306-307, to Lily Yeats, 25 December 1898.
135 Summerfield, *Russell*, pp. 159, 255-261, 279.
136 See Denson, MS. 9967, 72, 75, 85, 104, 111, 120; 9968, 368, 381, 390. Russell, *Letters*, pp. 28-30, 34-35. A.E., *Song and Its Fountains*, p. 94.
137 Gregory, *Seventy Years*, p. 325.
138 Russell, *Letters*, pp. 26-28, to W. B. Yeats, 10 February 1898.
139 Reid, *Private Road*, p. 194.
140 Denson, MS.9968, 419, to Thomas Sharp, 30 September 1925.
141 Yeats, *Essays and Introductions*, p. 415.
142 Ibid., p. 300.
143 Ann Saddlemyer, ed., *J. M. Synge: Collected Works IV* (London: Oxford University Press, 1968), p. 53.
144 Yeats, *A Vision* (B), p. 167.
145 George Roberts, 'J. M. Synge,' in W. R. Rodgers, ed., *Irish Literary Portraits* (London: British Broadcasting Corporation, 1972), p. 107. Hereafter Rodgers, ed., *Portraits*.
146 Moore, *Salve*, pp. 39-78.
147 Alan Price, ed., *J. M. Synge: Collected Works II* (London: Oxford University Press, 1966), pp. 49, 60, 100, 128, 151. See also Weldon Thornton, *J. M. Synge and the Western Mind* (Gerrards Cross: Colin Smythe, 1979), p. 93.
148 Russell, *Letters*, pp. 23-24, to W. K. Magee, 25 December 1895.
149 Ibid., pp. 28-29, to W. B. Yeats, [10 April 1898].
150 Yeats, *Letters*, pp. 294-295, to G. W. Russell, 22 January 1898.
151 Gregory, *Seventy Years*, p. 326.
152 Ibid., p. 326.
153 Summerfield, *Russell*, pp. 51-52.
154 See Yeats, *A Vision* (B), p. 176: 'What dialect was to Synge, [Russell's] practical work as a co-operative organizer was to him, and he found precise ideas and sincere emotion in the expression of conviction.'
155 Yeats, *Essays and Introductions*, pp. 474-475.
156 Yeats, *Autobiographies*, p. 249. See also J. B. Yeats, *Letters to His Son*, pp. 232-233, J. B. Yeats to Oliver Elton, 1 November 1916: 'I agree with you that there is a great deal of the statesman in George Russell. . . . [He] is an open air man, he keeps his windows and doors open, he keeps open house and welcomes ideas. Yet he is not quite big enough. There are more things in heaven and earth than are dreamt of in his philosphy. . . . There is just a touch of the mediocre in his mind, as there is in Shaw's and in all these Co-operative/Socialistic people. The fact is a man cannot go into public life and mingle in any of these movements without the danger of the mediocre. To keep out of the mediocre one must keep the single eye and love only truth. To wholly escape it a man must stick to Literature, if that, as in Russell's case, be his forte.' See also ibid., pp. 123, 134-136.
157 Note Ernest A. Boyd, *Appreciations and Depreciations: Irish Literary Studies*

(Dublin: The Talbot Press, 1917), p. 39: 'His contact with the routine of journalism and the essentially practical work of reorganization has by no means blunted his mystic sense. In fact, he has gained enormously by this diversity of occupation, which has saved him from exhausting his artistic faculty by writing in order to live, while poetry and painting prevent him from forgetting the aesthetic in the economic man.'

158   John Eglinton, W. B. Yeats, A.E., W. Larminie, *Literary Ideals in Ireland* (London: T. Fisher Unwin, 1899), pp. 10-11. Hereafter A.E., et. al., *Literary Ideals*.
159   Denson, MS.9967, 60, to W. B. Yeats, 14 September 1898.
160   Yeats, *Uncollected Prose*, II, pp. 127-128.
161   A.E., et. al., *Literary Ideals*, pp. 23-24, 26-27.
162   Denson, MS. 9967, 61, to W. B. Yeats, 11 October 1898.
163   Le Gallienne, ed., *Hallam*, pp. 96-98.
164   Yeats, *Uncollected Prose*, II, pp. 130-132; Yeats, *Memoirs*, pp. 179-180.
165   Denson, MS. 9967, 62, to W. B. Yeats, [29 October 1898]. The present writer has not been able to locate the controversy alluded to in this letter.
166   A.E., et. al., *Literary Ideals*, p. 46.
167   Denson, MS. 9967, 64, to W. B. Yeats, 7 November 1898. See also Yeats, *Letters*, pp. 303-305, to Lady Gregory, 6 November [1898].
168   A.E., et al., *Literary Ideals*, pp. 51-54.
169   Denson, MS.9967, 65, to W. B. Yeats, [13 November 1898].
170   A.E., et. al., *Literary Ideals*, pp. 57-65.
171   Misquotation. ' 'Tis the twilight of the ages and it's time to quit the plough. Oh the very sunlight's weary ere it lightens up the dew . . . ' A.E., *Collected Poems* (London: Macmillan, 1913), pp. 106-107.
172   A.E., et. al., *Literary Ideals*, pp. 69-74. See also Gregory, ed., *Ideals in Ireland*, pp. 87-102. Yeats wrote this essay in May 1899, and it is a fuller answer to Larminie's objections.
173   Yeats, *Poems*, p. 138.
174   A.E., et. al., *Literary Ideals*, pp. 79-88.
175   Yeats, *Letters*, pp. 306-307, to Lily Yeats, 25 December [1898].
176   Yeats, *Uncollected Prose*, II, p. 134.
177   Ibid., p. 135.
178   Ibid., p. 133.
179   A.E., *The Divine Vision*, pp. 24-25. In the 'Note', p. 94, Russell explains the 'Hound of Ulla' as 'Cuchulain, the great champion of the Red Branch cycle of tales.'
180   Yeats, *Poems*, p. 155.
181   Yeats, *Letters*, p. 63, to Katharine Tynan, 14 March [1888].
182   Yeats, *Poems*, pp. 199-200. See Joyce, *A Portrait*, p. 251. Stephen Dedalus conveniently ignores the poems written after 1902, and Yeats's extensive revision, in 1908, of almost everything he had written up till then.
182a The changing of the title, from 'The Autumn of the Flesh' to 'The Autumn of the Body', is itself significant.
183   Yeats, *Letters*, p. 402, to G. W. Russell, 14 May 1903.
184   Ibid., pp. 433-435, to G. W. Russell, [? April 1904].
185   Yeats, *Poems*, pp. 565-567. See also Ellmann, *Identity*, pp. 92-93.
186   Synge, *Works*, IV, pp. 53-54.
187   Yeats, *Uncollected Prose*, II, p. 26. Lady Gregory, *Our Irish Theatre: A Chapter of Autobiography* (Gerrards Cross: Colin Smythe, 1972), p. 20: "We propose to have performed in Dublin in the spring of every year certain Celtic and Irish plays, which whatever be their degree of excellence will be written with a high

ambition, and so to build up a Celtic and Irish school of dramatic literature."
... I think the word "Celtic" was put in for the sake of Fiona Macleod.' Hereafter Gregory, *Our Irish Theatre*.

CHAPTER VI: PLAYS AND CONTROVERSIES: ACT I

1. Yeats, *Poems*, p. 260.
2. B. C. Bloomfield, ed., *English Little Magazines No. 15: Beltaine, Number One to Number Three, May 1899 — April 1900 edited by W. B. Yeats* (London: Frank Cass and Co., 1970), p. 6. Hereafter Yeats, ed., *Beltaine*.
3. Joyce, *Ulysses*, p. 191.
4. Moore, *Salve*, p. 14.
5. Denson, MS.9967, 129, to Charles Weekes, [? January 1904].
6. Russell, *Letters*, p. 182, to L. R. Bernstein, 11 June 1929. Cf. Denson, MS.9968, 199, to T. B. Mosher, [June 1911]: 'I wrote [*Deirdre*] very hastily having been in a theatre about four times in my life previous to writing it.'
7. Holloway, *Diaries*, p. 44, entry for 7 September 1904.
8. Yeats, *Autobiographies*, pp. 47, 64-65.
9. Ellmann, *Man and Masks*, pp. 34-40, 48.
10. Hone, *Yeats*, pp. 108-110.
11. See Flannery, *Idea of a Theatre*, pp. 1-6.
12. Yeats, *Autobiographies*, p. 87.
13. Flannery, *Idea of a Theatre*, p. 288. See also Yeats, *Poems*, p. 262; and Finneran, ed., *Letters to Yeats*, I, p. 152 from G. W. Russell, [January 1906]: 'What I think is wrong about your way of getting a movement to work is that all movements need volunteers and you cannot afford to pay everyone, and when you talk in Dublin about "singing canaries" and "poultry gardens" it all comes back to the people for whom it was intended, and with very vivid exaggerations. There is probably not one of the younger people of whom you have not said some stinging and contemptuous remark. They may have been justified. But if you wish to lead a movement you can only do so by silence on points which irritate you or by suggestions to the people.'
14. Clarke, *Penny in the Clouds*, pp. 52-53. Warre Bradley Wells, *Irish Indiscretions* (Dublin: Maunsel and Roberts, 1923), pp. 140-141. Gibbon, *Yeats*, pp. 44-45, 51-52, 85, 111.
15. Maire Nic Shiubhlaigh, *The Splendid Years* (Dublin: James Duffy, 1955), pp. 14-15. Hereafter Nic Shiubhlaigh, *Splendid Years*.
16. O'Connor, *My Father's Son*, p. 142; cf. Clarke, *Penny in the Clouds*, p. 203; James H. Cousins and Margaret Cousins, *We Two Together* (Madras: Ganesh, 1950), p. 76.
17. Sir Maurice Bowra, *Memories* (London: Weidenfeld and Nicolson, 1966), pp. 237-238.
18. See George Roberts, 'A Meeting with AE', *Irish Times*, 13 July 1955. Anon, 'Talking to H.O. White', *Irish Times*, 7 April 1962. O'Connor, 'Two Friends,' pp. 70-71. Clarke, *Penny in the Clouds*, pp. 52-53, 95.
19. Yeats, *Memoirs*, p. 130.
20. Holloway, *Diaries*, pp. 39, 44-45, 74-75.
21. Yeats was guilty of a double standard. He was uneasy about Colum's *Broken Soil*, but enthusiastic about Lady Gregory's *Spreading the News*; he prevented the production of Cousins' *Sold*, but allowed Boyle's *The Building Fund*.

22 Moore, *Ave*, p. 281.
23 Quoted in Robert Hogan and James Kilroy, *The Modern Irish Drama: A Documentary History: Vol. III, The Years of Synge, 1904-1908* (Dublin: Dolmen, 1978), p. 36. Hereafter Hogan and Kilroy, III.
24 O'Connor, *My Father's Son*, p. 95.
25 Denis Gwynn, *Edward Martyn and the Irish Revival* (1930; rpt. New York: Lemma, 1974), pp. 127-128. Hereafter Gwynn, *Martyn*. Robert Hogan and James Kilroy, *The Modern Irish Drama: A Documentary History: Vol. I, The Irish Literary Theatre 1899-1901* (Dublin: Dolmen, 1975), pp. 26-27. Hereafter Hogan and Kilroy, I.
26 A.E., *Daily Express* (Dublin), 28 January 1899, p. 3.
27 Russell, *Irish Homestead*, V, 328-329, 6 May 1899.
28 Holloway, *Diaries*, pp. 5-6.
29 Hogan and Kilroy, I, pp. 48-52; Moore, *Ave*, p. 158.
30 Cugan, 'A Literary Dinner,' *United Irishman*, 20 May 1899, p. 2. Note National Library of Ireland, MS.13,493, Horace Plunkett to T. P. Gill, 6 May 1899: 'George Moore has been with me and will dine and make a speech. Get him and Russell together before the dinner. It will greatly improve the speech.'
31 Russell, *Irish Homestead*, V, 392-393, 3 June 1899. Summerfield, *Russell*, pp. 96-97 is misleading.
32 Russell, *Letters*, pp. 31-33, to W. B. Yeats, [April 1899].
33 A.E., *Imaginations and Reveries*, pp. 25-26. See also Denson, MS.9967, 121, to T. B. Mosher, March 1903. John Eglinton, *Confidential or Take It or Leave It* (London: The Fortune Press, 1951), p. 8: '[Yeats] hankered after the theatre but his true theatre was in his own mind.' Gregory, *Our Irish Theatre*, p. 16.
34 Quoted in Summerfield, *Russell*, p. 114.
35 Denson, MS.9967, 75, to W. B. Yeats, [? January 1900].
36 Denson. MS.9967, 41, to W. B. Yeats, [April-July 1896]. Yeats, *Memoirs*, p. 91.
37 Russell, *Letters*, pp. 26-28, to W. B. Yeats, 10 February 1898. See also National Library MS.15,600, 23, to G. W. Russell, [circa 26 November 1897]: 'Symons is becoming more and more of a mystical writer. He is writing now about a French mystic, who "lost the whole world and gained his own soul" or in other words went mad. He is living almost a srict life too.' See unpub. lettr., Yeats to Lady Gregory, [7 April 1898]: 'Russell and Symons seem to have got on excellently the other day.'
38 Hone, *Yeats*, p. 142. Joseph Hone, *The Life of George Moore: With an Account of His last Years by His Cook and Housekeeper, Clara Warville* (London: Gollancz, 1936), pp. 106-114. Hereafter Hone, *Moore*.
39 Russell, *Song and Its Fountains*, pp. 10-11.
40 Michael J. Sidnell, George P. Mayhew, and David R. Clark, eds., *Druid Craft: The Writing of 'The Shadowy Waters'* (Dublin: Dolmen; London: Oxford University Press, 1972), pp. 225-227. Hereafter Sidnell, et. al., eds., *Druid Craft*. Helmut E. Gerber, ed., *George Moore in Transition: Letters to T. Fisher Unwin and Lena Milman 1894-1910* (Detroit: University of Michigan Press, 1968), pp. 175-176. Hereafter Gerber, ed., *Moore in Transition*.
41 Moore, *Ave*, pp. 241-251.
42 Yeats, *Poems*, pp. 796, 810.
43 Russell, *Song and Its Fountains*, p. 11. Sidnell, et. al., eds., *Druid Craft*, pp. 4-15.
44 Sidnell, et. al., eds., *Druid Craft*, pp. 269-271. Gregory, *Seventy Years*, pp. 356-357: 'George Moore came in with a wild scheme for having *The Shadowy Waters* translated into Irish.'
45 Denson, MS.9967, 71, to W. B. Yeats, [September-November 1899].
46 Yeats, *Letters*, pp. 327-328, to G. W. Russell, November [1899].
47 Sidnell, et. al., eds., *Druid Craft*, pp. 288-289.

48 Ibid., pp. 290-300.
49 A.E., *Song and Its Fountains*, p. 11.
50 Moore, *The Unicorn*, p. 38.
51 Sidnell, et. al., eds., *Druid Craft*, pp. 10, 13, 14, 23, 24, 78, etc. See also Yeats, *Memoirs*, p. 40. Yeats, *Poems*, p. 199.
52 Ibid., pp. 268-271, 290-300.
53 Ibid., p. 224.
54 Yeats, *Letters*, p. 402, to G. W. Russell, 14 May 1903.
55 Ibid., p. 280, to Fiona Macleod [? early January 1897]; cf. p. 322, to Mrs Clement Shorter, 21 June 1899.
56 Ibid., p. 278, to Robert Bridges, 10 January [1898].
57 Ibid., p. 425, to Frank Fay, [? 20 January 1904].
58 A.E., et. al., *Literary Ideals*, p. 37. See also S. B. Bushrui, *Yeats's Verse Plays: The Revisions 1900-1910* (Oxford: Clarendon Press, 1965), p. 16. Hereafter Bushrui, *Yeats's Verse Plays*.
59 Sidnell, et. al., eds., *Druid Craft*, pp. 62-65.
60 Ibid., pp. 288-289.
61 Ibid., pp. 289, 299.
62 Ibid., p. 289.
63 Quoted in Bushrui, *Yeats's Verse Plays*, p. 18. See W. B. Yeats, *Plays and Controversies* (London: Macmillan, 1923), p. 187. Hereafter Yeats, *Plays and Controversies*.
64 Sidnell, et. al., eds., *Druid Craft*, pp. 288-289. See Holloway, *Diaries*, pp. 32-33.
65 Yeats, *Plays*, p. 340.
66 Russell, *Song and Its Fountains*, p. 11.
67 Sidnell, et. al., eds., *Druid Craft*, p. 317.
68 George Moore, *United Irishman*, 17 March 1900, p. 7. See also Yeats, *Autobiographies*, p. 447.
69 Yeats, *Letters*, pp. 335-337, to the Editor of *The Freeman's Journal*, 20 March 1900. Yeats, *Letters*, p. 338, to the Editor of the *Daily Express* (Dublin), 5 April 1900. Yeats, *Uncollected Prose*, pp. II, 211-213, to the Editor of the *United Irishman*, 21 April 1900.
70 Yeats, *Memoirs*, p. 113. Gregory, *Seventy Years*, pp. 310, 365-366. Yeats, *Autobiographies*, p. 368.
71 Gregory, *Seventy Years*, p. 310.
72 Yeats, *Letters*, pp. 335-337, to the Editor of *The Freeman's Journal*, 20 March 1900.
73 Ibid., p. 338, to the Editor of the *Daily Express* (Dublin), 5 April 1900.
74 Yeats, *Uncollected Prose*, II, pp. 211-213, to the Editor of the *United Irishman*, 21 April 1900.
75 Denson, MS.9967, 77, to W. B. Yeats, [April 1900].
76 See for example, Hone, *Yeats*, pp. 150-172. Malcolm Brown, *The Politics of Irish Literature: From Thomas Davis to W. B. Yeats* (Seattle: University of Washington Press, 1972), pp. 348-390.
77 See Hone, *Yeats*, pp. 165-166.
78 Unpub. lettr., Yeats to Lady Gregory, 27 May 1900.
79 Gregory, *Seventy Years*, p. 370.
80 Unpub. lettr., Yeats to Lady Gregory, 5 June 1900.
81 This claim is not strictly true. He did not complete *The Speckled Bird* or a proposed 200 page history of Irish Literature that was to be 'systematically political or national . . . throughout'. See Yeats, *Letters*, pp. 146-147, to John O'Leary, [26 December 1887].
82 Yeats, *Letters*, pp. 344-345, to Lady Gregory, [2 June 1900].
83 Yeats, *Memoirs*, p. 130.

84 Yeats, *Autobiographies*, p. 245.
85 Yeats, *A Vision* (B), p. 174.
86 Ibid., p. 175.
87 Ibid., p. 173
88 Monk Gibbon, 'AE (George Russell)' in Rodgers, ed., *Portraits*, p. 199.
89 Denson, MS.9967, 81, to T. B. Mosher, 7 June 1900. Hone, *Moore*, pp. 236-237.
90 Hone, *Moore*, p. 237.
91 Summerfield, *Russell*, p. 106.
92 Rupert Hart-Davis, ed., *George Moore: Letters to Lady Cunard 1895-1933* (London: Rupert Hart-Davis, 1957), pp. 30-31, to Lady Cunard, [Autumn 1900]. Hereafter Hart-Davis, ed., *Letters to Lady Cunard*.
93 George Moore, *Evelyn Innes* (London: T. Fisher Unwin, 1901), p. 103. Hereafter Moore, *Evelyn Innes* (1901).
94 George Moore, *Evelyn Innes* (London: T. Fisher Unwin, 1898), pp. 182, 237. Hereafter Moore, *Evelyn Innes* (1898). See also Yeats, *Letters*, pp. 300-301, to Lady Gregory, [29 June 1898]: 'Get Moore's *Evelyn Innes* from the library. I am "Ulick Dean" the musician.'
95 Moore, *Evelyn Innes* (1901), pp. 74, 117.
96 Moore, *Evelyn Innes* (1898), p. 243.
97 Moore, *Evelyn Innes* (1901), p. 117.
98 Moore, *Evelyn Innes* (1898), pp. 271, 305.
99 Ibid., p. 300.
100 Moore, *Evelyn Innes* (1901), p. 101, 103, 108.
101 Ibid., pp. 103-104. Note Denson, MS.9967, 168, to John Quinn, 1 October 1898: 'The *Farewell* book has been interrupted by the re-writing of *Evelyn Innes*, from which I have now disappeared (Thank Heaven!).'
102 Gregory, ed., *Ideals in Ireland*, pp. 45-51.
103 Ibid., pp. 87-107.
104 Ibid., p. 16.
105 Gregory, *Seventy Years*, p. 386. Yeats, *Letters*, p. 347, to George Moore, [? January 1901].
106 B. C. Bloomfield, ed., *English Little Magazines No. 14: Samhain, Number One to Number Seven, October 1901 to November 1908* (London: Frank Cass and Co., 1970), pp. 16-19. Hereafter Yeats, ed., *Samhain*. See also Hyde, *Literary History*, pp. 385-386.
107 Yeats, *Plays*, p. 1181.
108 Hogan and Kilroy, I, p. 102.
109 Ibid., p. 111. Anon., *Freeman's Journal*, 24 October 1901, p. 4.
110 Ibid., pp. 105, 111, 113. James Joyce wrote a vigorous attack on the final season of plays. See James Joyce, 'The Day of the Rabblement', in Richard Ellmann and Ellsworth Mason, eds., *The Critical Writings of James Joyce* (New York: The Viking Press, 1959), pp. 68-72.
111 Ibid., pp. 117-130. Anon., *Freeman's Journal*, 13 November 1901, pp. 5-6.
112 Anon., *Freeman's Journal*, 15 November 1901, p. 4.
113 Summerfield, *Russell*, p. 112. Yeats, *Autobiographies*, p. 449.
114 Robert Hogan and James Kilroy, *The Modern Irish Drama: A Documentary History: Volume II, Laying the Foundations 1902-1904* (Dublin: Dolmen, 1976), pp. 9-12. Hereafter Hogan and Kilroy, II.
115 Gerard Fay, *The Abbey Theatre: Cradle of Genius* (London: Hollis and Carter, 1958), pp. 32-35. Hereafter Gerard Fay, *Abbey Theatre*.
116 Nic Shiubhlaigh, *Splendid Years*, p. 5.
117 Hogan and Kilroy, I, p. 135.
118 Robin Skelton and Ann Saddlemyer, eds., *The World of W. B. Yeats: Essays in Perspective. A Symposium and Catalogue* (Victoria: Adelphi Bookshop Ltd.,

1965), pp. 110-111. Hereafter Skelton and Saddlemyer, eds., *World of Yeats*.
119 Ibid., p. 111. Nic Shiubhlaigh, *Splendid Years*, pp. 12-13.
120 Hogan and Kilroy, II, p. 9.
121 Ibid., pp. 9-10. Denson, *Bibliography*, p. 56. Moore, *Salve*, pp. 129 ff. Cousins, *We Two Together*, p. 66.
122 Denson, MS.9967, 132, to T. B. Mosher, [early 1904]: 'I did not expect you would like *Deirdre* as it was written hurriedly in a few days.' Denson, MS.9968, 199 to T. B. Mosher, [June 1911]: 'I wrote it very hastily having been in a theatre about four times in my life previous to writing it, but I should have spent a year over it instead of three or four days.'
123 Summerfield, *Russell*, pp. 112-113.
124 Yeats, *Letters*, pp. 364-365, to Lady Gregory, 20 January [1902].
125 Hogan and Kilroy, II, p. 12. Nic Shiubhlaigh, *Splendid Years*, p. 13 is inaccurate.
126 National Library of Ireland, MS.15,600, 48, to G. W. Russell, [26 January 1902]. Elizabeth Coxhead, *Lady Gregory: A Literary Portrait*, 2nd. ed. (London: Secker and Warburg, 1966), pp. 64-65 points out that the play was largely written by Lady Gregory. Hereafter Coxhead, *Gregory*. Vide Yeats, *Plays*, pp. 232-233; Ernest Boyd, *The Contemporary Drama of Ireland* (Boston: Little, Brown, and Co., 1917), p. 64. Hereafter Boyd, *Contemporary Drama*.
127 Yeats, *Letters*, pp. 364-365, to Lady Gregory, 20 January [1902]. Denson, MS.9968, 238, to John Quinn, 14 March 1914.
128 Denson, MS.9967, 96, 28 January 1902.
129 Hogan and Kilroy, II, pp. 12-15. Nic Shiubhlaigh, *Splendid Years*, p. 16.
130 Ibid., p. 12.
131 Ibid., pp. 14-16. Nic Shuibhlaigh, *Splendid Years*, p. 20. James Kilroy, *The 'Playboy' Riots* (Dublin: Dolmen, 1971), p. 87.
132 Quoted in Hogan and Kilroy, II, p. 41.
133 Frank Fay, 'Pélleas et Mélisande at the Theatre Royal', in Robert Hogan, ed., *Towards a National Theatre* (Dublin: Dolmen, 1970), p. 44. Hereafter Fay, *National Theatre*.
134 Hogan and Kilroy, II, p. 41.
135 Yeats, *Plays*, p. 176.
136 Yeats, *Uncollected Prose*, II, p. 292. Flannery, *Idea of a Theatre*, pp. 248-249. Nic Shiubhlaigh, *Splendid Years*, p. 19. Yeats, *Memoirs*, p. 276. Denson, MS.9967, 97, to Sarah Purser, 5 March 1902; and ibid., p. 98, to Sarah Purser, 4 April 1902.
137 Flannery, *Idea of a Theatre*, pp. 239-278. The 1903 production of *The Hour Glass* and the 1906 production of *The Shadowy Waters* were perhaps the most stylized and the most theatrically effective of the early sets.
138 Hogan and Kilroy, II, pp. 10-14.
139 Yeats, *Letters*, p. 367, to Lady Gregory, [22 March 1902].
140 Ibid., pp. 367-369, to Lady Gregory, [3 April 1902].
141 Yeats, *Autobiographies*, p. 450.
142 Yeats, *Letters*, pp. 368, to Lady Gregory, [3 April 1902]. Denson, MS.9967, 98, to Sarah Purser, 4 April 1902: 'Yeats likes *Deirdre* and recants all his criticisms and he and Martyn tell me it is beautifully constructed, so I feel proud as an old bard.'
143 Yeats, *Uncollected Prose*, II, p. 285.
144 Holloway, *Diaries*, pp. 14-25.
145 Fay, *National Theatre*, pp. 72, 77.
146 Yeats, *Uncollected Prose*, II, p. 285.
147 Quoted in Nic Shiubhlaigh, *Splendid Years*, pp. 190-192.
148 See Eleanor Hull, 'The Story of Deirdre, in its Bearing on the Social Development

of the Folk Tale,' *Folk Lore: Transactions of the Folk Lore Society: A Quarterly Review of Myth, Tradition, Institution, and Custom* (London: David Nutt, 25 March 1904), Vol. XV, pp. 33-34.
149 Ibid., pp. 25-26.
150 A.E., *Imaginations and Reveries*, p. 10.
151 Herbert V. Fackler, ed., *Deirdre: A Legend in Three Acts by George W. Russell (A.E.)* (Chicago: De Paul University, 1971), pp. 2-3 is incorrect. Hereafter Fackler, ed. *Deirdre*. See Theophilus O'Flanagan, *Deirdri, or, The Lamentable Fate of the Sons of Usnach, An Ancient Dramatic Irish Tale, One of the Three Tragic Stories of Erin; Literally Translated into English, from an Original Gaelic Manuscript, with Notes and Observations: To which is Annexed, The Old Historic Account of the Facts on Which the Story is Founded* (Dublin: Printed by John Barlow, 1808). Hereafter O'Flanagan, *Deirdre*. Whitley Stokes, *Irische Texte* — Zweite serie, 2, Heft, pp. 153-177. Hereafter Stokes, *Deirdre*. Eleanor Hull, *The Cuchullin Saga, Being a Collection of Stories Relating to the Hero Cuchullin Translated from the Irish by Various Scholars: Compiled and Edited with Introduction and Notes by Eleanor Hull* (London: David Nutt, 1898). Hereafter Hull, *Deirdre*.
152 Hull, *Deirdre*, p. 24.
153 Fackler, ed., *Deirdre*, pp. 3-6. Nic Shiubhlaigh, *Splendid Years*, p. 191.
154 Ibid., p. 18.
155 Ibid., p. 30.
156 Yeats, *Autobiographies*, p. 449.
157 Maurice Bowra, *The Heritage of Symbolism* (London: Macmillan, 1943), p. 181.
158 Fackler, ed., *Deirdre*, p. 18.
159 Boyd, *Appreciations and Depreciations*, p. 38.
160 Nic Shiubhlaigh, *Splendid Years*, p. 19.
161 Yeats, *Autobiographies*, p. 450.
162 Quoted in Hogan and Kilroy, II, p. 41.
163 Yeats's familiarity with the legend of Deirdre dates at least to his Introduction to the 1888 edition of *Fairy and Folk Tales*, p. 4: 'In this way stories have been handed down with such accuracy, that the long tale of *Deirdre* was, in the earlier decades of this century, told almost word for word, as in the very ancient MSS. in the Royal Dublin Society.'
164 A.E., *Imaginations and Reveries*, p. 21.
165 Yeats, *Plays*, p. 389. See Aubrey de Vere, *The Foray of Queen Maeve and Other Legends of Ireland's Heroic Age* (London: Kegan Paul, Trench and Co., 1882), p. ix.
166 Ibid., p. 375.
167 See Sir Samuel Ferguson, *Lays of the Red Branch: New Irish Library* (London: T. Fisher Unwin, and Dublin: Sealy, Bryers and Walker, 1897), pp. 35-91.
168 Yeats, *Plays*, p. 389.
169 Peter Ure, *Yeats the Playwright: A Commentary on Character and Design in the Major Plays* (1963; London: Routledge and Kegan Paul, 1969), pp. 43-58.
170 See Robin Skelton and David R. Clark, eds., *Irish Renaissance: A Gathering of Essays, Memoirs and Letters from the Massachusetts Review* (Dublin: Dolmen, 1965), pp. 147-148.
171 Yeats, *Plays*, p. 388. Note Yeats, *Letters to Dorothy Wellesley*, p. 51, 'Lady Gregory wrote the end of my "Deirdre" on my fundamental mass.'
172 See Holloway, *Diaries*, p. 55: '[*Kincora*] . . . loses much of its charm by repetition and has not the same witchery for me as say *Deirdre* had, for instance, even after seeing it many times.' Oliver St. John Gogarty to G. K. Bell, 26 November 1906 in Jeffares, ed., *Critical Heritage*, p. 159: 'I did not like [Yeats's]

Deirdre. His attempted conception of her is nauseating: he has whorified a fine old lover with little lascivities.' Alice Milligan, *Freeman's Journal*, 4 February 1907, in Kilroy, *The 'Playboy' Riots*, p. 79: 'Mr Yeats began it himself in *Deirdre*. Of this no more need be said than that, as the most brazen playgoers and play actors require acting expurgated editions of Shakespeare, acting expurgated versions of Yeats will be called for.' Finneran, ed., *Letters to Yeats*, I, p. 166, A.E.F. Horniman to Yeats, 14 August 1906: 'You authors, (some of you) really care, but Russell does not care . . . You know perfectly well that your "real passion for good work" gets no sympathy from the emotional people. It is the workship of sentiment and emotion which is used as a means of keeping down the artistic standard . . . It is as if you were to become satisfied with a *Deirdre* only rather better than Russell's scarecrow!'

173 Russell, *Letters*, pp. 41-42, to W. B. Yeats, 19 April 1902.
174 A.E., *Collected Poems* (London: Macmillan, 1913), p. 37.
175 Summerfield, *Russell*, p. 114.
176 A.E., *Imaginations and Reveries*, pp. 9-10.
177 Summerfield, *Russell*, p. 114.
178 See Gibbon, ed., *Living Torch*, pp. 154-158.
179 Hone, *Moore*, p. 241.
180 The present writer's conjecture.
181 Patricia Ann McFate and William E. Doherty, 'W.B. Yeats's *Where There is Nothing*: Theme and Symbolism,' *Irish University Review*, II, Autumn 1972, pp. 150-151. Hereafter McFate and Doherty, 'Yeats's *Where There is Nothing*.'
182 Yeats, *Autobiographies*, pp. 452-453.
183 Moore, *Salve*, pp. 161-165. Hone, *Moore*, pp. 242-247. Yeats, *Letters*, pp. 376-377, to A.H. Bullen, 27 June [1902].
184 Finneran, ed., *Letters to Yeats*, I, pp. 102-103, Frederick Ryan to W.B. Yeats, 10 August 1902. See also ibid., I, p. 152, G.W. Russell to W.B. Yeats, [January 1906]. Moore, *Salve*, p. 131.
185 Hone, *Yeats*, p. 185.
186 Yeats, *Autobiographies*, p. 453.
187 Present writer's conjecture based on Yeats, *Letters*, p. 381, to George Russell, 18 October [1902].
188 Yeats, *Uncollected Prose*, II, p. 296. Yeats, *Plays*, p. 1292. Flannery, *Idea of a Theatre*, p. 292.
189 See McFate and Doherty, 'Yeats's *Where There is Nothing*', pp. 150-152.
190 Yeats, *Plays*, p. 1140.
191 Ibid., p. 1144.
192 Finneran, ed., *Letters to Yeats*, I, pp. 104-108, John Quinn to W.B. Yeats, 27 September 1902. Denson, MS.9967, 111, to W.B. Yeats [22 September 1902]. Yeats, *Autobiographies*, p. 499.
193 Denson, MS.9967, 111, to W.B. Yeats, [22 September 1902].
194 Wade, *Bibliography*, p. 58.
195 Yeats, *Letters*, p. 380, to Lady Gregory, [4 October 1902].
196 Ibid., p. 381, to George Russell, 18 October [1902].
197 Clarke, *Penny in the Clouds*, p. 55.
198 Unpub. lettr., Yeats to Lady Gregory, [6] October 1902.
199 Denson, MS.9967, 112, to W.B. Yeats [28 September 1902]. Note however unpub. lettr., Yeats to Lady Gregory, 2 June 1904 which clearly indicates that the matter was not 'clearing up'. 'George Moore was at Symons' last night. He refused to shake hands and walked out of the room without a word. He had no time to think and was left to his natural impulses, which are bad. Symons

went to the door with him and thought he seemed undecided. Mrs Symons was furious.'
200 Moore, *Ave*, p. 244.
201 Ibid., p. 251.
202 Ibid., p. 281, and Moore, *Vale*, p. 178.
203 Ibid., p. 44.
204 Ibid., p. 149.
205 Ibid., p. 52.
206 Ibid., p. 242.
207 Moore, *Vale*, p. 244.
208 Moore, *Ave*, p. 45.
209 Yeats, *Autobiographies*, pp. 401-412, 422-454; Yeats, *Memoirs*, pp. 269-271.
210 Yeats, *Plays*, p. 797.
211 Yeats, *Autobiographies*, p. 402.
212 Ibid., pp. 404-405. For Yeats's most ribald jibe at Moore see Yeats, *Poems*, p. 792.
213 Ibid., p. 454.
214 National Library of Ireland, MS.15,600, 8, to George Russell, [? April 1904].
215 Moore, *Vale*, pp. 241-242. Hone, *Moore*, p. 331. Eglinton, *Memoir*, pp. 230-231. Summerfield, *Russell*, pp. 105-107. Yeats, *Letters*, p. 510, to John Quinn, 27 April 1908. Denson, MS.9968, 238, to John Quinn, 14 March 1914. Russell, *Letters*, pp. 202-203, to R.I. Best, 24 May 1933.
216 Russell, *Letters*, p. 91, to W.B. Yeats, 5 November 1913.
217 A.E., *Avatars*, pp. 169-172.

CHAPTER VII: PLAYS AND CONTROVERSIES: ACT II

1 Denson, MS.9967, 140, to W.B. Yeats, [April 1904].
2 Yeats, *Autobiographies*, p. 450.
3 Ann Saddlemyer, ed., *The Collected Plays of Lady Gregory in Four Volumes: Volume One: The Comedies* (Gerrards Cross: Colin Smythe, 1971), pp. 3-11, 279-289. Hereafter Gregory, *Plays*, I. Yeats, *Autobiographies*, p. 565. Coxhead, *Gregory*, pp. 66-67. Hogan and Kilroy, II, p. 137. Flannery, *Idea of a Theatre*, p. 325.
4 The present writer's conjecture. The play was opposed by Maud Gonne and Arthur Griffith, but only Maud Gonne was a member of the executive.
5 Prizes were announced in *United Irishman*, 8 November 1902, p. 1.
6 First published in *United Irishman*, 15 November 1902, p. 3.
7 Hogan and Kilroy, II, pp. 48-51. Flannery, *Idea of a Theatre*, p. 325.
8 Denson, MS.9967, 120, to W.B. Yeats, [February 1903].
9 National Library of Ireland, MS.15,600, 35, to George Russell, 21 February, 1903.
10 Holloway, *Diaries*, p. 32. Arthur Griffith resigned from the Theatre Society in protest.
11 Yeats, *Plays*, p. 594.
12 Russell, *Letters*, pp. 44-45, to W.B. Yeats, 2 March 1903.
13 See Curran Collection, University College Dublin, Cur. L.4., W.B. Yeats to Fay, 15 September [1903]: 'Tell Digges that the astrological allusions are out of the *Paradiso* by Dante. He attributes the seven sciences to the seven planets and for most part for reasons that are obvious to an astrological student, but would take too long to explain. For instance, Saturn who resides over the birth of contemplative natures has philosophy attributed to him and so on. Pronounce

the Latin words as they are pronounced by priests. I have written to Hyde, who has left, about the motto.' See Dante, *Paradiso*, cantos II, VIII; Milton, *Paradise Lost*, Bk. 3, ll. 481 ff.
14 Russell, *Letters*, pp. 44-45, to W.B. Yeats, 2 March 1903.
15 Yeats, *Plays*, pp. 622-624.
16 R.H.S., 'The New Irish Plays', *United Irishman*, 21 March 1903, p. 3.
17 Hogan and Kilroy, II, pp. 53-56.
18 Holloway, *Diaries*, pp. 23-24.
19 Nic Shiubhlaigh, *Splendid Years*, pp. 36-39. Gerard Fay, *Abbey Theatre*, pp. 53-59.
20 Russell, *Letters*, pp. 46-47, to W.B. Yeats, May 1903.
21 First published in *United Irishman*, 21 June 1902, p. 3. First performed by I.N.T.S. in the Antient Concert Rooms, Camden Street, Dublin, 29 October 1902.
22 First published in *United Irishman*, 5 July 1902, p. 3. First performed by I.N.T.S. in the Antient Concert Rooms, Camden Street, Dublin, 31 October 1902.
23 Alan Denson, *James H. Cousins (1873-1956) and Margaret E. Cousins (1878-1954): A Bio-Bibliographical Survey* (Kendal: privately printed, 1967), p. 256. Hereafter Denson, *Cousins*.
24 Yeats, *Letters*, p. 379, to Lady Gregory, [26 September 1902].
25 Ibid., p. 379.
26 Denson, MS.9967, 120, to W.B. Yeats, [February/March 1903].
27 First published in *United Irishman*, 27 December 1902, pp. 5-8. First performed in Cork by the local dramatic society, 26 and 27 December 1905. See also Denson, *Cousins*, pp. 257-258.
28 Cousins, *We Two Together*, pp. 74, 77-78.
29 First published in *United Irishman*, 2 May 1903, pp. 2-3. First performed by National Literary Society and Cumann na nGaedheal, 20 April 1903. Performance was reviewed: *Daily Express* (Dublin), 21 April 1903, p. 5; *Irish Times*, 21 April 1903, p. 6; *Freeman's Journal*, 21 April 1903, p. 7. See also Cousins, *We Two Together*, p. 91; *Daily Express* (Dublin), 3 November 1903, p. 6.
30 National Library of Ireland, MS.15,600, 3, to George Russell, [17 July 1903]. See also Flannery, *Idea of a Theatre*, p. 188. Hogan and Kilroy, II, p. 51.
31 Hogan and Kilroy, II, pp. 64-65. National Library of Ireland, MS.15,600, 35, to George Russell, 21 February 1903.
32 Ibid., p. 65.
33 National Library of Ireland, MS.15,600, 3, to George Russell, [17 July 1903].
34 Ibid., 4, to George Russell, [mid July 1903].
35 Denson, MS.9967, 140, to W.B. Yeats, [? July 1903].
36 Cousins, *We Two Together*, pp. 67-68, 126.
37 Russell, *Letters*, p. 229: 'Synge's Diary records four evenings spent with Russell; first with Yeats and Russell, 8 November 1897; second "at the Theosophical Society with Russell", 26 November 1897; third and fourth merely "an evening with AE", 12 and 30 October 1898.' In addition there were two or three occasions when Russell and Synge were house guests at Coole Park at the same time.
38 Synge, II, p. 380.
39 Hogan and Kilroy, II, p. 139.
40 Ibid., pp. 74-83.
41 Yeats, *Uncollected Prose*, II, pp. 306-308, 331-338. W.B. Yeats, *Explorations* (New York: Macmillan, 1962), pp. 114-123.
42 Hogan and Kilroy, II, p. 75. Gerard Fay, *Abbey Theatre*, pp. 60-61.
43 Maud Gonne, 'A National Theatre', *United Irishman*, 24 October 1903, pp. 2-3.
44 James Connolly, 'National Drama', *United Irishman*, 24 October 1903, p. 2.

45 Thomas Kettle, 'Mr Yeats and the Freedom of the Theatre', *United Irishman*, 15 November 1902, p. 3.
46 Russell, *Letters*, pp. 48-49, to John Quinn, 17 May 1903; Yeats, *Letters*, pp. 416-418, to Lily Yeats, 25 December 1903; Murphy, *Prodigal Father*, p. 260; Liam Miller, *The Dun Emer Press, Later the Cuala Press* (New Yeats Papers VII) (Dublin: Dolmen, 1973), pp. 33-35. Hereafter Miller, *The Dun Emer Press*.
47 Hogan and Kilroy, II, pp. 42-45. Denson, MS.9967, 145, to T.B. Mosher, [April 1905]. Yeats, *Memoirs*, pp. 147-148.
48 Ibid., pp. 87-92. Nic Shiubhlaigh, *Splendid Years*, pp. 45-46.
49 For example, see Cousins, *We Two Together*, pp. 92-93. See also Anne Saddlemyer, ed., *Theatre Business* (Gerrards Cross; Colin Smythe, 1982), pp. 42-43, Lady Gregory to Synge, [29 March 1903]: '. . . they are rehearsing a three act play of Colum's (very interesting, but very imperfect) . . .' Hereafter Saddlemyer, ed., *Theatre Business*.
50 Anon., 'Irish National Theatre: Last Night's Performances', *Freeman's Journal*, 4 December 1903, p. 4: 'In *Broken Soil* there is a distinct mark of originality and genius.' Anon., 'Irish National Theatre Society', *Irish Times*, 4 December 1903, p. 7: '*Broken Soil* . . . is a very cleverly constructed work.' Chanel, 'Broken Soil', *The Leader*, 12 December 1903, pp. 266-267: 'The great merit of the play is that it deals with ordinary persons . . . [but] it is liable to serious criticism in one respect. There is too great a complexity of motive.' 'The Mower', 'The Plays at the Molesworth Hall,' *United Irishman*, 12 December 1903, p. 6: 'There is much in the play to suggest that its light is the steely spark struck from the flint of intelligence, rather than the vibrant glow from the fire of loving conviction, but it is quite certain that the expression, whatever its source, is neither symmetrical nor abundant.' This review was strongly attacked by Oliver St. John Gogarty in *United Irishman*, 19 December 1903, p. 6. See also Holloway, *Diaries*, pp. 30-31, and Nic Shiubhlaigh, *Splendid Years*, pp. 45-47.
51 Denson, MS.9967, 120, to W.B. Yeats, [March 1903].
52 Yeats, *Letters*, p. 417, to Lily Yeats, 25 December 1903. See also Yeats, *Letters*, pp. 432-433, to Edward Garnett, 12 April 1904.
53 Skelton and Saddlemyer, eds., *World of Yeats*, p. 113.
54 Denson, MS.9967, 128, to W.B. Yeats, [January 1904]. See also Saddlemyer, ed., *Theatre Business*, pp. 48-49, Synge to Lady Gregory, 16 December 1903: 'Colum's play seems to have gone well . . .'
55 Ibid., 130, to John Quinn, 20 January 1904.
56 Ibid., 131, to John Quinn, [? 24 January 1904].
57 Finneran, ed., *Letters to Yeats*, I, pp. 137-139, George Russell to W.B. Yeats, [March 1904].
58 Ibid., Hogan and Kilroy, II, p.102. Kelly resigned from the Society.
59 Finneran, ed., *Letters to Yeats*, I, pp. 137-139, George Russell to W.B. Yeats, [March 1904].
60 Ibid., pp. 139, George Russell to W.B. Yeats, [March 1904]. See also Hogan and Kilroy, II, p. 114.
61 Reconstructed from Russell's correspondence as the present writer has not been able to locate Yeats's letter. See Denson, MS, 9967, 136, 138, 139.
62 Denson, MS.9967, 139, to W.B. Yeats, 30 March 1904.
63 Ibid., 142, to W.B. Yeats, [? 23 April 1904].
64 Ibid., 141, to George Roberts, Secretary, Irish National Theatre Society, 23 April 1904.
65 Yeats, *Letters*, pp. 433-435, to George Russell, [April 1904]; and National Library of Ireland, MS.15,600, 8, to George Russell, [April 1904].
66 Yeats, *Poems*, p. 369.

67 Yeats, *Autobiographies*, pp. 246-249.
68 Yeats, *Poems*, p. 495.
69 See, for example, *United Irishman*, 9 July 1904, p. 5.
70 At the time Russell was helping the Yeats sisters re-organize the Dun Emer Press. See Skelton and Saddlemyer, eds., *World of Yeats*, p. 146, and Liam Miller, *The Dun Emer Press, Later the Cuala Press* (Dublin: Dolmen, 1973), pp. 32-46.
71 James Flannery, *Miss Annie F. Horniman and The Abbey Theatre* (Dublin: Dolmen, 1970), pp. 7-15.
72 National Library of Ireland, MS.15,600, 47, to George Russell, 8 April 1904.
73 Hogan and Kilroy, II, pp. 104-112, 128-131. Holloway, *Diaries*, pp. 50-51. For a summary of some of the arguments about the opening programme see Saddlemyer, ed., *Theatre Business*, pp. 62-65, Synge to Lady Gregory, 11 November 1904.
74 Nic Shiubhlaigh, *Splendid Years*, pp. 62-63.
75 Gerard Fay, *Abbey Theatre*, pp. 93-100.
76 Denson, MS.9967, 145, to T.B. Mosher, [? April 1905]: 'Most of our writers here are turning their attention to drama. I feel rather sorry I ever helped get up the Irish National Theatre Society. If I had foreseen the vortex it has created drawing half a dozen good writers to it to write plays which don't interest me, I would have seen it perish in babyhood before I would have spent so much precious time and energy on it.'
77 Denson, MS.9967, 120, to W.B. Yeats, [March 1903]. Skelton and Saddlemyer, eds., *World of Yeats*, p. 131. Hogan and Kilroy III, pp. 36-37.
78 National Library of Ireland, MS.15,600, 40, to George Russell, 7 August 1905.
79 Ibid., 43, to George Russell, 3 August [1905].
80 Ibid., 40, to George Russell, 7 August [1905].
81 Ibid., 40, to George Russell, 7 August 1905; 42, to George Russell, 7 September [1905]. Unpub., lettr., Yeats to Lady Gregory, 29 September 1905. See also Saddlemyer, ed., *Theatre Business*, p. 79.
82 Ibid., 38, to George Russell, 19 September [1905]. Yeats, *Autobiographies*, p. 245.
83 Unpub. lettr., Yeats to Lady Gregory, 29 September 1905. Compare *Saddlemyer, ed., *Theatre Business*, pp. 78-80, Yeats to Synge, 9 September 1905: '. . . if we get things through in the form in which Russell proposed them at present, I think we will have quiet and a workman-like Society. To get them through it may be necessary for you and I and Lady Gregory and the Fays to stand in together, having come to a previous agreement.'
84 Skelton and Saddlemyer, eds., *World of Yeats*, p. 116. Peter Kavanagh, *The Story of the Abbey Theatre: From its Origins in 1899 to the Present* (New York: Devin-Adair; Toronto: Thomas Allen, 1950), p. 52. For a summary of the details see Saddlemyer, ed., *Theatre Business*, pp. 82-83.
85 Unpub. lettr., Yeats to Lady Gregory, 21 December 1905.
86 National Library of Ireland, MS.15,600, 46, to George Russell, 6 January 1906.
87 Finneran, ed., *Letters to Yeats*, I, pp. 151-152, George Russell to W.B. Yeats, [January 1906]. Hogan and Kilroy, III, p. 61. Compare Saddlemyer, ed., *Theatre Business*, pp. 270-271, Synge to Yeats, 12 January 1908: 'I am still in favour of some democratic method with the Company — Payne said to me last year that discipline would never be got in the Abbey unless we organize the public spirit of the Company. I entirely agree with him; coercion has never been a success in Ireland . . .'
88 Yeats, *Letters*, p. 466, to George Russell, [8 January 1906]. For details of Yeats's arguments with Synge and Lady Gregory see Saddlemyer, ed., *Theatre Business*, pp. 85-102.

89 Murphy, *Prodigal Father*, p. 299. See also Saddlemyer, ed., *Theatre Business*, pp. 104-106, Lady Gregory to Colum, 9 January [1906].
90 Ibid., p. 299.
91 Ibid., p. 298.
92 Ibid., p. 299-300.
93 Nic Shiubhlaigh, *Splendid Years*, pp. 75-79. The resignations had been foreshadowed as early as March 1906. See Saddlemyer, ed., *Theatre Business*, pp. 117-118, Synge to Lady Gregory, 1 March [1906], and Synge to Yeats, 7 March [1906].
94 Unpub. lettr., Russell to Lollie Yeats, n.d. Gregory Papers, Special Collections Dept., Robert W. Woodruff Libr., Emory University.
95 Murphy, *Prodigal Father*, pp. 306-307.
96 Yeats, *Memoirs*, pp. 10, 161.
97 Kilroy, *'Playboy' Riots*, pp. 88-89.
98 O'Connor, *My Father's Son*, pp. 94-95.
99 See Kilroy, *'Playboy' Riots*, p. 92.
100 Ibid., pp. 91-94.
101 S.L.M., 'Dramatic Rivalry', *Sinn Fein*, p. 1, 8 May 1909.
102 Murphy, *Prodigal Father*, pp. 346-347.
103 Ibid., p. 347.
104 Nic Shiubhlaigh, *Splendid Years*, p. 77.
105 Russell, *The Irish Statesman*, pp. 459-460, 19 December 1925.
106 Yeats, *Letters*, p. 536, to J.B. Yeats, 10 October 1909.

CHAPTER VIII: 'BUT FRIENDSHIP NEVER ENDS'

1 Yeats, *Poems*, p. 351.
2 Ibid., p. 392.
3 Ibid., p. 315.
4 Ibid., p. 256.
5 Ibid., p. 267.
6 Ibid., p. 289.
7 Ibid., p. 315.
8 For example see Yeats, *Letters*, p. 474, to Stephen Gwynn, 13 June 1906; Yeats, *Poems*, p. 262; and Yeats, *Memoirs*, pp. 221-222.
9 Bolger, *Irish Co-Operative Movement*, p. 99.
10 Ibid., p. 103.
11 See for example, Russell, 'Peace or War', *Irish Homestead*, I, 289, 18 November 1911.
12 Russell, *Letters*, p. 91, to W.B. Yeats, 5 November 1913.
13 Yeats, *Letters to Dorothy Wellesley*, p. 13, to Dorothy Wellesley, 26 July [1935].
14 Ibid., p. 13.
15 Yeats, *Poems*, p. 473.

INDEX

Abbey Theatre 222, 224, 227, 230, 232.
AE see Russell, George William.
Aherne, Owen 113.
All-Ireland Review, The 193, 194.
Allingham, William 24, 35, 132.
anima mundi 69, 81, 127, 147, 148.
anti-self 86, 89.
Archer, William 196, 214
Arnold, Edwin 18.
Arnold, Matthew 31, 64, 69, 163. 'On the Study of Celtic Literature', 61, 129.
Arrow, The 171.
Art Schools 1, 2, 3, 5, 6, 8, 29, 30, 62.
Ashe King, Richard 60.
Auden, Wystan Hugh 102.
avatar 10, 110–111, 119, 125–126.

Balzac, Honoré de 232.
Bax, Clifford 18.
Beardsley, Aubrey 180.
belief 20, 146, 147, 149–152.
Beltaine 171.
Besant, Annie 39.
Best, Richard 172.
Bhagavad Gita, The 18, 32, 34.
Blake, William 2, 3, 15, 18, 28, 33, 72, 79, 81, 82, 89, 91, 97, 124, 146, 147, 168, 181, 190, 191. Yeats/Ellis edition, 20, 38, 60, 69, 89.
Blavatsky, Helena Petrovna 9, 10, 12, 14, 16, 33, 39, 45, 54–57, 58, 69, 106, 110, 122, 125, 126. *Isis Unveiled*, 9. *The Secret Doctrine*, 9, 69, 141.
Boehme, Jacob 33, 60.
Boer War 185.
Book of Leinster, The 198, 199, 201.
Book of the Rhymers' Club, The 37–38.

Bookman, The 39, 94, 96, 97, 100.
Boston Pilot, The 23, 129.
Boucicault, Dion (Lardner) 194.
Bowra, Sir Maurice 176, 201.
Boyd, Ernest 14. *Ireland's Literary Renaissance*, 14, 84.
Boyle, William 224.
Bridges, Robert 102, 166, 183.
Browning, Robert 102, 166.
Buffon, Comte de 53, 167.
Burne-Jones, Sir Edward 184.
Byrne, William 36.
Byron, George Gordon, Lord 3, 28, 69.

Castiglione, Count Baldassare 235.
Catholic Church 58, 94, 111, 119.
Castle of Heroes, The 117–125, 134.
Caulfield, C. 220.
celtic 24, 26, 61–68, 72, 77, 104, 106, 109, 117, 122, 127, 128–137, 149, 154, 155, 163, 169–171, 190, 237.
Celtic Christmas, The 194.
Chatterjee, Mohini 17–18.
Clarke, Austin 42, 113, 208.
Coates, Caroline Clements see Rea, Carrie.
Coffey, George 194.
Coleridge, Samuel Taylor 29, 44, 69.
Collins, Mabel 15.
Colum, Padraic 211, 215, 218, 225, 229, 230. *Broken Soil*, 218–219. *The Land*, 224. *The Saxon Shillin'*, 211, 219.
Connolly, James 217.
Constant, Alphonse Louis 49–50, 53.
Contemporary Club 22, 23.
Co-Operative Movement see I.A.O.S.
Cousins, James 77, 194, 214–215. *The Racing Lug*, 214. *The Sleep of the King*, 214. *Sold*, 215. *The Sword of Dermot*, 215.

Craig, Gordon 196.
Cumann na nGeadheal 215, 217.

Daily Chronicle, The 196.
Daily Express (Dublin), *The* 163–167, 169.
Dante Alighieri 50, 73, 132, 166, 213.
Davis, Thomas 23, 42, 109.
Dick, Frederick 59.
Digges, Dudley 215, 217, 220.
Dillon, John 154.
Dowden, Professor Edward 51, 69.
Dowson, Ernest 101.
druids 90, 118, 120.
Dublin Hermetic Society, The 14–17, 94–95.
Dublin Theosophical Society, The 16.
Dublin University Review, The 22, 128.
Duffy, Sir Charles Gavan 24.
Dun Emer Press 218.
Dunlop, Daniel 155.
Dwyer, Arthur 59.

Eglinton, John see Magee, William Kirkpatrick
Eliot, George see Evans, Mary Ann
Ellis, Edwin 39, 94. Yeats/Ellis edition, 20, 38, 60, 69, 89.
Emerson, Ralph Waldo 31.
English Review, The 87.
Européen, L' 216.
Evening Herald, The 193.
Evening Telegraph (Dublin), *The* 28, 104.
Evans, Mary Ann 9, 15.
Evans-Wentz, W.Y. 82–83.

Fay, Frank 194, 195, 197, 201, 208, 211, 215, 225.
Fay, William 177, 194, 196, 211.
Fainne an Lae 157.
Farr, Florence 39, 106.
Ferguson, Sir Samuel 24, 42, 165, 202.
Flower, Robin 36.
folklore 4, 23, 47, 69, 103, 106, 112, 137, 151, 178.
Fortnightly Review, The 193.
Freeman's Journal, The 193, 198.
French, Cecil 32.

Gaelic League 130.

Gael, The 23.
Gibbon, Monk 36, 37, 82, 189. *The Seals*, 37.
Goethe, Johann Wolfgang von 31, 36, 46, 48, 98, 166, 187.
Gonne, Maud 39, 60, 73, 76, 122, 150, 183, 194, 195, 210, 211, 215–217.
Gosse, Edmund 134.
Gregory, Lady (Augusta) 27, 29, 113, 120, 121, 123, 130, 131, 140, 151–153, 155, 157, 158, 160, 162, 163, 169, 174, 175, 178, 179, 180, 185–187, 191, 197, 206, 209, 210–212, 222, 224–228, 230, 232, 237. *Kincora*, 224. *Spreading the News*, 224. *Twenty-five*, 211–212, 214.
Gregory, Robert 123, 151.
Griffith, Arthur 210, 211, 218, 230.
Gwynn, Stephen 25, 193, 236.
Gyles, Althea 60, 168.

Hallam, Arthur (the younger) 44, 164.
Hardy, Thomas 102.
Harvey, Rev. Arnold 123.
Hegel, Georg Wilhelm Friedrich 91.
Henley, William Ernest 39.
Hermetic Order of the Golden Dawn 57–58, 60, 69, 73, 79, 84, 89, 106, 113, 123, 124, 174–175, 181.
Hermetic Society 117, 125.
Holloway, Joseph 113, 173, 195, 197, 201, 214.
Hone, Joseph 58, 189, 206.
Hopkins, Gerard Manley 102.
Hopper, Nora 132.
Horniman, Annie 224.
Horton, William Thomas 58.
Household, The 58–62, 94–95, 107, 108, 114, 153.
Hughes, John 2, 26, 41.
Hull, Eleanor 199.
Hyde, Douglas 22–23, 28, 41, 61, 119, 206. *Love Songs of Connacht*, 140.

Ideals in Ireland 191.
imagination 1, 17, 78, 79, 142, 146, 148, 151, 165, 196.
Irish Independent, The 217.
Inginidhe-na-hEireann 194, 218.
Internationalist, The 139–140, 157.

Index

Irish 25–26, 61, 128–131, 149, 170–171.
Irish Agricultural Organization Society (I.A.O.S.) 126, 152–163, 172, 174, 231, 235, 237.
Irish Homestead, The 53, 132, 135, 153, 158, 159, 162, 172, 178, 235.
Irish Literary Society (London) 25, 214. See also National Literary Society (Dublin).
Irish Literary Theatre, The 131, 163, 178–180, 192–193.
Irish Minstrelsy 37.
Irish National Dramatic Society 194, 203.
Irish National Theatre Society 205, 209, 210–212, 214–222, 234.
Irish Parliamentary Party 154.
Irish Statesman, The 29, 162, 232.
Irish Theosophist, The 34, 93, 97, 104, 106–108, 112, 115, 157, 162.
Irish Volunteers 232.
Irish Weekly Independent, The 104.
Irish Worker, The 236.
Isle-Adam, Count Villiers de l' 183.

Jackson, Holbrook 129.
James, William 85.
Johnson, Lionel 39, 46, 101, 132.
Johnston, Charles 10, 14, 16, 28, 53, 54, 60, 108. 'The Speech of the Gods', 17, 60.
Joyce, James 52, 78, 92, 113, 217. *Ulysses*, 172.
Joyce, Robert Dwyer 24.
Judge, William Quan 110.

Kabbalah 9, 75, 181.
Kalidasa 12, 20.
Keats, John 29, 44, 164.
Kelly, P.J. 220.
Kettle, Thomas 217, 229. 'Mr Yeats and the Freedom of the Theatre', 217–218.
Kipling, Rudyard 166.

Lane, Sir Hugh 232, 234.
Larminie, william 166–167.
Levi, Eliphas see Constant, Alphonse Louis.
Little, Philip Francis 114, 204–206.
Lucifer 55, 56, 57.

Lugné-Poe, Aurélien 195.
Lynch, Hannah 28–29.

Macleod, Fiona see Sharp, William.
MacNeice, Louis 42.
Maeterlinck, Maurice 183, 195.
Magee, William Kirkpatrick 2, 156, 161, 163–166, 172.
magic 48–51, 78–84, 87–91, 92, 94, 98, 107, 148.
Mallarmé, Stéphane 167.
Manchester Courier, The 38.
Mangan, James Clarence 24, 42.
Mannin, Ethel 84.
Martyn, Edward 178, 181, 288–229. *The Heather Field*, 178. *The Tale of a Town*, 177.
mask 46–47, 86, 89, 174, 176.
Mathers, MacGregor 39, 80–81, 112, 123.
Mathers, Moira 60.
Mathews, Elkin 38.
Mill, John Stuart 11.
Milligan, Alice 194.
Milton, John 54, 99. *Paradise Lost*, 54. *Samson*, 165.
Mitchell, Susan 53, 231.
Moore, George 42, 44, 45, 82, 113, 161, 177, 178–193, 196, 205–209, 231. *Confessions of a Young Man*, 180. *A Drama in Muslin*, 209. *Evelyn Innes*, 190–191. *Hail and Farewell*, 208. *Ave*, 181. *Salve*, 173, 190. *Vale*, 45, 209. *The Lake*, 209. *A Mummer's Wife*, 180. *Parnell and his Island*, 180. *The Untilled Field*, 205.
moods 97, 146–149, 152, 174.
Moore, Thomas 24, 133.
Moran, D.P. 130.
More, Henry 83.
Moreau, Gustave 8.
Morris, William 39, 132.
Murphy, William Martin 236.
mystic 26, 30, 48–51, 84, 85, 90, 156, 174, 237.
mysticism 13, 18, 30, 36, 48–51, 78–79, 84, 94, 189.
mythology 16, 20, 73, 106.

Nation, The 24, 133.

National Literary Society (Dublin), The 25, 103, 134, 215.
National Observer 39, 61, 70.
neo-Plattonism 9, 75, 77, 106, 148.
New Ireland Review, The 26.
Nic Shiubhlaigh, Maire see Walker, Mary.
Nietzsche, Friedrich 171, 235.
Nobel Prize 27.
North, Violet see Russell, Violet.
North American Review, The 182.

O'Casey, Sean 98.
occult 58, 87, 112, 115, 118, 125, 147, 165.
O'Connor, Frank see O'Donovan, Michael.
O'Curry, Eugene 108.
O'Donnell, Frank Hugh 130, 178.
O'Donovan, Michael 40, 113, 176, 177, 234.
O'Faolain, Sean 18, 40, 87, 89.
O'Flanagan, Theophilus 199.
O'Grady, Standish 69, 219.
Oldham, Charles Hubert 21, 22.
O'Kelly, Seamus 203.
O'Leary, John 23, 33, 41, 93, 112, 115, 128, 185, 186, 235.
O'Sullivan, Seamus see Starkey, James Sullivan.

Pall Mall Gazette, The 134.
Parnell, Charles Stewart 154.
Pascal, Blaise 50.
Pater, Walter 42, 44, 69, 147.
Pearse, P.H. 229.
phantasmagoria 68–72, 76–78, 81.
Phillips, Stephen 134.
Pim Brothers Ltd. 120, 155, 237.
Plato 20, 60, 74, 77, 88, 116, 160.
Plotinus 50, 135, 136.
Plunkett, Sir Horace 152–153, 155, 158, 163, 178, 235, 237.
Pollexfen, George 119.
Pollexfen, Isabella 10.
Porter, Arthur Kingsley 83.
Powell, F. York 38.
Providence Sunday Journal, The 23.
Pryse, James Morgan 107–108.
psychometry 107.
Purser, Sarah Henrietta 154.

Quinn, John 219.
Quinn, Maire T. 215, 217, 220.

Raftery, Anthony 76, 206.
Rea, Carrie 10, 11, 14, 15, 16, 28, 31, 34–35, 53–54.
Reichenbach, Baron von 53.
reincarnation 149–152.
Renan, Ernest 132. *La vie de Jésus*, 9, 11. 'The Poetry of the Celtic Races', 61, 64.
Rhymers' Club 39, 59, 73, 94.
Rhys, Ernest 39, 105.
Roberts, George 182, 184, 226, 228.
Robartes, Michael 111–115, 154.
Rossetti, Dante Gabriel 2, 166.
Rousseau, Jean Jaques 61.
Royal Hibernian Academy 3, 34, 38, 232.
Russell, George William paintings, 1–2. visions, 2, 3, 6–8, 12, 19, 81–87, 113, 122, 157. PLAYS: *Britannia Rule-the-Wave*, 230–231. *The Countess of the Wheel*, 178. *Deirdre*. 169, 173, 194–201, 203–204, 220–222, 229. POEMS: *By Still Waters*, 229. 'By the Margin of the Great Deep', 99, 101. 'Carrowmore', 137–139, 167. *Collected Poems*, 160. 'Connla's Well', 133, 134. 'Dana', 141–143. 'Dawn', 99. 'Destiny', 20. *The Divine Vision and Other Poems*, 140, 169. 'Dream Love', 134. 'Duality', 134. 'Dusk', 19. *The Earth Breath*, 134–136, 196. 'Echoes', 73. 'A Farewell', 169. 'Forgiveness', 73, 74–78, 98. 'Germinal', 47. 'The Gift', 134. 'The Great Breath', 98, 101. *Homeward: Songs by the Way*, 20, 92–101, 103, 107, 117, 134, 169, 237. 'How', 59. 'Illusion', 134. 'Janus', 134, 136. 'The Last Hero', 102. 'Magic', 19. 'The Master Singer', 141–143. 'A Memory', 218. 'Mystery', 100. *New Songs*, 170. *The Nuts of Knowledge*, 169, 218, 229. 'On a Hill-top', 19. 'Our Thrones Decay', 103. 'Pain', 101. 'Parting', 71, 73. 'The Place of Rest', 103. 'Pity', 73. 'Recall', 138–139. 'The Robing of the King',

135. 'Sacrifice', 101. 'The Secret', 19. 'Star Teachers', 116, 134. 'Sung on a By-Way', 19, 136. 'Symbolism', 19. To a Spiritual Woman', 70–71. 'To One Consecrated', 73. 'Truth', 101. 'The Unknown God', 101. 'The Veils of Maya', 101. 'The Vesture of the Soul', 19. 'The Well of Ballykeele', 126. PROSE: *The Avatars*, 126, 209. *The Awakening of the Fires*, 155. *The Building Up of a Rural Civilization*, 235. *The Candle of Vision*, 7, 78, 82. *Co-operation and Nationality*, 235. 'The Dramatic Treatment of Legend', 204. 'The Enchantment of Cuchullain', 108. *Ideals in Ireland: Priest or Hero*, 154. *Imaginations and Reveries*, 25. 'Literary Ideals in Ireland', 165. 'Nationality and Cosmopolitanism in Literature', 167–168. 'A Poet of Shadows', 41. 'Some Characters of the Irish Literary Movement', 51. *Song and Its Fountains*, 7, 8, 18, 26, 35, 43, 93, 148, 183, 234. 'The Speech of the Gods', 17, 34, 60. *To the Masters of Dublin*, 162.
Russell, Thomas Elias 5, 38.
Russell, T.W. 230, 235.
Russell, Violet 58, 209.
Ryan, Frederick 205.

Samhain 171.
Sankara 17, 20.
Savoy, The 108–111, 117, 139, 180.
Scott, Sir Walter 132.
séances 51, 54, 55, 83, 90.
Shakespear, Olivia 40.
Shakespeare, William 29, 99, 118, 166, 191, *Hamlet*, 172.
Sharp, Thomas 160.
Sharp, William 120, 123, 160, 168.
Shaw, George Bernard 174, 234.
Sheehan, James 28.
Shelley, Percy Bysshe 3, 18, 29, 44, 51, 82, 151, 164, 191. *Prometheus Unbound*, 16.
Sinn Fein 125.
Sinn Fein 230, 231.
Sinnett, Alfred Percy 8, 10–12, 16. *Esoteric Buddhism*, 8, 10–11, 17,

150. *The Occult World*, 10, 12, 15.
Sketch, The 29, 135, 136.
spiritual 1, 9, 10, 12, 15, 30, 31, 35, 37, 48, 50, 54, 56, 59, 65, 71, 72, 74, 75, 78, 92, 95, 98, 103, 116, 148, 149, 164, 165, 166, 167, 188, 191.
spiritual marriage 183.
Spiritualism 54–57, 87, 89, 124.
Stella Matutina 124. see also Hermetic Order of the Golden Dawn.
Stephens, James 113, 236.
Stokes, Whitley 199.
style 43–44, 114, 140–144, 146, 209.
Swedenborg, Emmanuel 60, 81, 124, 151, 162, 168.
symbol 69, 79, 97, 148, 181, 184.
Symbolism 77, 79, 83, 98, 147, 165, 166, 167, 168, 183.
Symons, Arthur 39, 108, 109, 117, 134, 180, 188, 189.
Synge, John Millington 27, 130, 140, 156, 159, 161, 163, 169, 171, 203, 210, 216, 217, 218, 219, 224, 225, 228, 230, 234, 235, 237. *The Aran Islands*, 161. 'Le Mouvement Intellectuel Irlandais', 216. *The Playboy of the Western World*, 217, 230, 234. *The Shadow of the Glen*, 216, 219. 'The Vagrants of Wicklow', 66. *The Well of the Saints*, 224.

Tennyson, (Lord) Alfred 39, 44, 129, 164, 166, 201.
Tery, Simone 48.
Theatre of Ireland, The 229, 231.
Theosophical Society 11, 17, 25, 56, 57, 58, 89, 135, 155, 216. Esoteric Section, 54, 56–57.
Theosophist (Madras), *The* 17, 34.
Theosophist 57, 106, 119, 150, 155.
Theosophy 8–13, 16, 17, 20, 55, 93, 141, 156, 163.
Thoreau, Henry David 18, 31, 157.
Tingley, Katherine 155, 157.
Tynan, Katharine 22, 28, 33, 39, 41, 45, 129, 158.

Underhill, Evelyn 30, 48, 49, 85, 145.
United Irishman, The 178, 186, 196, 207, 214, 217, 218.

United Ireland 61.
Unity of Being 42, 86, 89, 147.
Upanishads, The 9, 17, 19–20, 32, 34, 95, 108.
Ure, Peter 202.

Vedas 9, 124, 141.
Victoria, Queen 155, 185–186, 230.
visions 41, 49, 82–83, 113, 120, 121, 146. see also George William Russell, visions.
visionary 3, 4, 6–8, 35, 61–68, 81–82, 94, 148, 168.

Walkley, Arthur 214.
Walker, Mary 175, 201, 226, 229, 231.
Wallace, Henry 159.
Weekes, Charles 15, 56, 93, 108, 173.
Weekly Review, The 57.
Wellesley, Lady Dorothy 236.
Whitman, Walt 168, 169.
Wilde, Oscar 39, 46. The Decay of Lying, 39.
Wordsworth, William 18, 20, 31, 164, 166.
Wright, Claude Falls 15, 111.

Yeats, Elizabeth Corbet (Lollie) 229.
Yeats, Susan Mary (Lily) 13, 159, 219.
Yeats, John Butler 2, 11, 13, 16, 22, 29, 38, 87, 89, 147, 148, 228, 231, 232.
Yeats, William Butler PLAYS: At the Hawk's Well, 80. The Cat and the Moon, 208. Cathleen ni Houlihan, 80, 195, 204, 220, 224, 230. The Countess Cathleen, 178, 181, 196. The Death of Cuchulain, 67. Deirdre, 201–204. Diarmuid and Grania, 169, 179, 192–193, 195. The Epic of the Forest, 174. The Equator of Olives, 14. The Hour Glass, 212–214, 218, 220. The King's Threshold, 216. The Land of Heart's Desire, 112, 174. Love and Death, 174. On Baile's Strand, 224. The Pot of Broth, 218, 220. The Shadowy Waters, 80, 180–185. The Unicorn from the Stars, 209. Vivien and Time, 174. Where There is Nothing, 32, 204–209, 210. POETRY:

'Adam's Curse', 140, 149. 'All Souls' Night', 27, 238. 'Anashuya and Vijaya', 12–13, 20. A Book of Irish Verse, ed., 96, 103, 134, 140. The Book of the Rhymers' Club, 38.
'The Cap and Bells', 80. 'A Cradle Song', 142. 'The Choice', 223. 'The Coming of Wisdom with Time', 63. 'Coole Park, 1929', 28. 'Coole Park and Ballylee, 1931', 27. 'Crazy Jane and Jack the Journeyman', 102. 'Crossways', 42, 104, 174. The Countess Cathleen and Various Legends and Lyrics, 38, 111, 128. 'The Dedication to a book of Stories selected from the Irish Novelists', 24. 'The Double Vision of Michael Robartes', 114. 'Easter 1916', 24. 'Ego Dominus Tuus', 223. 'The Everlasting Voices', 102. 'A Faery Song', 5. 'The Folly of Being Comforted', 140, 169–170. 'He bids his Beloved be at Peace', 101. 'He hears the Cry of the Sedge', 116. 'He mourns for the Change that has come upon him and his Beloved, and longs for the End of the World', 126–127. 'The Hosting of the Sidhe', 103. 'Into the Twilight', 15. In the Seven Woods, 169, 218, 231. 'The Lake Isle of Innisfree', 39. 'The Lamentation of the Old Pensioner', 65, 67. Last Poems, 66. 'Love's Loneliness', 67. 'The Man who Dreamed of Faeryland', 39. 'Meditations in Time of Civil War', 24. The Municipal Gallery Revisited', 27. 'On Woman', 151. The Oxford Book of Modern Verse, ed., 20. 'The Phases of the Moon', 113. Poems and Ballads of Young Ireland, ed., 23, 37, 129. 'The Rose', 73. 'The Rose of the World', 75–77. 'The Sad Shepherd', 4. 'Sailing to Byzantium', 88. 'The Secret Rose', 106–107. 'September 1913', 235. 'She Who Dwelt Among the Sycamores', 6. 'Shepherd and Goatherd', 151. 'The Solitary Fairy', 6. 'The Song of the Happy Shepherd', 3, 4. 'The Statues', 91. 'The Stolen Child', 15, 36. 'Summer

Index

and Spring', 67. 'To Ireland in the Coming Times', 24, 42, 83–84. 'To the Rose Upon the Rood of Time', 73. 'The Tower', 88. *The Tower*, 127. 'The Unappeasable Host', 102. 'Vacillation', 84–85, 91. *The Wanderings of Oisin and Other Poems*, 38, 39, 41, 227. 'The White Birds', 101. 'The Wild Swans at Coole', 37, 68. *The Wind Among the Reeds*, 63, 169, 179, 209, 227. *The Winding Stair and Other Poems*, 91. PROSE: *Autobiographies*, 2, 7, 8, 11, 38, 42, 45, 47, 59, 84, 85, 86, 87, 93, 95, 162–163, 188, 208, 223, 230, 234. 'The Autumn of the Body', 170. 'The Autumn of the Flesh', 130, 166–167, 170. 'Blake's Illustrations to Dante', 146. 'The Celtic element in Literature', 20, 129, *The Celtic Twilight*, 61, 62, 71, 73, 80, 129, 131, 205. 'The Crucifixion of the Outcast', 112. *Dhoya*, 37, 61. *Dramatis Personae*, 200–201. 'Dublin Fanaticism', 236. 'Dublin Mystics', 96–97. *Early Poems and Stories*, 5, 32, 42, 66. 'The Eaters of Precious Stones', 80. *Essays and Introductions*, 95. *Estrangement*, 234. *Fairy and Folk Tales of the Irish Peasantry*, ed. 41, 61. 'A General Introduction for My Work', 20, 68, 77. *Ideas of Good and Evil*, 205. *Ideals in Ireland*, 191–192. 'Ireland After Parnell', 60, 64. 'The Irish Dramatic Movement', 27. 'Irish National Literature III: Contemporary Irish Poets', 97, 128. 'An Irish National Theatre', 217. 'The Irish National Theatre and Three Sorts of Ignorance', 217. 'An Irish Visionary', 61, 62–72, 84, 92, 114, 128. *Is the Order of R.R. & A.C. to Remain a Magical Order?*, 57. 'John Eglinton and Spiritual Art', 164. *John Sherman*, 37, 43. *Journal*, 53. 'Magic', 67, 152. *Memoirs*, 150. 'My Friend's Book', 160. 'A New Poet', 94–96. 'Noble and Ignoble Loyalties', 186. 'The Old Men of the Twilight', 112. 'Out of the Rose', 80. *Per Amica Silentia Lunae*, 118. 'The Poems and Stories of Miss Nora Hopper', 163. 'The Poetry of A.E.', 136–137. 'Popular Ballad Poetry of Ireland', 23. 'A Reckless Century. Irish Rakes and Duellists', 68. 'Regina, Regina Pigmeorum, Veni', 80. *Reveries Over Childhood and Youth*, 81. 'Rosa Alchemica', 80, 111–115, 116–117. *The Secret Rose*, 80, 115, 116–117, 189. 'Speaking to the Psaltery', 103. *The Speckled Bird*, 78, 80, 124–125, 140. *Stories from Carleton*, ed., 37. 'A Symbolic Artist and the Coming of Symbolic Art', 130, 168–169. 'The Symbolism of Poetry', 147. 'The Theatre, the Pulpit and the Newspapers', 217. 'Three Irish Poets', 132–136. *The Trembling of the Veil*, 188. *A Vision*, 8, 60, 84, 87, 88, 89, 114, 161, 188. 'Where There is Nothing, There is God', 112.

Young, Elizabeth 220.
Young Ireland Society 23, 24.
Young Ireland Poets 42, 92.

Zimmermann, Georges-Denis 76.